KOSTAS DIMITRIOU Phd & MARKOS HATZITASKOS MSc

CORE COMPUTER SCIENCE

For the IB Diploma Program
(International Baccalaureate)

Express Publishing

Published by Express Publishing

Liberty House, Greenham Business Park, Newbury,
Berkshire RG19 6HW, United Kingdom
Tel.: (0044) 1635 817 363
Fax: (0044) 1635 817 463
email: inquiries@expresspublishing.co.uk
www.expresspublishing.co.uk

First published 2015
Fifth impression 2019

Made in EU

ISBN 978-1-4715-4209-1

Copyright page

List of licensed IB material used:

1. DP Computer Science Guide (first exams 2014):

TOPIC 1- SYSTEM FUNDAMENTALS,1.1 SYSTEMS IN ORGANIZATIONS, Planning and system installation,1.1.1 The context for which a new system is planned,1.1.2 The need for change management,1.1.3 Compatibility issues resulting from situations including legacy systems or business mergers,1.1.4 Different systems implementation,1.1.5 Alternative installation processes,1.1.6 Problems that may arise as a part of data migration,1.1.7 Various types of testing, User focus,1.1.8 Importance of user documentation,1.1.9 Different methods of providing user documentation,1.1.10 Different methods of delivering user training System backup,1.1.11 Causes of data loss.,1.1.12 Consequences of data loss in a specified situation,1.1.13 Range of methods that can be used to prevent data loss Software deployment,1.1.14 Strategies for managing releases and updates,1.2 SYSTEM DESIGN BASICS, Components of a computer system,1.2.1 Hardware, software, peripheral, network, human resources,1.2.1 The roles that a computer can take in a networked world,1.2.3 Social and ethical issues associated with a networked world System design and analysis,1.2.4 Relevant stakeholders when planning a new system,1.2.5 Methods of obtaining requirements from stakeholders.,1.2.6 Appropriate techniques for gathering the information needed to arrive at a workable solution,1.2.7 Suitable representations to illustrate system requirements,1.2.8 Purpose of prototypes to demonstrate the proposed system to the client,1.2.9 Importance of iteration during the design process,1.2.10 Possible consequences of failing to involve the end-user in the design process.,1.2.11 Social and ethical issues associated with the introduction of new IT systems Human interaction with the system,1.2.12 Usability,1.2.13 Usability problems with commonly used digital devices,1.2.14 Methods that can be used to improve the accessibility of systems,1.2.15 Range of usability problems that can occur in a system,1.2.16 Moral, ethical, social, economic and environmental implications of the interaction between humans and machines, TOPIC 2 COMPUTER ORGANIZATION,2.1 COMPUTER ORGANIZATION - COMPUTER ARCHITECTURE,2.1.1 The central processing unit (CPU) and its elements,2.1.2 RAM and ROM,2.1.3 The cache memory,2.1.4 The machine instruction cycle, SECONDARY MEMORY,2.1.5 Persistent storage and secondary memory OPERATING AND APPLICATION SYSTEMS,2.1.6 Functions of an operating system,2.1.7 Software application,2.1.8 Common features of applications, BINARY REPRESENTATION,2.1.9 Bit, byte, binary, decimal and hexadecimal,2.1.10 Data representation, SIMPLE LOGIC GATES,2.1.11 Boolean operators,2.1.12 Truth tables using Boolean Operators,2.1.14 Logic diagrams using logic gates, TOPIC 3. NETWORKS,NETWORK FUNDAMENTALS,3.1.1 Different types of networks,3.1.2 Importance of standards in the construction of networks,3.1.3 Networks, communication and layers,3.1.4 Technologies required to provide a VPN,3.1.5 Use of a VPN,DATA TRANSMISSION,3.1.6 Protocol and data packet,3.1.7 Necessity of protocols,3.1.8 Speed of data transmission across a network.,3.1.9 Compression of data,3.1.10 Characteristics of different transmission media,3.1.11 Packet switching, WIRELESS NETWORKING,3.1.13 Advantages and disadvantages of wireless networks,3.1.14 Hardware and software components of a wireless network,3.1.15 Characteristics of wireless networks.,3.1.16 Different methods of network security,3.1.17 Advantages and disadvantages of each method of network security, TOPIC 4. COMPUTATIONAL THINKING,4.1 GENERAL PRINCIPLES, Thinking procedurally,4.1.1 Procedure appropriate to solving a problem,4.1.2 Order of activities and required outcome,4.1.3 The role of sub-procedures in solving a problem Thinking logically,4.1.4 Decision-making in a specified situation,4.1.5 Decisions required for the solution to a specified problem,4.1.6 Iteration associated with a given decision in a specified problem,4.1.7 Decisions and conditional statements,4.1.8 Logical rules for real-world, Thinking ahead,4.1.9 Inputs and outputs required in a solution,4.1.10 Pre-planning in a suggested problem and solution,4.1.11 Need for pre-conditions,4.1.12 Pre- and post-conditions,4.1.13 Exceptions that need to be considered Thinking concurrently,4.1.14 Parts of a solution that could be implemented concurrently,4.1.15 Concurrent processing and problem solution,4.1.16 Decision to use concurrent processing in solving a problem Thinking abstractly,4.1.17 Examples of abstraction,4.1.18 Abstraction and computational solutions for a specified situation,4.1.19 Abstraction from a specified situation,4.1.20 Real-world and abstraction,4.2 CONNECTING COMPUTATIONAL THINKING AND PROGRAM DESIGN,4.2.1 Searching, sorting and other algorithms on arrays,4.2.2 Standard operations of collections,4.2.3 Algorithm to solve a specific problem,4.2.4 Analyse an algorithm presented as a flow chart,4.2.5 Analyse an algorithm presented as pseudocode,4.2.6 Construct pseudocode to represent an algorithm,4.2.7 Suggest suitable algorithms to solve a specific problem,4.2.8 Deduce the efficiency of an algorithm in the context of its use,4.2.9 Determine number of iterations for given input data,4.3 INTRODUCTION TO PROGRAMMING, Nature of programming languages,4.3.1 State the fundamental operations of a computer,4.3.2 Distinguish between fundamental and compound operations of a computer,4.3.3 Explain the essential features of a computer language,4.3.4 Explain the need for higher level languages,4.3.5 Outline the need for a translation process from a higher level language to machine executable code Use of programming languages,4.3.6 Variable, constant, operator, object,4.3.7 Define various operators,4.3.8 Analyse the use of variables, constants and operators in algorithms,4.3.9 Develop algorithms using loops, branching,4.3.10 Describe the characteristics and applications of a collection,4.3.11 Develop algorithms using the access methods of a collection,4.3.12 Discuss the importance of sub-programmes and collections within programmed solutions.,4.3.13 Construct algorithms using pre-defined sub-programmes, one-dimensional arrays and/or collections, TOPIC 5 OBJECT ORIENTED PROGRAMMING,D.1 OBJECTS AS A PROGRAMMING CONCEPT,D.1.1 The general nature of an object,D.1.2 Distinguishing between object and instantiation,D.1.3 & D.1.4 UML diagrams,D.1.5 Process of decomposition,D.1.6 Relationships between objects,D.1.7 Need to reduce dependencies between objects,D.1.8 Constructing related objects,D.1.9 Data types,D.1.10 Data items passed as parameters,D.2 FEATURES OF OOP,D.2.1 Encapsulation,D.2.2 Inheritance,D.2.3 Polymorphism,D.2.4 Advantages of encapsulation,D.2.5 Advantages of inheritance,D.2.6 Advantages of polymorphism,D.2.7 Advantages of libraries,D.2.8 Disadvantages of OOP,D.2.9 Use of programming teams,D.2.10 Advantages of modularity in program development,D.3 PROGRAM DEVELOPMENT,D.3.1 Class, identifier and variables,D.3.2 Method, accessor, mutator, constructor, signature and return value,D.3.3 Private, protected, public, extends and static,D.3.4 Uses of the primitive data types and the string class,D.3.5 Code examples for D.3.1 - D.3.4,D.3.6 Code example for selection statements,D.3.7 Code examples for repetition statements,D.3.8 Code examples of arrays,D.3.9 Features of programming languages that enable internationalization,D.3.10 Ethical and moral obligations of programmers

2. DP Computer Science guide (first exams 2004) pages 100-102:

```
static void output(String info),{  System.out.println(info);,},static void
output(char info),{  System.out.println(info);,},static void output(byte info),{
System.out.println(info);,},static void output(int info) {
System.out.println(info); },static void output(long
info),{  System.out.println(info);,},static void output(double
info),{  System.out.println(info);,},static void output(boolean info),{
System.out.println(info);,},static String input(String prompt),{  String inputLine
= "";,System.out.print(prompt);,try,{inputLine = (new java.io.BufferedReader( new
java.io.InputStreamReader(System.in))).readLine();},catch (Exception e),{ String
err = e.toString();,System.out.println(err);,inputLine = "";,},return
inputLine;,},static String inputString(String prompt) { return input(prompt);
},static String input(),{ return input("");,},static int inputInt(),{ return
inputInt(""); }, static double inputDouble(), { return inputDouble(""); },static
char inputChar(String prompt),{ char
result=(char)0;,try{result=input(prompt).charAt(0);},catch (Exception e){result =
(char)0;},return result;,},static byte inputByte(String prompt),{ byte
result=0;,try{result=Byte.valueOf(input(prompt).trim()).byteValue();},catch
(Exception e){result = 0;},return result;,},static int inputInt(String prompt),{
int result=0;,try{result=Integer.valueOf(,input(prompt).trim()).intValue();},catch
(Exception e){result = 0;},return result;,},static long inputLong(String prompt),{
long result=0;,try{result=Long.valueOf(input(prompt).trim()).longValue();},catch
(Exception e){result = 0;},return result;,},static double inputDouble(String
prompt) { double result=0; try{result=Double.valueOf(
input(prompt).trim()).doubleValue();},catch (Exception e){result = 0;},return
result;,},static boolean inputBoolean(String prompt) { boolean result=false;
try{result=Boolean.valueOf( input(prompt).trim()).booleanValue();},catch (Exception
e){result = false;},return result;,}
```

KOSTAS DIMITRIOU Phd & MARKOS HATZITASKOS MSc

CORE COMPUTER SCIENCE

For the IB Diploma Program

(International Baccalaureate)

Express Publishing

Kostas' Dimitriou Dedication

Dedicated to my father who taught me the value of human dignity and to my mother who taught me the value of truth.

Markos' Hatzitaskos Dedication

Dedicated to my grandmother Elissavet, my mother Eleni-Maria and my brother Kostis, who have always been there for me.

Preface

Kostas Dimitriou holds a PhD in Spatial Decision Support Systems and Environmental Planning, and has taught computer science courses in various undergraduate and postgraduate University courses. He has participated in many scientific conferences and workshops, twenty research projects, and presented sixty scientific articles. He teaches the IB computer science course in the Hellenic American Educational Foundation since 2002. He is a Microsoft Certified Educator, Microsoft Expert Educator and Microsoft Expert Education Trainer. {kdimitriou@haef.gr}

Markos Hatzitaskos holds an MSc in Advanced Computing and has taught computer science courses throughout all school levels (from primary to high school and the I.B.). He currently teaches in the Hellenic American Educational Foundation since 2011. In his free time, whenever that might be, he develops mobile applications and attends the Athens School of Fine Arts as an undergraduate. {markosh@haef.gr}

The authors would like to thank the Board of Directors and the Administration of the Hellenic American Educational Foundation (HAEF) for providing an ideal working environment. Thanks are also due to Alkis Dialismas who checked our documents for improper citation or potential plagiarism using Turnitin, and Kostas Ziogas who gave us some valuable advice. Both authors would like to express their gratitude to the employees of Express Publishing and especially to our friend Tzeni Vlachou.

The authors would like to acknowledge the support of John Woodcock, former HAEF IB coordinator, and Sophia Arditzoglou, current HAEF IB coordinator, over the years. A lot of Computer Science students contributed with valuable ideas, comments and suggestions on early drafts. The computer science class of 2014 encouraged us to start this book.

The purpose of this document is to facilitate learning and help our colleagues and CS students around the world. This book is based on the IB computer science syllabus and follows the IB computer science syllabus. The authors did their very best to cite all resources used. If you find a source that is not properly cited please report it to authors. This book was inspired by the book[1]: Jones, R & A. Meyenn. (2004). Computer science Java Enabled. International Baccalaureate. Series, IBID press, Victoria.

---

[1] Jones, R & Meyenn, A. (2004). Computer science Java enabled. International Baccalaureate. Series, IBID press, Victoria.

The following IBO documents were used during the development of this book:

1. International Baccalaureate Organization. (2004). IBDP Computer Science Guide.
2. International Baccalaureate Organization. (2012). IBDP Computer Science Guide.
3. International Baccalaureate Organization. (2012). IBDP Approved notations for developing pseudocode.
4. International Baccalaureate Organization. (2012). IBDP Java Examination Tool Subset.
5. International Baccalaureate Organization. (2012). IBDP Pseudocode in examinations.

Table of contents

Chapter 1

TOPIC 1 – SYSTEM FUNDAMENTALS

© IBO 2012

Topic 1- system fundamentals[1]

System life cycle

System life cycle refers to the stages through which the development of a new system passes through. Figure 1.1 presents a system life cycle specifically for software, whereas Figure 1.2 presents a more general system life cycle. Although most systems begin with the analysis stage and continue with the design, implementation, operation and maintenance, sometimes it might be necessary to backtrack and return to an earlier stage.[2]

Figure 1.1: Software life cycle

[1] International Baccalaureate Organization. (2012). IBDP Computer Science Guide.
[2] International Baccalaureate Organization. (2004). IBDP Computer Science Guide.

Although the software and system life cycles are not directly presented in the new IB Computer Science curriculum, they are briefly mentioned in the first section of this chapter so as to inspire some fruitful discussions between teachers and students.

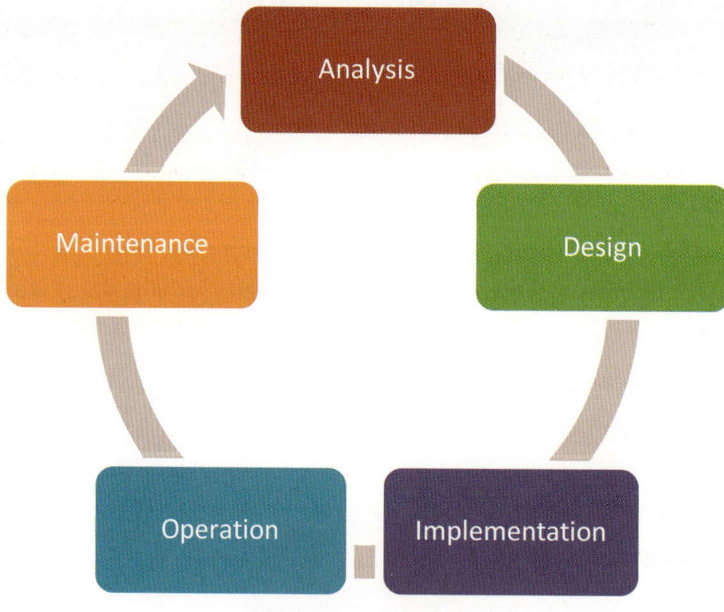

Figure 1.2: System life cycle

Figure 1.3: Some stages of the Software life cycle

The first Topic of the new computer science guide[1] and the section of the new computer science guide[1] that explain the internal assessment requirements directly refer only to four phases of the software life cycle as depicted in Figure 1.3.

1.1 Systems in organizations

Planning and system installation

1.1.1 The context for which a new system is planned

Exit skills. Students should be able to[1]:
Investigate and outline the framework of a new system. Describe the limitations of a proposed system. Present various organizational issues that relate to the installation of a new system. Identify the importance of a new system for various users. Outline the technologies involved.

A *new system* can be created in order to replace a system that is inefficient, no longer suitable for its original purpose, redundant or out-dated. The purpose of a new system can also be to increase productivity or quality of the output or even to minimize costs. The new system should reduce the errors or flaws of the existing one. The development of most large systems involves a huge amount of time and effort and contains a lot of different stages.

A computer system includes hardware, software, people working with it or using it and the immediate environment. So updating a computer system may involve actions like training employees to use the new system, changing the physical location of a server, or even firing employees.

Planning a new system is the process of thinking about various details and organizing the activities required to achieve the desired goal.

Planning should anticipate potential organizational issues such as:

Image 1.1: Feasibility study and its components

- lack of guiding organizational and business strategies
- lack of stakeholder and end-user participation
- lack of end-user 'ownership' of system
- lack of attention to required training
- lack of attention to various organizational issues, such as organizational culture

- lack of attention to the design of tasks and jobs, allocation of information system tasks, and the overall usability of the system.

At this stage a feasibility report or feasibility study should be conducted. The feasibility study evaluates and analyzes a project and its potential, based on various technical, economical, legal, operational and scheduling criteria. It is used to decide whether the proposed project should be pursued.[3]

T	Technical feasibility: Is the existing technology sufficient to implement the proposed system?
E	Economic feasibility: Is the proposed system cost effective?
L	Legal feasibility: Are there any conflicts between the proposed system and any regulations/laws?
O	Operational feasibility: Are the existing organizational practices and procedures sufficient to support the maintenance and operation of the new system?
S	Schedule feasibility: How long will we wait?

Example 1.1:
Question: A bookstore uses door-to-door salespersons to collect various orders from various customers. The orders are taken to the company's offices and are input by a secretary. The bookstore has decided to change this department and will ask the salespersons to input the orders at home, using their personal computers. Discuss the various effects of these changes.

Answer: The bookstore will no longer need the secretary or any physical space to accommodate the relevant department. Utility bills will be reduced and probably a smaller office will be enough for the company. The secretary will have to find a new job, or another position in the company. Salespersons will have to acquire some computer skills and they will need to have a PC with an internet connection. New computer software and hardware will also have to be obtained by the company, which will also need to find a secure way (network) to allow the salespersons to connect to the server. Staff working from home may ask for extra pay.

1.1.2 The need for change management

Exit skills. Students should be able to[1]:
Identify factors that are involved. Justify the need for change management. Investigate and outline success factors.

[3] Feasibility study. (2014, November 21). In *Wikipedia, The Free Encyclopedia*. Retrieved 18:03, November 23, 2014, from http://en.wikipedia.org/w/index.php?title=Feasibility_study&oldid=634775631

Change management involves various parameters and is a process of shifting individuals, teams, departments and organizations from the present state to a desired state. Successful change management guarantees that all stakeholders accept and embrace changes in their working environments. The goal is to maximize benefits and minimize the negative impacts of change on individuals.

For example, in a small business, if the operating system changes, the employees need to get proper training before they are able to use it in their everyday working schedule. In a school environment a new printer that is able to automatically print both sides could reduce costs but someone would have to inform teachers and students about this new functionality. Some people often feel threatened by a new completely computerized system, because they are afraid that they might lose their jobs. Unfortunately, sometimes their fears come true.

1.1.3 Compatibility issues resulting from situations including legacy systems or business mergers

Exit skills. Students should be able to[1]:

Describe the importance of compatibility.
Identify the way legacy systems interact with modern systems.
Suggest strategies for successful integration during business mergers.
Identify the international dimension of software compatibility.

The term *legacy system* refers to an old technology, hardware, computer system, or application program. Some systems that belong to this category may still play an important role in an organization. Such a system may still be in use because its data cannot be converted to newer formats, or its applications cannot be upgraded. Keeping a legacy system in operation involves various maintenance challenges. Even high technology agencies such as NASA use legacy systems because the system still provides for the users' needs, even though newer or more efficient technologies are available[4]. It is clear that the exchange of data between legacy and new systems is a factor that the administration needs to pay special attention to.

Business merger is the combining of two or more business entities. The main reason companies merge is to reduce costs. During this process all departments of both companies need to ensure that all subsystems are compatible.

[4] (n.d.). Retrieved November 23, 2014, from https://www.fbo.gov/index?s=opportunity&mode=form&id=e2cd8e7c507a2bbd3614ede86beb5666&tab=core&_cview=0

Four Strategies for Integration[5]

1. Keep both information systems, and develop them to have the same functionality (high maintenance cost)
2. Replace both information systems with a new one (increased initial cost).
3. Select the best information systems from each company and combine them (it is very difficult for the employees to work with information systems from another company).
4. Select one company's information systems and drop the other companies' (policy problems).

Nowadays information technologies offer enormous potential for the world economy and society. Most organizations interact with individuals and other organizations that are located in different countries. *Language differences* greatly increase communication problems, even if individuals have some knowledge of the others' mother language. Language is not only a form of communication but also a way of thinking and defining the world.

Software incompatibility is a situation where different software entities or systems cannot operate satisfactorily, cooperatively or independently, on the same computer, or on different computers linked by a local or wide area computer network.

1.1.4 Different systems implementation

Exit skills. Students should be able to:
Define SaaS (Software-as-a-Service). Define on premise software. Relate and analyze the difference between SaaS (Software-as-a-Service) and on premise software solutions.

Image 1.2: SaaS

Business software can operate installed on a client's infrastructure and premises or hosted on dedicated servers that belong to a company that provides such services. A locally hosted system is the most appropriate solution for larger and complex systems. A remotely hosted system is the most

[5] Legacy System Integration. (n.d.). Retrieved November 23, 2014, from http://www.coleyconsulting.co.uk/merge.htm

appropriate solution where there is no necessary hardware equipment in place or in cases where the administration wishes to outsource responsibilities for maintenance, support, backups, security, etc.

SaaS (Software-as-a-Service) or "on-demand software" is a contemporary delivery method that allows software and data to be hosted and managed centrally on a remote datacenter. Users pay to access the services provided on a subscription basis. SaaS solutions reside on the cloud and need a web browser and a broadband Internet connection to be accessed.[6]

Image 1.3: SaaS use versus on premise installation

SaaS is less expensive because it has a low initial cost and requires few investments in installation, maintenance and upgrading. Companies have to pay only for the SaaS subscription, which is cheaper in the short-to-medium term. SaaS provides a scalable solution, since a company has only to adjust its monthly SaaS subscription as required. In most cases only a web browser and a broadband internet connection are required to access SaaS applications. A wide range of desktop, portable and mobile devices also support SaaS solutions. SaaS requires few IT personnel and all software updates take place far away from company's premises. SaaS is considered a safe solution because applications and data reside in the cloud service of the provider's datacenter. However, there is a possibility of data loss, if a SaaS provider goes out of business. The performance of a web browser-based application that is hosted in a distant datacenter that is accessed via an Internet connection is low when compared to software running on a local machine or over the company's local area network. SaaS integration with other SaaS solutions or software installed locally is always difficult.

1.1.5 Alternative installation processes

Exit skills. Students should be able to[1]:
Explain the major installation processes Suggest with reasons different installation processes Explain the pros and cons of each installation process

The installation of a new system is a situation that most enterprises, organizations and individuals will face one or more times. During this process the old system will be retired and the new system will take its place.

[6] Software as a service. (2014, November 17). In *Wikipedia, The Free Encyclopedia*. Retrieved 18:05, November 23, 2014, from http://en.wikipedia.org/w/index.php?title=Software_as_a_service&oldid=634189323

Example 1.2:

Question: A medical company is very satisfied from the technical performance of its current information technology infrastructure. Is there any reason to change it?

Answer: Maybe, the current system may be too expensive to run and maintain. So a new system may decrease the total expenses of the company.

Example 1.3:

Question: What is meant by the term "operational feasibility" found in a feasibility report?

Answer: A feasibility report should examine the "operational feasibility" of the proposed system. This part should examine whether the existing organizational practices and procedures are sufficient to support the maintenance and operation of the new system.

Example 1.4:

Question: What is meant by the term "merger"?

Answer: The combining of two or more corporations or business enterprises into a single corporation.

Example 1.5:

Question: What is meant by the term "software incompatibility"?

Answer: It is a situation where different software entities or systems cannot operate satisfactorily, cooperatively or independently, on the same computer, or on different computers linked by a local or wide area computer network.

Example 1.6:

Question: State five advantages of "SaaS".

Answer: Lower initial cost, easy to upgrade, ease of access from anywhere, easy to predict the cost of initial implementation (subscription), the application is ready to use.

Example 1.7:

Question: State five possible disadvantages of "SaaS".

Answer: Dependence on a third party, security and confidentiality, dependence on Internet connection, risk of data loss, not as powerful as on premise solutions.

One critical decision when moving from an old system to a new one is the choice of *implementation (conversion, changeover) method*. Changeover is the process of putting the new system online and retiring the old one. The reason for an organization to choose one implementation method in favour of another is often a trade-off between costs and risk.
It should be mentioned that in most cases there might be resistance by employees or customers to change and planning should try to minimize the negative effects.

The types of changeovers are:

- *Parallel.* The main characteristic of Parallel Changeover is that both systems work in parallel for a short period of time. This method is very popular because of the limited risk. Outputs of both systems can be compared to ensure that the new system is functioning properly. If the new system fails, the company can revert or return to the old system. When the company is satisfied with the output of the new system, the old system can be terminated. Running two different systems simultaneously means extra costs and workload because it requires that the two systems run parallel for a certain period of time. The company has to maintain two different systems and this results in various organizational tasks. This method is not efficient if the old and the new systems have completely different processing tasks, functions, inputs, or outputs.
- *Big Bang or Direct (immediate).* This changeover is very risky since the company plugs in the new system and unplugs the old one at the same time. Once the administration has decided to use this method and has prepared all the necessary procedures, the changeover begins. Obviously there are dangers associated with this method if the new system does not function as expected. This method is preferred when the system is not critical. With this approach, all users need to be trained appropriately before the switch takes place, in order to use the new information system efficiently.

Example 1.8:

Question: A nuclear station is equipped with a highly automated control system. This system should be replaced by a new system. Suggest a suitable implementation method. Justify your answer.

Answer: The correct answer is parallel changeover because the main characteristic of this conversion method is the limited risk. The cost of operation and maintenance of both systems will be higher but this is of limited importance in this particular situation. Direct method of implementation is not appropriate because of the high risk of failure and the absence of a trusted backup system. The scenario described in the question does not imply the existence of multiple sites so the pilot method is not considered as an alternative.

- *Pilot.* The pilot method is mostly used in large organizations that have multiple sites. The new system is introduced in one of the sites and extended to other sites over time. The risk of this method is low and the pilot sites can serve as models for the rest of the company. The first group that adopts the new system is called the pilot site or the pilot group. After the system proves successful at the pilot site, it is implemented into the rest of the company using a changeover method (usually direct).
- *Phased.* With the phased conversion method, a company converts one module of the system at a time, meaning that different parts of the system are converted at

different times. The training period is extended and the adoption of the new system takes longer, since each phase must be implemented separately. The installation of the new system is done per module, per department etc.

1.1.6 Problems that may arise as a part of data migration

Exit skills. Students should be able to[1]:
Define data migration. Identify the importance of incompatibility and incompleteness. Provide a balanced analysis of different data migration scenarios.

Data migration refers to the transfer of data between different formats, storage types and computer systems. It usually takes place in an automatic manner so as to achieve efficient use of human resources. Data migration happens when an organization changes, upgrades or merges its information systems (for example, due to a merger or takeover).[7] Many problems may arise when transferring data from one system to another. First of all, there may be incapability of moving the information due to parameters such as incompatibility with the new system or non-recognizable data structures. Also, data may be lost or not transferred due to an incomplete data transfer or errors during the process. In addition, data can also be misinterpreted due to incompatibilities, caused by the different conventions of each country concerning date, time and measurement units.

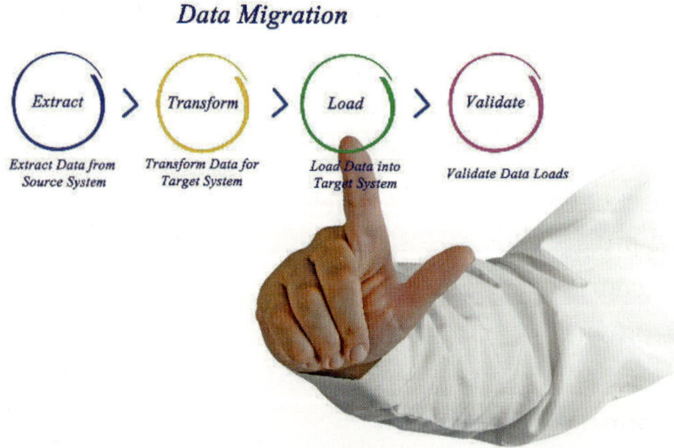

Image 1.4: Data migration

[7] Database Glossary - D. (n.d.). Retrieved November 23, 2014, from http://www.nwdatabase.com/database-glossary-d.htm

PLAN

- While the planning stage depends on the extend and purpose of the migration, the planning process should also include determining the requirements of the migration. Parameters such as the identification of the future environment, the development and the documentation of the migration plan should be considered.

MIGRATE

- During the migration phase, the Information Technology department will need to communicate its plans, obtain, install and configure any necessary software and hardware, and proceed to the data migration.

VALIDATE

- A pre-migration test to validate data is highly recommended, in addition to post-migration validation testing. These tests will check that the data is in the same state after the migration as it was before the migration.

Figure 1.2: Data migration stages[8]

1.1.7 Various types of testing

Exit skills. Students should be able to[1]:

Identify the importance of testing.
Define major testing types.
Suggest the best testing for a proposed scenario.

Testing can happen in different ways and in different phases.

Functional testing tests individual commands, text input, menu functions, etc. confirms that they perform and function correctly according to the design specifications. For example, if a choice is made to add a client, does the program go to the "add clients module"?
Data testing is when normal, abnormal and extreme data is put into the system. Suppose that there is a program that accepts a student's percentage in a math exam and gives a "pass" message if the number entered is greater than or equal to sixty; otherwise it prints a "fail" message. This program can be tested with[9, 10]:

- *Normal Data* such as 76 will be used to check if "pass" and "fail" messages are appropriately provided.
- *Data at the Limits* should also be used, for this particular problem 0, 59, 60, 100 are all examples of normal data at the limits.

Useful Information: Some authors describe as "extreme/boundary data the data at the limits of acceptability/validity" and as "abnormal/erroneous data the data outside the limits of acceptability/validity." cf. David Watson and Helen Williams, 2012, page 79.

[8] Adopted by: IBM, 2007, Best practices for data migration. http://www-935.ibm.com/services/us/gts/pdf/bestpracticesfordatamigration-wp-gtw01275-usen-01-121307.pdf
[9] IB Computing Home Page. (n.d.). Retrieved November 23, 2014, from http://www.ib-computing.com
[10] Watson D., H. Williams, 2012, Cambridge IGCSE Computer Studies Revision Guide, Cambridge University Press.

- *Extreme Data* will be outside the normal limits; -10, 104, 1223 are examples. These data should be rejected during validation testing. The user may not input such data because they're wrong, and it's easy to press a key twice by mistake.
- *Abnormal Data (illegal data)* will be the type of data that we really didn't expect. For this particular program it could be data that looks like a string, a character and not an integer. This data would not usually be entered. A naive user may enter *"two"*, which seems unlikely but he/she could also hit the spacebar and enter *"4 5"*, instead of *"45"*, for example.

Alpha testing is done before the software product is made available to the general public. Normally, Alpha testing will be carried out by the company that develops the software in a laboratory type environment and not by the end users in their usual workplaces[11, 12].

Beta testing includes comments and suggestions of the users. Unlike Alpha testing, users outside the company are involved in the testing. Their feedback is valuable and can be used to fix defects and errors that were missed, and also contributes in the preparation of support teams that will deal with expected issues. Frequent beta testing results in last minute software changes. In some cases, the Beta version will be made available to the general public. This can provide vital real-world information and feedback[11, 12].

Dry-run testing is conducted using pen-and-paper by the programmer. During dry run testing the programmer mentally runs the algorithm. He examines the source code and decides on what the output of a run should be (execution).

During *unit testing,* individual parts of the system are tested separately.

During the *integration testing,* the entire system is tested at the same time to verify that that all components can work together.

User acceptance testing is used to determine if the system satisfies the customer needs and in most cases is conducted in user premises before accepting transfer of ownership. This type of testing is the last stage of the software testing process.

Debugging is a systematic process of finding and correcting the number of bugs (errors) in a computer program.
It is important to mention that there are computer programs that can automatically test other programs. This makes the testing process faster and cheaper.

[11] Alpha vs. Beta Testing. (n.d.). Retrieved November 23, 2014, from http://www.centercode.com/blog/2011/01/alpha-vs-beta-testing/
[12] (n.d.). Retrieved November 23, 2014, from http://ezinearticles.com/?Alpha-Testing-and-Beta-Testing&id=433

Example 1.9:

Question: Several verification and validation checks are performed on data being entered into a database by a bank employee. The database contains an "age" field and a "name" field. Give two examples of invalid data and one example of valid data for the field "age", and explain how this field could be validated.

Answer: All "age" entries should be checked to see if they are positive numbers and for consistency with a minimum/maximum range (e.g. 18-110). This process includes a type and a range check. Invalid data for the age field could be "Y" and "234" while valid data would be "25".

Question: How the "name" field could be verified?

Answer: It could be typed twice and the two entries compared. If both entries are the same then the "name" is verified. This process is called double entry and reduces data entry errors.

Validation and verification in relation to data input[2]

- *Validation* is the process of evaluating whether data input follows appropriate specifications and is within reasonable limits.
- *Verification* is the process of ensuring that the data input is the same as the original source data. A way of ensuring data verification is through double entry.

Verification vs. validation software testing

Verification is the confirmation that a computer product meets identified specifications, while validation is the confirmation that a computer product meets its design function or is appropriate for the intended use.

- Validation: Are we developing the correct system?
- Verification: Are we developing the system correctly?
- Validation: Does the product meet the customer-needs?
- Verification: Does the product comply with a specific regulation or condition?

User focus

1.1.8 Importance of user documentation

Exit skills. Students should be able to[1]:
Identify the importance of proper user documentation. Describe the way proper documentation affects implementation.

Programs and systems may become increasingly complex as their aim gets more and more and convoluted. Additionally, the user's way of thinking may differ from the developers'; hence the way the product functions may not be clear to the user. All of the above may lead to serious problems during the implementation or operational stage of the Software Life Cycle (SLC). The user might not know how to use the product to its full capacity, and even specialized technicians may not be able to set up the new system properly for the firm they work for. With appropriate external documentation, these issues can be easily countered, since there will be a user manual explaining every component of the product.

A systematic and organized software development procedure ensures that all supporting documents are produced in an orderly and methodical fashion. *It is very important to distinguish between internal documentation and external documentation.*

Internal documentation is the code comprehension features and details provided as part of the source code itself. Proper internal documentation includes:

- Appropriate module headers
- Appropriate comments
- Useful and meaningful variable names
- Useful module, classes, methods and function headers
- Appropriate code indentation
- Appropriate code structuring
- Appropriate use of enumerated types
- Appropriate use of constant identifiers
- Appropriate use of data types defined by the user

It is very difficult and likely impossible for the source code to be read by the final user.

External documentation is typically written as a separate document from the program itself. It is provided through various types of user supporting documents such as a users' guide, software requirements specification document, detailed description of the design and implementation features of the program and test document.

1.1.9 Different methods of providing user documentation

Exit skills. Students should be able to[1]:
Identify the importance of proper user documentation. Suggest various methods of user documentation. Describe the way propped documentation affect implementation.

User documentation can either be in a written or in an online form, so that the user can search the document more easily and quickly. The user documentation should include all the instructions that are mandatory for the system to operate and should contain frequently asked questions, which are always necessary for new users. The document should be well structured and divided into the appropriate categories.

Image 1.5: Different methods of user documentation

Manuals

These can be provided online or offline. One of the advantages of online manuals is the potential use of multimedia features. Manuals can also be provided online as pdf files which one can download and print. The advantage of a printed manual is that it can be read without the use of a PC or an internet connection.

Email support

Online support is an asynchronous type of support and can be provided via an email address. Users contact the support team of the company to resolve any problems with the help of specialized technicians.

Embedded Assistance or integrated user assistance

Software suites like MS Office have inbuilt help systems (tool tips and dynamic page content within the system itself). One example is when the user hovers the mouse over an icon a small text box appears with valuable help information. This kind of assistance is considered an excellent way to increase the usability of a software application. Embedded user assistance is context-specific, task-specific, and does not require novice users to ask the right question to find the suitable answer.

Frequently Asked Questions

Frequently Asked Questions (FAQ) are listed questions and answers, all supposed to give users answers to a common set of problems and pertaining to a particular topic. The format is commonly used on online forums. The list of questions contains questions that tend to recur.

Live chat sessions

Online support is a type of real time support that is extremely useful for emergency situations. A live chat technician will ask for the description of the occurring problem, and try to present a list of possible solutions. A telephone call, a live chat session or a video session provides a feeling of being supported by a real person, which is preferred by many users.

Online portals or web portals

Online support is provided in many ways, depending on the product or service that is being documented. Online portals can provide updated manuals, support pages and FAQ pages.

Remote desktop connections

Remote Desktop is a function that enables a specialized person to connect to the user's PC across the Internet from virtually any computer. Remote Desktop will actually allow a specialized technician to take control of the user's PC as though he/she was sitting directly in front of it. This solution is ideal if the user is not very experienced. This solution has some security disadvantages because the technician is allowed to have full access over the user's PC.

1.1.10 Different methods of delivering user training

Exit skills. Students should be able to[1]:
Identify the importance of proper user training Suggest various methods of user training Describe the way propped user training affect implementation

It is impossible to take full advantage of a new advanced IT system without proper training. Moreover even the highest investment in technology requires users that are able and wish to use it. User training is extremely important in almost every case.

All the staff must be familiar with the new system as they will make mistakes if they are not properly trained. Staff can be trained by self-instruction, formal classes or online training. Furthermore, the developers of the new software have to create clear educational material for solving any kind of questions a user might have.

User training can be delivered in a number of different ways depending on a variety of factors, such as the number of the students, the availability of instructors, the size of the business, and the training budget.

Self-Instruction or self-study

Self-instruction allows the user to learn in his/her own time, until he/she achieves mastery of the subject. Printed manuals, books, e-books or other resources such as video tutorials or online exercises can be provided and used whenever the user needs to improve his skills.

A user can benefit a lot through self-study. First of all, there is no tuition fee. Furthermore the user can study whenever he/she wants (no formal class at a fixed time and a fixed place). The disadvantages include lack of guidance or teacher support and the final result depends on the motivation of the user and their ability to learn on their own.

Image 1.6: Different methods of user training

Formal classes

A formal class offers an interactive setting that promotes open and free discussion between students and the teacher (instructor). Having several students learning in the same classroom has the additional advantage of allowing students to exchange ideas with one another. Direct interaction with the expert allows for ideas to be exchanged easily and without any technical communication barriers.

A classroom situation may disadvantage shy members. The classroom can also obstruct one's ability to learn by allowing other, more self-assured students to dominate the discussion environment.

Remote/distance learning/online training[13]

The main benefit of asynchronous online learning is that it allows participants to take part in high quality courses from anywhere in the world provided they have a PC and Internet connection. This type of Virtual Classroom is accessible 24/7/365. Time efficiency and time management are valuable strengths of distance learning. Students can access their virtual courses, lectures, course materials, and class discussions at any time, day or night. The use of interactive learning environments contributes to self-direction and promotes critical thinking, and thus is highly supported by the literature of adult education and training.

An online educational program requires participants who are able to access the online learning environment. Lack of the required infrastructure will exclude otherwise eligible students from the online course. Students and instructors must possess a minimum level of IT skills in order to function effectively in an online environment. Online asynchronous education places greater responsibility on the student and gives students control over their learning experience, and thus is considered inappropriate for more dependent and immature learners.

---

[13] Illinois Online Network: Educational Resources. (n.d.). Retrieved November 23, 2014, from http://www.ion.uillinois.edu/resources/tutorials/overview/

System backup

1.1.11 Causes of data loss.

Exit skills. Students should be able to[1]:
Identify the negative impact of data loss. Identify various causes of data loss.

Data loss[14] refers to an error condition where data is lost or destroyed due to system failure, storage negligence, or even transmission or processing errors. Various precautions can be taken, in order to prevent or restore data loss, through both hardware and software. The cost of data loss depends on how costly it may be to go on without the data, how costly it may be to recreate the data, as well as how costly it may be to notify users of data loss.

Causes	Comments/Solutions
Accidental deletion	• Very common cause of data loss • Use of file recovery software
Administrative errors	• Need for care
Poor data storage organization system (misplacement)	• Data can't be found • Restructure data organization
Building fires	• Rare • Store data in two locations
Closing the program without saving the file	• Very common cause of data loss • Need for care, use of autosave features
Computer viruses	• Very common cause of data loss • Need for antivirus software • Regular backups
Continued use after signs of failure	• Need for Self-Monitoring, Analysis and Reporting Technology (SMART) • Need for PC checkup • Regular backups
Data corruption	• Errors in computer data • Regular backups
Firmware corruption	• Hard disk failure • Regular backups
Natural disasters (floods, earthquakes)	• Rare • Store data in two locations • Regular backups
Outsiders wanting to delete, alter or steal the information.	• Regular backups • Need for a firewall • Need for authentication methods
Physical damage of the storage device (intentionally or not)	• Regular backups • Need for care
Power failure	• Need for UPS (uninterruptible power supply) • Regular backups

[14] Data loss. (2014, August 25). In *Wikipedia, The Free Encyclopedia*. Retrieved 18:06, November 23, 2014, from http://en.wikipedia.org/w/index.php?title=Data_loss&oldid=622747408

1.1.12 Consequences of data loss in a specified situation

Exit skills. Students should be able to[1]:
Outline the negative impact of data loss in various situations. Identify various consequences of data loss in a given scenario.

In all cases data loss is something that we want to prevent, but there are cases where data loss could have extremely serious consequences. For example, if the medical records of a patient in a hospital are lost, then the patient's life can be in danger if the data cannot be retrieved, and some painful examinations might have to be repeated. Data loss is not that dangerous in all cases, but retrieval is time consuming and might not always be possible, which is a problem. Imagine a situation where a client books a hotel room over the phone. But when he/she arrives at the hotel, the receptionist informs him/her that there is no record of his/her booking and no rooms are available. The client (after the initial shock) has to search for another hotel perhaps informing friends and colleagues on social media of his/her discomfort and disappointment.

1.1.13 Range of methods that can be used to prevent data loss

Exit skills. Students should be able to[1]:
Define failover systems, redundancy, removable media, offsite storage and online storage. Give details about the methods used to prevent loss of data.

Image 1.7: Data loss

In the case of system or hard drive crashes, the data we have stored in them can be lost forever, or are inaccessible. In order to prevent this, specialists have created different methods by which one can be prepared for the above situation:

- Regular backup of files using hard disks or magnetic tapes
- Firewall installation
- Data storage in two or more locations (*offsite* storage)
- Removed hard copies (printed versions of data)
- Installation of an Antivirus program for antivirus protection

Example 1.10:

Question: A bank uses a database server that provides database services to various computers. Describe a secure strategy for backing up and restoring the data on the database server after a failure.

Answer: A secure back-up strategy would be to use high-capacity magnetic tapes because the tapes are very cheap per Gigabyte and have great longevity. The first step is to back up the files of the hard disks to tapes every night. The back-up process should be completely automated and the tapes should be secured and stored off-site in a fire-proof room. A suitable strategy for restoring the data after the failure would be to use these tapes to restore the database on the server.

- Human error reduction techniques and/or failsafe (accidentally deleted files)
- *Online* auto save backup (iCloud, Dropbox)

Image 1.8: Removable media backup tape (high-capacity magnetic tape)

In computers science, *redundancy* is the duplication of storage devices and stored data of a computer system with the intention of securing the stored data. It is considered as a failsafe method.

Diskettes, Blu-ray discs, CDs, DVDs, USB (Universal Serial Bus) are *removable media* that are used for fast data backup and data storage. These removable media can store data permanently and are non-volatile.

A *failover system* is a computer system which is on standby capable of switching to a spare computer system upon hardware failure, network failure, or any other type of error, such as software malfunction. The main difference between a failover and a *switchover* is the degree of needed human intervention. Typically, a failover is automatic and handles abnormal situations without human interference. In a failover system when primary server fails the standby server is made primary. In a switchover system the primary and the secondary server interchange the primary role. Critical systems typically allow for failover to take place on system failure so as to provide reliability and continuous availability.[15]

[15] Failover. (2014, June 25). In *Wikipedia, The Free Encyclopedia*. Retrieved 18:07, November 23, 2014, from http://en.wikipedia.org/w/index.php?title=Failover&oldid=614395973

Software deployment

1.1.14 Strategies for managing releases and updates

Exit skills. Students should be able to[1]:
Define updates, patches, upgrades and releases. Give details about the management of updates and releases. Describe automatic update process.

There are several ways in which updates can be made available. First of all, most of the times the purchasing of a product means access to free online updates, released by the company. There are automatic updates that function through the net. These types of updates usually aim to improve the product, fix various deficiencies or perform minor changes. When the company decides that it no longer wishes to support software and wishes to promote a newer version, it stops releasing updates (the life cycle of the new system having started some time before).

Arrow points from smaller to larger alterations.

- ***Patches*** are used by software companies to update applications by fixing known bugs and vulnerabilities. Be aware that, patches may introduce new bugs as side effects.[16]
- ***Updates*** improve a product in a minor way by adding new functionalities or fixing known bugs. In most cases updates are free.[17]
- ***Upgrades*** always contain novel functionalities or characteristics, as well cumulative bug fixes. In most cases upgrades need to be bought.[17]
- ***Releases*** are final, working versions of software applications. These applications have already gone through alpha and beta software testing. Releases relate to new or upgraded applications.[18]

[16] Patch (computing). (2014, November 11). In *Wikipedia, The Free Encyclopedia*. Retrieved 18:08, November 23, 2014, from http://en.wikipedia.org/w/index.php?title=Patch_(computing)&oldid=633351269

[17] What is the difference between and Upgrade and an Update? (n.d.). Retrieved November 23, 2014, from http://www.enfocus.com/en/support/knowledge-base/what-is-the-difference-between-an-upgrade-and-an-update/

[18] Release. (n.d.). Retrieved November 23, 2014, from http://searchsoftwarequality.techtarget.com/definition/release

Example 1.11:

Question: State two stages of the "data migration process".

Answer: Plan and validate

Example 1.12:

Question: State one difference between "alpha" and "beta testing".

Answer: Alpha testing takes place inside the company which develops the software while beta testing includes selected users that are not employees of the software company and test the software in their premises.

Example 1.13:

Question: Does a programmer needs a computer to conduct "dry run testing"?

Answer: No, because dry run testing is conducted manually using a pencil and a paper in most cases.

Example 1.14:

Question: State one difference between "internal" and "external" documentation.

Answer: Internal documentation facilitates programmers while external documentation focuses on the user of the product.

Example 1.15:

Question: state one major advantage of "formal classes"

Answer: Direct interaction with the expert allows immediate answer to students' questions without any technical communication barrier.

Example 1.16:

Question: State three methods that can be used to prevent "data loss".

Answer: Regular backup of files using hard disks or tapes, online auto save backup, Data storage in two or more locations (offsite storage).

1.2 System design basics

Components of a computer system

1.2.1 Hardware, software, peripheral, network, human resources

Exit skills. Students should be able to[1]:
Give the precise meaning of the terms hardware, software, peripheral, network and human resources.

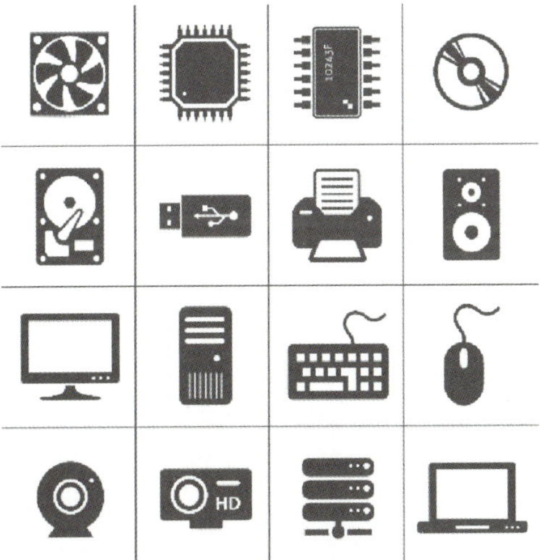

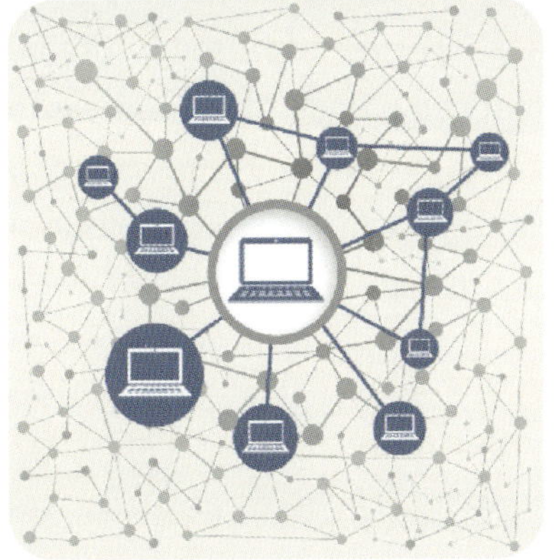

Image 1.9: Hardware, software & network

Computer *hardware*: The physical elements of a computer, e.g. screen, CPU etc.

Software: A series of instructions that can be understood by a CPU. These instructions guide the CPU to perform specific operations. Software is comprised of both programs and data.[19]

Peripheral device: any auxiliary device that can communicate and work with a computer. For example: input/output devices, printers, etc. A peripheral device extends the capabilities of the computer system it is connected to. The peripheral is not a core, essential, part of the computer.[1]

Computer Network: A set of computer systems that are interconnected and share resources, as well as data. For example: Local Area Network, Wide Area Network, etc.[1]

Human Resources: People who are used or could be used in an organization, business or economy.

[19] Software. (2014, November 19). In *Wikipedia, The Free Encyclopedia*. Retrieved 18:09, November 23, 2014, from http://en.wikipedia.org/w/index.php?title=Software&oldid=634491568

1.2.2 The roles that a computer can take in a networked world

Exit skills. Students should be able to[1]:
Define client, server, email server, DNS server, router and firewall. Describe the different roles that a computer can take.

The computer can assume several roles in a networked world. It can function as a client, server, e-mail server, domain name system server (DNS server), router or firewall.

A *dumb terminal* is a device that usually consists of a keyboard, a monitor, and a network card that is connected to a server or a powerful computer. Dumb terminals depend entirely on the computer to which they are connected for computations, data processing and data management.

A *thin client* is a relatively low performance terminal, which heavily but not entirely, depends on the server to which it is connected.

A *client* receives data via the network, whereas the *server* has saved data on it and offers it to clients. A server may be a program or a computer that provides services requested by clients connected over a network while a client is an average computer or terminal (dumb terminal, thin client) used to access a computer-based system.

An *email server* is the equivalent of a post office that manages the flow of email in and out of the network, checks that an email address is valid, allows users to access their email, etc.

A *router* is a networking device that accepts incoming quanta of information (data packets), reads their destination address and distributes them across networks, according to a routing table or routing policy (policy based routing). A router identifies the destination of messages and sends them via an appropriate route and is used to forward data packets between networks.

A *Domain Name System Server* attributes names to network addresses and therefore resolves names by assigning them to the appropriate network entity (a resource that is part of the network). A DNS server allows you to type names into the address bar of your web browser like "mit.edu" and the web browser automatically finds that address on the Internet. The *Domain Name System* is a protocol within the set of the TCP/IP protocol suite and is used for managing public names of web sites. One can always bypass a DNS lookup by entering the Internet Protocol (IP) address directly into a browser.

A *firewall* is a hardware or software network infrastructure that controls data flow access among network entities. The firewall is mainly used to offer protection and limit access to a network. The ideal firewall system configuration consists of hardware and software components.

A *client-server* refers to a software network architecture system where clients request information and servers perform tasks in order to provide the information. At least one server machine is required as a prerequisite for the client-server architecture. The main difference between server and clients is that servers share their resources, whereas clients do not.[1, 20]

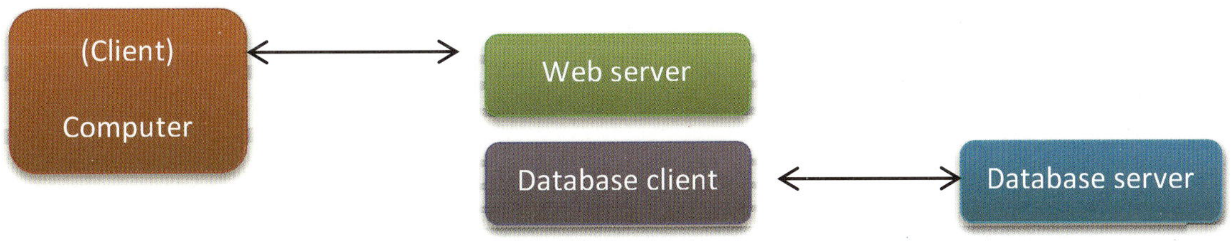

Figure 1.3: Client Server example[21]

Example 1.17: Figure 1.5 depicts a client server example that includes a client computer running a web browser (Internet Explorer, Firefox, Chrome etc.) and a server computer running a database server. The user on the client computer needs to access the bank central server. In order to do that, the web browser of the client sends a specific request to the web server of the bank. The web server receiving the request needs to access the central database of the bank and sends its own request through the database client. The requested information is then returned from the central database to the database client and from the web server to the client through the web browser.

1.2.3 Social and ethical issues associated with a networked world

Exit skills. Students should be able to[1]:
Give the precise meaning of IT subjects of social and ethical significance. Develop a balanced and thorough review of a given scenario that involves social and ethical issues. Explain the effects that are associated with continued developments in IT.

Issues of social and ethical significance can arise whenever information technology is used. These issues have positive and negative ethical and social impacts. Many people can be affected and it is sometimes difficult to identify the person who is to be held responsible. An

[20] Client–server model. (2014, October 7). In *Wikipedia, The Free Encyclopedia*. Retrieved 18:09, November 23, 2014, from http://en.wikipedia.org/w/index.php?title=Client%E2%80%93server_model&oldid=628622834

[21] Experts you should follow. (n.d.). Retrieved November 23, 2014, from http://www.wikianswers.com/Q/In_a_client_server_environment_what_is_a_server

introduction of a new system may affect the life of thousands, millions, or even billions of users (take for example the Internet). The IT subjects of social and ethical significance are[22]:

- *Reliability*, which refers to how well an IT system functions. Computer failures cause data loss, time loss, money loss, injury or even death. The reliability of IT systems determines confidence in their value.
- *Integrity*, which refers to protecting the completeness and accuracy of data. Data lacks integrity if it is incomplete, out of date, or has been purposely or unintentionally altered.
- *Inconsistency*. Problems may also arise if information is duplicated in a database and only one copy is updated, causing inconsistency (e.g. telephone field).
- *Security*, which refers to the protection of hardware, software, peripherals and computer networks' from unauthorized access. Biometrics, proprietary tokens, passwords, firewalls, and locks are some of the most common security systems placed to restrict access to IT systems.
- *Authenticity*, which involves a person proving their identity to gain access to a computer system beyond reasonable doubt. It is important to mention that requiring more than one independent factor increases the difficulty of providing false credentials.[23]
- *Privacy*, which is the ability to control how and to what extent data is used and disseminated to others. It includes issues such as: how long data is stored, who has access to the data and how the data is used.

Image 1.10: Anonymity

- *Anonymity*. Privacy becomes anonymity when, for instance, an individual uses an IT system to conceal his/her true identity in order to cyber-bully another person, commit illegal actions or crimes, hack computers, commit terrorism etc.
- *Intellectual property*, which refers to ideas, discoveries, scientific endeavours, photographs, films, essays, and art works. Copyright laws are designed to protect intellectual property from unauthorized and illegal reproduction. Modern "copy and paste" and file-sharing practices and devices make it easy to break copyright laws.
- *The Digital Divide and Equality of Access.* The growth and the use of IT systems have not developed at the same rate for everybody in all parts of the world, or in all areas of the same country. Even within advanced countries there are people who lack access to IT infrastructures, and online services. Economic costs, financial costs, lack of literacy, lack of language skills (English) and lack of basic resources such as electricity are the main reasons that sustain the digital divide.

---

[22] IBDP, 2010, ITGS Guide, International Baccalaureate Organization.

[23] Multi-factor authentication. (2014, November 6). In Wikipedia, The Free Encyclopedia. Retrieved 18:12, November 23, 2014, from http://en.wikipedia.org/w/index.php?title=Multi-factor_authentication&oldid=632725562

- *Surveillance*, which involves using IT to monitor individuals or groups of people either with or without (also a privacy issue) their knowledge or permission. Governments, law enforcement, private groups, employers, traffic control etc. may perform surveillance.
- *Globalization and Cultural Diversity*. IT helps to diminish the importance of geographical, political, economic and cultural boundaries while speeding up the global spread of political, financial, sport and cultural news. Traditional cultures and values may diminish gradually over time.

Image 1.11: Surveillance and addiction

Useful Information Multi-factor authentication (MFA) is an authentication technique used to control computer access. A user can enter by exhibiting authentication factors from at least two of the three categories:

- *Something you know. Knowledge* factors ("things only the user *knows*"), passwords
- *Something you have. Possession* factors ("things only the user *has*"), ATM cards
- *Something you are. Inherence* factors ("things only the user *is*"), biometrics

- *IT Policies*. Policies are enforceable procedures and measures that promote the appropriate use of computers, networks, information systems and technologies. Governments, public authorities, local authorities, businesses, private groups or individuals are developers of various IT policies. The fast pace of Information Technology progression means policies often quickly made obsolete.

Example 1.18:

Question: Is it possible to use two or more authentication methods to control a computer access?

Answer: Yes, multifactor authentication technique is used when there is a need for advanced security.

- *Standards and Protocols*, which are predefined technical rules and conventions that developers of hardware and software should follow. Standards and protocols allow for compatibility, facilitate communication and interoperability. They are needed to ensure different systems are compatible with each other (examples: GIF, USB, ASCII etc.).
- *People and machines*. Internet addiction is a social impact. The use of AI in military or law-enforcement situations is also an issue of social concern. This subject analyzes all aspects of the interaction between IT and humans.
- *Digital Citizenship*, which covers appropriate behavior in a digital world. Appropriate behavior includes using IT ethically, in a way that respects society, the law and does not expose any person to threats, danger, or a contravention of their human rights.

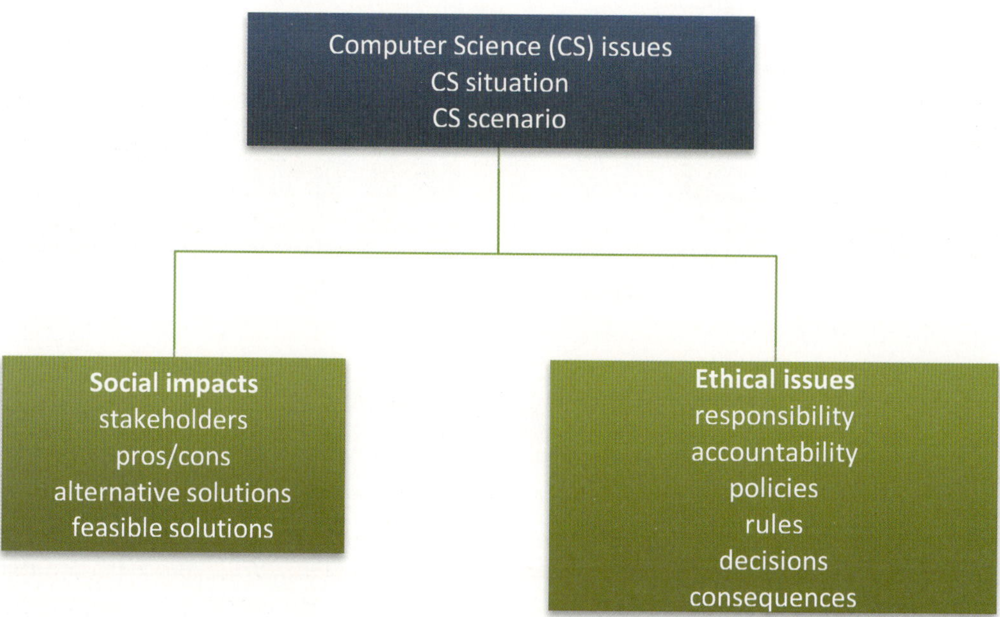

Figure 1.4: A possible diagram to be used when anlysing different CS and IT scenerios

The following tables illustrate some very simple examples. An IT system has pros and cons.

Cause	Positive Effects
Constant exposure to communication technology	• Citizens better informed about the world
Internet	• Email, WWW
Use of smartphones	• Easier communication in emergencies • Use of useful applications (GPS application for example)
Gaming	• Better hand-eye coordination
Mobile phones	• Easier communication with family (children, elderly) • Easier communication in emergencies

Cause	Negative Effects
Constant exposure to communication	• Psychological impacts such as stress, poor concentration and short attention span

technology	• Obstacle to personal one-to-one relationships
Internet addiction	• Neglected real life • Social media obsession
Use of smartphones	• Anxiety • Increasing expense of hardware
Gaming addiction	• Lower levels of concentration because of lack of sleep • Social desensitization • Neglected education and personal development
Overuse of mobile phones	• Possible health consequences • Possible car accidents

Example 1.19:

Question: There is a vast amount of scientific information and educational material available on the WWW. Discuss the advantages and disadvantages of students having unrestricted and unsupervised access to a PC that is connected to the Internet.

Answer:

- Pros:
  - Allows students to learn at their own speed
  - Allows students to access information to help with their studies
  - Allows students to access educational videos, podcasts, etc.
  - Facilitates communication
- Cons:
  - Some sites do not give accurate information
  - Some sites encourage and facilitate illegal or inappropriate activities (illegal downloading of videos, photos or music, ordering drugs, watching pornography)
  - Some sites facilitate plagiarism or cheating
  - Usually students that spend too much time on the Internet are deprived of "real" social contact and social skills
  - Typing and using the computer display for prolonged periods of time may cause health problems such as RSI or eye problems

System design and analysis

1.2.4 Relevant stakeholders when planning a new system

Exit skills. Students should be able to[1]:
Give the precise meaning of the terms end-user and stakeholder. Distinguish between the end-user and the stakeholder in a given scenario. Outline the role of individuals when planning a new computer system.

Stakeholders are individuals, teams, groups or organizations that have an interest in the realization of a project or might be affected by the outcome of a project[24]. So, any person who has interests in an existing or proposed information system can be described as a stakeholder of the system. The *end-user* is the person who is going to use the product. A relevant stakeholder can also be a frequent user of the current system. He/she will be able to identify flaws and errors of the current system or inconveniences that he/she has spotted. He/she will be able to propose some improvements that will be crucial to the update of the system. The manager or supervisor of the procedure that the system performs may also have some comments. Specialists who have dealt with a similar situation in the past can be asked for their advice.

Example 1.20:

Question: Most university students have computers with Internet access. The WWW can be a useful resource when researching educational information for classwork and homework and can be used to communicate by chatting online. Discuss possible advantages to university students when chatting online.

Answer: One possible benefit for university students using the Internet for chatting online is that they can exchange ideas, ask other students or scientists questions about courses and lectures, and get answers or clarifications. Also, other students may suggest useful sites to find educational material and scientific information. Chatting on-line facilitates making acquaintances and connections from all over the world (social and business networking). In most countries it is considered a cheaper way of communication than using the telephone, since if the user's home is equipped with a broadband connection, a fixed amount is paid to the Internet Service Provider (ISP) regardless of how long the user spends online (connected to Internet).

1.2.5 Methods of obtaining requirements from stakeholders.

Exit skills. Students should be able to[1]:
Describe processes that involve surveys, interviews and direct observations. Distinguish between the different methods of obtaining requirements. Outline the role of different stakeholders during the data gathering process.

[24] How to Identify stakeholders. (n.d.). Retrieved November 23, 2014, from http://www.prince2.com/blog/how-identify-stakeholders

Gathering various details about an existing system and obtaining stakeholder requirements for a planned system, will involve[25]:

- *Interviewing stakeholders*. An *interview* is a direct face-to-face procedure that focuses on obtaining reliable and valid data in the form of verbal responses from a person or a group (group of stakeholders).
    - *Structured interviews* are strictly standardized and prescribed. A set of prepared questions is presented in the same manner and order to each stakeholder.
    - *Unstructured interviews* are flexible. Stakeholders are encouraged to express their thoughts and personal beliefs freely.

Image 1.12: Interview

An interview is a time-consuming conversational process that allows the interviewer to clarify questions and to observe verbal and non-verbal behaviors of the stakeholders. A disadvantage is that unstructured interviews often yield data too difficult to summarize, evaluate or perform any form of statistical analysis on them.

- The use of *questionnaires* is effective when the questions are carefully constructed so as to elicit unambiguous responses. *Survey methodology* refers to a domain of applied statistics that focuses on taking samples from a population, as well as improving on the various data collection techniques (e.g. questionnaires).[26]

  Closed or restricted questionnaires involve "yes" or "no" answers, short response questions and box checking. Such a questionnaire facilitates statistical analysis, tabular presentation of data, and summarizing processes.

Image 1.13: Questionnaire

Open or unrestricted questionnaires involve free response questions but allows for greater depth of responses from the stakeholder. Such a questionnaire is difficult to interpret or summarize and makes statistical analysis impossible.

Questionnaires guarantee uniformity of questions and therefore yield data that is easier comparable than information obtained through

---

[25] Data Tools. (n.d.). Retrieved November 23, 2014, from http://www.okstate.edu/ag/agedcm4h/academic/aged5980a/5980/newpage16.htm

[26] Survey methodology. (2014, August 18). In *Wikipedia, The Free Encyclopedia*. Retrieved 18:13, November 23, 2014, from http://en.wikipedia.org/w/index.php?title=Survey_methodology&oldid=621707547

an interview. It is a time-saving, cost-efficient method to obtain data and reach a lot of stakeholders quickly. However, respondents' motivation is difficult to assess and stakeholders may not respond at all, answer only some questions, or misinterpret the question.

- *Direct observation of current procedures* involves spending time in different departments. It is considered as a time-and-motion study that can show where procedures and processes could be made more efficient, or where possible bottlenecks may be present. Direct observation makes possible the collection of different types of data and information. Being on-site over a period of time familiarizes the analyst with the case study, thereby facilitating involvement in all activities and processes. Observation is independent of user bias but is a time-consuming method.

  However, people sometimes change their behavior when they know they are observed. The term "*Hawthorne effect*" is used to describe situations where workers better perform when they know that they are participating in an observation process.[27]

Example 1.21:

Question: Suppose a supermarket wants to develop a new system for online ordering with free delivery. Who are the stakeholders?

Answer: System owners, system users (clerical employees, service workers, technical staff, professional staff, customers, suppliers), system designers (security experts, database administrators, web architects), system builders (application programmers, network administrators), system analysts, system testers, etc.

1.2.6 Appropriate techniques for gathering the information needed to arrive at a workable solution

Exit skills. Students should be able to[1]:
Describe processes that are involved to arrive at a workable IT solution. Describe methods and techniques used to examine current systems, competing products, organizational capabilities and the use of literature searches. Distinguish between the different methods for gathering data and information.

Examining current systems is a process that involves the detailed examination of the current system, analysis of its functions and procedures, studying the business and system

[27] Hawthorne effect. (2014, November 9). In *Wikipedia, The Free Encyclopedia*. Retrieved 18:14, November 23, 2014, from http://en.wikipedia.org/w/index.php?title=Hawthorne_effect&oldid=633077463

documents such as current order documents, logistics documents, and computer systems procedures and reports used by operations and senior managers.

According to Auston et al (1992) *literature search* refers to the identification, retrieval and management of various sources in order to find information on a topic, areas that might be interesting for further studies, derive conclusions, as well as develop guidelines for practices.[28]

Nowadays the most efficient way to identify published studies and to search for specific information is with the use of online databases, search engines etc.

Examining *competing products* may include the analysis of competitive factors, their benefits, vulnerabilities, successful characteristics, the breakthroughs that they introduce, their design features as well as the users' and stakeholders' acceptance.

Example 1.22:

Question: Compare unstructured interviews and restricted questionnaires as methods of data collection.

Answer:

Interviews	Questionnaires
More complete data can be collected	A lot of people can be reached in a short period of time
It is a time consuming method	A lot of employees may not respond
Clarifications may be given	Easy to perform statistical analysis

Example 1.23:

Question: State three possible ways to conduct surveys.

Answer: Online, face-to-face and telephone surveys.

During the analysis and design phases all critical *organizational capabilities* that are essential to support effective planning and developing of the new IT system should be identified. A successful IT system should result in a *competitive advantage*. According to Hall (2011) organizational capabilities such as sense-making, decision-making, asset availability, and operations management are completely associated with effective implementation of an information system, which in turn positively affects organizational performance. Information systems used in modern companies play a critical role and most companies use data and

[28] Ione Auston, MLS, Marjorie A. Cahn, MA, Catherine R. Selden, 1992, MLS, National Library of Medicine, Office of Health Services Research Information, prepared for Agency for Health Care Policy and Research, Office of the Forum for Quality and Effectiveness in Health Care, Forum Methodology Conference. December 13-16, 1992. Retrieved November 23, 2014, from http://www.nlm.nih.gov/nichsr/litsrch.html.

information as assets to gain competitive advantage. We should keep in mind that a modern information system should be planned to[29]:

- increase client trust
- preserve brand strength
- preserve organization reputation
- maintain corporate resiliency
- enhance organizational piece

1.2.7 Suitable representations to illustrate system requirements

Exit skills. Students should be able to[1]:
Develop system flow charts, data flow diagrams and structure charts for a given scenario. Distinguish between different diagrams used in computer science. Suggest the optimal way to represent system requirements.

System requirements are specified through a document called a *requirements specification document*. This document defines the specific customer requirements of a computer system. It is included within the system analysis and may be later used to test the system, after implementation, in order to evaluate it.[2]

Before proceeding with the various representations that are used to illustrate system requirements, it is very useful to examine the types of processing.

Types of processing: According the IBDP Computer Science Guide (2004)[2] there are three types of processing. The following table contains the equivalent definitions:

Online processing (interactive)	Data processing performed by a single processor through the use of equipment that it controls. For example: airline reservation.
Real-time processing	Data processing performed on-the-fly in which the generated data influences the actual process taking place. For example: aircraft control.
Batch processing	Data processing performed on data that have been composed and processed as a single unit. For example: payroll.

[29] Examining Impacts of Organizational Capabilities in Information Security: 2011, A Structural Equation Modeling Analysis by Hall, Jacqueline Huynh, Ph.D., THE GEORGE WASHINGTON UNIVERSITY, 2011, 204 pages; 3449269. Retrieved November 23, 2014, from http://gradworks.umi.com/34/49/3449269.html

Example 1.24:

Question: State two applications of real time processing.

Answer: Aircraft control, heart-rate monitoring.

***System flowcharts*[2]**

A system flowchart refers to the description of a data processing system, including the flow of data through any individual programs involved, but excluding the details of such programs. System flowcharts are frequently constructed during analysis activities and represent various computer programs, files, databases, associated manual processes, etc. They are able to show batch, real-time and online processing, and they are the only way to refer to hardware.

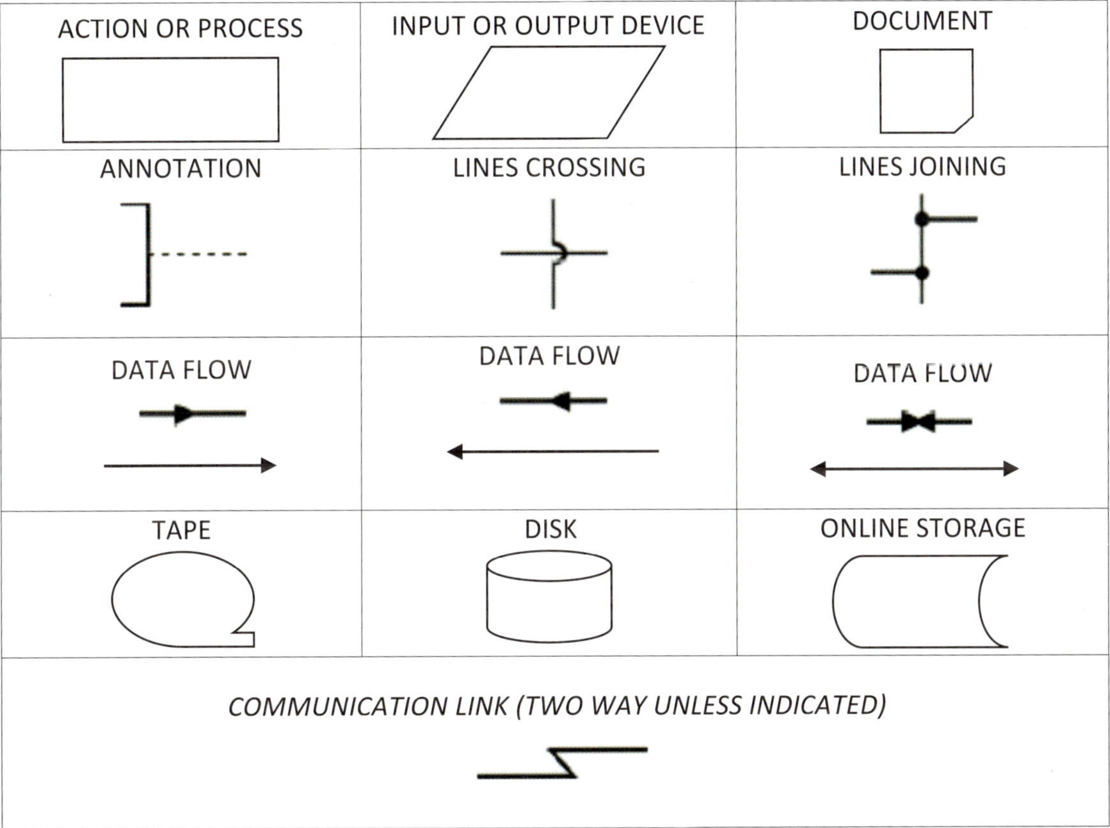

Table 1.1: System flowchart symbols

Example 1.25: The following system flowchart describes the hardware and software components of a system that is used to extract upcoming client birthdays from an online database. A computer program, "Calculate", reads the clients' file ("Clients") from the online database and writes the names to a new online file called "Birthday". The date is entered through a keyboard. All errors are sent in an error report to a monitor.

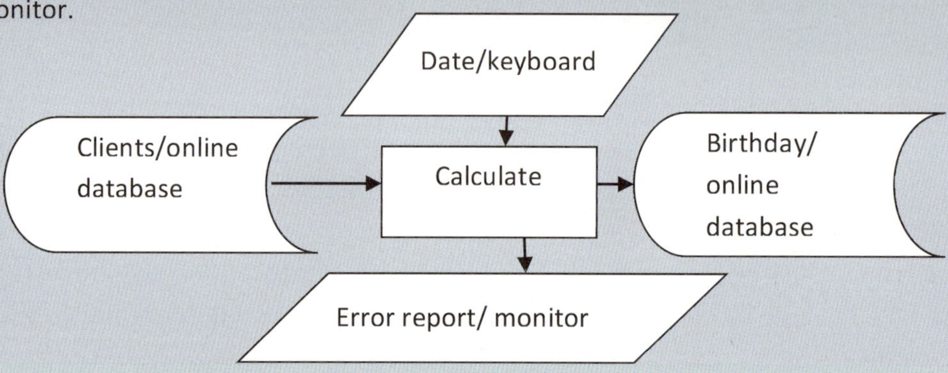

Example 1.26: (System flowchart) During the preparation of the monthly payroll run, the hours of each employee are entered through a keyboard. A validation and a verification process takes place. The name of this process is "Check". After this process data is stored in a transaction file on a local hard disk. If the "Check" process finds errors an error report is sent to a monitor. The "Calculate" program reads the transaction file and updates the master file, held on an online magnetic disk. All transfer details are stored on a magnetic tape and all pay slips are printed. A printout for each employee is created.

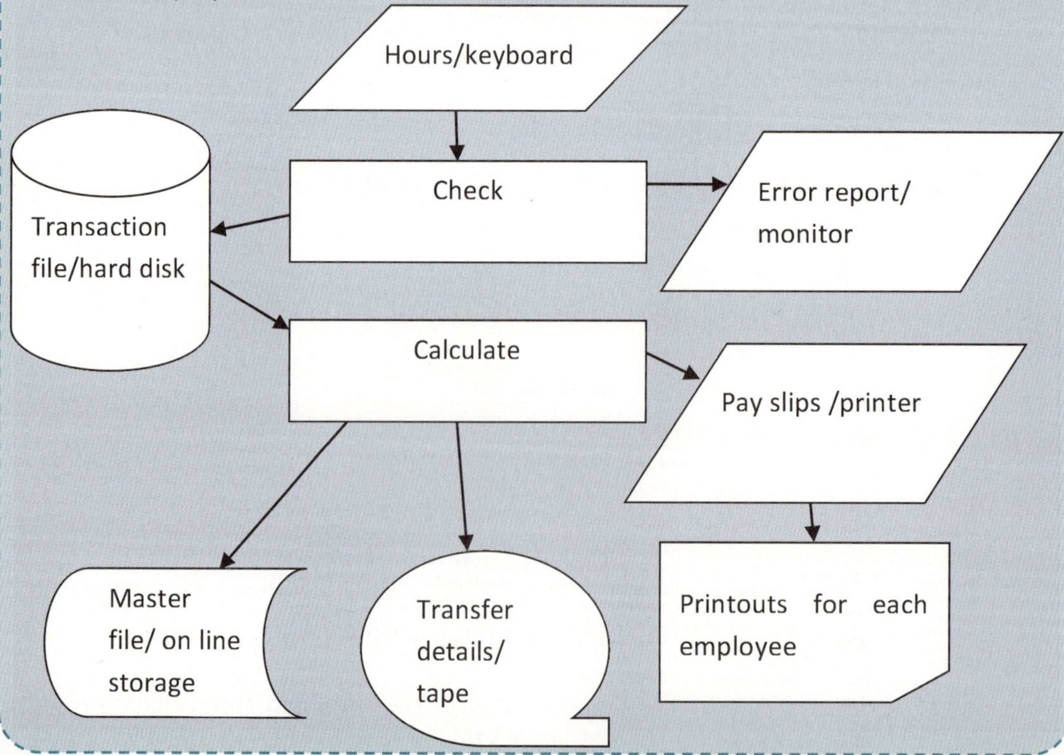

Data Flow Diagrams (DFD)

A DFD may usually be used to describe the problem to be solved (analysis). A DFD shows how data moves through a system and the data stores that the system uses. A DFD does not specify the type of the data storage and the type of data.

Data flow diagram element	Symbol
Process An operation performed on the data VERB	Calculate
Data flow Direction of data flow NOUN	Name →
Data store File held on disk or a batch of documents NOUN	Details
External entity Data source or destination NOUN	Person

Example 1.27: (<u>use of a DFD</u>). Drivers can apply to renew their driving license using a specialized national web site. Drivers input their personal details and various checks are made to ensure that the driver has all necessary qualifications (age and medical examinations). If the results are acceptable the online application is approved otherwise it is rejected.

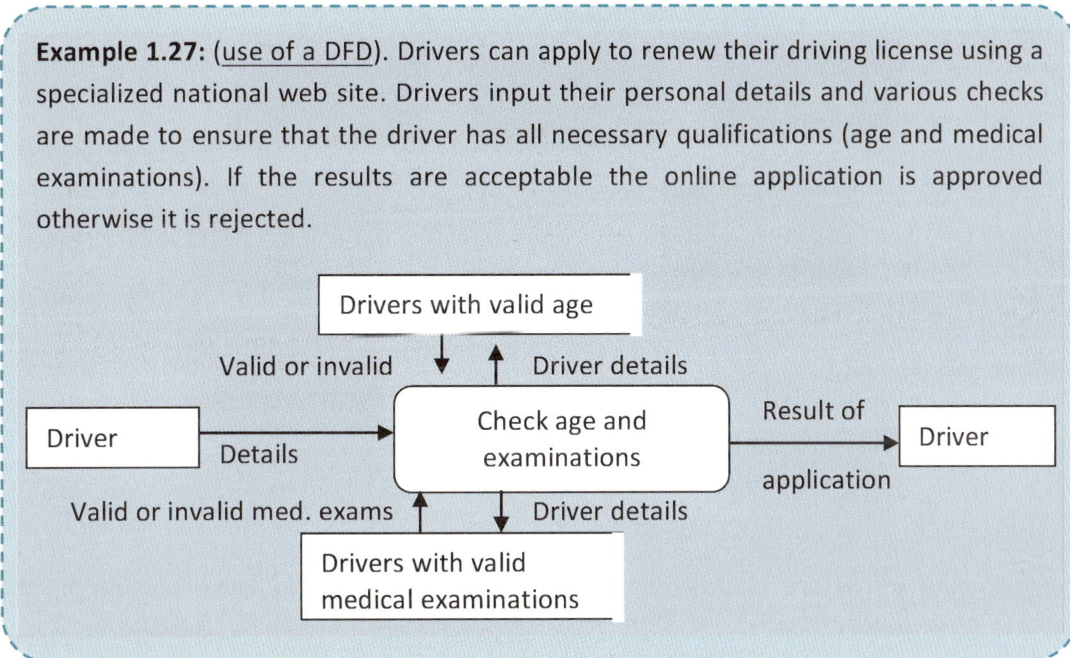

Structure charts

A structure chart describes functions and sub-functions of a system, as well as the relationships between modules of a computer program. The organization of a structure chart is straightforward, allowing the analyst to split a large problem into smaller ones. Each module performs a specific function and each layer in a program performs specific activities. A structure chart makes the modular design development much easier.

Modular design is the process of designing system modules individually and then combining the modules to form a solution to an overall problem.

Example 1.28: (use of a DFD). Students applying for a scholarship complete an online application form. The institution checks the student's marks with the help of an external consultant and contacts the student's school to confirm their grades. A decision is then made to approve or decline the scholarship application.

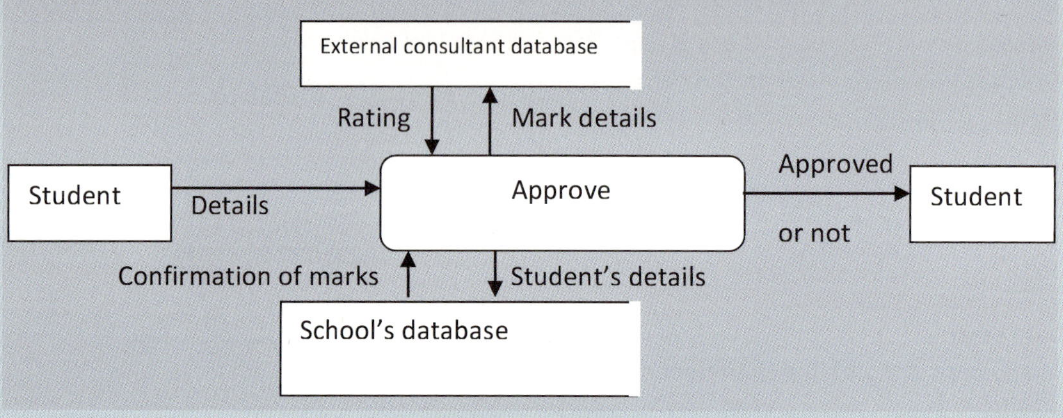

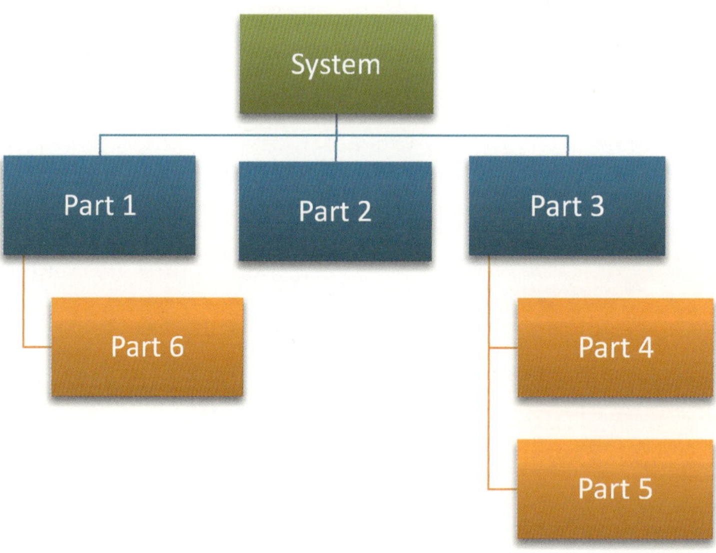

Figure 1.5: A structure chart

The following terms are closely related to modular design and were present in the previous CS IB guide (2004)[2]:

- *Top-down design* or "stepwise refinement" is a software design and problem solving technique that involves the partition of a problem into smaller sub-problems. Each sub-problem is further broken down until all sub-problems are detailed enough and no more partitioning is required. Programmers are able to attack its sub-problem and develop the equivalent programming code.[2]
- *Pseudocode* is an artificial language that is not directly related to any particular hardware and is used to describe algorithms. Pseudocode does not follow the grammar of any specific computer language and requires conversion to a computer language before the resulting program can be used.[2]

- *Module* is a complete and independent part of a program or an algorithm. [2]
- *Modular programming* or "Modularity" is the method of partitioning a computer program into separate sub-programs. The main advantage is that each sub-program can be easily modified and maintained without the necessity to alter other sub-programs of the program. [2]
- *Modular language* is a language that supports modular programming. [2]

Example 1.29:

Question: State two high-level computer languages that support modularity.

Answer: Java, JavaScript.

1.2.8 Purpose of prototypes to demonstrate the proposed system to the client

Exit skills. Students should be able to[1]:
Explain the need of prototyping during the design stage. Describe the need for user/client feedback. Explain the need for effective collaboration.

Image 1.14: Prototype creation

There are many advantages to creating a *prototype*. A prototype is either a working or non-working preliminary version of the final product or a simple version of the final system that is used as part of the design phase to demonstrate how the final product will work.

A prototype:

- Attracts the attention of the client, since it encourages them to use it and "get a feel for it"
- Provides just enough of the concept for the investors to decide if they want to fund the full production or not
- Encourages active participation between users and developers
- Gives an idea of the final product
- Helps in the identification of problems with the efficiency or the design
- Increases system development speed

Example 1.30:

Question: A robot company develops various robotic systems. In most cases a test prototype is produced.

1. Suggest a situation where the development of a prototype is justified and needed, and a situation where the development of a prototype will not help
2. Suggest an alternative testing method

Answer: Answers may include:

1.a. A prototype will help: Robotic cleaner, robotic kit (LEGO NXT), robotic lawnmower, security robots. Justification: All these robots would be developed for sale to the general public in large quantities; all these can be produced easily.

1.b. A prototype will not help: A robot that will carry out dangerous tasks in a nuclear reactor, a robot that will be used in a specific space mission. Justification: Immediate need, time and money taken to produce and test a prototype may be considerable, special operational circumstances unable or too dangerous to be reproduced.

2. Computer simulation that will be based on detailed mathematical models. Use of the computer simulation for testing purposes.

1.2.9 Importance of iteration during the design process

Exit skills. Students should be able to[1]:
Define iteration. Explain the importance of iteration during the system and software lifecycle. Explain the importance of iteration during the design process.

Iteration refers to the repetition of a set of instructions for a specific number of times or until the operations yield a desired result[2]. It is impossible to design a system, an interface or software that has no initial functional or usability problems. During the design process, the designers of the product may have to step back several times and reconsider choices they have made. Even the best designers cannot design perfect products in a single attempt, so an iterative design methodology should be adopted. As they proceed to decide how the product will finally look and function, they may stumble on several difficulties or inconsistencies that will force them to return to previous steps or versions and modify them, or even start the process from the very beginning. Iterative development of software involves steady improvement of the design based on various evaluation and testing methods (e.g. user testing). Hence, to make sure that everything works as it should, the producer may have to run through the process again and again.

Useful Information: It is a good idea to read the article: "Iterative user interface design" by Jacob Nielsen. *Originally published in IEEE Computer* Vol. 26, *No. 11 (November 1993), pp. 32-41.*

http://www.nngroup.com/articles/iterative-design/

1.2.10 Possible consequences of failing to involve the end-user in the design process.

Exit skills. Students should be able to[1]:
Explain the importance of end-user involvement during the design stage. Identify possible consequences when the end-user does not actively participate in the design process. Discuss the importance of clearly defined goals.

For a system to be successful, the analysis and the design must involve all key stakeholders including the *client* (the person or organization paying for the project) and the *end users* (people who will use the system). Involvement, collaboration and active participation are critical because a project with poorly-defined stakeholder goals is unlikely to be successful. The developed system may either solve a different problem, or deal with issues that are outside of the project's scope.

Example 1.31:
Question: A school saves its student records and files on paper, which are kept in file cabinets. The school hires a system analyst to help on the computerization and automation of the file storing process. Explain why the school administration has to work together with the analyst to define the problem accurately.

Answer: The school administrator is the expert on the problem, while the system analyst is the computer expert and responsible for the analysis phase. Both parties need to collaborate to come up with a clear and precise definition of the problem. They have to predefine the outcomes and the criteria of success so that when the system is realized there is a concrete set of criteria to use for evaluation.

1.2.11 Social and ethical issues associated with the introduction of new IT systems

Exit skills. Students should be able to[1]:
Explain the importance of the introduction of new IT systems. Analyse the social and ethical issues that relate to a given scenario. Identify possible consequences associated with new IT systems.

Tip: It would be a good idea to revise section 1.2.3 - IT subjects of social and ethical significance.

Automated Teller Machines (ATM) replaced bank tellers, E-pass systems replaced highway toll collectors, internet travel sites replaced small travel agencies, automated voice systems replaced service representatives, email replaced mail carriers, voice recognition systems replaced typists, and reporters are being replaced by blogs and "citizen journalists" and social media users. Machines are replacing humans in countless tasks, forcing millions of individuals into unemployment. A counterargument is that jobs don't vanish, but change. Finally, advances in robotics and artificial inteligence may eventually replace an increasingly large amount of workers with smart robots. This could create social disturbance similar to that during the Industrial Revolution (when the introduction of machines had a similar impact on society).

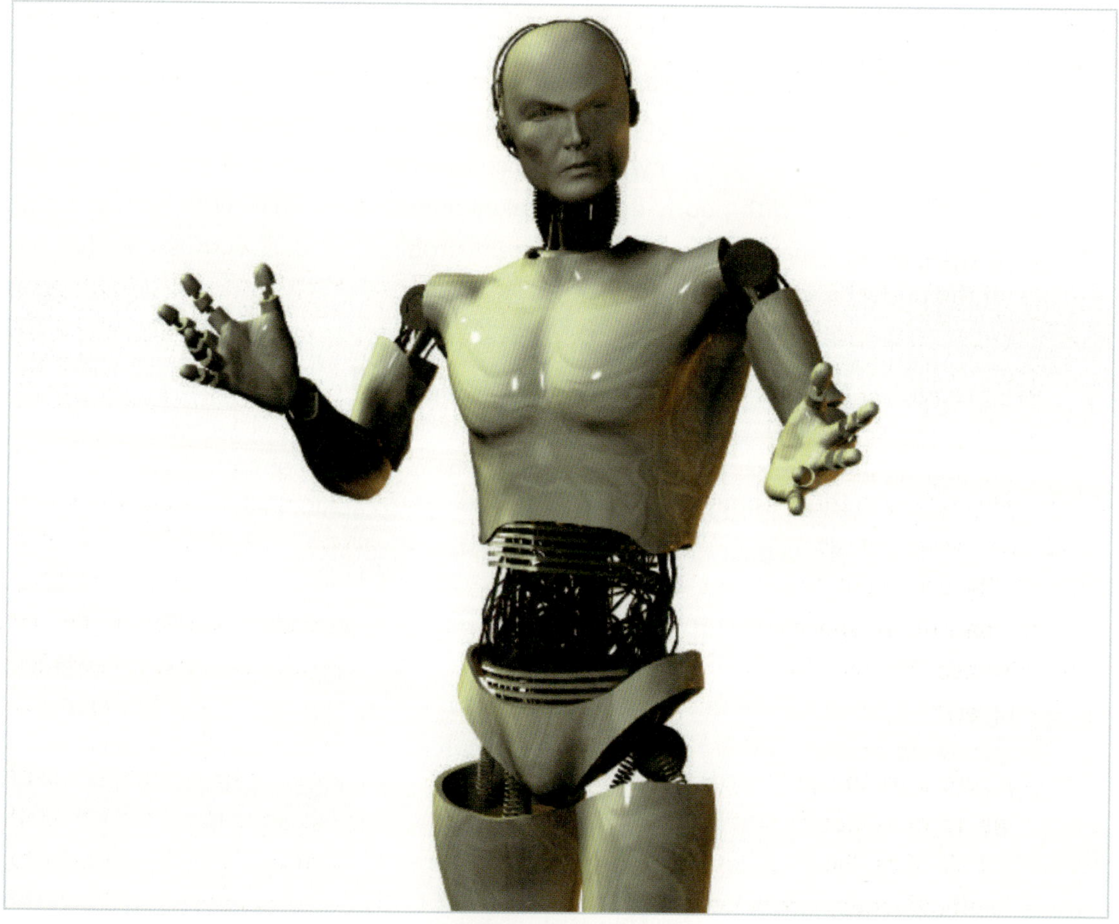

Image 1.15: A robot

Introducing new information technology systems and applications (or constantly developing old ones) certainly has a great impact on society and starts to pose ethical questions about the extent to which this uncontrollable development can or should continue. Take the creation of Facebook and Twitter, for instance. These social networks became increasingly popular, penetrating users' social and personal lives, ultimately becoming a vital component of them. Facebook changed the way social interractions occur. It is important to mention that social interaction is also an essential element of social change that affects ideas, beliefs, moral values etc. Other IT developments may have a more indirect social impact, but still, since the primary purpose of developing information technology systems should be to improve human life, this impact should be examined.

Continuous development of computerized systems may absorb people and cause them to drift apart from the physical world and become enclosed in virtual environments. Participation in virtual environments may completely disorient some users. In addition, automated environemnts, such as the "smart home",which takes care of everyday tasks like checking the refrigerator contents and making appropriate orders of supplies, may deprive people of socialization and interaction opportunities that these tasks once offered to them. Considering these possible outcomes, further moral and ethical questions arise.

A surprising finding is that in a business environment, the introduction of a new improved information system often places more stress on the personnel because they have to study, learn, and familiarize themselves with the new system while completing their regular duties.

The extent to which IT advances are benefical must be determined in order to be sure that it will not affect human society negatively.

Human interaction with the system

1.2.12 Usability

Exit skills. Students should be able to[1]:
Give the precise meaning of the term usability, ergonomics and accessibility.

Accessibility refers to the potential of a service, product, device or environment to serve and meet the needs of as many individuals as possible. A system characterized by high accessibility can meet the needs of many people, while a system with low accessibility presents barriers to specific groups of people. Frequently, accessibility is studied in parallel with disabled people (people with special needs) and the use of various assistive technologies.[30]

Usability refers to the potential of a product, application or website to accomplish user goals. The term is not limited to computer science but extends to other products and services of all kinds. Factors that influence usability are described in section 1.2.13. Usability relates to effectiveness, efficiency and satisfaction in a specified context of use.[31]

---

[30] Accessibility. (2014, September 22). In *Wikipedia, The Free Encyclopedia*. Retrieved 18:19, November 23, 2014, from http://en.wikipedia.org/w/index.php?title=Accessibility&oldid=626601064
[31] Usability. (n.d.). Retrieved November 23, 2014, from http://searchsoa.techtarget.com/definition/usability

Ergonomics or human engineering refers to the design of safe and comfortable products, systems or processes, specifically for people. For example, computer hardware, such as keyboards, are shaped by ergonomic consideration in order to improve users' comfort.[32]

1.2.13 Usability problems with commonly used digital devices

Exit skills. Students should be able to[1]:
Explain the effect of usability problems. Identify usability problems in modern devices.

Students should analyze the overall usability of a device using the eight quality components of usability[33, 34]:

1. *Complexity/Simplicity*: Amount of effort to find a solution or get a result.
2. *Effectiveness*: Comparison of user performance against a predefined level.
3. *Efficiency*: Task completion time after the initial adjusting period.
4. *Error*: Number of errors, type of errors and time needed to recover from errors.
5. *Learnability*: Time used to accomplish tasks on the first use.
6. *Memorability*: Time, number of button clicks, pages, and steps used by users when they return to the device after a period of not using it.
7. *Readability/Comprehensibility*: Reading speed.
8. *Satisfaction*: Attitude of users toward applications after using them; i.e. if users like it.

Image 1.16: Usability problems with different devices

USABILITY PROBLEMS – DIFFERENT DEVICES

GPS/navigation systems

1. Small screen.

---

[32] Ergonomics. (n.d.). Retrieved November 23, 2014, from http://www.webopedia.com/TERM/E/ergonomics.html

[33] (n.d.). Retrieved November 23, 2014, from http://userpages.umbc.edu/~zhangd/Papers/IJHCI1.pdf

[34] Nielsen Norman Group. (n.d.). Retrieved November 23, 2014, from http://www.nngroup.com/articles/usability-101-introduction-to-usability/

2. Low-quality speakers.
3. Antenna with poor performance that makes it difficult to receive a satellite signal.
4. Inaccurate geographical data.
5. Outdated street data.
6. Inefficient routing software.

TABLETS

1. Accidental touches leads to undesired selections.
2. Difficult to learn different gesture features' of various manufacturers.
3. Bad or poor scaling and zoom control.
4. Difficult-to-use control features.
5. Small side buttons.
6. Poorly written instructions.

Game consoles

1. Some portable game consoles have relatively small screens.
2. Buttons may be too small.
3. Difficult to use outdoors (insufficient brightness).
4. Short battery life.

PCs:

1. Excessive keyboard use may lead to RSI (Repetitive Strain Injury) syndrome.
2. Excessive use of a large, bright screen may cause eyesight problems or tire the eyes.
3. Poor room lighting conditions may lead to distracting reflections on the screen.
4. The mouse of a PC is designed for right-handed people, making its use difficult for left-handed people.

Digital Cameras:

1. Incorrect calibration of touch screen menus.
2. The need to hold the camera vertically, does not allow convenient navigation through the touch-screens. An auto rotate screen option would increase usability.
3. If a camera does not have a flash capability or it is equipped with an inadequate flash, then the user has to purchase and carry an extra hardware component.
4. The buttons are too small, making it difficult to push them.
5. Some cameras require specific software to connect them with a computer and store or transfer files (no drag and drop files option).

Mobile phones

1. The keyboard of a mobile phone is very small and as a result many novice users elderly people or users with bad eyesight struggle to use it.
2. Some users don't really need all the special features; they just need a basic device for calls and SMS messaging.

MP3 Devices:

1. Tiny buttons.
2. Insufficient memory.
3. Fragile.
4. Lack of a screen in “micro” or “shuffle” devices.
5. Overall usability can be improved by use of NLP (natural language processing) and making the overall interface more intuitive, so that even people not familiar with technology can use them.
6. Use of acceleration sensors or gesture control to enhance functionality (e.g. shaking the device to change the song).

Example 1.32:
Question: Tablets are often too small to have a usable virtual keyboard. Most of them provide the option of handwriting recognition for input. Discuss whether this input method is convenient for tablets.

Answer: Handwriting recognition is a suitable form of input on tablets as it is quicker and easier for the user. This means that the touch screen on tablets can have smaller dimensions than a keyboard, allowing the whole tablet to be smaller. On the other hand, handwriting recognition is not always accurate and it takes time to train the software to understand a user’s handwriting. Also, a user’s handwriting may be different in difficult and demanding circumstances, for example when writing quickly or writing on a moving bus. In most cases the tablet would still require an alternative input method (such as the small virtual keyboard) to input a word if not successfully recognized using handwriting recognition.

Example 1.33:
Question: State some health and safety issues that secretaries and typists (keyboard operators) should be aware of. Suggest measure that can be taken to improve the working conditions.

Answer:

- Issues: RSI, dry eyes, back problems, headaches
- Measures: regular breaks, properly-designed chairs, wrist supports

1.2.14 Methods that can be used to improve the accessibility of systems

Exit skills. Students should be able to[1]:
Explain the importance of accessibility. Identify how different devices improve accessibility.

Useful Information: A keyboard that is mounted too high to be used by children lacks accessibility. A laptop that weights 20 kilos is not portable. These are straightforward examples. The following notes focus on methods that make the use of IT easier for disabled individuals.

The World Health Organization (WHO) suggested the following definitions[35]:

- "*Impairment*: a loss or abnormality of psychological, physiological, or anatomical structure or function.
- *Disability*: any restriction or lack (resulting from an impairment) of the ability to perform an activity in the manner or within the range considered normal for a human being."

Some critical aspects to consider when evaluating the accessibility of an IT system (according to Burgstahler, 2012)[36]:

1. **Visual impairment, from blindness to colour vision deficiency**

   Input methods and devices:

   Braille input devices are available. Most blind people or seeing-impaired use touch type with standard keyboards.

   Output methods and devices:

   Speech output devices can read the screen text. Screen readers are commonly used to convert text to speech using speech synthesizers. A braille display is a device that allows for braille characters to be displayed using pins, in order for blind users to be able to read text.[37] For people with colour blindness the capability to adjust the colour of the display or change the background and foreground colours is also of great value.

2. **Hearing and speech impairments**

   Input methods and devices:

   No problem with commonly used devices

---

[35] UN Enable : First 50 Years : Chapter II - What is a disability? (n.d.). Retrieved November 23, 2014, from http://www.un.org/esa/socdev/enable/dis50y10.htm

[36] Adopted by: Burgstahler, S., 2012, Working Together: People with Disabilities and Computer Technology, Retrieved November 23, 2014 from http://www.washington.edu/doit/Brochures/Technology/wtcomp.html

37 Refreshable braille display. (2014, August 27). In Wikipedia, The Free Encyclopedia. Retrieved 18:20, November 23, 2014, from http://en.wikipedia.org/w/index.php?title=Refreshable_braille_display&oldid=623037113

Output methods and devices:

Replace sound signals with visual effects. Use of subtitles to replace audio speech track.

3. **Cognitive Problems and learning disabilities**

Input and output methods and devices:

Special software that provides active participation, multi-sensory experiences, strong interaction, positive reinforcement, personalized instruction, individualized instruction, and repetition can be useful in skill building. A basic word processor can be a useful tool for persons with dysgraphia or dyslexia.

4. **Mobility impairments, limited hand mobility, Parkinson disease**

Input methods and devices:

Specialized disk guides can assist while inserting and removing CDs, DVDs, diskettes etc.

Disabled people that cannot use a normal keyboard can instead use a pointing device to press keys and control a personal computer. Mouth and head-sticks can also be used to control a personal computer if needed.[36]

Left-handed and right-handed keyboards are available for individuals who lack one arm or who have lost the ability to use one arm, and those who have fine motor control but lack a range of motion great enough to use a standard keyboard or suffer from severely reduced strength. These keyboards provide more efficient key arrangements than usual keyboards designed for two-handed users.

Track balls and specialized input devices such as wearable computer interfaces can replace mouse and keyboard. Modified gloves are wearable computer interfaces that facilitate people with mobility impairments.

Image 1.17: Disabilities

For individuals who cannot move their fingers independently, all fine motor skills will be affected. They may not be able to use conventional keyboards or keypads, etc. Some special devices and hardware modifications completely replace the common input devices (mouse, keyboard) for individuals who cannot operate these input devices.

Expanded keyboards equipped with larger keys can replace usual keyboards for users with limited fine motor control.

Scanning and Morse code input that emulate the keyboard are suitable for people with severe mobility impairment or reduced ability to coordinate the movements of the arms and hands.

In some cases, special knobs rely on a muscle whose action is normally controlled by the individual's will (voluntary control). To make selections, disabled users take advantage of knobs activated by movement of the head, neck, finger, foot, lips, tongue, breath, etc.

Another assistive technology includes the sip-and-puff (SNP), which can be used to control using air pressure by inhaling and exhaling through a tube. Disabled users input Morse code by activating specialized switches (e.g., a sip-and-puff mechanism registers a "dot" with a sip and "dash" with a puff). A translation process converts Morse code into a computer understandable form.[38]

Natural language processing, voice recognition and speech-recognition are emerging alternatives for people with disabilities. These technologies allow disabled users to interact with their PCs by speaking or spelling words.

People with mobility impairments can take advantage of word prediction software that can reduce text input difficulties for commonly-used words. Word-prediction software predicts entire words after several keystrokes and auto-completes users' frequently-used words and phrases. This makes typing faster, and orthographically correct, and thereby reduces effort.

Output methods and devices:
There is no necessity for different output devices.

Useful Information: *The computer science department of the Colorado State University is making an effort to provide accessible distance classes, and on campus classes to students. http://www.cs.colostate.edu/accessi/?page=index*

1.2.15 Range of usability problems that can occur in a system

Exit skills. Students should be able to[1]:
Explain the effect of usability problems Identify usability problems in various systems.

Tip: It would be a good idea to recall the "eight quality components of usability" (1.2.13)

[38] Sip-and-puff. (2014, August 22). In *Wikipedia, The Free Encyclopedia*. Retrieved 18:21, November 23, 2014, from http://en.wikipedia.org/w/index.php?title=Sip-and-puff&oldid=622302284

If a website is difficult to use, or if a website fails to clearly state what a company offers and what users can do, users will leave. If users get lost on various pages of the site then the website will not serve its original purpose. If a site's information is hard to read, doesn't answer users' key questions or contains irrelevant information, then the site has low or no usability. If an interface is not appealing then it will not attract users. For websites that serve e-commerce it is important for the users to quickly locate a product. Successful intranets increase employee productivity and decrease time wasted.

Ticketing systems:

Important: Ticketing systems may refer to public transportation ticketing systems, to theater ticketing systems etc. or to helpdesk software that tracks customer requests. (Known as "support tickets").

Usability quality component	Usability considerations
Complexity/ Simplicity: Amount of effort to find a solution.	Unclear instructions on how to obtain a ticket. Lack of built-in help.
Effectiveness: Comparison of user performance against a predefined level.	Not abiding to international standards. Foreign people find it difficult.
Efficiency: Task completion time after the initial adjusting period.	Complicated site that makes user perform unnecessary actions.
Error: Number of errors, type of errors and time to recover from errors.	The user books more tickets than he/she wishes and he/she has to restart the booking process.
Learnability: Time used to accomplish tasks at first use.	The first time someone enters the site, gets confused and it takes him/her some time to understand the required procedure.
Easy to remember: Time, number of button clicks, pages, and steps used by users when they return to the device after a period of not using it.	People get confused and it takes some time to remember the required procedure.
Readability/ Comprehensibility: Reading speed.	The font and the background selected are not appropriate.
Satisfaction: Attitude and satisfaction of users after using the application.	Unsatisfied customers because of poor system.

Online payroll systems:

Usability quality component	Usability considerations
Complexity/ Simplicity: Amount of effort to find a solution.	Unclear instructions on how to calculate taxes. Lack of built-in help.
Effectiveness: Comparison of user performance against a predefined level.	The system is designed for another country. Other systems have been localized.

Efficiency: Task completion time after the initial adjusting period.	The system is not suitable for the user's needs and he/she has to perform a lot of modifications every time he/she needs to use it.
Error: Number of errors, type of errors and time to recover from errors.	No verification and validation rules. Prone to errors.
Learnability: Time used to accomplish tasks at first use.	The design of menus is not straight-forward.
Easy to remember: Time, number of button clicks, pages, and steps used by users when they return to the device after a period of not using it.	The interface is not intuitive
Readability/ Comprehensibility: Reading speed.	Hard-to-read interface.
Satisfaction: Attitude and satisfaction of users after using the application.	Difficult to use, unhappy users.
It would be a good idea to read http://neoinsight.com/blog/2009/05/16/usability-catastrophe-payroll-calculator/ to understand more about how usability is very important.	

Scheduling systems:

Usability quality component	Usability considerations
Complexity/ Simplicity: Amount of effort to find a solution.	Unclear instructions on how to use the system. Lack of built-in help.
Effectiveness: Comparison of user performance against a predefined level.	Other applications have better synchronization capabilities.
Efficiency: Task completion time after the initial adjusting period.	System may be difficult to understand making a simple task, like organizing your schedule, complex.
Error: Number of errors, type of errors and time to recover from errors.	Time to reschedule a wrong appointment (entry).
Learnability: Time used to accomplish tasks at first use.	Complicated menus.
Memorability: Time, number of button clicks, pages, and steps used by users when they return to the device after a period of not using it.	Difficult to remember the optimal way to add a task.
Readability/ Comprehensibility: Reading speed.	Very small characters.
Satisfaction: Attitude and satisfaction of users after using the application.	Ideal for another country with different time/date/distance unit format.

Voice recognition systems:

Usability quality component	Usability considerations
Complexity/ Simplicity: Amount of effort to find a solution.	Lack of built-in help.
Effectiveness: Comparison of user performance against a predefined level.	Other competing solutions produce better results.

Efficiency: Task completion time after the initial adjusting period.	Poor word-recognition performance.
Error: Number of errors, type of errors and time to recover from errors.	Prone to errors.
Learnability: Time used to accomplish tasks at first use.	It takes time for the software to recognize the voice of a new user. The user has to be very patient during the initial use of the system.
Memorability: Time, number of button clicks, pages, and steps used by users when they return to the device after a period of not using it.	Sometimes the software needs retraining.
Readability/ Comprehensibility: Reading speed.	N/A
Satisfaction: Attitude and satisfaction of users after using the application.	The user needs to speak loudly, which results in problematic and embarrassing situations when in public places.

Systems that provide feedback:

Usability quality component	Usability considerations
Complexity/ Simplicity: Amount of effort to find a solution.	Lack of intuitive interface. No support of native language. Difficult to obtain feedback.
Effectiveness: Comparison of user performance against a predefined level.	Give incorrect or irrelevant feedback.
Efficiency: Task completion time after the initial adjusting period.	Give feedback when the user can't use it. Give feedback rarely.
Error: Number of errors, type of errors and time to recover from errors.	Difficult to re-enter information after a wrong input.
Learnability: Time used to accomplish tasks at first use.	Difficult to learn.
Memorability: Time, number of button clicks, pages, and steps used by users when they return to the device after a period of not using it.	Difficult to remember.
Readability/ Comprehensibility: Reading speed.	Difficult to read the instructions.
Satisfaction: Attitude and satisfaction of users after using the application.	Inconvenient interface, menus etc.

Tip: It would be a good idea to study some case studies from this web site: http://www.usabilityfirst.com/about-usability/usability-roi/case-studies/

Also, read http://www.designprinciplesftw.com/ to learn the 10 usability heuristics for user interface design.

1.2.16 Moral, ethical, social, economic and environmental implications of the interaction between humans and machines

Exit skills. Students should be able to[1]:
Explain the difference between ethics and moral. Identify moral, ethical, social, economic and environmental implications of the interaction between humans and machines in a given scenario. Develop a balanced and thorough review of a given scenario that involves moral, ethical, social, economic and environmental implications.

Tip: It would be a good idea to revise section 1.2.3 - IT subjects of social and ethical significance.

Artificial Intelligence (AI) and robotics are two computer science fields that point towards a very different future. A difficult question yet unanswered is: how can we replicate living beings using silicon chips, computer networks, and software? Advances in AI make it possible to predict that in the near future, computers will achieve a kind of intelligence. Artificial life does not have two of the principal characteristics associated with organic planetary life. It is not carbon and water based. Furthermore, it has not evolved along with others forms of life. Many scientists are concerned that advances in AI might lead to unpredictable and dangerous situations with no human control over AI robots.

Imagine a situation where manipulation of sound, picture or video fools your senses to experience something that has never happened. It is acceptable to watch a science fiction movie or listen to digitally-augmented vocals, but it is unacceptable to blackmail someone using a digitally-altered video.

Useful Information[39]: Although ethics and morals both refer to "wrong and right" they should be considered under different frameworks. Religion, society, profession and family set the ethic framework, while one owns principles set morals.

Despite predictions to the contrary, I.T. has dramatically increased the amount of printed-paper. Even when users are careful about printing, vast reams of paper ends up in the recycling bin every day. Even recycling paper requires extensive use of chemicals and energy. The environmental consequences should be considered when printing documents from the computer. Furthermore, electronic waste contains lead, cadmium, mercury, chromium, PVC, and other dangerous chemicals that end up in landfills causing pollution.

The digital divide exists not only between high and low income households but also between countries. Laptops, tablets, smart-phones, interactive whiteboards, multimedia, wireless technologies, search engines, social networks, file sharing, digital music and photography, and other cutting-edge information technologies are part of everyday life for the fortunate, but just a dream for many more. The consequences of the digital divide result in increasing inequality and reduced opportunities for education, entertainment and income.

---

[39] Ethics vs. Morals. (n.d.). Retrieved November 23, 2014, from http://www.diffen.com/difference/Ethics_vs_Morals

Example 1.34:

Question: A hospital holds a lot of confidential information about patients. The administration stores this information on a computer system. Explain the measures and methods that the administration should take to ensure that such information remains absolutely confidential.

Answer: Use of passwords, only qualified staff are allowed to access patients' files, use of physical locks, use of encrypted data, use of firewall, etc.

Example 1.35:

Question: A secret intelligence agency is highly concerned about security and keeps biometric details of all visitors and personnel on a database system. The agency is introducing the use of biometric features as a security measure and has recently installed iris scanning and recognition equipment at the entry points of their building. Describe any resulting issues.

Answer: Agents should be scanned at least once per working day and this may raise concerns about their health. The long-term effects of daily scanning of photographing a person's iris are not yet fully researched. Social issues include concern over the storage of visitors' biometric information on the database system.

Example 1.36:

Question: Compare and contrast the suitability of humans and computers in relation to various tasks.

Answer:

- Computers are more consistent than humans
- Computers are very good at repetitive tasks
- Computers can make precise calculations
- Computers can perform accurate calculations
- Computers can perform complex calculations
- Computers can process large volume of quantitative data in short periods of time
- Computers don't need breaks
- Computers have the ability to work in conditions too dangerous for a human
- Humans adapt
- Humans can easily identify shapes
- Humans can easily process sounds

Answer cont.:

- Humans can handle unexpected circumstances
- Humans can process qualitative data
- Humans have creativity
- Humans have emotions
- Humans have senses (debate differences from sensors)

Example 1.37:

Question: Some governments are introducing e-passports. Such a passport stores personal and biometric data about the passport holder. What is meant by the term biometric property? Give an example of a biometric property.

Answer: A biometric property of a person that can be used to identify him/her. Facial structure, fingerprint, iris pattern, DNA profile and voice profile.

Example 1.38:

Question: Identify a mission that could be carried out by a robot.

Answer: Any of the following:

- Mission that requires consistent task completion
- Mission that requires continuous operation
- Mission that is dangerous
- Mission that is repetitive
- Mission that is unpleasant
- Mission that requires precise movement
- Mission that requires a robot able to operate in environments humans cannot work in
- Mission that requires robots to act faster than humans
- Mission that requires robots to provide increased productivity

Example 1.39:

Question: A chemical company decides to adopt a fully automated system. Before the introduction of the new system the company reassigns daily tasks and assignments to each worker. Describe the effects on the workers.

Answer:

- Administrators will be able to check up on their daily work through the new system; good for some workers, not for others
- Anxiety about being made redundant

Answer cont.:

- Fear that they will not be able to cope with new system
- Tedious tasks will be performed by the new system, not the workers
- Various tasks may be made safer
- Workers will have to learn new skills
- New skills will mean better qualifications
- New skills will mean better salaries

Example 1.40:

Question: Why is working from home better than working from an office? Justify your answer.

Answer:

- <u>Economic issues and implications for the company</u>
    - No need for large and expensive offices
    - Lower utility bills
    - No need for parking fees
    - Training costs (use of technologies)
- <u>Social issues and implications</u>
    - Global workforce
    - Group working can become difficult
    - Employees lose social interaction
    - More time can be spent with family
- <u>Environmental issues and implications</u>
    - Less traffic and less pollution
- <u>Moral issues and implications</u>
    - Harder to monitor what employees are doing
    - Greater security issues (insecure home network and Internet connection)
- <u>Ethical issues and implications</u>
    - Some employees will need to take important decisions without the presence of their coworkers
    - Some employees will have difficulties keeping pace without continuous supervision
    - Employees feel like their own boss
- <u>Health issues and implications for the employees</u>
    - Less stress
    - Quality of life improved with peace and quiet

Example 1.41:

Question: A company decides to build a web-site for marketing purposes. An analyst is asked to help. Explain what information the analyst must collect before the design process.

Answer: Languages, format, possible colour scheme, information and data that the site will include, internal and external links etc.

Example 1.42:

Question: State some new IT solutions in the Banking sector that benefit the client.

Answer:

- Mobile banking
- Online banking
- ATMs

Example 1.43:

Question: State some new IT solutions in the Banking sector that benefit the employees.

Answer:

- Automatic validation and verification of transactions
- Online databases that do not allow duplicate entries
- Automatic balancing

Example 1.44:

Question: State some new IT solutions in the education sector that benefit students.

Answer:

- Use of simulation educational software facilitates the deeper understanding of difficult concepts
- Use of tablets to better organize all resources and access multimedia content
- Use of Learning Management Systems to collaborate with peers

Example 1.45:

Question: State some new IT solutions in the education sector that benefit teachers.

Answer:

- Spreadsheets could be used to effectively calculate grades
- Use of Smart Boards to enhance student participation and interest
- Use of online resources to enrich teaching material and content

Example 1.46:

Question: State one disadvantage of continuous development of computerized systems.

Answer: The participation in virtual environments may completely disorient users.

Chapter References

1. International Baccalaureate Organization. (2012). IBDP Computer Science Guide
2. International Baccalaureate Organization. (2004). IBDP Computer Science Guide
3. Feasibility study. (2014, November 21). In Wikipedia, The Free Encyclopedia. Retrieved 18:03, November 23, 2014, from http://en.wikipedia.org/w/index.php?title=Feasibility_study&oldid=634775631
4. (n.d.). Retrieved November 23, 2014, from https://www.fbo.gov/index?s= opportunity&mode=form&id=e2cd8e7c507a2bbd3614ede86beb5666&tab=core&_cview=0
5. Legacy System Integration. (n.d.). Retrieved November 23, 2014, from http://www.coleyconsulting.co.uk/merge.htm
6. Software as a service. (2014, November 17). In Wikipedia, The Free Encyclopedia. Retrieved 18:05, November 23, 2014, from http://en.wikipedia.org/w/index.php?title=Software_as_a_service&oldid=634189323
7. Database Glossary - D. (n.d.). Retrieved November 23, 2014, from http://www.nwdatabase.com/database-glossary-d.htm
8. IBM, 2007, Best practices for data migration. Retrieved November 23, 2014, from http://www-935.ibm.com/services/us/gts/pdf/bestpracticesfordatamigration-wp-gtw01275-usen-01-121307.pdf
9. IB Computing Home Page. (n.d.). Retrieved November 23, 2014, from http://www.ib-computing.com
10. Watson D., H. Williams, 2012, Cambridge IGCSE Computer Studies Revision Guide, Cambridge University Press.
11. Alpha vs. Beta Testing. (n.d.). Retrieved November 23, 2014, from http://www.centercode.com/blog/2011/01/alpha-vs-beta-testing/
12. (n.d.). Retrieved November 23, 2014, from http://ezinearticles.com/?Alpha-Testing-and-Beta-Testing&id=433
13. Illinois Online Network: Educational Resources. (n.d.). Retrieved November 23, 2014, from http://www.ion.uillinois.edu/resources/tutorials/overview/
14. Data loss. (2014, August 25). In Wikipedia, The Free Encyclopedia. Retrieved 18:06, November 23, 2014, from http://en.wikipedia.org/w/index.php?title=Data_loss&oldid=622747408
15. Failover. (2014, June 25). In Wikipedia, The Free Encyclopedia. Retrieved 18:07, November 23, 2014, from http://en.wikipedia.org/w/index.php?title=Failover&oldid=614395973
16. Patch (computing). (2014, November 11). In Wikipedia, The Free Encyclopedia. Retrieved 18:08, November 23, 2014, from http://en.wikipedia.org/w/index.php?title=Patch_(computing)&oldid=633351269
17. What is the difference between and Upgrade and an Update? (n.d.). Retrieved November 23, 2014, from http://www.enfocus.com/en/support/knowledge-base/what-is-the-difference-between-an-upgrade-and-an-update/
18. Release. (n.d.). Retrieved November 23, 2014, from http://searchsoftwarequality.techtarget.com/definition/release
19. Software. (2014, November 19). In Wikipedia, The Free Encyclopedia. Retrieved 18:09, November 23, 2014, from http://en.wikipedia.org/w/index.php?title=Software&oldid=634491568

20. Client–server model. (2014, October 7). In Wikipedia, The Free Encyclopedia. Retrieved 18:09, November 23, 2014, from http://en.wikipedia.org/w/index.php?title=Client%E2%80%93server_model&oldid=628622834

21. Experts you should follow. (n.d.). Retrieved November 23, 2014, from http://www.wikianswers.com/Q/In_a_client_server_environment_what_is_a_server

22. International Baccalaureate Organization. (2010). IBDP ITGS Guide

23. Multi-factor authentication. (2014, November 6). In Wikipedia, The Free Encyclopedia. Retrieved 18:12, November 23, 2014, from http://en.wikipedia.org/w/index.php?title=Multi-factor_authentication&oldid=632725562

24. How to Identify stakeholders. (n.d.). Retrieved November 23, 2014, from http://www.prince2.com/blog/how-identify-stakeholders

25. Data Tools. (n.d.). Retrieved November 23, 2014, from http://www.okstate.edu/ag/agedcm4h/academic/aged5980a/5980/newpage16.htm

26. Survey methodology. (2014, August 18). In Wikipedia, The Free Encyclopedia. Retrieved 18:13, November 23, 2014, from http://en.wikipedia.org/w/index.php?title=Survey_methodology&oldid=621707547

27. Hawthorne effect. (2014, November 9). In Wikipedia, The Free Encyclopedia. Retrieved 18:14, November 23, 2014, from http://en.wikipedia.org/w/index.php?title=Hawthorne_effect&oldid=633077463

28. Ione Auston, MLS, Marjorie A. Cahn, MA, Catherine R. Selden, 1992, MLS, National Library of Medicine, Office of Health Services Research Information, prepared for Agency for Health Care Policy and Research, Office of the Forum for Quality and Effectiveness in Health Care, Forum Methodology Conference. December 13-16, 1992. Retrieved November 23, 2014, from http://www.nlm.nih.gov/nichsr/litsrch.html.

29. Examining Impacts of Organizational Capabilities in Information Security: 2011, A Structural Equation Modeling Analysis by Hall, Jacqueline Huynh, Ph.D., THE GEORGE WASHINGTON UNIVERSITY, 2011, 204 pages; 3449269. Retrieved November 23, 2014, from http://gradworks.umi.com/34/49/3449269.html

30. Accessibility. (2014, September 22). In Wikipedia, The Free Encyclopedia. Retrieved 18:19, November 23, 2014, from http://en.wikipedia.org/w/index.php?title=Accessibility&oldid=626601064

31. Usability. (n.d.). Retrieved November 23, 2014, from http://searchsoa.techtarget.com/definition/usability

32. Ergonomics. (n.d.). Retrieved November 23, 2014, from http://www.webopedia.com/TERM/E/ergonomics.html

33. (n.d.). Retrieved November 23, 2014, from http://userpages.umbc.edu/~zhangd/Papers/IJHCI1.pdf

34. Nielsen Norman Group. (n.d.). Retrieved November 23, 2014, from http://www.nngroup.com/articles/usability-101-introduction-to-usability/

35. UN Enable: First 50 Years: Chapter II - What is a disability? (n.d.). Retrieved November 23, 2014, from http://www.un.org/esa/socdev/enable/dis50y10.htm

36. Burgstahler, S., 2012, Working Together: People with Disabilities and Computer Technology, Retrieved November 23, 2014 from http://www.washington.edu/doit/Brochures/Technology/wtcomp.html

37. Refreshable braille display. (2014, August 27). In Wikipedia, The Free Encyclopedia. Retrieved 18:20, November 23, 2014, from http://en.wikipedia.org/w/index.php?title=Refreshable_braille_display&oldid=623037113

38. Sip-and-puff. (2014, August 22). In Wikipedia, The Free Encyclopedia. Retrieved 18:21, November 23, 2014, from http://en.wikipedia.org/w/index.php?title=Sip-and-puff&oldid=622302284

39. Ethics vs. Morals. (n.d.). Retrieved November 23, 2014, from http://www.diffen.com/difference/Ethics_vs_Morals

Chapter 2

TOPIC 2 – Computer Organization

© IBO 2012

Topic 2 Computer organization[1]

Computer Architecture

2.1.1 The central processing unit (CPU) and its elements

Exit skills. Students should be able to[1]:
Define the terms CPU, ALU, CU, MAR, MDR, Address Bus and Data Bus. Develop a diagram of the CPU showing connections between the elements mentioned above.

Computer systems consist of hardware and software components and follow the concept of the *input, process, output and storage model.* This means that a computer system takes in some data as input, processes it in a manner that we have requested and outputs the result in some way. During the processing phase, other data, may be needed apart from the inputted. This data will exist in the storage of the computer system and will be used during the processing phase. Furthermore, any new information that may arise from the processing phase may also be saved in the storage.

Example 2.1: Imagine that we have a digital camera which is a sort of computer system. In order to take a picture the system, follows the input, process, output and storage model.
The *input* is the pressing of the shutter button to notify the system that we want to take a photograph. The *process* that the computer system performs is to capture the light through the camera lens and transform it to create digital image. This transformation requires instructions that exist in the storage. These instructions are loaded and used by the processing phase. Finally, the *output* is the digital image that we view on the monitor screen of the camera. This output is also *saved* on the storage (memory).

The input, process and output model is shown in Figure 2.1, outlining the relationship between the components of a computer system. More specifically, a computer system accepts data or instructions as input from an input device (from a keyboard, a sensor, a

[1] International Baccalaureate Organization. (2012). IBDP Computer Science Guide

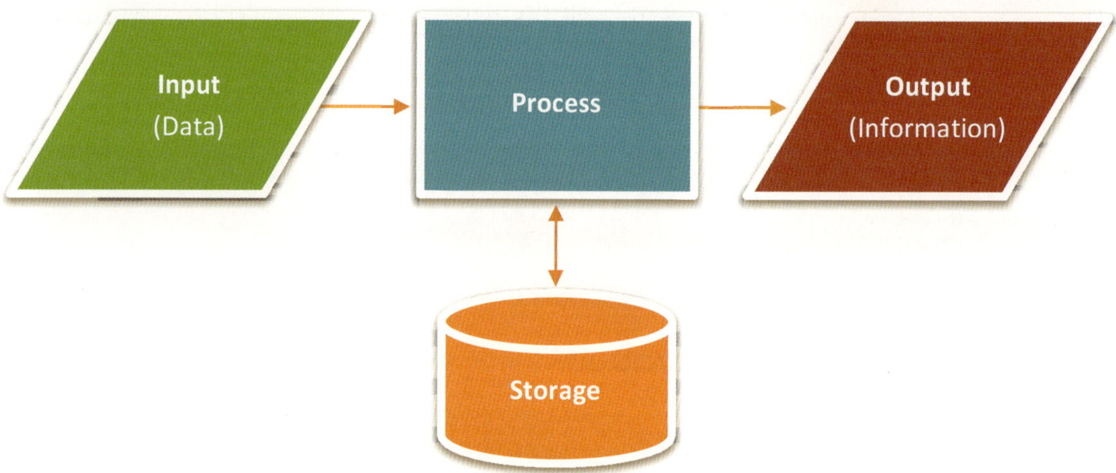

Figure 2.1: The input, process and output model

digital camera button etc.). Data or instructions are then processed by the computer system. It may be the case that other data or instructions, apart from the input, are necessary during processing. These exist in the storage and may be loaded and used. Finally, the computer system outputs the processed data into information that we can see and use (using a monitor, speakers, a printout, etc.). This output is also saved on the storage (memory).

Data or instructions that are processed by a computer system in the process phase of the input, process, output and storage model are processed by the *central processing unit (CPU)*. The CPU is a hardware component of a computer system and can perform basic arithmetic, logical or input/output operations, in order to process data from input devices into useful information. The CPU is the "brain" of a computer system and can process data very quickly but can only process data by following instructions – it cannot think for itself. The CPU can also be referred to as the *processor* or *chip. A block diagram* can be created to represent the elements that compromise it. This block diagram is shown in Figure 2.2. The CPU functions in the process phase of the input, process, output and storage model. It retrieves and saves data and information from and to the storage, which is the primary memory of the computer system. Any data or information that is to be saved on or retrieved from some storage medium (ex. hard disk, CD, DVD, floppy disk, USB stick) first has to pass through the primary memory in order to be accessed by the CPU. As such, the CPU can retrieve data only from the input or primary memory of the computer system.

The CPU contains the:

- control unit (CU)
- arithmetic logic unit (ALU)
- memory address register (MAR)
- memory data register (MDR)

The *control unit (CU)* is responsible for the operation of the CPU. It controls the retrieval of instructions from the primary memory as well as the sequence of their execution.

The *arithmetic logic unit (ALU)* performs all the basic arithmetic, logical or input/output operations. The CU is responsible for providing the ALU with the data that needs to be processed as well as the instructions of how the data should be processed.

As shown in Figure 2.2 the primary memory used as storage contains two types of memory -

The terms bit (b), Byte (B) and their multiples

Computer systems are binary systems. That means that all the data and instructions that are stored in a computer system are stored in sequences of binary digits that can take only two possible values, 1 and 0. Thus a **bi**nary digi**t** **(bit)** is the basic unit of information in computer systems and can have only two values: either 1 or 0. Eight bits form a **byte**.

1 Byte = 8 bits

A **bit** is denoted by the small letter **b**, whereas a **byte** is denoted by the capital letter **B**. Thus, 1B = 8b. **One byte can store a single character** (ex. the letter A).

In a 64 bit computer each memory location holds 64 bits. A 64 bit Memory (Address) Bus transfers 64 bits at any one time (which are the contents of a memory location in a 64 bit computer system).

In computer systems we describe everything in bits and bytes. As such, they are used to denote file sizes stored on memory or disks (ex. a 12MB file) or even connection speeds (ex. 50Mbps). However, since files can become quite large and connection speeds quite fast, multiples of bits and bytes are used. The following table depicts the prefixes that can be used to denote multiples of bits and bytes.

Term	Size in binary system	Size approximation
Kilo (K)	1,024	1,000
Mega (M)	$1,024^2$	1,000,000
Giga (G)	$1,024^3$	1,000,000,000
Tera (T)	$1,024^4$	1,000,000,000,000

In the decimal system, one kilometer is 1,000 meters. However, since computer systems are binary, a "Kilo" is 1,024. Since these two values are close there is a tendency to use multiples of 1,000 instead of 1,024 in the binary system as well.

It is important not to mix the meaning of bits and bytes and their multiples. For example, the values of 12Mb (twelve mega bit) and 12MB (twelve mega bytes) are different.

12 Mb = 12 * $1,024^2$ bits whereas 12 MB = 12 * $1,024^2$ Bytes

Since 1 Byte is equal to 8 bits, 12MB is an amount 8 times greater than 12Mb.

the *random access memory (RAM)* and the *read only memory (ROM)*.

The RAM stores the executing program instructions as well as any data that is needed. Instructions and data in the RAM are stored in unique memory locations and every such location has an *address* as well as *content*. The content is where the instructions and data reside, whereas the memory location is used by the CU to find, retrieve and access the data in order to send it to the ALU for processing.

Similar to the RAM, the ROM holds instructions and data in unique memory locations. Every such location has an address as well as content. Unlike the RAM however, the ROM is used to store permanent instructions and data that cannot be changed and are used to boot and operate the computer. As such, nothing can be altered in the ROM.

Example 2.2: In order to move from higher prefixes to lower prefixes, we multiply by 1,024. For example, if a file has a size of 2GBs the file size in KBs will be 2 * 1,024 * 1,024. We multiply 2 by 1024 in order to get the file size in MBs and then multiply by 1,024 again to get the file size in KBs.

2GBs = 2 * 1,024 MBs = 2,048 MBs = 2,048 * 1,024 KBs = 2,097,152 KBs

In order to move from lower prefixes to higher prefixes, we divide by 1,024. For example, if a file has a size of 2KBs the file size in GBs will be (2 / 1,024) / 1,024. We divide 2 by 1,024 in order to get the file size in MBs and then divide by 1,024 again to get the file size in GBs.

2KBs = 2 / 1,024 MBs = 0.001953125 MBs = 0.001953125 / 1,024 GBs = 0.0000019073486328125 GBs

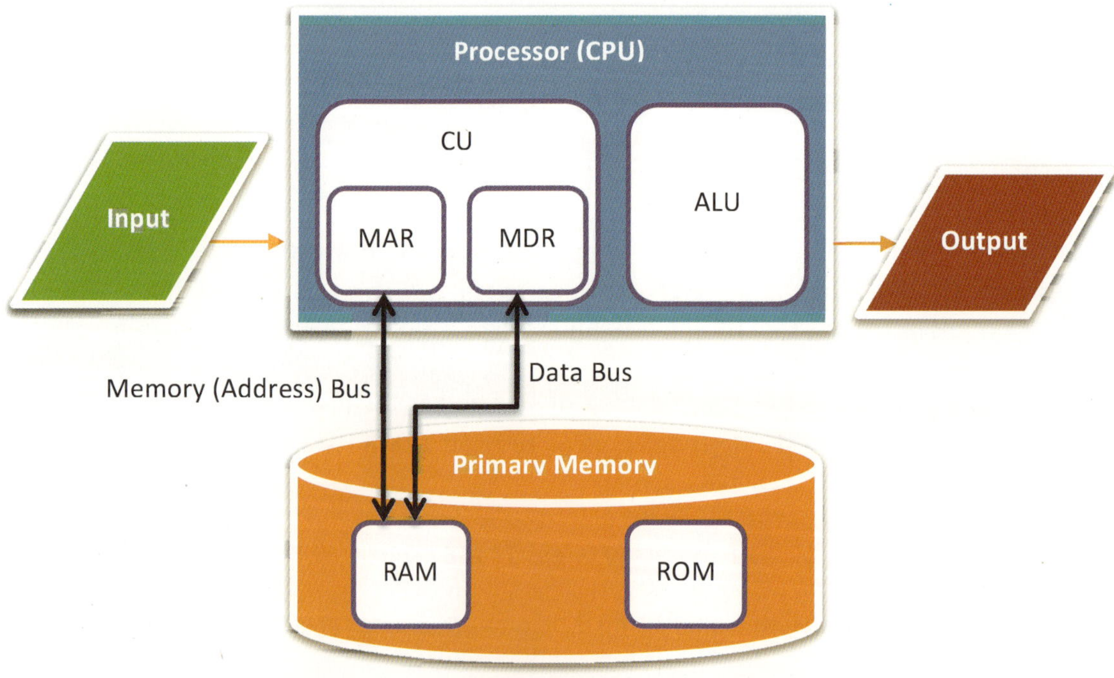

Figure 2.2: CPU block diagram

The CU contains various *registers*. In general, a register is a small storage location that can hold data, usually a multiple of 8 bits. For example, a 64 bit computer has 64 bit registers. The size of the register in bytes is known as a *word*. For example, the 64 bit register holds 64 bits = 8 * 8 bits and since 1 byte is equal to 8 bits, 64 bits = 8 Bytes. Thus, a 64 bit computer system has a word size of 8 bytes. This means that each memory location will hold 64 bits (or 8 Bytes).

The basic registers in the CU are the *memory address register (MAR)* and the *memory data register (MDR)*.

The MAR holds the memory address of the data to be used by the ALU, so that the ALU can fetch the corresponding content from the memory and process it accordingly. The MAR may also hold the memory address of where data that has been processed will need to be stored. In order for the MAR to communicate with the primary memory, a connection is necessary. This connection is accomplished by the Memory (Address) Bus.

The MDR holds the data that is to be used by the ALU and then saved to the RAM. The MDR is closely related to the MAR, since whichever memory address location the MAR is holding, the corresponding data will be loaded onto the MDR for processing by the ALU. After the processing has taken place, the ALU places the result onto the MDR and the data is copied to the memory address location in RAM specified by the MAR. The connection between the RAM and the MDR is accomplished by the Data Bus.

Example 2.3:

Question: Describe the function of the data bus found in a PC.

Answer: It carries data to the MDR and then to the ALU from memory and from ALU to the MDR and then to memory.

Example 2.4:

Question: Outline the function of the ALU (arithmetic logic unit).

Answer: The ALU performs arithmetical and logical operations. It performs various calculations and comparisons using various logic gates.

2.1.2 RAM and ROM

Exit skills. Students should be able to[1]:
Explain the use of primary memory. Define the terms RAM and ROM. Explain the differences between RAM and ROM.

The *primary memory* is the only storage that is directly accessible by the CPU. At any point in time, the primary memory may hold both data and instructions that are currently running on the computer system. These data and instructions are stored in the primary memory as binary machine code (i.e. a series of 0s and 1s).

As depicted in Figure 2.2 the primary memory consists of two types of memory:

- *Random Access Memory (RAM)*
- *Read Only Memory (ROM)*

Image 2.1: RAM

RAM is a general-purpose storage area meaning that the data stored can be over-written. This allows data and instructions to be loaded for execution and used whenever they are necessary. However, RAM is volatile, which means that whenever power is lost the contents of its memory are wiped clean (ex. if an unsaved document with changes is open when the power is lost, all the changes will be lost).

On the other hand, ROM is used to store instructions and data and cannot be over-written. This means that the instructions that are embedded in ROM cannot be changed, even if power is lost, and as such is considered non-volatile memory. ROM is used to store programs and instructions that do not need to be updated or changed (ex. the start-up instructions of the operating system).

Example 2.5:

Question: Identify some differences between ROM and RAM found in a PC.

Answer:

- ROM cannot be written to, but RAM can be written to.
- ROM holds the (BIOS) Basic Input / Output System, but RAM holds the programs running and the data used.
- ROM is much smaller than RAM.
- ROM is non-volatile (permanent), but RAM is volatile.

2.1.3 The cache memory

Exit skills. Students should be able to[1]:
Define cache memory. Explain the function of cache memory. Describe various types of cache memory.

RAM has two main types:

- *Dynamic RAM (DRAM)*
- *Static RAM (SRAM)*

SRAM is faster but more expensive than DRAM, and as such DRAM is preferred for the main RAM of a computer system. However, a small amount of SRAM is placed between the main RAM and the processor and it is called *cache* (Figure 2.3). As such, cache is a smaller and faster RAM (SRAM) that temporarily stores instructions and data so that the processor does not need to access the slower main memory (DRAM).

Cache holds the information from the RAM that is most actively used, and accessed most frequently. The computer system will run faster as the slower main memory will need to be accessed less frequently. When the processor needs to read from the main memory, it first checks if a copy of the data exists in the cache. If so, the processor reads from the cache, instead of reading from main memory. This action speeds up the process. If the data to be read do not exist in the cache, the data are first copied to the cache and then used. When the processor needs to write to the main memory it does so through cache memory.

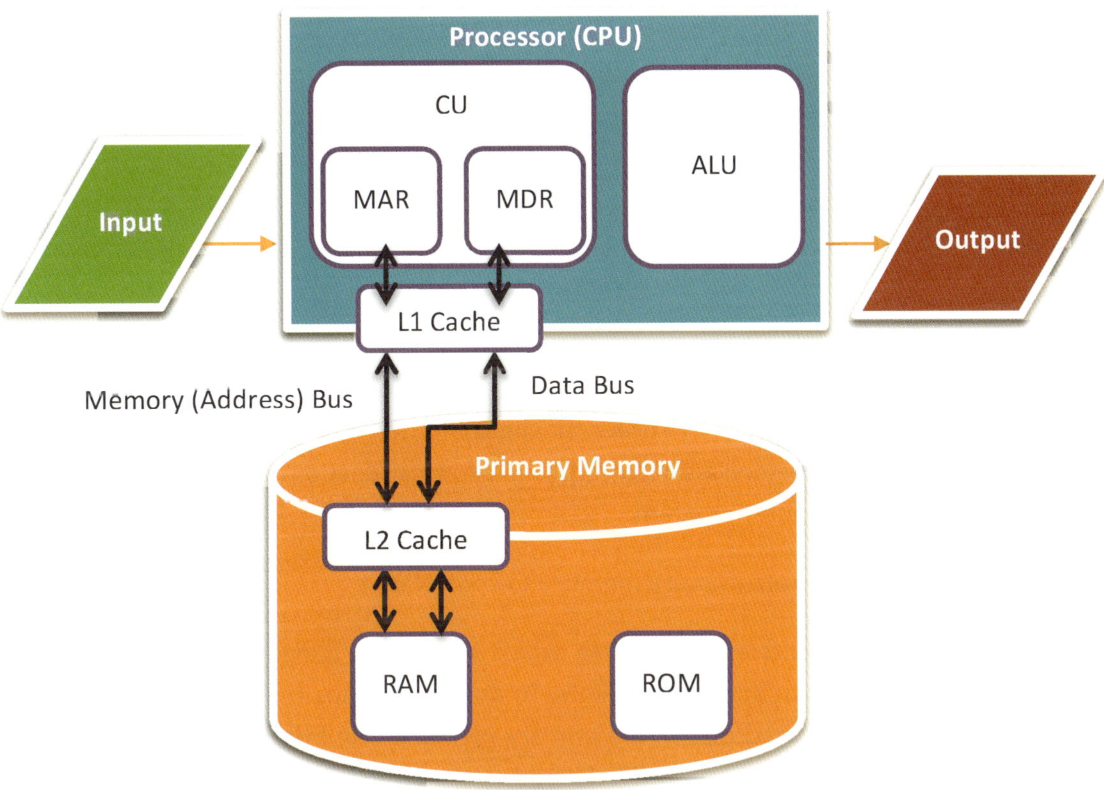

Figure 2.3: Cache

Example 2.6:
Question: State some differences between Cache Memory and RAM.

Answer:

- Cache memory is nearer to the CPU than RAM.
- Cache memory is much faster than RAM.
- Cache memory is more expensive than RAM.
- Cache memory is separated in L1 and L2.

We are interested in two types of cache memories that reside between the main RAM and the processor. These two types are *L1* cache and *L2* cache. L1 cache is placed on the microprocessor itself whereas L2 cache is placed between the primary memory and the microprocessor.

2.1.4 The machine instruction cycle

Exit skills. Students should be able to[1]:
Define machine instruction cycle. Describe machine instruction cycle. Explain the use of data bus and address bus during the machine instruction cycle.

Computer programs are stored in the primary memory as a series of instructions in machine code. These instructions, as well as any other necessary data, have to be moved from the primary memory and into the CPU in order for the computer program to operate. In order for that to happen, specific steps are followed. The following functions are carried out by the CPU in order to run a computer program:

1. **Fetch instruction from primary memory to control unit**

The CPU is responsible for knowing which instruction it needs to take from the primary memory in order to operate correctly. To do that it sends the appropriate address through the memory (address) bus to the primary memory. The instruction that resides in the specific address is then copied into the data bus and sent to the control unit (CU).

2. **Decode instruction in control unit**

The instruction that has been received by the CU is then decoded. Decoding an instruction allows the CPU to be aware of any additional data that are necessary for the execution of the instruction. Any required data that need to be loaded from the primary memory in order for the instruction to be executable are then fetched. The addresses of these data are placed into the memory (address) bus and the data from these addresses are received by the CPU through the data bus.

3. Execute instruction

The CPU executes the instruction using the necessary data that have been loaded and calculates a result. Depending on the result, additional data may be needed. These data are fetched from the primary memory for further calculations. As before, the addresses of these data are placed into the memory (address) bus and the data from these addresses are received by the CPU through the data bus.

4. Store result of execution and check for next instruction

After executing the instruction and computing the result the CPU then stores the result in the primary memory. To do so, it specifies the address where the result will reside in the primary memory, using the memory (address) bus and sends the data through the data bus. The CPU then checks for the next instruction and repeats the steps described above by fetching, decoding, executing and finally storing the result.

The four steps presented above describe the machine instruction cycle.

Example 2.7:

Question: What is an instruction cycle?

Answer: It is the basic operation cycle of a computer, taking place in a definite time period, during which one instruction is fetched from memory and executed. It typically consists of four stages: fetch, decode, execute and store.

Secondary Memory

2.1.5 Persistent storage and secondary memory

Exit skills. Students should be able to[1]:
Define persistent storage. Explain the need for persistent storage. Define virtual memory. Explain the use of virtual memory.

As described in section 2.1.2 the primary memory of a computer system consists of both random access memory (RAM) and read only memory (ROM). The primary memory is the only storage that is directly accessible by the CPU, meaning that any data that is stored elsewhere needs to first be copied onto the RAM, since the ROM cannot be written to but only read from, in order to be used by the CPU. RAM however is volatile, meaning that whenever power is lost the contents of the memory are wiped. Furthermore, RAM is a relatively fast memory but has only a restricted capacity to hold data. As instructions and data are saved onto the RAM, the RAM will inevitably become full at some point. At that point some instructions or data from the RAM will need to be moved in order to make space for new instructions or data. This is where secondary memory comes into play.

Secondary memory (a.k.a. secondary or auxiliary storage) is a relatively slow memory that may be written to (just like the RAM) but is also *non-volatile* (just like the ROM); meaning that the contents of the memory are not wiped if power is lost but are persistent. That is why secondary memory is also known as *persistent storage*. Furthermore, secondary memory has a relatively high capacity to hold data compared to the primary memory.

When the computer starts-up the RAM is empty. Instructions and data (such as the operating system) need to be copied into the RAM in order for the computer system to run. In most computer systems these are copied from the secondary memory. Secondary memory is thus what provides persistent storage to computer systems. This is very important since if secondary memory did not exist a computer system would be unable to store instructions and data persistently. Whenever it shut down all the contents of the only existing primary memory would be lost.

Without the availability of secondary memory only ROM, would be able to store programs and instructions. That would mean that since ROM cannot be over-written, a computer would only be able to perform fixed operations and any user data would have to be re-inputted every time the user wished to use them. This would be acceptable for devices such as simple calculators, but imagine a mobile telephone user, who would have to re-enter the names and telephone numbers every time the mobile telephone was powered on. Such a system would be very hard or impossible to use as the user would have to remember all the telephone numbers or carry an address book everywhere!

Since data is very important, if not critical, for computer systems to function correctly, the loss of data would be detrimental. As such, computer systems that need to hold persistent data and not have data loss cannot function properly just with primary memory.

Figure 2.4 depicts the way that the CPU, primary and secondary memories are connected. The CPU can only access the volatile primary memory that is relatively fast but moderate in capacity. The primary memory is connected to the non-volatile secondary memory that is relatively slower but has a higher capacity to hold data.

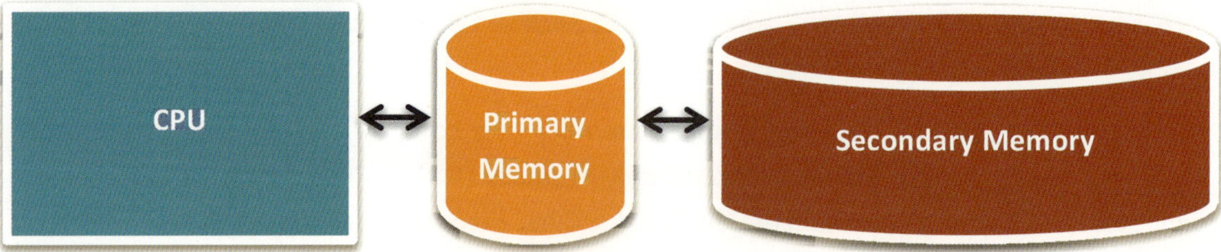

Figure 2.4: CPU, Primary and Secondary Memory

Example 2.8: Imagine that we have a computer system that has a primary memory of 4GBs. When the system is off the volatile primary memory is empty. When the system is turned on various programs are loaded into the memory (including the operating system) in order for the computer system to run correctly. Say that these programs need 2GBs of primary memory. There are only 2GBs of primary memory left for any other programs we might use.

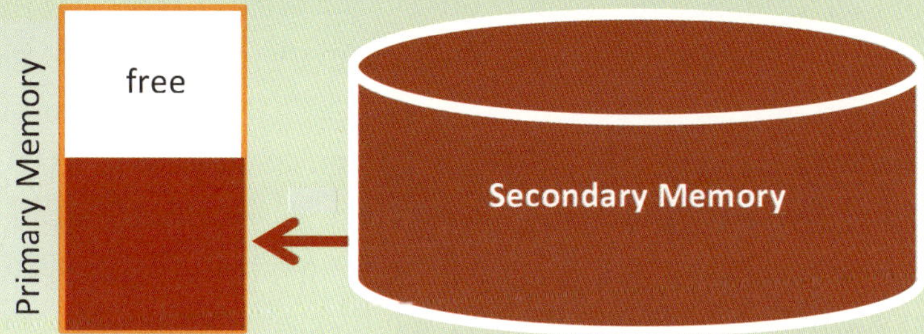

Imagine that we need to design a new logo for our school. We run a web browser so as to look for other logos and get some ideas. Assume the web browser needs around 500MBs (0.5GBs) of primary memory in order to run. There are only 1.5GBs of primary memory left for any other programs we might use.

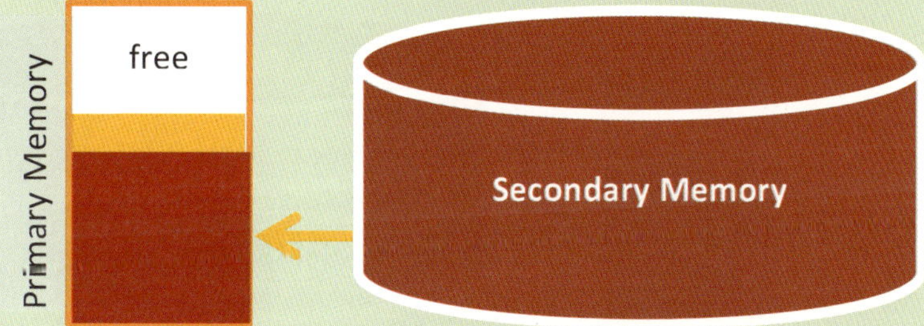

After we look at a few other logos, we decide on an idea for our logo and we also run a graphic design program that will allow us to create the logo. However, we decide to keep the web browser running so as to look at the other logos as we go along. Assume the graphic design program needs around 1GB of primary memory in order to run. There are only 500MBs (0.5GBs) of primary memory left for any other programs we might use.

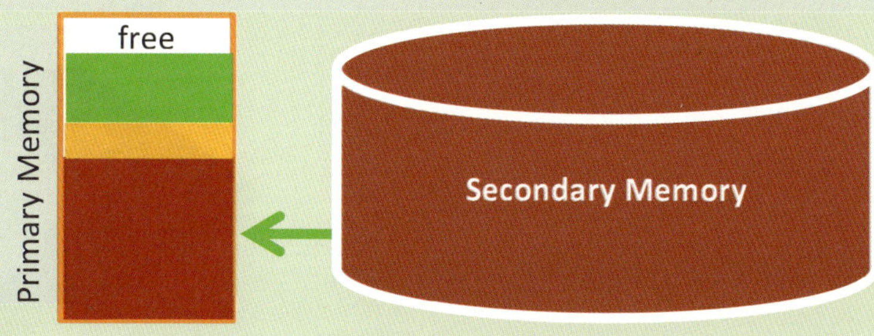

While designing our logo in our graphic design program, we decide that a 3D sphere would look great. In order to create the 3D sphere, we would need to run a 3D modeling program. Assume this program needs around 1GB of primary memory in order to run. However, we only have 500MBs (0.5GBs) of primary memory left.

If secondary memory did not exist, we would not be able to run the 3D modeling program without closing some of the other programs in order to release some primary memory. However, the secondary memory allows us to run all these programs concurrently and seamlessly. Since there is not enough space in the primary memory to load the 3D modeling program, some other program loaded by the user (either the web browser or the graphic design program) is copied into secondary memory, this making space for the 3D modeling program to be loaded into primary memory. Whenever the program that was moved into the secondary memory is needed, some other program in the primary memory is copied to the secondary memory. The first program is again copied back into the primary memory and is ready to be used by the user. The process described above is called ***Virtual memory*** and can be defined as the use of secondary memory as if it was primary memory.

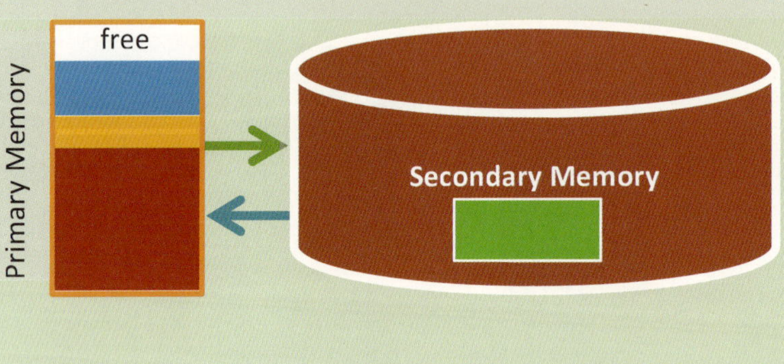

As depicted in the example, secondary memory is required to hold information that may not be needed all of the time or may be too large to fit as a whole in primary memory (*virtual memory*). This makes secondary memory a necessity in most computer systems.

There are a number of different secondary memory (storage) devices. The main ones are listed below:

- Hard drive (a.k.a. hard disk)
- CD-RW, DVD-RW
- USB Flash drive
- Secure Digital (SD) or Compact Flash (CF) card
- Zip disk
- Floppy disk
- Magnetic tape

Image 2.2: Hard drive

Different storage devices

Image 2.3: An old 5.25 inch floppy disk

Image 2.4: A loaded DVD drive

Image 2.5: An old 3.5 inch floppy disk

Image 2.6: Multipe Compact flash memory cards

Image 2.7: A ZIP drive with a disk

Image 2.8: A solid state drive (SSD) for notebook and a hard disk drive (HDD) for desktop computer

Image 2.9:Various USB sticks

As secondary memory is obviously crucial to computer systems it becomes apparent that advances in the technology surrounding secondary memory are beneficial to computer systems as a whole. New technologies appear and existing ones strive to become more efficient, robust, and faster, as well as to hold more data than before.

As the modern world is characterized by an increasing amount of computer systems, masses of data are produced continuously which have to be stored somewhere. All these data have to be stored in non-volatile secondary (storage) memory. As such, the need for such memory is ever-increasing.

Example 2.9:

Question: State some differences between primary and secondary memory.

Answer:

- Most computers are equipped with a smaller amount of primary memory and a larger amount of secondary memory.
- Primary memory is volatile, which means it does not retain data when the power is turned off.
- Primary memory is more expensive compared to secondary memory.
- Primary memory is much faster than secondary memory.
- Primary memory is directly accessed by the CPU.
- Secondary memory is not directly accessible by the CPU.
- Secondary memory is non-volatile, which means it retains data when the power is turned off.

Operating and application systems

2.1.6 Functions of an operating system

Exit skills. Students should be able to[1]:
Define operating system. Explain the main functions of an OS.

An *Operating System (OS)* is a set of software that controls the computer's hardware resources and provides services for computer programs. It is a very important part of a computer system since it acts as an intermediary between software applications (i.e. programs) and the computer hardware.

This relation is shown in Figure 2.5. In a computer system a user would interact with an application that has been designed to meet the user's needs. This application would require an operating system in order to function. This operating system would allow the application to interact with the hardware of the computer system thanks to a number of services.

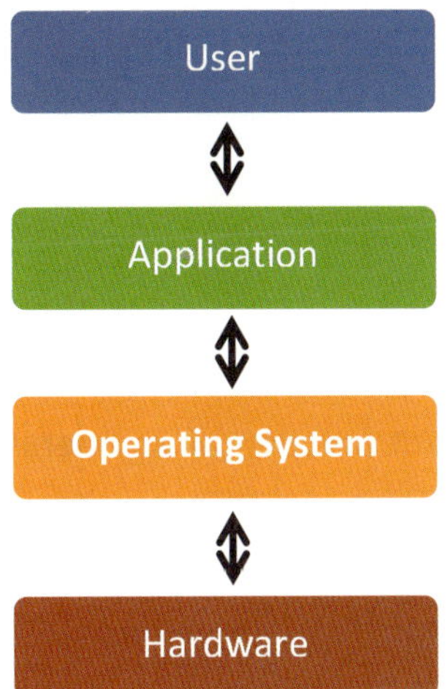

Figure 2.5: User, application, operating system and hardware interaction

The main services that an operating system provides are listed and described below:

- Peripheral communication
- Memory management
- Resource monitoring and multitasking
- Networking
- Disk access and data management
- Security

Peripheral communication

Peripheral devices are all the hardware components of the computer system that reside outside the CPU. Examples of peripheral devices include keyboards, monitors, mice, printers, microphones, etc. The operating system is responsible for communicating directly with the hardware and providing an interface between hardware devices and applications. This allows for applications to use hardware devices in a trouble-free manner.

Memory management

An Operating System (OS) is responsible for all the memory that is available in a computer system. This means that an OS manages how the memory is used by applications and ensures that one application does not interfere with memory that is being used by some other application. If one application interferes with another application's memory, the latter may stop functioning or its data may be affected or overwritten.

Resource monitoring and multitasking

An application that is running on a computer system takes up resources. These resources include the amount of memory the application is occupying, or how much processor time it needs in order to function properly. An OS is responsible for the efficient allocation of resources so that an application can run as effectively as possible on a particular computer system.

Multiple applications may run on a computer system at any one time, appearing as though they are performing tasks simultaneously. Most computer systems however have a single CPU that can perform a single action at any particular time. That means that applications must share the CPU time in order to accomplish their goal. This is known as multitasking and it is a core OS service.

Networking

An operating system manages connections to and interactions with networks of other computer systems so as to allow the sharing of resources (such as files and printers). Networking is essential to modern computer systems, most connected with either a local area network or the Internet. An operating system acts as an intermediary between applications and networks, allowing applications to interact with networks in a straightforward manner.

Disk access and data management

An important function of an operating system is its ability to access data stored in memory and disks. Data are stored using files, which are structured in such a way so as to make better use of the space available to the system, as well as to provide reliability and fast access times. The OS is responsible for keeping track of these files, as well as which files are being used by which applications so that an application does not overwrite another applications' files. The OS is also responsible for coordinating the transfer of data from the disk files into the primary memory and vice versa.

Security

Apart from allowing applications to run successfully, the operating system is also responsible for the overall security of a computer system. The most common but effective method of protection is to provide some form of identity to the user that will allow his/her authentication. Most often a username and a password must be provided. However, other methods of authentication may be used, such as magnetic cards or biometric data. Apart from authentication methods, an additional security measure is the use of *log files* that keep trace of the activity of any user in the computer system. Anything a user does (reads, writes or deletes files, changes some settings, etc.) is recorded so that unauthorized users and activities may be discovered.

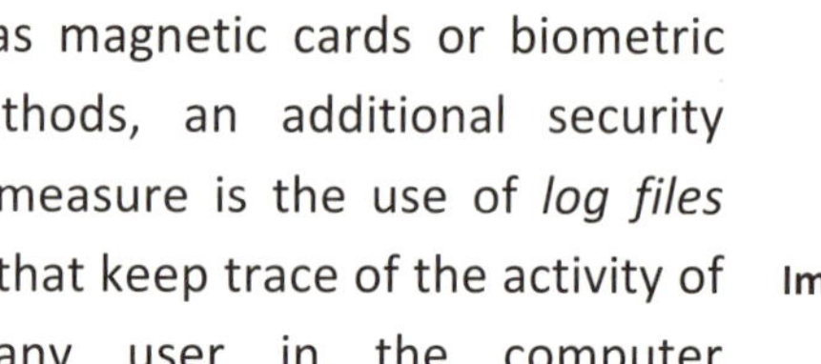

Image 2.10: OS logos

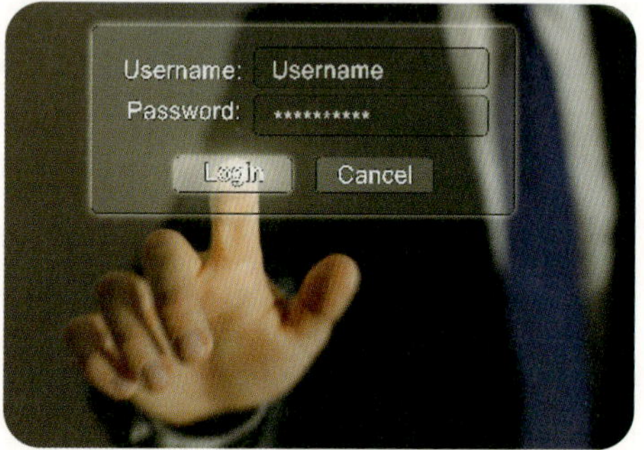

Image 2.11: Security

Some important examples of major operating systems at the moment are OS X, Linux, UNIX and Microsoft Windows.

Example 2.10:

Question: Outline the operating system ensures that files are only accessed by the users allowed.

Answer: The OS deals with different passwords and the equivalent access levels. This ensures that only appropriate users can access particular files. Different uses have different access levels and different rights (add, edit, delete, view a file etc.).

2.1.7 Software application

Exit skills. Students should be able to[1]:
Define the term application software. Define the terms word processors, spreadsheets, database management systems, email, web browsers, computer-aided design (CAD) and graphic processing software, and describe the use of these applications.

A computer system has the ability to run at least one software application, which has been installed by the manufacturer, to complete some predefined tasks. For example, a digital camera is on its own a computer system. It consists of both hardware and software components and follows the input, process, output and storage model as described in the example of section 2.1.1. The software components of the digital camera are preloaded when it is manufactured and complete predefined tasks (ex. when the shutter button is pressed, the software is run that is responsible for capturing the image in digital form and storing it into memory after processing it is run). These software components of the digital camera can only be altered by receiving their updated versions from the manufacturer.

However computer systems include devices such as desktop and laptop computers, tablets, mobile smart phones etc. These allow the user to install a large number of software applications on to them. This allows for the use of a range of software applications on them, instead of being able to complete only one predefined task.

Application software are programs designed for the end-user that enable the completion of various tasks in order to increase productivity. The main software applications that may be installed on such computer systems include:

- Word processors
- Spreadsheets
- Database management systems
- Web browsers
- Email
- Computer Aided Design (CAD)
- Graphic processing software

Word processors

A word processor is a software application that is used for the production of any sort of document. It includes tools for the composition, editing, formatting and possibly printing of documents. Word processing, is the action of creating documents using a word processor. This is the most common of all the main software applications that can be installed on a computer system.

Some well-known word processing applications are Microsoft Word (see Figure 2.6) and Apple iPages.

Figure 2.6: Microsoft Word, an example of a word processor

Spreadsheets

A spreadsheet is a software application that is used for the organization and analysis of data. The data in a spreadsheet application is represented as *cells*, organized in rows and columns. These cells may contain numbers, text or results of formulas that calculate and display values automatically on the basis of the contents of other cells. Spreadsheet software applications allow not only for the fundamental operations of arithmetic and mathematical

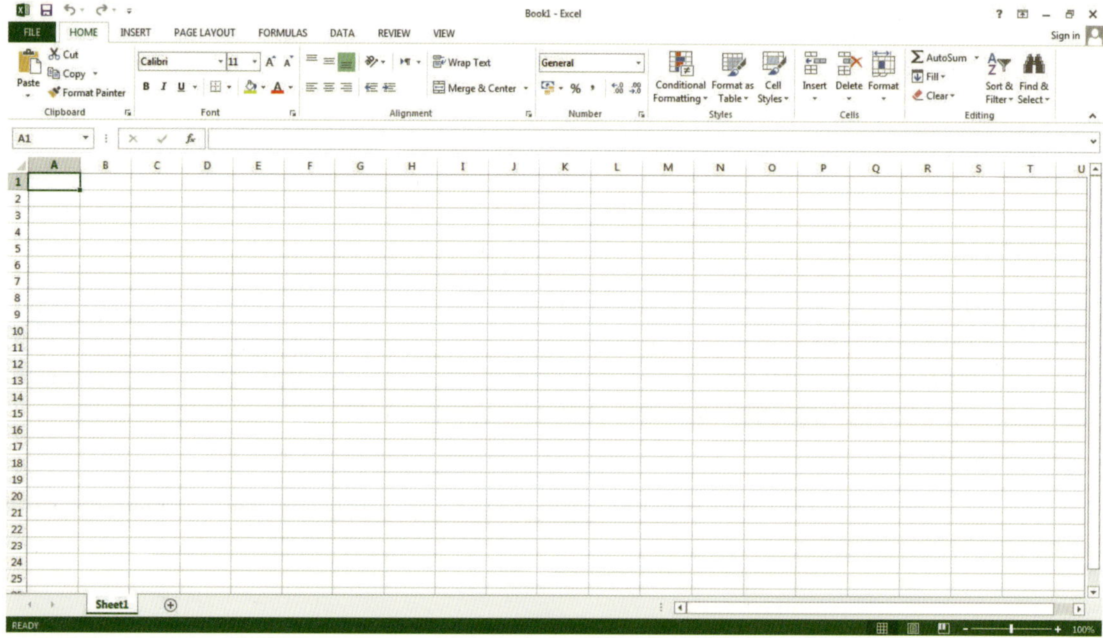

Figure 2.7: Microsoft Excel, an example of a spreadsheet application

functions to be shown but also provide common financial and statistical operations and can display graphical data as well. Spreadsheet software applications are used not only in accounting or finance, but also in any context that requires arithmetic data to be entered, processed and presented.

Some well-known spreadsheet applications are Microsoft Excel (see Figure 2.7) and OpenOffice Calc.

Database management systems (DBMS)

A database management system (DBMS) is a software application that manages (creates, queries, updates stores, modifies, and extracts information) databases and is designed to provide an interface between users and a database. A well-known DBMS is MS ACCESS (Figure 2.9).

A *database* can be defined as an organized collection of data. This data is organized into *records* and model some relevant aspect of reality. For example, a database can store information about a school. All the data will be organized in records with each student's information organized in one record as shown in Figure 2.8.

Student ID	First Name	Last Name	Telephone Number
1572	Tom	Jones	510-572-8276
1573	John	White	510-537-3456
1574	Wendy	Stevens	510-591-6374

Figure 2.8: A database with three records (rows)

The database in Figure 2.8 represents structured data items in a table. It contains three records (also called rows or tuples) and four *fields* (also called columns). Each record represents a set of related data, which in this example is the information about a specific student. A key feature of a database is the unique key. A unique key is one (or more) specific fields that uniquely identify each record. In our example, the Student ID field is the unique

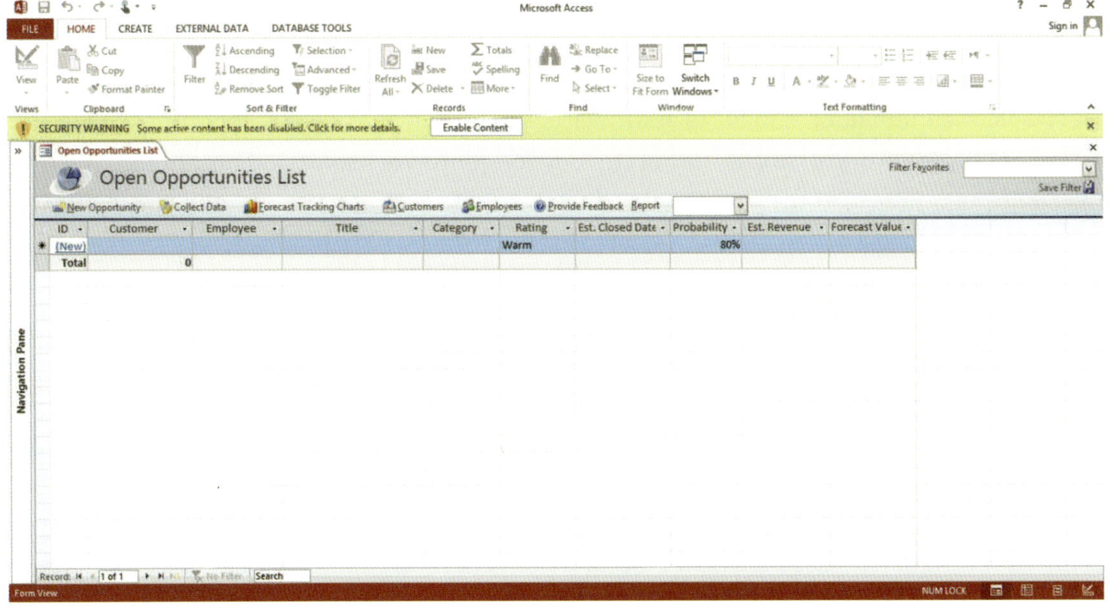

Figure 2.9: Microsoft Access, an example of a DBMS application

key because each student will have a specific unique Student ID that can identify him/her and differentiate him/her from all the other students in the school.

Web browsers

A web browser (or browser) is a software application used to access, retrieve, and present content on the World Wide Web. This content may be web pages, images, videos or other files and may be identified by a URI (Uniform Resource Identifier). An example of a URI is http://en.wikipedia.org/. The web browser uses a URI to connect to the appropriate web servers and request the wanted information. The web servers send back the information which the web browser then displays to the user.

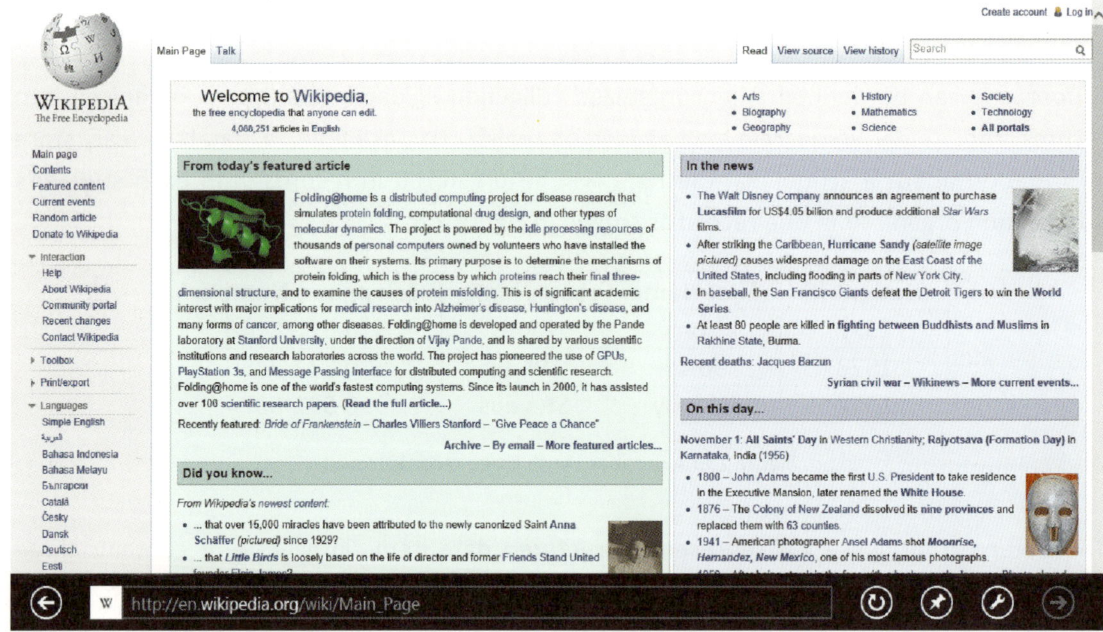

Figure 2.10: Microsoft Internet Explorer, an example of a web browser application

Some major web browsers are Microsoft Internet Explorer (see Figure 2.10), Google Chrome, Mozilla Firefox and Apple Safari.

Email

Electronic mail (email or e-mail) is a software application that allows for the exchange of digital messages from a single author to one or more recipient(s). The author and the recipient(s) do not need to be online simultaneously to exchange the email. The author of the email sends the email to the email server of the recipient(s), and when the latter connects to the server, they will receive the message.

An email consists of three components: the envelope, the header and the body. In order for an email to be transferred from the author to the recipient(s), the *Simple Mail Transfer Protocol (SMTP)* is used. This protocol communicates delivery parameters using the message envelope. The message header contains information about the sender and recipient(s) addresses, as well as the subject field and a date/time stamp. Finally, the message body contains the actual message which the author wants to send to the recipient(s).

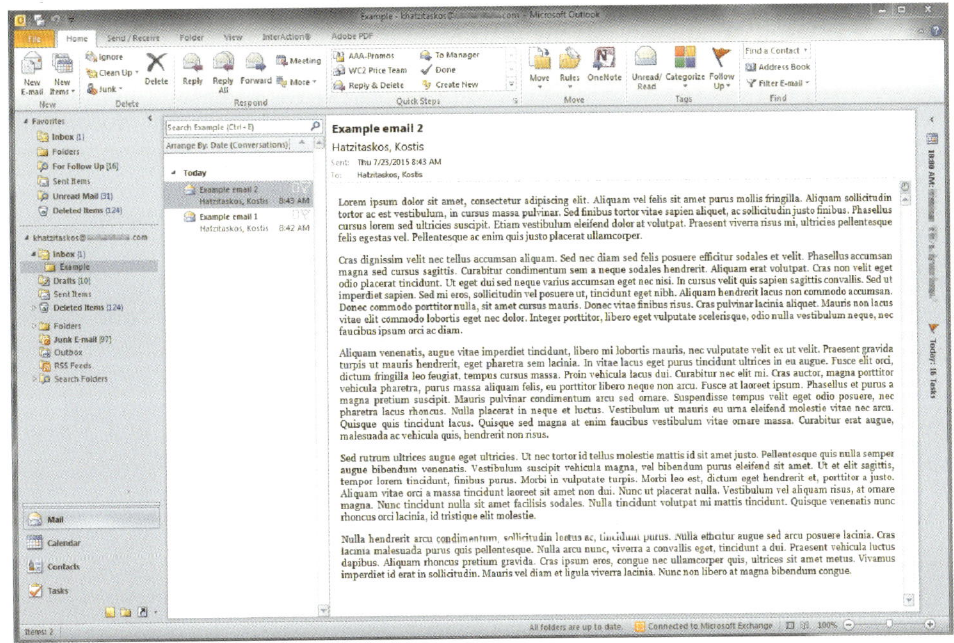

Figure 2.11: Microsoft Outlook, an example of an email application

Email software applications can be web-based, or as software that is installed on a personal computer system. *Web-based email* (a.k.a. webmail) can be accessed by any computer system that supports a web browser. The main disadvantage of web-based email software applications is the need to be connected to the internet while using it.

Some important software applications for email are Microsoft Outlook (see Figure 2.11) and for web-based email Google Gmail.

Computer Aided Design (CAD)

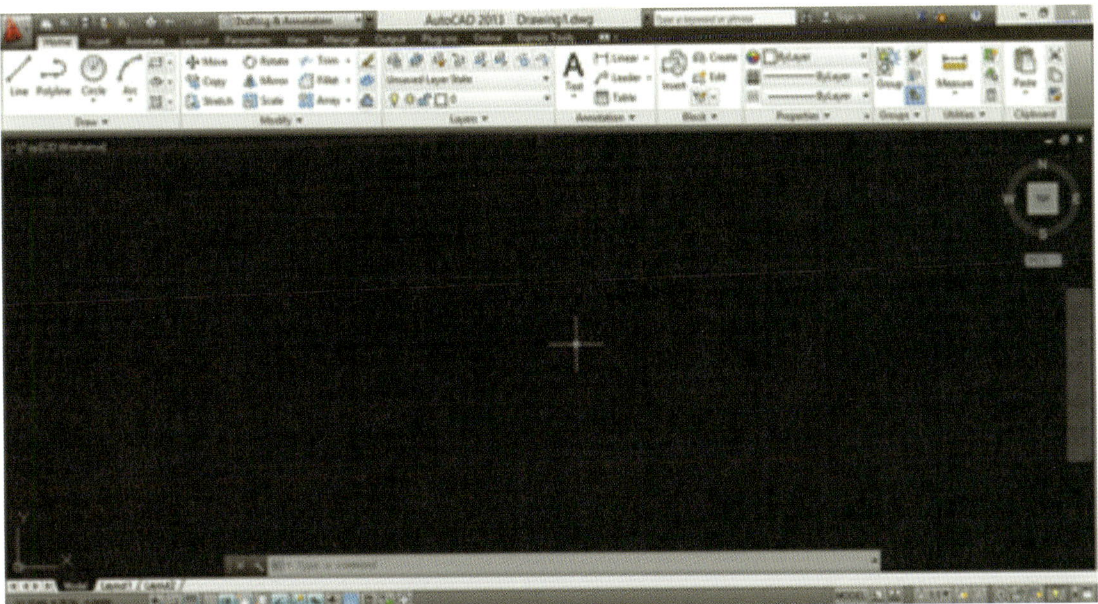

Figure 2.12: Autodesk AutoCAD, an example of a CAD application

A computer-aided design (CAD) application is a software application that assists engineers to create, modify, analyze and optimize a design. CAD is used in many fields and its purpose is to increase the productivity of the designer and the quality of the resulting design. Some examples of circumstances where CAD applications are used include automotive, shipbuilding, architectural design, and many more.

CAD applications allow engineers to inspect a design from any angle or position. Computer-aided designs can convey more than just shape information. Materials, dimensions, tolerances can all be represented in such a way that when an engineer changes one value all the other dependent values automatically change accordingly.

Some major CAD applications are Autodesk AutoCAD (see Figure 2.12) and Dassault Systèmes Solid Works.

Example 2.11:

Question: State some difference between a Spreadsheet software application and a Database Management System.

Answer:

- A Database Management System could be used for various data associations that cannot be created with spreadsheets.
- A Database Management System manages databases and serves a lot of users.
- A Database Management System preserves data integrity easier.
- A spreadsheet can be used to produce charts and graphs using automated software tools.
- A spreadsheet can hold a limited amount of information.
- A spreadsheet usually serves the needs of a single person.
- Spreadsheet software can perform a lot of mathematical functions and perform data analysis.

Graphic processing software

Graphic processing software (aka graphics software or image editing software) allows a user to manipulate visual images on a computer. A user can edit an image with the use of tools in various ways, such as selecting and moving, cropping, scaling, erasing, etc.

Some popular graphic processing software applications are Adobe Photoshop (see Figure 2.13) and Corel Draw.

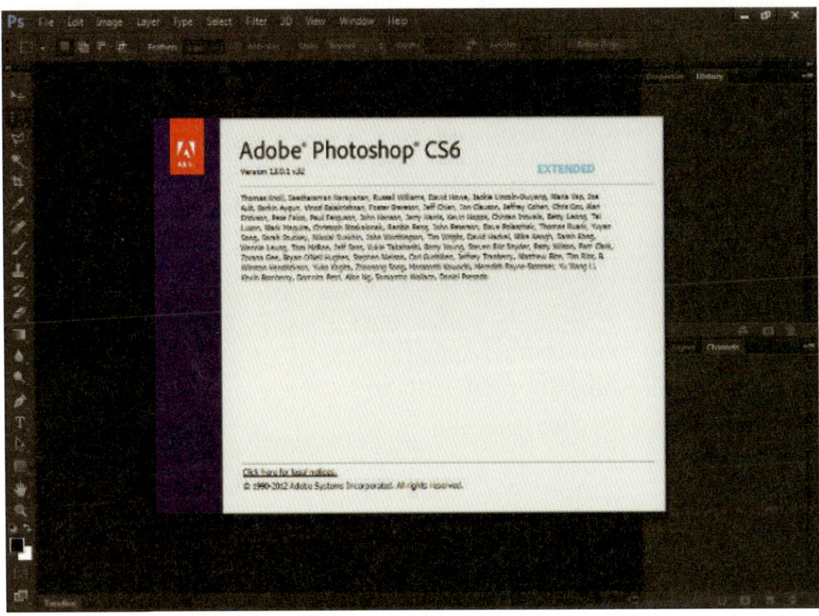

Figure 2.13: Adobe Photoshop, an example of a graphic processing software application

2.1.8 Common features of applications

Exit skills. Students should be able to[1]:
Define the terms toolbars, menus, dialogue boxes, graphical user interface (GUI) and command line interface (CLI). Identify features that are provided by the application software and features that are provided by the operating system.

Software applications installed in computer systems, as described in 2.1.7, typically include a *graphical user interface (GUI)* to allow the user to interact with them in a number of ways, instead of just typing in commands. A GUI includes components such as graphical icons and visual indicators, as well as toolbars, menus, and dialogue boxes. These allow the interaction between the user and the software application to be performed more smoothly through direct manipulation of the graphical elements.

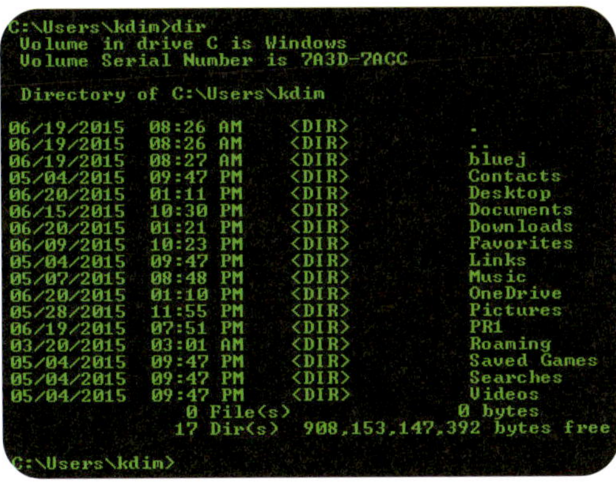

Figure 2.14: Example of a Command Line Interface

Software applications have improved greatly over the years. Early software applications operated with commands that had to be typed in, which we call *command line interfaces (CLIs)*. Later ones took advantage of GUIs. An example of a CLI is shown in Figure 2.14. Both CLIs and GUIs have pros and cons which are described in Table 2.1.

	Command Line Interfaces (CLIs)	Graphical User Interfaces (GUIs)
Pros	• Easier to implement by a programmer • Requires less memory to run • Can be run on computer systems without a graphical monitor • Quicker to type in a command than to use a mouse – experienced users may find it useful	• Users do not need to remember specific commands – easier for new users to use • Users use icons to remember commands • Commands are grouped in menus and toolbars
Cons	• Users need to remember specific commands – hard for new users to use	• More complex to implement by a programmer • Requires more memory • Requires a graphical monitor and a pointing device

Table 2.1: Pros and Cons of CLIs and GUIs

Common GUI elements include the following:

- Toolbar
- Menu
- Dialogue box

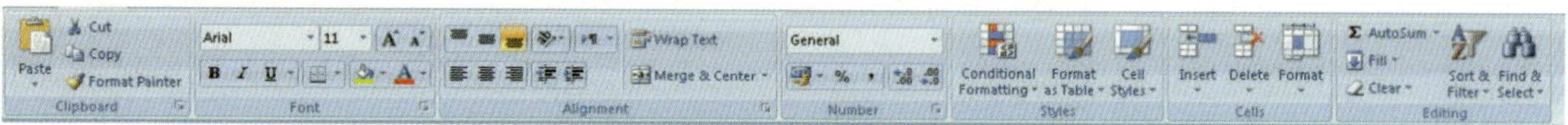

Figure 2.15: Microsoft Office Word Toolbar

A *toolbar* is a GUI element on which buttons, icons, menus, or other input or output elements are placed. An example of a toolbar is shown in Figure 2.15.

A *menu* is a GUI element that displays a list of commands that can be chosen by the user to perform various functions. An example of a typical menu that displays operations related to creating, opening, closing and saving a file is shown in Figure 2.16.

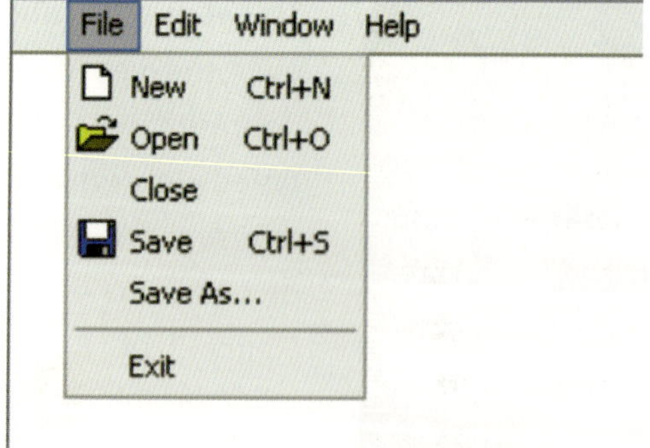

Figure 2.16: A generic menu

A *dialogue box* is a GUI element that is used to communicate information to the user and allow him/her to respond by choosing an option from a list of specific choices. An example of a dialogue box that notifies the user that the file that is about to be closed is unsaved and allows the user to select from a list of possible events is shown in Figure 2.17.

Figure 2.17: A dialogue box

GUIs provide ways that allow users to understand and interact with computer systems in a more direct and natural way than CLIs. GUIs are described using the acronym *WIMP*, which stands for *Windows, Icons, Menus and Pointers*.

These, and other GUI elements are common and can be found in almost every software application. Since this is the case, it would be a waste of time for every software application programmer to have to go through implementing these common GUI elements over and over again for every separate software application. Therefore, some common GUI elements, such as toolbars, menus, dialogue boxes, windows, etc., are provided by the operating system, so that the programmer only needs to state their existence. For example, a programmer that wants to implement a program which will run in a window and have some menus needs to specify what commands the menus will include, what will happen when the user initiates them by clicking them, as well as where they will reside within the window. However, the actual menus and windows themselves are provided by the operating system, as well as what happens when the window is minimized or moved.

The fact that some features are provided by the application software and some by the operating system not only saves time for the programmer. It also improves usability for the users, since all these features (toolbars, menus, dialogue boxes, windows, etc.) are displayed in a familiar way across the software applications. This minimizes the possibility of confusion and provides a smoother learning curve for each new software application. For example, the steps for creating a new document, saving or closing it is the same in almost all programs: under the file menu on the upper left corner of the application toolbar.

Computer Organization – Binary representation

2.1.9 Bit, byte, binary, decimal and hexadecimal

Exit skills. Students should be able to[1]:
Define the terms bit, byte, binary, denary/decimal, and hexadecimal. Perform various conversions between different numbering systems.

bit and Byte

The terms bit and Byte where initially encountered in 2.1.1. In this section we restate the terms for bit and Byte provided in 2.1.1 and look into further definitions.

Computer systems are binary systems that use sequences of bits to represent data. A *binary digit (bit)* is the basic unit of information in computer systems and can have only two values: either *1* or *0*. Eight bits form a byte.

1 Byte = 8 bits

A bit is denoted by the small letter *b*, whereas a Byte is denoted by the capital letter *B*. Thus, **1B = 8b**. One Byte can store a single character (ex. the letter "A").

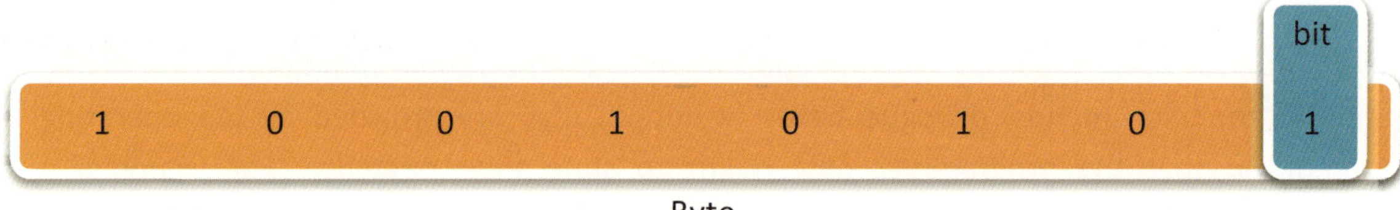

Byte

Decimal number system

The decimal number system is a positional system that uses ten digits (0, 1, 2, 3, 4, 5, 6, 7, 8, and 9) to represent any number, no matter how large or small. The decimal number system (or *base-10*) has ten as its base and it is the most widely-used number system. The digits in the decimal number system can be used with a decimal separator to represent a fractional part, as well as a plus/minus sign (+/-) sign to indicate whether the number represented is greater or less than zero.

Since base-10 is a positional system, the position of each digit within a number provides the multiplier by which that digit is multiplied. Table 2.2 shows the initial four place values in the decimal number system. Note that the multiplier is always a power of ten, with a base of 10 and an exponent that increases by one compared with the exponent of the position to its right. Thus, each position has a value ten times that of the position to its right.

multiplier (power of ten)	10^3	10^2	10^1	10^0
multiplier	1000	100	10	1
multiplier (in writing)	thousands	hundreds	tens	units

Table 2.2: Initial place values in the decimal number system

An example of a number in the decimal number system is 6275 base 10 or 6275_{10}. All numbers should state the base in which they belong (10 in this example). However, since the decimal number system is the most widely used number system if the base is omitted it is assumed that the number is in the base-10 system.

Example 2.12: Imagine that we need to understand what quantity is represented by the number 0.627 base 10 or 0.627_{10}. The table below depicts the digits of the number as well as the multiplier.

multiplier (power of ten)	10^{-1}	10^{-2}	10^{-3}
multiplier	0.1	0.01	0.001
digits	6	2	7

The value represented by the number 0.627_{10} is:

6*0.1 + 2*0.01 + 7*0.001 = 0.627

In the same manner, fractional quantities to the right of the decimal point can be represented. The position of each digit within a number again provides the multiplier with which that digit is multiplied. Table 2.3 shows the initial three place values in the fractional part of the decimal number system. Note that the multiplier is always a power of ten, with a base of 10 and an exponent that decreases by one compared with the exponent of the position to its left. Thus, each position has a value ten times less that of the position to its left.

multiplier (power of ten)	10^{-1}	10^{-2}	10^{-3}
multiplier	0.1	0.01	0.001
multiplier (in writing)	one tenth	one hundredth	one thousandth

Table 2.3: Initial place values in the decimal number system

Apart from the decimal number system, which is base-10 and uses ten digits to represent any number, there exist a couple of other useful number systems that are used widely in computer systems. These two are the binary and hexadecimal number systems. The binary is base-2 whereas the hexadecimal is base-16. We look into both.

Example 2.13: Imagine that we need to understand what quantity is represented by the number 6275 base 10 or 6275_{10}. The table below depicts the digits of the number as well as the multiplier.

multiplier (power of ten)	10^3	10^2	10^1	10^0
multiplier	1000	100	10	1
digits	6	2	7	5

The value represented by the number 6275_{10} is:

6*1000 + 2*100 + 7*10 + 5*1 = 6275

Binary number system

The binary number system is a positional system that uses two digits (0 and 1) to represent any number. The binary number system (or base-2) has two as its base. It is the most widely used number system in computer science. Numbers represented in this system are known as binary numbers. Since base-2 is a positional system, the position of each digit within a number provides the multiplier with which that digit is multiplied. Table 2.4 shows the initial eight place values in the binary number system. Note that the multiplier is always a power of two, with a base of 2 and an exponent that increases by one compared with the exponent of the position to its right. Thus, each position has a value two times that of the position to its right.

multiplier (power of two)	2^7	2^6	2^5	2^4	2^3	2^2	2^1	2^0
multiplier	128	64	32	16	8	4	2	1

Table 2.4: Initial place values in the binary number system

An example of a number in the binary number system is 101110 base 2 or 101110_2. The base number cannot be omitted in the binary number system.

Image 2.12: All computer processes are in binary form

Example 2.14: Imagine that we need to convert the number 101110 base 2 or 101110_2 to a decimal integer equivalent. The table below depicts the digits of the binary number as well as their multiplier, depending on their respective positions.

multiplier (power of two)	2^7	2^6	2^5	2^4	2^3	2^2	2^1	2^0
multiplier	128	64	32	16	8	4	2	1
digits			1	0	1	1	1	0

To calculate the decimal value represented by the binary number 101110_2 we must multiply every digit of the number with its respective multiplier and then sum the results, as such:

$$0*1 + 1*2 + 1*4 + 1*8 + 0*16 + 1*32 = 46_{10}$$

Example 2.15: In a similar manner we may need to convert the number 46_{10} to a binary number equivalent. We can do this in two ways:

1) Repeatedly divide the decimal number by two and retain the remainders. When the number to be divided is zero, the algorithm stops. Reading the retained remainders from last to first gives us the decimal number as a binary number.

46 divided by 2 gives 23 and remainder 0
23 divided by 2 gives 11 and remainder 1
11 divided by 2 gives 5 and remainder 1
5 divided by 2 gives 2 and remainder 1
2 divided by 2 gives 1 and remainder 0
1 divided by 2 gives 0 and remainder 1
0 divided by 2 – algorithm has finished

The result (reading the remainders from last to first) is $46_{10} = 101110_2$.

2) Write the powers of two from right to left, starting with 2^0 and incrementing the exponent by one. The list of eight elements would be the following:

128	64	32	16	8	4	2	1

Pick the value from the list that is closest but not greater than the decimal number. In our example, 32 is closest to 46 but not greater. Write a 1 under that number and subtract it from the initial value. Repeat the above steps until the initial value is reduced to zero. We put a 0 under any numbers that do not have a 1 under them. Reading the list of 1s and 0s from left to right gives us the binary number.

In our example, we add a 1 under 32 and subtract 32 from 46. 46 - 32 = 14.

128	64	32	16	8	4	2	1
		1					

Then, we add a 1 under 8 and subtract 8 from 14. 14 - 8 = 6.

128	64	32	16	8	4	2	1
		1		1			

Then, we add a 1 under 4 and subtract 4 from 6. 6 - 4 = 2.

128	64	32	16	8	4	2	1
		1		1	1		

Then, we add a 1 under 2 and subtract 2 from 2. 2 - 2 = 0.

128	64	32	16	8	4	2	1
		1		1	1	1	

The initial value has been reduced to zero. We put a 0 under 16 and 1.

128	64	32	16	8	4	2	1
		1	0	1	1	1	0

The result (reading the list of 1s and 0s from left to right) is $46_{10} = 101110_2$.

Binary number system and negative numbers

Two's complement is the way most modern computers represent signed binary numbers. The main advantage of this representation is that addition, subtraction and multiplication are carried out easily. Suppose that an 8 bit register stores the number 28. In this representation, positive binary numbers start with 0 while negative binary numbers start with 1.

128	64	32	16	8	4	2	1
0	0	0	1	1	1	0	0

In this example the *MSB* (*most significant bit*) is 0. The MSB is the bit position in a binary number having the greatest value while the *LSB* (*least significant bit*) is the bit on the right, which gives us what we call the units value. In binary arithmetic it is easy to understand from the LSB whether the number is even or odd.

Example 2.16: Suppose we want to find -28 (8 bit register). 28 in an 8-bit register is:

0	0	0	1	1	1	0	0

First we invert the digits. All ones become zeros and all zeros become ones.

1	1	1	0	0	0	1	1

Then we add 1.

+	1	1	1	0	0	0	1	1
	0	0	0	0	0	0	0	1

And the output is

1	1	1	0	0	1	0	0

So this is -28 in two's complement representation. It is important to mention that in a 16 bit register -28 would be 1111111111100100_2

Example 2.17: Suppose we want to find -56 (8 bit register).

56 in binary is:

0	0	1	1	1	0	0	0

First we invert the digits. All ones become zeros and all zeros become ones.

1	1	0	0	0	1	1	1

Then we add 1.

+	1	1	0	0	0	1	1	1
	0	0	0	0	0	0	0	1

And the output is

1	1	0	0	1	0	0	0

So this is -56 in two's complement representation.

Example 2.18: This method also works when we want to convert a negative number to its positive equivalent. Suppose we want to convert 11000000_2 which is -64_{10} to 64 (using an 8 bit register).

1	1	0	0	0	0	0	0

First we invert the digits. All ones become zeros and all zeros become ones.

0	0	1	1	1	1	1	1

Then we add 1.

+	0	0	1	1	1	1	1	1
	0	0	0	0	0	0	0	1

And the output is

0	1	0	0	0	0	0	0

So this is 64 in two's complement representation.

Using two's complement the largest positive number that can be stored in an 8 bit register is: 01111111→$+127_{10}$

Using two's complement the largest negative number that can be stored in an 8 bit register is: 11111111→-1_{10}

Using two's complement the smallest positive number that can be stored in an 8 bit register is: 00000001→1_{10}

Using two's complement the smallest negative number that can be stored in an 8 bit register is: 10000000→-128_{10}

Binary fractions

Unsigned numbers

In the binary system and in the decimal system the radix point is used to separate the fractional from the whole part. For example the number 4.5 has 4 in its integer part and ½ in its fractional part. Suppose we want to convert this to binary. Assume that we will work using 8 bits. We are going to use 4 bits for the integer part and 4 bits for the fractional part. So this is a *fixed point representation* method.

4 is 0100_2

0.5 or 0.½ is 2^{-1}

2^3	2^2	2^1	2^0	2^{-1}	2^{-2}	2^{-3}	2^{-4}
8	4	2	1	½	¼	1/8	1/16
0	1	0	0	1	0	0	0

So the output is 0100.1000_2

Example 2.19: Suppose we want to find 12.3125

12 is 1100_2

0.3125 is 0.25+0.0625 or $2^{-2}+2^{-4}$

2^3	2^2	2^1	2^0	2^{-1}	2^{-2}	2^{-3}	2^{-4}
1	1	0	0	0	1	0	1

So the output is 1100.0101_2

Signed numbers

The two's complement method will be used to represent signed binary fractions. The fixed point method will be used.

Suppose we want to find- 2.75

First we will find 2.75

2 is 0010_2

0.75 is 0.5+0.25 or $2^{-1}+2^{-2}$

2^3	2^2	2^1	2^0	2^{-1}	2^{-2}	2^{-3}	2^{-4}
0	0	1	0	1	1	0	0

Then we invert the digits. All ones become zeros and all zeros become ones.

1	1	0	1	0	0	1	1

After that we add 1.

+	1	1	0	1	0	0	1	1
	0	0	0	0	0	0	0	1

And the output is

1	1	0	1	0	1	0	0

So this is -2.75_{10} in two's complement representation.

Example 2.20:

Question: Write the representation of the decimal number 4.25, in fixed-point, using 8 bits, where 4 bits are used for the fractional part, in two's complement representation method.

Answer:

4_{10} is 0100_2

$0.25_{10}=0100_2$

0100.0100_2 result

Example 2.21:

Question: Write the representation of –4.25, in fixed-point, using 4 bits for the fractional part, in two's complement representation method.

Answer:

0100.0100 convert 0 to 1 and 1 to 0

1011.1011 add 1

1011.1100_2 result

Hexadecimal number system

The hexadecimal number system is a positional system that uses 16 digits (0, 1, 2, 3, 4, 5, 6, 7, 8, 9, A, B, C, D, E and F) to represent any number. Digits A to F represent quantities from 10 to 15, thus A = 10, B = 11, C = 12, D = 13, E = 14 and F = 15. The hexadecimal number system (or base-16) has sixteen as its base and is used in computer science. Numbers represented in this system are known as hexadecimal numbers.

Since base-16 is a positional system, the position of each digit within a number provides by the multiplier which that digit is multiplied. Table 2.5 shows the initial five place values in the hexadecimal number system. Note that the multiplier is always a power of sixteen, with a base of sixteen and an exponent that increases by one compared with the exponent of the position to its right. Thus, each position has a value sixteen times that of the position to its right.

multiplier (power of sixteen)	16^4	16^3	16^2	16^1	16^0
multiplier	65536	4096	256	16	1

Table 2.5: Initial place values in the hexadecimal number system

Example 2.22: Imagine that we need to convert the number 1EB5 base 16 or $1EB5_{16}$ to a decimal integer equivalent. The table below depicts the digits of the binary number as well as their multiplier, depending on their respective positions.

multiplier (power of sixteen)	16^3	16^2	16^1	16^0
multiplier	4096	256	16	1
digits	1	E	B	5

To calculate the decimal value represented by the hexadecimal number $1EB5_{16}$ we must multiply every digit of the number with its respective multiplier and then add all of the results, like so:

1*4096 + E*256 + B*16 + 5*1

= 1*4096 + 14*256 + 11*16 + 5*1 (since E = 14 and B = 11)

= 4096 + 3584 + 176 + 5

= 7861_{10}

Example 2.23: In a similar manner we may need to convert the number 7861_{10} to a hexadecimal number equivalent. Below, we describe the way to achieve this. Note that the algorithm followed is similar to the one that converts decimal to binary numbers.

Repeatedly divide the decimal number by sixteen and retain the remainders. When the number to be divided is zero the algorithm stops. Reading the retained remainders from last to first gives us the decimal number as a hexadecimal number.

7861 divided by 16 gives 491 and remainder 5
491 divided by 16 gives 30 and remainder 11 (11 = B)
30 divided by 16 gives 1 and remainder 14 (14 = E)
1 divided by 16 gives 0 and remainder 1
0 divided by 16 – algorithm has finished

The result (reading the remainders from last to first) is 7861_{10} = $1EB5_{16}$.

An example of a number in the hexadecimal number system is 1EB5 base 16 or $1EB2_{16}$. The base number cannot be omitted in the hexadecimal number system.

Example 2.24:

Question: An 8-bit register is used to store integers in two's complement. Calculate $8F_{16} + 2B_{16}$. Is it possible to store the result in this 8-bit register?

Answer: The output is BA_{16}. This is 186 in the decimal number system. The maximum number that can be stored in this register is 127. So it is impossible to store this result in this register.

Example 2.25:

Question: Determine the value of A_{10} in the following expression:

$A_{10} = A3_{16}+23_{16}$

Answer:

$A_{10} = A3_{16}+23_{16}=C6_{16}=198_{10}$

OR

$A_{10} = A3_{16}+23_{16}=163_{10}+35_{10}=198_{10}$

or

$A_{10} = 1010\ 0011_2+0010\ 0011_2=1100\ 0110_2=198_{10}$

Example 2.26: Imagine that there is a computer system that uses 1 bit to represent text characters.

With 1 bit, the possible number of different representations that can be achieved is 2, since this one bit can take the values:

0 or 1

With only two different representations it would mean that the computer system would only be able to distinguish between only two different states. One state could be used to represent the capital letter "A", the other the capital letter "B", but there would not be any other different states to represent all the other letters in the Latin alphabet.

If the computer system uses 2 bits to represent text characters, the number of different representations that can be achieved is 4, since these two bits can take the values:

00, 01, 10, or 11

Clearly, a sequence of 2 bits is still not enough to represent as many different representations as are needed.

A larger sequence of bits is needed. The important thing to understand is that a larger sequence of bits used to represent something in a computer system allows for a larger possible number of distinct representations.

2.1.10 Data representation

Exit skills. Students should be able to[1]:
Outline the way in which strings, integers, characters and colours are represented in the computer. Outline the space required to store strings, integers, characters and colours in a computer Describe the relation between the hexadecimal colour code and the number of colours available.

Computer systems are binary systems, meaning that there are only two possible values that they can represent: the values 0 and 1. These two values can be represented by a single binary digit (bit). In order for such systems to represent more complex data, sequences of binary digits are used. The length of these binary digit sequences determines the possible number of different representations that can be achieved.

The relationship that exists between the number of bits used by a computer system and the number of different representations that can be achieved is the following:

2^n where n is the number of bits used

Table 2.6 presents the number of different representations that can be achieved when n number of bits are used, where n takes the values from 1 to 8.

Number of bits used	1	2	3	4	5	6	7	8
Distinct representations	2^1	2^2	2^3	2^4	2^5	2^6	2^7	2^8
	2	4	8	16	32	64	128	256

Table 2.6: Distinct representations with n number of bits

In order for computer systems to effectively communicate and exchange data, the way they represent data must be consistent and similar. For example, imagine that a computer system uses 8 bits to represent the letter "A" while another computer system uses the same 8 bits to represent the letter "B". Whenever the second computer system receives a text file from the first, all the "A" symbols would be represented as "B", and the text file would not be consistent between the two computer systems. As such, it is important that there is consistency between computer systems in how they represent and exchange data. That is why the standard formats exist.

Some of these standard formats are the following:

Integers

Table 2.6 represents the number of different representations for "n" number of bits, where "n" is between 1 and 8. The relationship 2^n can be used to calculate the number of different representations for any number of bits "n".

Imagine that we use 8 bits to represent an integer number. That means that there can be 2^8 = 256 different representations, which means that 256 integer numbers can be represented.

This would allow us to represent all the unsigned positive integers from 0 to 255, thus 256 different integer numbers.

Examples of unsigned positive integers represented with 8 bits:

$00000001_2 = 1_{10}$

$00000101_2 = 5_{10}$

$00011001_2 = 25_{10}$

$11111111_2 = 255_{10}$

The twos complement method was presented in the previous section. However, we may wish to represent both positive and negative numbers using the "sign-and-magnitude number representation". This method represents a number's sign by allocating the left-most bit as a sign bit to represent the sign. As mentioned before, the left-most bit is termed the most significant bit (MSB). The MSB is set to 0 for a positive number or 1 for a negative number. The rest of the bits indicate the magnitude of the number. As such, if we use 8 bits to represent an integer number and the MSB is the sign bit, only 7 bits remain for the magnitude, which means that $2^7 = 128$ absolute values can be represented. This allows for numbers -127 to +127 to be represented.

Examples of integers using the "sign-and-magnitude number representation" represented with 8 bits:

$00000001_2 = 1_{10}$

$10000001_2 = -1_{10}$

$11111111_2 = -127_{10}$

$01111111_2 = 127_{10}$

$10000000_2 = 0_{10}$ and $00000000_2 = 0_{10}$

As can be seen from the last example, in this approach there are two ways to represent the number zero. Overall, in this representation the MSB is comparable with the common way of showing a sign (0 for "+" and 1 for "-").

Characters

The American Standard Code for Information Interchange (ASCII) is a character-encoding scheme originally based on the English alphabet. This means that ASCII is used to represent text in computer systems. To do that a number is assigned to each letter from 0 to 127. For example letter K is assigned the number 75. ASCII uses 7 bits to represent each character which means that it can achieve $2^7 = 128$ different representations (i.e. 128 different characters). It holds the Latin alphabet, (lower case letters a-z and capital letters A-Z) as well as all the digits of the decimal numbering system 0-9.

Since the Latin alphabet has only 26 letters, 52 different representations are needed for both lower case and capital letters. Furthermore, 10 more different representations are needed for the decimal digits. The remaining 66 different representations are used to hold the space and punctuation characters, as well as some control characters. An example of a control character is the carriage return character that is used to indicate that the rest of the document should start from a new line. Table 2.7 represents the ASCII character-encoding scheme.

Code	Char	Code	Char	Code	Char	Code	Char	Code	Char
0	NULL	**26**	SUB	**52**	4	**78**	N	**104**	h
1	SOH	**27**	ESC	**53**	5	**79**	O	**105**	I
2	STX	**28**	FS	**54**	6	**80**	P	**106**	j
3	ETX	**29**	GS	**55**	7	**81**	Q	**107**	k
4	EOT	**30**	RS	**56**	8	**82**	R	**108**	l
5	ENQ	**31**	US	**57**	9	**83**	S	**109**	m
6	ACK	**32**	[Space]	**58**	:	**84**	T	**110**	n
7	BEL	**33**	!	**59**	;	**85**	U	**111**	o
8	BS	**34**	"	**60**	<	**86**	V	**112**	p
9	TAB	**35**	#	**61**	=	**87**	W	**113**	q
10	LF	**36**	$	**62**	>	**88**	X	**114**	r
11	VT	**37**	%	**63**	?	**89**	Y	**115**	s
12	FF	**38**	&	**64**	@	**90**	Z	**116**	t
13	CR	**39**	‘	**65**	A	**91**	[	**117**	u
14	SO	**40**	(	**66**	B	**92**	\	**118**	v
15	SI	**41**	)	**67**	C	**93**	]	**119**	w
16	DLE	**42**	*	**68**	D	**94**	^	**120**	x
17	DC1	**43**	+	**69**	E	**95**	_	**121**	y
18	DC2	**44**	,	**70**	F	**96**	`	**122**	z
19	DC3	**45**	-	**71**	G	**97**	a	**123**	{
20	DC4	**46**	.	**72**	H	**98**	b	**124**	|
21	NAK	**47**	/	**73**	I	**99**	c	**125**	}
22	SYN	**48**	0	**74**	J	**100**	d	**126**	~
23	ETB	**49**	1	**75**	K	**101**	e	**127**	DEL
24	CAN	**50**	2	**76**	L	**102**	f		
25	EM	**51**	3	**77**	M	**103**	g		

Table 2.7: The ASCII character-encoding scheme

There are other character-encoding schemes available that allow for additional characters to be represented. This allows non-English characters, graphic symbols and mathematical symbols to be represented. For example, the most widely known character-encoding scheme is Unicode.

Strings

In a computer system, a string is a sequence of characters. If the UTF-8 encoding-scheme is used, each character will consist of 8 bits, and assuming that the average length of a word in the English language is 5 letters, then on average 5*8 bits = 40 bits will be needed for each word to be stored.

Colours

Many computer systems have a video display unit or monitor as an output device in order to communicate with the user. Monitors use pixels to display information and have a specific display resolution, such as 1024 x 768, that represents width x height in pixels (ex, a monitor having a resolution of 1024 x 768 has a width of 1024 pixels and a height of 768 pixels). A pixel is the smallest controllable element in a display or of a picture represented on the screen. Figure 2.18 demonstrates how an image is made up of individual pixels rendered as small squares. We can see this by enlarging the image until the pixels become apparent.

Example 2.27

Question: Why is the Unicode character-encoding scheme needed?

The ASCII character-encoding scheme can represent 128 different characters. This is enough for the lowercase and capital letters of the 26-letter Latin alphabet, as well as the space, punctuation and control characters.

However, not all languages are written with the Latin alphabet. For example, the Arabic alphabet consists of 28 letters, very different from the Latin alphabet, and it is written from right to left. In the same manner, the Greek alphabet consists of 24 letters, which also are different from both the Latin and the Arabic characters.

In order to incorporate all these different characters as well as the space, punctuation, mathematical and control characters into a single character-encoding scheme, it is necessary to represent far more than the 128 different characters of ASCII. That is why the Unicode character-encoding scheme was designed and is necessary throughout computer systems.

The Unicode character-encoding scheme contains all the ASCII characters as well as more specialized Latin letters with diacritics, as well as a number of other alphabets such as Greek, Hebrew and Arabic.

Every pixel in a computer colour monitor may have only one colour at any moment. However, each colour is made up of a combination of shades of red, green and blue. Each pixel stores information about its state and colour in a memory location. There are many ways to represent and store an individual colour.

Figure 2.18: When an image is enlarged pixels become apparent

One such way is in the hexadecimal RGB colour values that specify the amount of Red, Green and Blue light that need to appear at a pixel, in order to produce a specific colour. By combining different shades of Red, Green and Blue a large variety of colours can be displayed.

Each colour value is represented as a hexadecimal value of two digits that may take up values from 00 to FF. Thus, in order to describe a colour value in this way, a six-digit hexadecimal number is needed such as 70EF5A, which is shown in Figure 2.19. The first two hexadecimal digits represent the Red colour, the next two the Green colour and the last two the Blue colour. A little red (112), a lot of green (239) and a little of red (90) combines to make a "lime" shade of green (Figure 2.19).

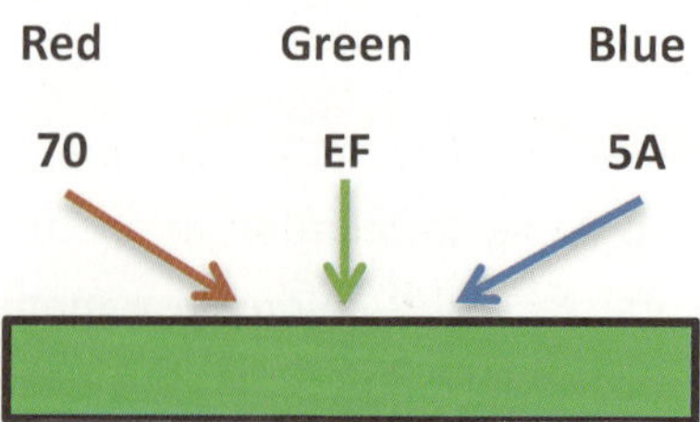

Figure 2.19 Representation of hexadecimal RGB colour value 70EF5A

The range of a two-digit hexadecimal number is from 00 to FF, which in decimal is from 00_{16} = 0*16 + 0*1 = 0_{10} to FF_{16} = 15*16 + 15*1 = 255_{10}. The range of a six digit hexadecimal number is from 000000_{16} to $FFFFFF_{16}$. Since two hexadecimal numbers can represent 256 colours (from 0 to 255), six hexadecimal numbers (which are used to describe colours in computer monitors) can represent 256*256*256 = 16777216_{10} distinct colours.

Example 2.28:

Question: Does binary represent an example of a lingua franca?

Answer: A *lingua franca* is a language that is used as a "bridge" language to make communication possible between people who do not have the same mother tongue. For example, English is the native language in the United Kingdom, but it is used as a lingua franca in the Philippines in order for all foreigners and natives to communicate with each other.

Binary allows the representation of data as a series of 0s and 1s. This includes text, which means that binary is actually used to represent letters, sentences and paragraphs of text. This text could be created by a user in one place of the earth and read by some other user, of different nationality, residing in another place. Thus, binary is used to represent any digital data that we want and allows us to communicate with other people. From this point of view one could argue that binary does represent an example of a lingua franca.

However, binary is not used as a language by people, but rather by computers in order to represent (amongst other things), languages used by people. That is, the user of one computer would draft a document in a specific language (such as English) and not in binary, so that when another user opened up the document he/she would still need to be able to read the specific language (English in this case) rather than the binary. So Binary is used to represent data, including languages, and not as a communicative language itself. Binary would be extremely difficult for people to use as they would need to know a specific character-encoding scheme (such as Unicode) by heart and be able to use it. But comprehending and writing in a language of 0s and 1s would be tremendously hard, as it was when the first programmers had to write programs in binary. As such, seen from this point of view binary does not represent an example of a lingua franca.

Example 2.29:

Question: A photograph measures 80 by 100 pixels and is stored as a graphic file. The colour representation is 15-bit high colour and uses 5 bits for Red, 5 bits for Green and 5 bits for Blue. An extra bit is set aside for an *alpha channel which* is normally used as an opacity channel. As such, the colour representation uses 16-bits in total, which is 2 Bytes. Determine how many different colours can be represented. Calculate the size of the file assuming that each pixel of this photograph uses two bytes.

Answer:

- $2^5*2^5*2^5$= 32768 possible colours
- SIZE = Bytes used * Dimensions =2*80*100=16000 Bytes

Simple logic gates

2.1.11 Boolean operators

Exit skills. Students should be able to[1]:
Define the Boolean operators: AND, OR, NOT, NAND, NOR and XOR. Develop truth tables for the Boolean operators: AND, OR, NOT, NAND, NOR and XOR.

Computer systems are made up of electrical circuits and use the binary system to represent and store data. In order to do so, electrical circuits have been designed to receive one or more binary numbers as their inputs and produce a single output. The logical operations of these circuits are governed by the rules of Boolean logic.

There are six Boolean operators available: AND, OR, NOT, NAND, NOR and XOR. In order to understand how they work, look at the simple electrical circuit in Figure 2.20. It involves a single switch, a light, a battery and some connecting cables. Since both a light and a switch can either be on or off, the circuit can be in one of the two states, and as such resembles the binary system used in computer systems.

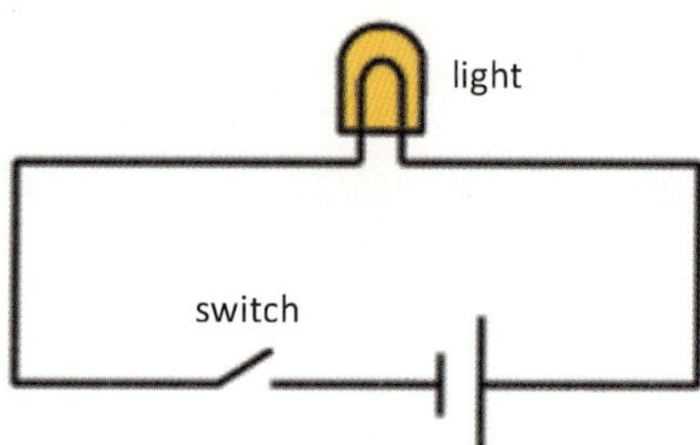

Figure 2.20: Simple electrical circuit

There are only two states that both the switch and the light can have at any point in time:

- When the switch is open, the light is off. In the binary system, the switch and the light in this state are represented by a 0.
- When the switch is closed the light is on. In the binary system, the switch and the light in this state are represented by a 1.

In Table 2.8 we represent the above two states in a table that is known as a *truth table*. In this example we only have one input (the switch, and whether it is open or closed) and one output (the light, and whether it is on or off).

Input	Output
Switch	**Light**
Open (0)	Off (0)
Closed (1)	On (1)

Table 2.8: Simple truth table

The electrical circuit in Figure 2.20 described above is the simplest electrical circuit. It resembles a simple on/off switch. Computer systems however demand more complex circuitry in order to accomplish their tasks and so we must examine the six Boolean operators and their truth tables.

Another way to represent Boolean operators is with the use of Venn diagrams. One is shown in Figure 2.21. There is one circular region for each input variable (the switch in our example). The interior of the circular region corresponds to when the input variable is 1/true (in our example the switch is closed) and the exterior to when the input variable is 0/false (in our example the switch is open). The shaded region denotes when the single output (in our example the light) will be 1/true, and the white region denotes when the output will be 0/false.

Figure 2.21 represents exactly the same information that the truth table in Table 2.8 describes. The output (the light) is 1/true when the input (the switch) is 1/true (the inside of the circular region) and 0/false when the input (switch) is 0/false.

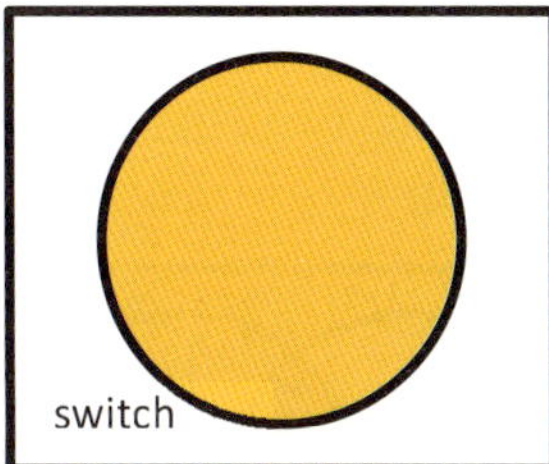

Figure 2.21: Venn diagram of the simple truth table

The *AND* Boolean operator

The AND Boolean operator, shown in Figure 2.22, is slightly more complicated than the simple electrical circuit of the on/off switch. The main difference is that there are two switches, instead of one, *in series*.

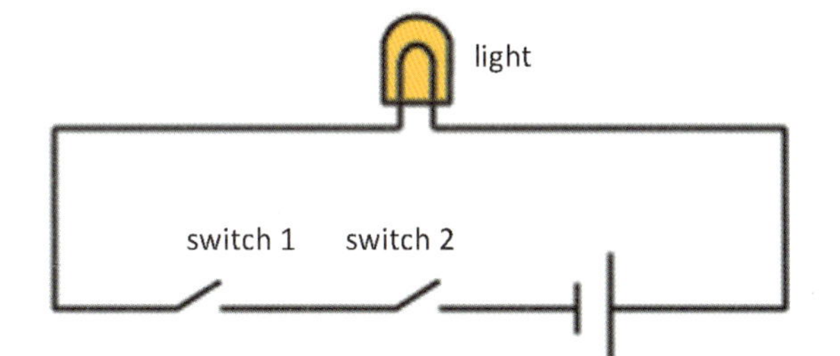

Figure 2.22: Electrical circuit representing the AND Boolean operator

There are four states that the switches and the light can have at any point in time:

- When both switches are open (0) the light is off (0)
- When switch number 1 is open (0) and switch number 2 closed (1) the light is off (0)
- When switch number 1 is closed (1) and switch number 2 open (0) the light is off (0)
- When both switches are closed (1) the light is on (1)

We can represent the above four states in Table 2.9. We have two inputs (switch 1 and switch 2) and one output (the light).

Inputs		Output
Switch 1	**Switch 2**	**Light - AND**
Open (0)	Open (0)	Off (0)
Open (0)	Closed (1)	Off (0)
Closed (1)	Open (0)	Off (0)
Closed (1)	Closed (1)	On (1)

Table 2.9: AND truth table

From the truth table we can understand that only when both switches are closed (1) the light will be on (1). The AND Boolean operator is also denoted by the symbol "·".

As a Venn diagram, the AND Boolean operator can be described as shown in Figure 2.23. There are two circular regions, since there are two inputs (switch 1 and 2). The inside of these regions represent when the respective input has a value of 1/true. Where they overlap both inputs have a value of 1/true (both switches are closed) and the output is 1/true (the light is on). That is where the shaded region appears. Only when both switches are closed is the light on.

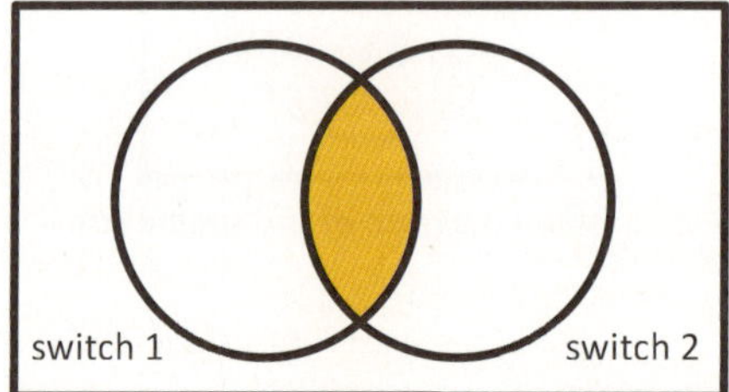

Figure 2.23: Venn diagram of the AND truth table

The *OR* Boolean operator

The OR Boolean operator, shown in Figure 2.24, has two switches, like the AND Boolean operator. But instead of having them in series, the OR Boolean operator has the two switches *in parallel*.

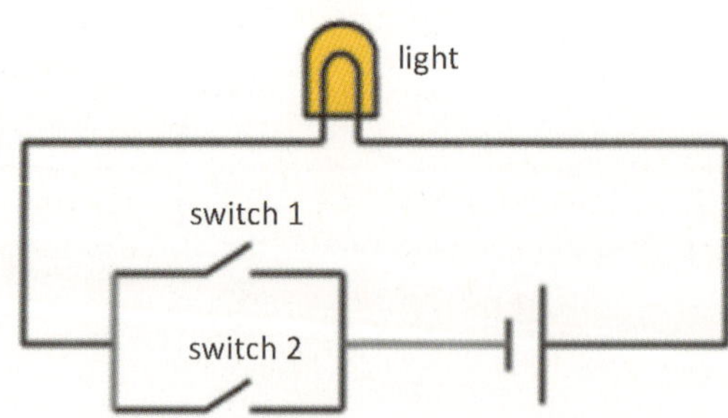

Figure 2.24: Electrical circuit representing the OR Boolean operator

There are four states that the switches and the light can have at any point in time:

- When both switches are open (0) the light is off (0)
- When switch number 1 is open (0) and switch number 2 closed (1) the light is on (1)
- When switch number 1 is closed (1) and switch number 2 open (0) the light is on (1)
- When both switches are closed (1) the light is on (1)

We can represent the above four states in Table 2.10. We have two inputs (switch 1 and switch 2) and one output (the light).

Inputs		Output
Switch 1	**Switch 2**	**Light - OR**
Open (0)	Open (0)	Off (0)
Open (0)	Closed (1)	On (1)
Closed (1)	Open (0)	On (1)
Closed (1)	Closed (1)	On (1)

Table 2.10: OR truth table

From the truth table we can understand that only when both switches are open (0) the light will be off (0). Otherwise, if one or both of the switches are closed (1) the light will be on (1). The OR Boolean operator is also denoted by the symbol "+".

As a Venn diagram the OR Boolean operator can be described as shown in Figure 2.25. The shaded region appears inside the circular regions since whenever at least one switch is closed (1/true) the light will be on (1).

Figure 2.25: Venn diagram of the OR truth table

The *NOT* Boolean operator

This Boolean operator has a single input and a single output. What this operator accomplishes is to take the input and output the reverse. If the input is 1/true the output will be 0/false, and if the input is 0/false the output will be 1/true. We can represent the above two states in Table 2.11. We have one input and one output.

Input	Output - NOT
0 (false)	1 (true)
1 (true)	0 (false)

Table 2.11: NOT truth table

The NOT Boolean operator is also denoted by a bar on top of an input (ex.$\overline{\text{switch}}$).

As a Venn diagram, the NOT Boolean operator can be described as shown in Figure 2.26. The shaded region appears outside the circular region, since whenever the input is 1/true the output is 0/false and vice versa.

Figure 2.26: Venn diagram of the NOT truth table

The *NAND* Boolean operator

The NAND Boolean operator is similar to the AND Boolean operator, but with its outputs inverted. As in the AND Boolean operator, the NAND Boolean operator has four states that it can be in, which are described in Table 2.12. Instead of having an output of 1/true when both the inputs are 1/true, as is the case for the AND Boolean operator, the NAND Boolean operator has an output of 1/true when one or both inputs are 0/false.

Inputs		Output
Input 1	**Input 2**	**NAND**
Open (0)	Open (0)	On (1)
Open (0)	Closed (1)	On (1)
Closed (1)	Open (0)	On (1)
Closed (1)	Closed (1)	Off (0)

Table 2.12: NAND truth table

As a Boolean operator NAND is very important in computer science since any Boolean function can be implemented by using a combination of NAND gates. The NAND Boolean operator is denoted by a bar on top of an AND symbol (ex. $\overline{\text{Input 1} \cdot \text{Input 2}}$).

As a Venn diagram the NAND Boolean operator can be described as shown in Figure 2.27. The shaded region appears outside the intersecting circular region since whenever the inputs are both 1/true the output is 0/false. Otherwise the output is 1/true.

Figure 2.27: Venn diagram of the NAND truth table

The *NOR* Boolean operator

The NOR Boolean operator is similar to the OR Boolean operator but with its outputs inverted. As in the OR Boolean operator the NOR Boolean operator has four states that it can be in, which are described in Table 2.13. Instead of having an output of 1/true when one or both inputs are 1/true, as is the case for the OR Boolean operator, the NOR Boolean operator has an output of 1/true when both inputs are 0/false.

Inputs		Output
Input 1	**Input 2**	**NOR**
Open (0)	Open (0)	On (1)
Open (0)	Closed (1)	Off (0)
Closed (1)	Open (0)	Off (0)
Closed (1)	Closed (1)	Off (0)

Table 2.13: NOR truth table

The NOR Boolean operator is denoted by a bar on top of an OR symbol (ex. $\overline{\text{Input 1} + \text{Input 2}}$).

As a Venn diagram the NOR Boolean operator can be described as shown in Figure 2.28. The shaded region appears outside the circular regions since whenever both inputs are 0/false the output is 1/true.

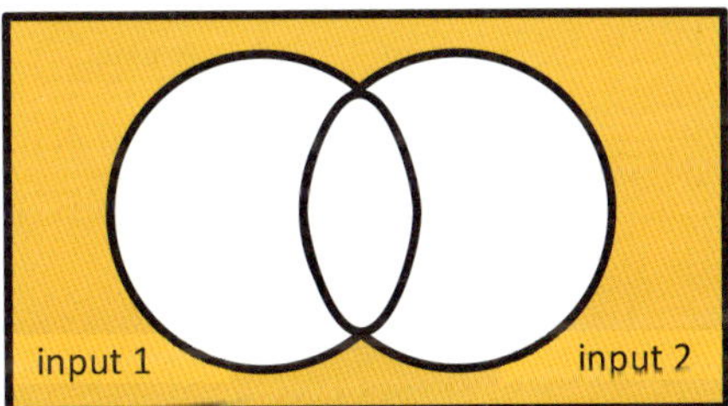

Figure 2.28: Venn diagram of the NOR truth table

The *XOR* (exclusive OR) Boolean operator

The XOR Boolean operator can be thought of as one or the other but not both. As in the OR Boolean operator, the XOR Boolean operator has four states that it can be in, which are described in Table 2.14.

Inputs		Output
Input 1	**Input 2**	**XOR**
Open (0)	Open (0)	Off (0)
Open (0)	Closed (1)	On (1)
Closed (1)	Open (0)	On (1)
Closed (1)	Closed (1)	Off (0)

Table 2.14: XOR truth table

The XOR Boolean operator is denoted by the following Boolean expression: $\overline{\mathrm{A}} \cdot \mathrm{B} + \mathrm{A} \cdot \overline{\mathrm{B}}$.

As a Venn diagram, the XOR Boolean operator can be described as shown in Figure 2.29. The shaded region appears inside the circular regions but not where they overlap, since the output is 1/true only when input 1 or input 2 are 1/true but not both.

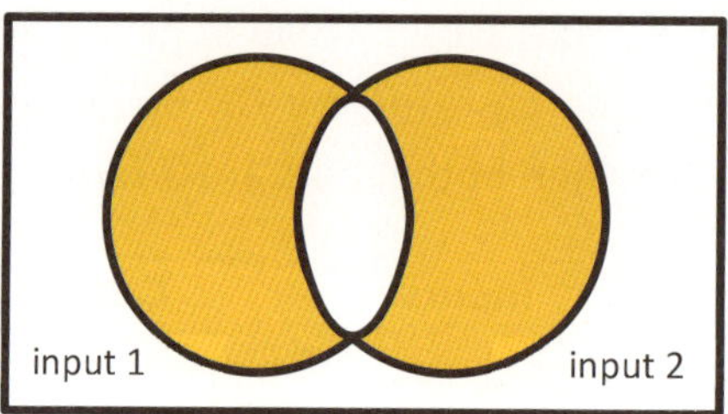

Figure 2.29: Venn diagram of the XOR truth table

Various symbols and shapes used for Boolean operators

It is very useful to know that various symbols are used to represent the Boolean operators described in the previous part. Table 2.15 depicts these symbols. It should be mentioned that the IB computer science guide[1] clarifies that when constructing logic diagrams "The gate should be written as a circle with the name of the gate inside it".

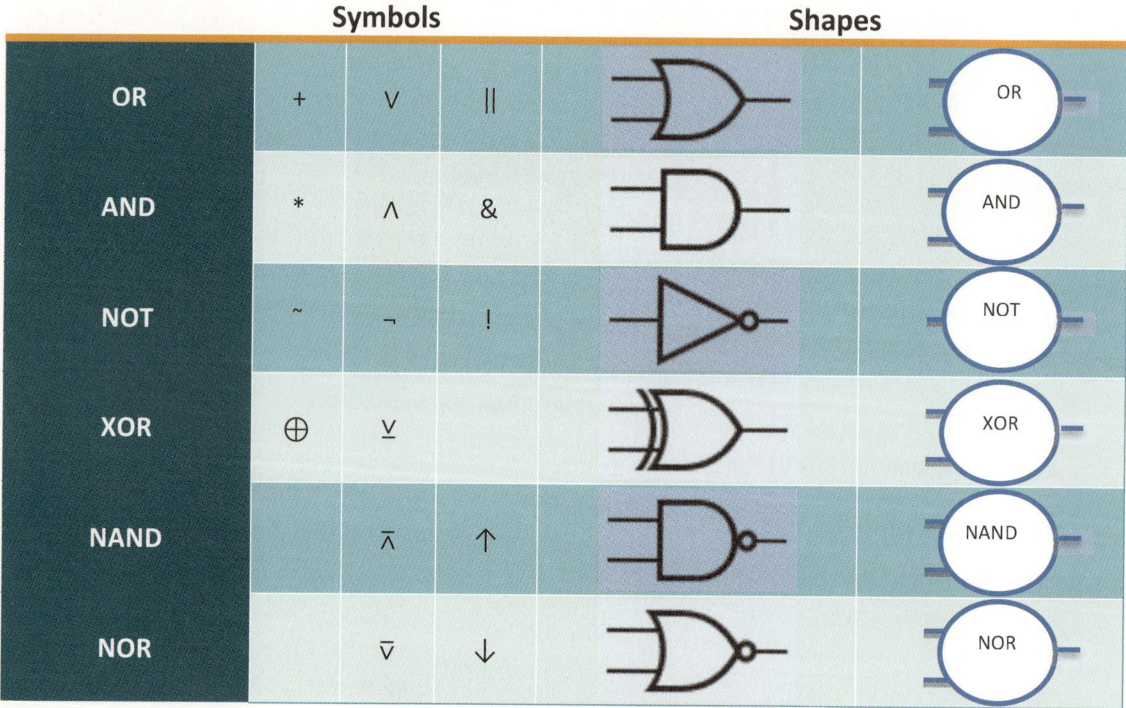

	Symbols			Shapes	
OR	+	∨	||		OR
AND	*	∧	&		AND
NOT	~	¬	!		NOT
XOR	⊕	⊻			XOR
NAND		⊼	↑		NAND
NOR		⊽	↓		NOR

Table 2.15: Logical Operations and gates

2.1.12 Truth tables using Boolean Operators

Exit skills. Students should be able to[1]:
Convert sentences to Boolean expressions. Develop and evaluate Boolean expressions using truth tables. Develop truth tables by combining the various Boolean operators: AND, OR, NOT, NAND, NOR and XOR.

Using the six Boolean Operators described in section 2.1.11 (AND, OR, NOT, NAND, NOR and XOR), one can construct truth tables that represent the inputs and single output of more complex logical statements such as "Tania won't go to play if it is cold and raining, or if he/she has not done her homework".

Before we move on, let us take note of an interesting fact about truth tables. Table 2.8: Simple truth table and Table 2.11: NOT truth table had one input each that could be either 0/false or 1/true. This is so because we are working with Boolean operators that resemble the binary system, and each input can have only one of two values: 0/false or 1/true. As such they had two rows describing the possible combinations of inputs. All the other truth tables for the Boolean operators had two inputs, and had four rows describing the possible combinations of inputs. Truth tables can be built to have as many inputs as necessary but we are interested only in truth tables with up to three inputs, which will have eight rows describing the possible combinations of inputs, as shown in Tables 2.16-2.18. There is always only one output.

Input	Output
0 (false)	0 (false)
1 (true)	1 (true)

Table 2.16: Truth table with one input

Inputs		Output
Input 1	Input 2	OR
0 (false)	0 (false)	0 (false)
0 (false)	1 (true)	1 (true)
1 (true)	0 (false)	1 (true)
1 (true)	1 (true)	1 (true)

Table 2.17: Truth table with two inputs

Inputs			Output
Input 1	Input 2	Input 3	(Input 1 AND Input 2) OR Input 3
0 (false)	0 (false)	0 (false)	0 (false)
0 (false)	0 (false)	1 (true)	1 (true)
0 (false)	1 (true)	0 (false)	0 (false)
0 (false)	1 (true)	1 (true)	1 (true)
1 (true)	0 (false)	0 (false)	0 (false)
1 (true)	0 (false)	1 (true)	1 (true)
1 (true)	1 (true)	0 (false)	1 (true)
1 (true)	1 (true)	1 (true)	1 (true)

Table 2.18: Truth table with three inputs

Let's look into the earlier statement in detail in order to figure out the inputs and outputs:

"Tania won't go to play if it is cold and raining, or if she has not done her homework"

We are interested in whether Tania will not go to play. As such, this is our output. Whether Tania goes to play or not depends on whether it's *cold* **and** *raining* (pay attention to the AND Boolean operator) **or** if she has **not** done her *homework* (pay attention to the OR and NOT Boolean operators). The inputs of this statement are 1) whether it's cold, 2) whether it's raining and 3) whether the homework is done.

The statement under consideration could be re-written, using the notation for the Boolean operators as follows:

$$\text{Will not go to play} = (\text{Cold} \cdot \text{Raining}) + (\overline{\text{Homework}})$$

As such we can construct the following truth table:

Input					**Output Will not go to play**
Cold	Raining	Cold **AND** Raining	Homework	**NOT** Homework	(Cold **AND** Raining) **OR** (**NOT** Homework)
0	0	0	0	1	1
0	0	0	1	0	0
0	1	0	0	1	1
0	1	0	1	0	0
1	0	0	0	1	1
1	0	0	1	0	0
1	1	1	0	1	1
1	1	1	1	0	1

Table 2.19: Complex truth table

The approach described above with the truth table of Table 2.19 can be used in any statement. This allows us to examine all the possible inputs and outputs that can appear.

- So, *'if it is hot and sunny, then we will go for a walk'* becomes
  - *'If (it is hot • it is sunny) = go for a walk'*
  - *A • B = C where A = sunny, B = hot, C = walk*
- So, *'if it is hot or it is sunny, then we'll go for a walk'* becomes
  - *if (it is hot + it is sunny) = go for a walk'*
  - *A + B = C where A = sunny, B = hot, C = walk*
- So, *'if it's hot and it's not raining, then we'll go for a walk'* becomes
  - *if (it's hot •* $\overline{\textit{it's raining}}$*) = go for a walk'*
  - *A •* $\bar{B}$ *= C where A = hot, B = rain, C = walk*
- So, *'if it's hot or sunny, but not both, we'll go for a walk'* becomes
  - *'if (it's hot ⊕ it's sunny) = we'll go for a walk'*
  - *A ⊕ B = C where A = hot, B = sunny, C = walk*

The sentence "If the airplane is late and there are no taxis in the airport, then we will have to cancel our meeting tomorrow" could be analysed with the help of the following table.

Propositions (statements)	NOT (sentence)
A = Airplane is late	NOT A = Airplane NOT late
B = Taxis are not available	NOT B = NOT (Taxis are not available)
F = Cancel our meeting	NOT F =NOT (Cancel our meeting)

Table 2.20: Logical analysis of sentence

The logical expression that describes this sentence is: A AND B = F

The equivalent truth table follows:

	A	B	Cancel meeting
Airplane NOT late – NOT (taxis are not available)	0	0	FALSE - 0
Airplane NOT late – taxis are not available	0	1	FALSE - 0
Airplane late – NOT (taxis are not available)	1	0	FALSE - 0
Airplane late – taxis are not available	1	1	TRUE - 1

Example 2.30:

Question: A chemical factory is equipped with three safety mechanisms. These safety mechanisms are used to warn the local authorities for a potential accident. If safety mechanism A or safety mechanism B are in the OFF position and if safety mechanism C is in the ON position, then there is no reason to worry about an upcoming accident. Construct a truth table for this scenario.

Answer: Assume that ON position is 1 and OFF position is 0. It is possible to convert this problem into a logic statement. Suppose that "no worry" is depicted with W, then:

$$W = (\overline{A} + \overline{B}) * C$$

A	B	C	F = NOT A OR NOT B	W = F AND C
0	0	0	1	0
0	0	1	1	1
0	1	0	1	0
0	1	1	1	1
1	0	0	1	0
1	0	1	1	1
1	1	0	0	0
1	1	1	0	0

Example 2.31:

Question: Construct truth tables for the following two Boolean expressions and determine if they are equivalent.

X= A⊕C

Y= A + C

Answer:

A	C	X= A⊕C	Y= A + C
0	0	0	0
0	1	1	1
1	0	1	1
1	1	0	1

Two Boolean expressions are equivalent when the equivalent columns are identical. These two expressions are not equivalent. When A = 1 and C =1, X value is not equal to Y value (fourth row).

Example 2.32:

Question: Construct truth tables for the following two Boolean expressions and determine if they are equivalent.

A = P XOR Q OR R

B = P OR Q OR R

Answer:

P	Q	R	A	B
1	1	1	1	1
1	1	0	0	1
1	0	1	1	1
1	0	0	1	1
0	1	1	1	1
0	1	0	1	1
0	0	1	1	1
0	0	0	0	0

These two expressions are not equivalent.

Example 2.33:

Question: An alarm system has three inputs Q, W, R and one output I. When signal at Q is FALSE then the output at I is the same as input signal R. When signal at Q is TRUE then the output at I is the same as input signal W. Construct the truth table for this alarm system and then write the equivalent Boolean expression.

Answer:

Q	W	R	I
0	0	0	0
0	0	1	1
0	1	0	0
0	1	1	1
1	0	0	0
1	0	1	0
1	1	0	1
1	1	1	1

I = Q'*W'*R+Q'*W*R+Q*W*R'+Q*W*R

Example 2.34:

Question: Construct a truth table for the expression: p OR q AND r

Answer:

p	q	r	$p \vee (q \wedge r)$
1	1	1	1
1	1	0	1
1	0	1	1
1	0	0	1
0	1	1	1
0	1	0	0
0	0	1	0
0	0	0	0

Example 2.35:

Question: Construct a truth table for the expression: (p XOR q) AND r

Answer:

p	q	r	$(p \veebar q) \wedge r$
1	1	1	0
1	1	0	0
1	0	1	1
1	0	0	0
0	1	1	1
0	1	0	0
0	0	1	0
0	0	0	0

Example 2.36:

Question: Construct a truth table for the expression: p AND q AND r

Answer:

p	q	r	p ∧ q ∧ r
1	1	1	1
1	1	0	0
1	0	1	0
1	0	0	0
0	1	1	0
0	1	0	0
0	0	1	0
0	0	0	0

Example 2.37:

Question: Construct a truth table for the expression: (p OR q) AND r

Answer:

p	q	r	(p ∨ q) ∧ r
1	1	1	1
1	1	0	0
1	0	1	1
1	0	0	0
0	1	1	1
0	1	0	0
0	0	1	0
0	0	0	0

Example 2.38:

Question: Construct a truth table for the expression: (NOT p OR q) AND NOT r

Answer:

p	q	r	(¬p ∨ q) ∧ ¬r
1	1	1	0
1	1	0	1
1	0	1	0
1	0	0	0
0	1	1	0
0	1	0	1
0	0	1	0
0	0	0	1

Example 2.39:

Question: Construct a truth table for the expression:

NOT (p OR q) AND (NOT r AND NOT p)

Answer:

p	q	r	¬(p ∨ q) ∧ (¬r ∧ ¬p)
1	1	1	0
1	1	0	0
1	0	1	0
1	0	0	0
0	1	1	0
0	1	0	0
0	0	1	0
0	0	0	1

Example 2.40:

Question: Construct a truth table for the expression:

NOT (p OR q) AND NOT (r AND NOT p)

Answer:

p	q	r	¬(p ∨ q) ∧ ¬(r ∧ ¬p)
1	1	1	0
1	1	0	0
1	0	1	0
1	0	0	0
0	1	1	0
0	1	0	0
0	0	1	0
0	0	0	1

Example 2.41:

Question: Construct a truth table for the expression: (p NAND q) NOR r

Answer:

p	q	r	$(p \barwedge q) \veebar r$
1	1	1	0
1	1	0	1
1	0	1	0
1	0	0	0
0	1	1	0
0	1	0	0
0	0	1	0
0	0	0	0

Example 2.42:

Question: Construct a truth table for the expression: r XOR (p NAND q) **Answer:**

p	q	r	r ⊻ (p ⊼ q)
1	1	1	1
1	1	0	0
1	0	1	0
1	0	0	1
0	1	1	0
0	1	0	1
0	0	1	0
0	0	0	1

Example 2.43:

Question: Construct a truth table for the expression: A XOR B **Answer:**

p	q	A ⊻ B
0	0	0
0	1	1
1	0	1
1	1	0

2.1 (Additional Section) Simplification and Boolean expressions

Exit skills. Students should be able to[1]:
Use simplification rules to simplify a Boolean expression.

The following table shows some properties of algebra used to simplify Boolean expressions.[2]

Property	EXPRESSION 1	EXPRESSION 2
Absorption	A + A * B = A	A * (A + B) = A
Adjacency	A * B + A * B'= A	(A + B) * (A + B') = A
Associative	A + (B + C) = (A + B) + C	A * (B * C) = (A * B) * C
Commutative	A + B = B + A	A * B = B * A
Complement	A + A' = 1	A * A' = 0
Consensus	(A * X) + (A' * Y) + (X * Y) = (A * X) + (A' * Y)	(A + X) * (A' + Y) * (X + Y) = (A + X) * (A' + Y)
DeMorgan	(A + B)' = A' * B'	(A * B)' = A' + B'
Distributive	A * (B + C) = A * B + A * C	A + B * C = (A + B) * (A + C)
Idempotency	A + A = A	A * A = A
Identity	A + 0 = A	A * 1 = A
Involution	(A')' = A	
Null	A + 1 = 1	A * 0 = 0
Simplification	A + A' * B = A + B	A * (A' + B) = A * B

Table 2.21: Properties of algebra

[2] Marcovitz, A. (2009). Introduction to Logic Design. McGraw-Hill.

Example 2.44:

If it rains, or it does not rain and is very cloudy, I will need an umbrella

The parts of this sentence are:

A = If it rains
A' = does not rain
B = is very cloudy
F = I will need an umbrella.

So the Boolean expression for this sentence is:

F = A + A' * B

Using the Simplification property from the previous table

F = A + A' * B = A + B

So the sentence could be simplified us

If it rains or is very cloudy I will need an umbrella

Example 2.45:

If it rains or it doesn't rain I will need an umbrella

A + A' = 1 (complement property). Always true so always need umbrella.

Example 2.46:

If it rains and it doesn't rain I will need an umbrella

A * A' = 0 (complement property). Impossible to have both conditions at the same time in the same place, so the output is always false. No need for umbrella.

Example 2.47: Construct the truth table and simplify the following Boolean expression:

F = A * B * C + A' * B * C' + A' * B * C

Solution

A	B	C	F
0	0	0	0
0	0	1	0
0	1	0	1
0	1	1	1
1	0	0	0
1	0	1	0
1	1	0	0
1	1	1	1

Exercise 2.47 cont.

By applying the rules of the previous table:

F = A’ * B * C’ + A’ * B * C + A * B * C = A’ * B * C’ + B * C * (A’ + A) = A’ * B * C’ + B * C * 1 =
A’ * B * C’ + B * C = B * (A’ * C’ + C) = B * (A’ + C) = B * A’ + B * C

Example 2.48: Construct the truth table and simplify the following Boolean expression:

F = A’ * B’ * C’ + A’ * B * C’ + A * B’ * C + A * B * C

Solution

A	B	C	F
0	0	0	1
0	0	1	0
0	1	0	1
0	1	1	0
1	0	0	0
1	0	1	1
1	1	0	0
1	1	1	1

By applying the rules of the table 2.21,

F = A’ * B’ * C’ + A’ * B * C’ + A * B’ * C + A * B * C =
A’ * C’ * (B + B’) + A * C * (B + B’) = A’ * C’ + A * C

Example 2.49: Simplify the following Boolean expression: F = A + B’ * A + B * A

By applying the rules of table 2.21, F = A + B’ * A + B * A = A + A * (B’ + B) = A + A = A

Example 2.50: Simplify the following Boolean expression:

F = (A * B)’ + A’ + B’ + A * (A + B) + B * (A + B)

By applying the rules of table 2.21,

F = (A * B)’ + A’ + B’ + A * (A + B) + B * (A + B) =
A’ + B’ + A’ + B’ + A * (A + B) + B * (A + B) =
A’ + B’ + A * (A + B) + B * (A + B) =
A’ + B’ + A + B = 1

2.1.13 Logic and Venn diagrams using logic gates

Exit skills. Students should be able to[1]:
Use AND, OR, NOT, NAND, NOR and XOR gates to develop a logic or Venn diagram. Convert a Boolean expression to logic or Venn diagram.

A variety of electrical circuits are used to build a computer system. These electrical circuits require binary inputs and produce a single binary output. Electrical circuits are constructed using the Boolean operators discussed in section 2.1.11 and are implemented by what are known as *logic gates*. A logic gate is a real electrical circuit that simulates a specific Boolean operator. There are six logic gates, as there are six Boolean operators.

The six logic gates are written as a circle with the name of the gate inside it, as bellow:

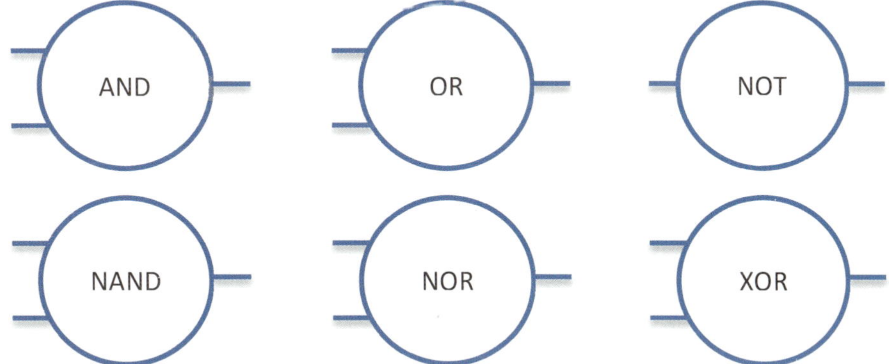

All the logic gates have a single output on their right, indicated by a line. The NOT gate has a single input on the left, whereas all the other gates have two inputs, indicated by the two lines on the left of the circle.

Let's create a logic diagram using some of the above logic gates for the statement we encountered in section 2.1.11:

"Tania won't go to play if it is cold and raining, or if she has not done her homework"

In section 2.1.12 we saw that the statement under consideration could be re-written, using the notation for the Boolean operators, as follows:

$$\text{Will not go to play} = (\text{Cold} \cdot \text{Raining}) + (\overline{\text{Homework}})$$

Looking at the above statement we identify that we need an AND gate, an OR gate and a NOT gate in order to create the logic diagram.

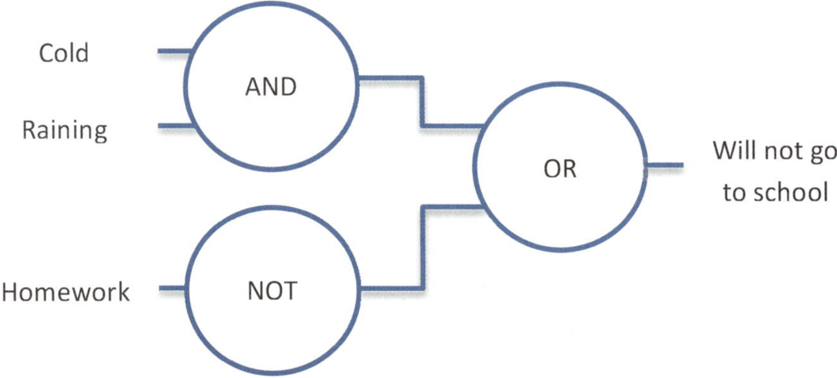

Inputs are shown on the left hand side whereas the output is shown on the right hand side. Problems associated with constructing logic diagrams will require an output dependent on no more than three inputs.

Example 2.51: Draw the logic circuit for the expression: (p OR q) and (r XOR s)

Logic circuit for expression: $(p \lor q) \land (r \veebar s)$

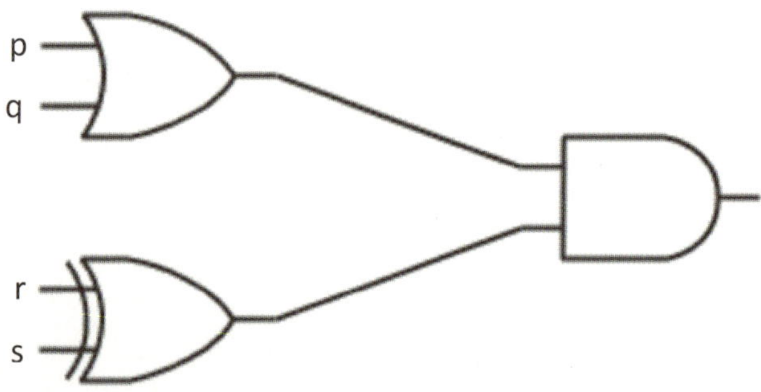

Example 2.52: Draw the logic circuit for the expression: (p AND NOT q) OR NOT s

Logic circuit for expression: $(p \land \neg q) \lor \neg s$

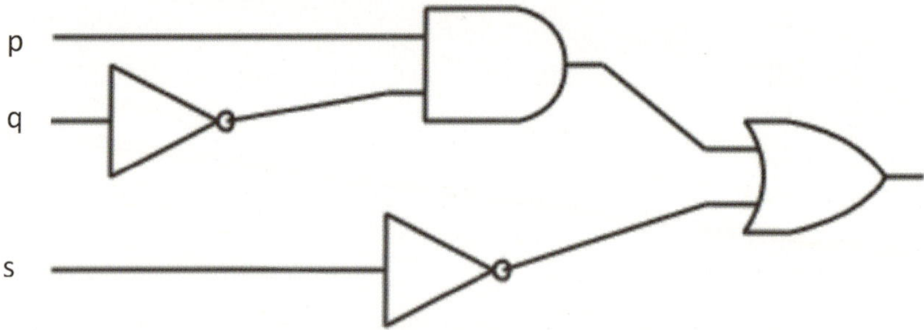

Example 2.53: Draw the logic circuit for the expression: (p OR NOT q) and NOT (r XOR s)

Logic circuit for expression: $(p \lor \neg q) \land \neg(r \veebar s)$

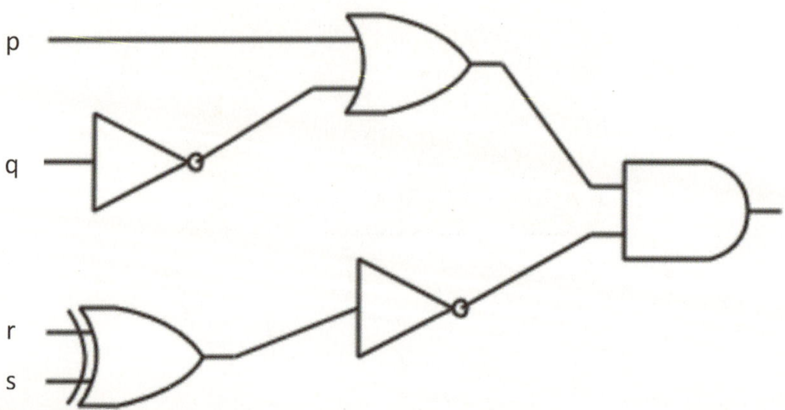

Example 2.54: Draw the logic circuit for the expression: p OR (NOT q AND p AND q)

Logic circuit for expression: $p \lor (\neg q \land p \land q)$

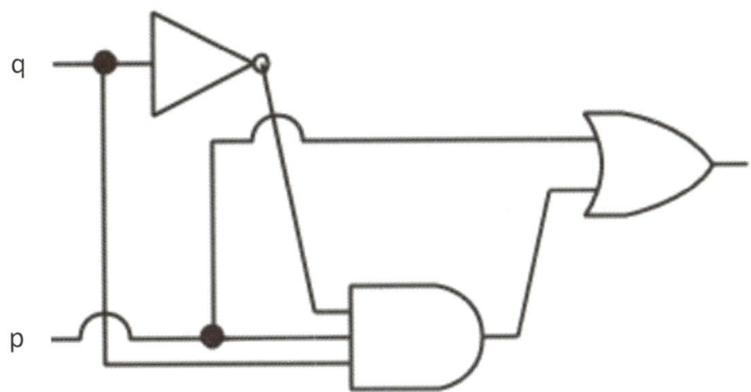

Example 2.55: Draw the circuit for the expression:
(p AND q) OR (q XOR (p AND r AND q))

Logic circuit for expression $(p \land q) \lor (q \veebar (p \land r \land q))$

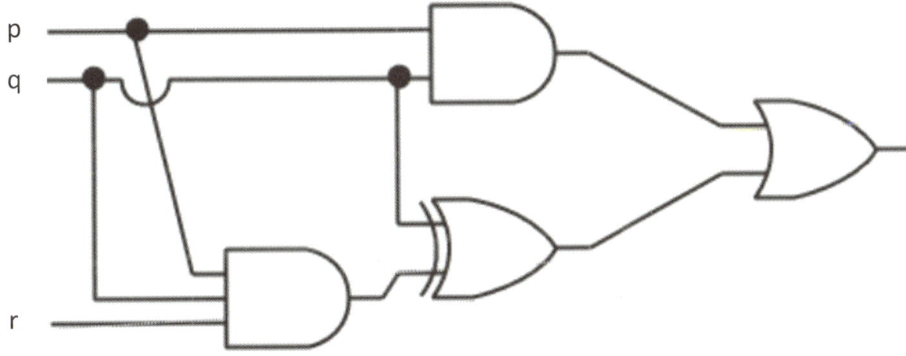

Example 2.56: Draw the Venn diagram for the expression: p AND NOT q OR NOT s

Venn diagram:

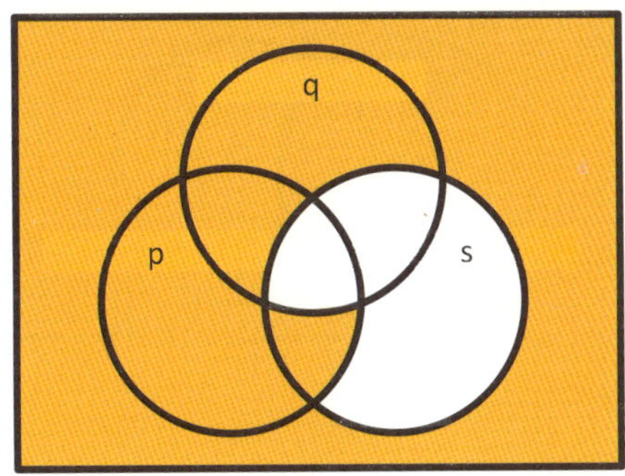

Example 2.57: Draw the Venn diagram for the expression:
q OR p AND NOT p OR s AND NOT s

Venn diagram:

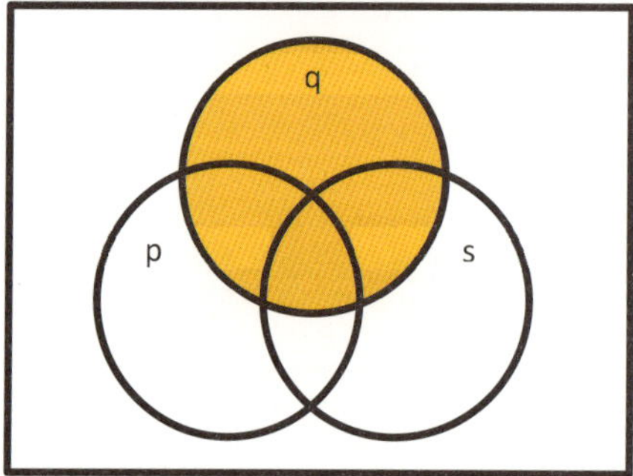

Example 2.58: Draw the Venn diagram for the expression: p OR NOT q AND p AND q

Venn diagram:

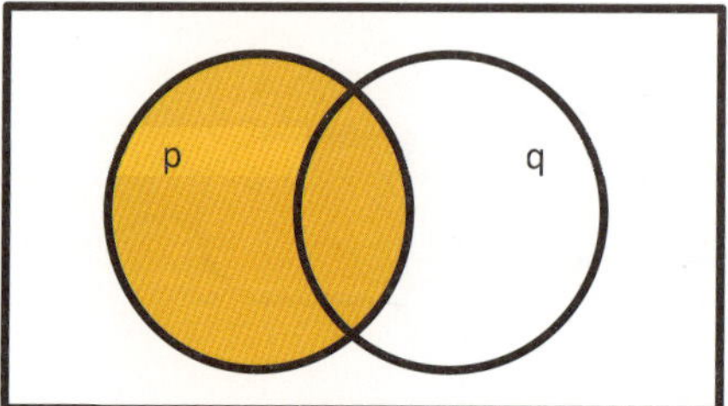

Example 2.59: Draw the Venn diagram for the expression: p OR NOT q

Venn diagram:

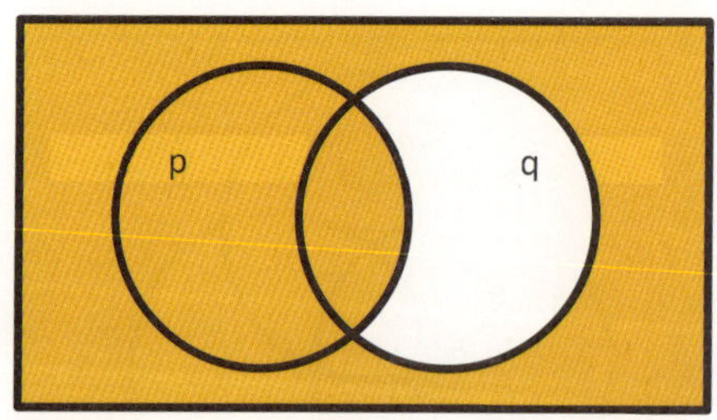

Chapter references

1. International Baccalaureate Organization. (2012). IBDP Computer Science Guide.
2. Marcovitz, A. (2009). Introduction to Logic Design. McGraw-Hill.

TOPIC 3 – NETWORKS

Topic 3. Networks[1]

Introduction and some definitions

Exit skills. Students should be able to:

Define the terms: bus topology, cable, check digit. data integrity, check sum, data packet, gateway, handshaking, hub, ISDN (integrated services digital network), local area network, microwave transmission, modem, network, packet, packet switching, networking, parity bit, protocol, TCP/IP (transmission control protocol/ Internet protocol) and wide area network (WAN).

Image 3.1: Aristotle

Aristotle said[2] "Man is by nature a social animal; an individual who is unsocial naturally and not accidentally is either beneath our notice or more than human. Society is something that precedes the individual. Anyone who either cannot lead the common life or is so self-sufficient as not to need to, and therefore does not partake of society, is either a beast or a god." The ways in which we interact are continually altering and evolving. Technological advancements influence communication methods. Today the Internet is the major driving factor and the change agent that determines our everyday communication habits. Sounds and gestures are transformed into bits and bytes and allow us to live in a networked world. The extended influence and the reduced cost of information exchange across the Internet have changed the way people interact. Early data networks were limited to exchanging character-based information between interconnected computer systems. Modern networks have developed to carry voice, music, video streams, text, and graphics between different devices such as computer systems, smartphones, tablets, etc. Instant messaging, blogs, podcasting, wikis, intranets, extranets, on-line gaming, on line movie rentals, collaboration tools and CMSs have this in common; they are all network dependent. The following table contains some definitions from the old syllabus (2004)[3]. These terms are also used in the new syllabus.

Term	Definition
bus topology	Computer network in which a "bus" connects all the devices together through a common cable.
cable	Copper wire (usually coaxial and twisted pair) and fibre (fibre

[1] International Baccalaureate Organization. (2012). IBDP Computer Science Guide.
[2] Copied by: A quote by Aristotle. (n.d.). Retrieved December 21, 2014, from http://www.goodreads.com/quotes/183896-man-is-by-nature-a-social-animal-an-individual-who
[3] International Baccalaureate Organization. (2004). IBDP Computer Science Guide.

	optic cable-made from glass). Cables allow for the connection of computers over a network.
check digit	Extra digit added to numerical data that is used to check data integrity after input, transmission, storage and processing.
data integrity	The accuracy of data after input, transmission, storage or processing.
check sum	Error-detecting procedure that generates a sum from the digits of a number.
data packet	Portion of a message that is transmitted through a network. Contains data such as check digits and destination address.
gateway	Link that resides between computer networks and is responsible for converting data passing through into the appropriate format so it can be understood by the receiving network.
handshaking	Exchange of predetermined signals to signify that a connection has been established between two systems.
hub	Network connection point for devices. Data arriving at a hub is copied and send to all the devices on the network.
ISDN (integrated services digital network)	International communications standard that allows for the transmission of audio/video and other data over digital telephone lines.
local area network (LAN)	Computer network where all the connected computers are within a limited geographical area (ex. a home, school, etc.). Connection between the computers may be through cables and/or microwave transmission.
microwave transmission	Electronic communication without the need for cables.
modem (abbreviation of modulator/demodulator)	Electronic equipment that converts computer digital signals into audio signals and back. The audio signals are transmitted over telephone lines, which allows for distant communication.
network	Computer systems that are interconnected and can share resources and data.
packet	Group of bits. May Include control signals, error control bits, coded information, as well as the destination for the data.
packet switching	Network communication method that creates and transmits small units of data, called packets, through a network, independently of the overall message.
networking	Making use of a network.
parity bit	Error-detecting procedure that appends a binary digit to a group of binary digits. The sum of all the digits, including the appended binary digit, establishes the accuracy of the data after input, transmission, storage or processing.
protocol	International rules that ensure the transfer of data between systems. A protocol that is recognized as the standard for a specific type of transfer is called standard protocol. For example: TCP/IP is a standard protocol.
TCP/IP (transmission control protocol/ internet protocol)	Communications protocols used to connect hosts on the Internet.
wide area network (WAN)	Computer network where all the connected computers are in a larger geographic area than that served by a LAN or a MAN (metropolitan area network).

Table 3.1: Definitions from the syllabus

Network fundamentals

3.1.1 Different types of networks

Exit skills. Students should be able to[1]:
Identify and define local area network (LAN), virtual local area network (VLAN), wide area network (WAN), storage area network (SAN), wireless local area network (WLAN), internet, extranet, virtual private network (VPN), personal area network (PAN) and peer-to-peer (P2P).

A computer network is comprised of two or more computer systems that are connected and able to communicate and exchange data. Such computer systems are connected by using either cable or wireless media. There are two key terms in computer networks that play an important role:

- **Server**
- **Client**

***Server*[4]**

A server can either be a computer system or a software application that provides a service to the other computer systems connected to the same network. For example, a server can provide the ability to the rest of the computers on the network to store and to share files, taking the role of a file server.

***Client*[3]**

A client can either be a computer system or a software application that requests a service from a server connected to the same network. For example, an email client software application can request from an email server software application to fetch any new emails that may have been received.

In summary, a server computer system is a host running server software applications and sharing its resources with clients that make requests. A client, on the other hand, does not share any of its resources but requests content from a server. Servers thus wait for incoming requests for content from clients.

There are a number of ways that one can connect two or more computer systems in order to create a network. However, the following three are the most commonly used network components that play an essential part in the creation of a network: Hub, Switch and Router. Although all three components have been integrated into a single box, they remain different devices that are essential to networking and with significant differences between them. A typical box hosting a hub or a switch and a wired or wireless router would be similar to the device depicted in Figure 3.1.

---

[4] Client/server (client/server model, client/server architecture). (n.d.). Retrieved December 23, 2014, from http://searchnetworking.techtarget.com/definition/client-server

Figure 3.1: A device that includes a hub or a switch and a wireless router

Hub[5]

A hub is the connection point for devices on a single network. Network devices and computer systems connect to a hub using Ethernet cables that attach to a port. For example, the hub in Figure 3.1 has eight ports, which means that eight devices or computer systems can connect to it. Thus, a hub consists of multiple ports. When a network device wishes to send data to some other device on the network, it sends the data to the hub. The hub then copies the data and sends it to all devices connected to its ports. The device waiting to receive the data accepts the data. All the other devices just ignore it. Although passing the data along to every port ensures that it will reach its destination, a lot of traffic is generated on the network, since all the other ports that just ignore the data have to nevertheless receive it. This slows down the network.

Switch[4]

A switch is also the connection point for multiple devices on a single network. However, unlike a hub, the switch can identify which network device is connected to which *port*. This allows the switch to transmit data to the exact port and network device for which it is intended. This means that when a network device wishes to send data to some other device on the network, it sends the data to the switch and the switch sends the data to the appropriate receiver rather than all the ports and devices connected to those ports. As such, networks connected with a switch are faster than networks connected with a hub.

Router[4]

A router is a more sophisticated device than both a hub and a switch. Its use is to join multiple networks and serve as an intermediary between these networks so that data can be exchanged effectively and efficiently between network devices of those networks. For example, a router is used to connect a home network to the Internet. A hub or switch would not be able to accomplish such a task in a simple manner.

As stated, a hub or a switch and a router are commonly integrated into a single box, allowing the creation of a wired or wireless network, as well as connection of that network to other networks, such as the Internet.

---

[5] How do hubs, switches, routers, and access points differ? - Windows Help. (n.d.). Retrieved December 23, 2014, from http://windows.microsoft.com/en-us/windows/hubs-switches-routers-access-points-differ#1TC=windows-7

There are various different types of networks that can be established, as well as different protocols or "rules" that need to be followed in order for the computer systems involved to exchange data efficiently.

The network types that will be described briefly are the following:

- Local Area Network (LAN)
- Wireless Local Area Network (WLAN)
- Virtual Local Area Network (VLAN)
- Wide Area Network (WAN)
- Storage Area Network (SAN)
- Internet
- Extranet
- Virtual Private Network (VPN)
- Personal Area Network (PAN)
- Peer-To-Peer (P2P)

All of the network types described below have assisted in the globalization phenomenon of the recent decades. Globalization has been accelerated by the technical advances linked to network development. All of these different networks have played their part in interconnecting computer systems, whether locally or globally, and thus allowing people across the globe to communicate, do business and so on.

Example 3.1:

Question:

Describe some characteristics of the Internet.

Answer:

The Internet is a global collection of countless types of computers and computer networks that are connected together. Billions of interconnected devices form a network of solutions for various human problems and boost information exchange, marketing solutions, educational advances, health endeavors etc. WWW, email, file transferring, peer to peer networks are services that are supported by the Internet infrastructure. The Internet has no centralized control but governments have the power to restrict what citizens in their countries can access. Internet service providers can also restrict access to specific sites.

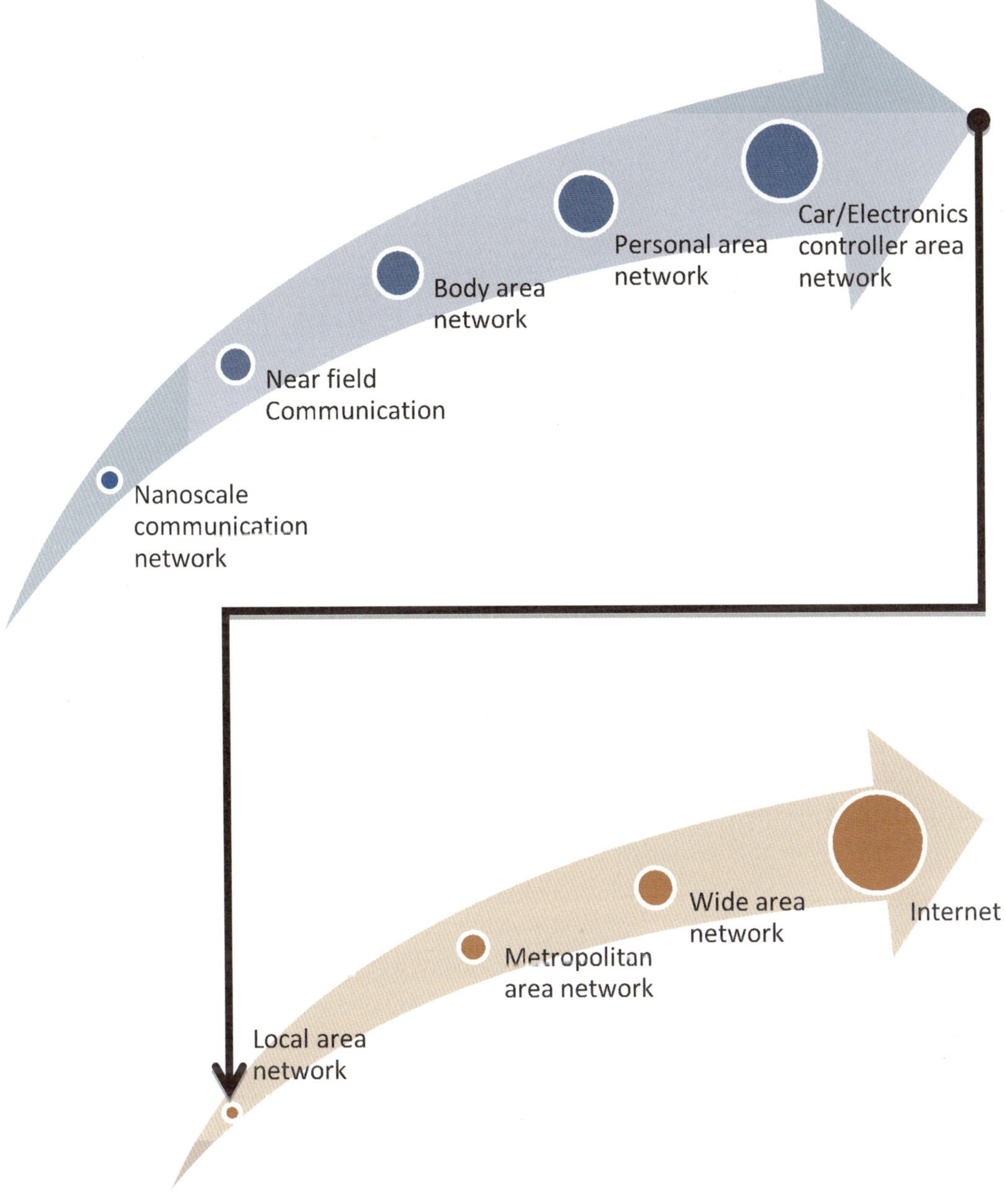

Figure 3.2 and Figure 3.3: Computer network types by spatial scope

Local Area Network (LAN)[6]

LAN is a computer network that connects computer systems that are within a limited geographical area such as a room, a home, an office building or a school. Computer systems interconnected with a LAN usually have high data-transfer rates between them.

A client-server mode of operation is commonly used. This allows for a single computer system to act as the server and be responsible for supplying various services to the clients in the network.

---

[6] Local area network. (2015, May 16). In *Wikipedia, The Free Encyclopedia*. Retrieved 16:43, June 15, 2015, from https://en.wikipedia.org/w/index.php?title=Local_area_network&oldid=662633873

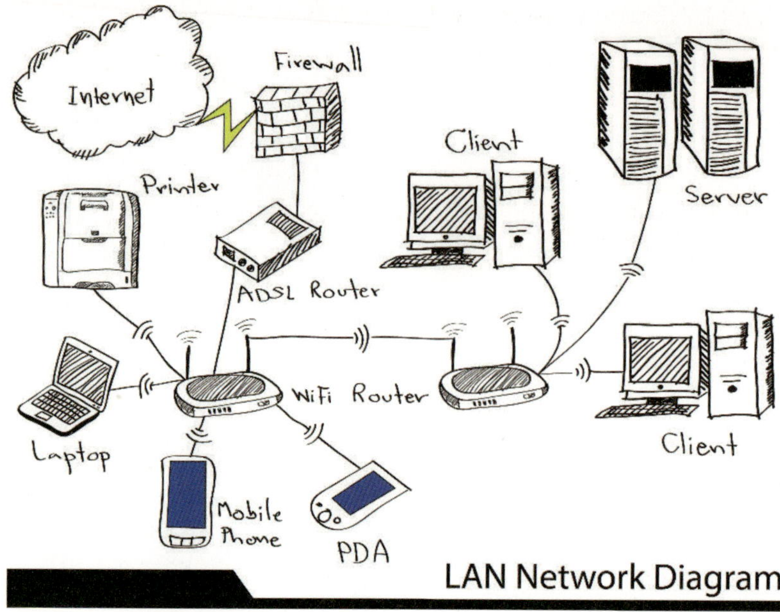

Image 3.2: Local Area Network

LANs allow the sharing of peripheral devices between the connected computer networks. That means that peripheral devices, such as printers, scanners or external hard drives, can be used by any computer system in the LAN that is desired. This eliminates the need to buy certain peripheral devices for every computer system used. For example, instead of having to buy a number of printers, one printer can be bought and connected to the server of the LAN, with the rest of the computer systems, the clients, accessing and sharing the printer through the server.

Another benefit of forming a LAN is that, apart from peripheral devices, data can also be shared. This allows for the exchange of data between clients, thus eliminating the need to physically send data using other means, such as by exchanging CDs or memory sticks. This increases flexibility and reduces wasted time.

The most common technology used to build wired LANs is a hub or a switch using Ethernet cabling. Figure 3.4 presents a wired LAN comprised of one server, three clients and a printer connected to the server though a hub or a switch.

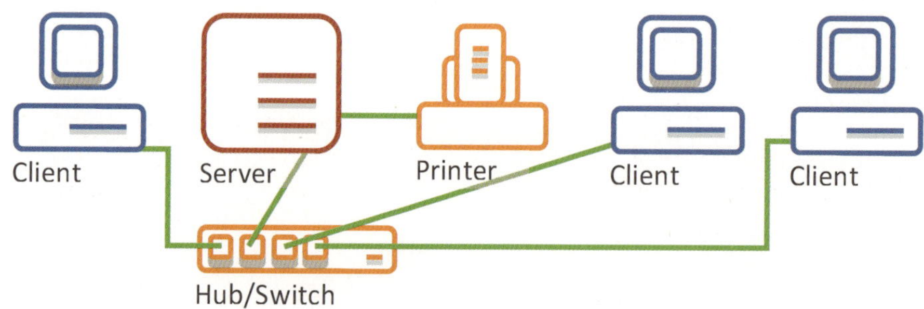

Figure 3.4: A local area network (LAN)

Wireless Local Area Network (WLAN)[7]

A WLAN links two or more computer systems within a limited geographical area, similar to LAN. The difference from a LAN is that WLAN devices are connected using some sort of

[7] Wireless LAN. (2015, June 14). In *Wikipedia, The Free Encyclopedia*. Retrieved 16:46, June 15, 2015, from https://en.wikipedia.org/w/index.php?title=Wireless_LAN&oldid=666879923

wireless connection method. This allows users to have mobile devices and laptops connected to the network and be able to move around.

WLANs have all the benefits of LANs, as well as the ease of wireless connection that allows the use of mobile devices on the move. However, WLANs can be less secure than wired LANs since a potential intruder does not require having a physical connection to the network. For example, an intruder may try to access a school WLAN even outside the school premises if the wireless network signal is strong enough.

The most common technology to build wireless LANs is Wi-Fi, which allows the exchange of data between computer systems using radio waves. Figure 3.5 presents a LAN comprised of one server, three clients and a printer connected to the server. Two of the clients are connected wirelessly through a wireless hub or switch.

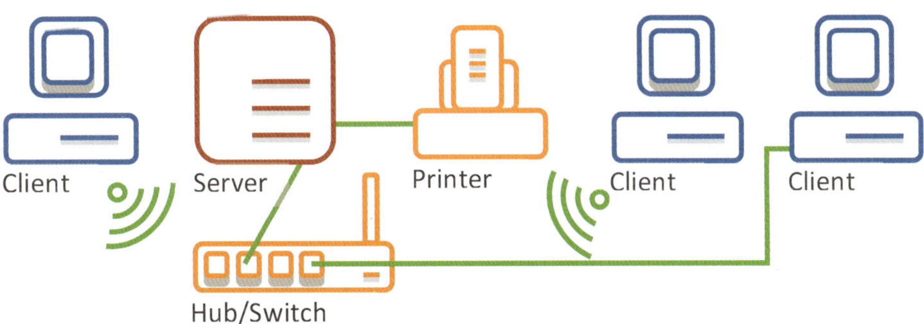

Figure 3.5: A local area network (LAN)

Example 3.2: Compare and contrast the similarities and differences between LAN and WLAN.

Answer:

	Similarities	Differences
LAN-WLAN	Both act on a local level.	They use different transmission medium.
	Both allow communication.	A LAN is safer.
	Both used to connect devices	The LAN is faster.
	Both allow sharing of resources	WLANs offer greater flexibility.

Virtual Local Area Network (VLAN)[8]

Imagine that a business has created a LAN and has connected all its computer systems and departments together. Departments such as accounting, human resources, sales and production have all been interconnected and all of the computer systems, from any department, can have access to any shared resources from any department. That may not

[8] VLAN (Virtual Local Area Network). (n.d.). Retrieved December 23, 2014, from http://orbit-computer-solutions.com/VLAN-and-Trunking.php

be desirable, since departments may not want or need to exchange any data with other, and having access to each other's shared resources may confuse instead of help.

The solution to this problem would be to set up a LAN for every department, so each department will have its own isolated network that cannot be accessed from the outside. These LANs could be connected together, connecting the switch from every LAN to a central switch, so as to be able to communicate between them whenever necessary without having access to each other's shared resources.

Instead of having to set up switches and cabling in order to create separate LANs for every department, a VLAN can be used to partition the initial LAN, where every department is connected, into *logical separate networks*. Each logical separate network cannot see the computer systems or the *shared resources* of other such logical separate networks, without specific set up that allows it to see them.

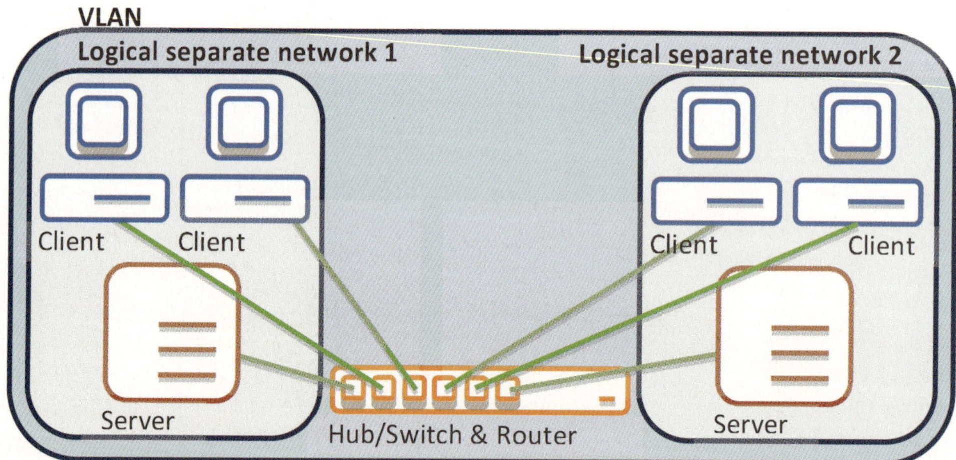

Figure 3.6: A virtual local area network (VLAN) with two logical separate networks

Example 3.3: Compare and contrast the similarities and differences between LAN and VLAN.

Answer:

	Similarities	Differences
LAN-VLAN	Both act on a local level.	A VLAN delivers better performance.
	They both have the same attributes.	A VLAN is safer.
	Both allow communication.	The formation of virtual workgroups is easy.
	Both used to connect devices	VLANs offer greater flexibility. Even if someone who is using a laptop moves to another place he/she will remain in his/her dedicated VLAN.
	Both allow sharing of resources	The partitioning of resources is easier.
		VLANs are independent on the medium and the physical topology of the network.
		Sometimes the management/administration of a VLAN is complex.

Figure 3.6 presents a VLAN comprised of two servers (each for a different department in a business) and four clients (two at each department). The VLAN is set up in such a way so that the LAN is segmented into two smaller logical separate networks.

Example 3.4: Compare and contrast LAN and VLAN.

Answer:

LAN		VLAN	
Pros	**Cons**	**Pros**	**Cons**
Sometimes the management of a LAN is easier	A LAN delivers worst performance.	A VLAN delivers better performance.	Sometimes the management of a VLAN is complex.
	A LAN is not that safe.	A VLAN is safer.	A network can accommodate a maximum number of VLANs (this number is big and so it is not a real disadvantage.)
	It does not provide formation of virtual workgroups.	The formation of virtual workgroups is easy.	
	LANs offer less flexibility.	VLANs offer greater flexibility. Even if someone who is using a laptop moves to another place he/she will remain in his/her dedicated VLAN.	
	The partitioning of resources is harder.	The partitioning of resources is easier.	
	LANs are dependent of the medium and the physical topology of the network.	VLANs are independent on the medium and the physical topology of the network.	

Wide Area Network (WAN)[9]

WAN is a computer network that connects computer systems that are within a large geographical area. The most obvious example of a WAN is the Internet. A WAN covers a broad area, such as a city, a country or even a network of countries allowing individuals, businesses and governments to carry out their daily business regardless of location. A WAN typically consists of LANs connected together over a broad geographical area. Figure 3.7 presents a WAN comprised of four LANs connected together throughout the globe.

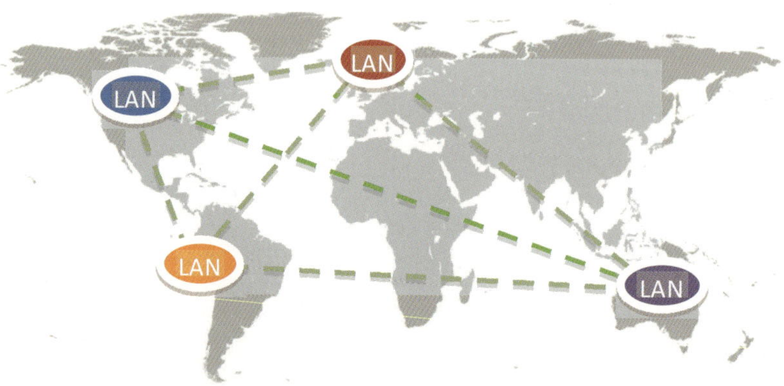

Figure 3.7: A wide area network (WAN) that consists of four LANs that are scattered around the globe

Storage Area Network (SAN)[10]

Image 2.3: Storage Area Network

A SAN is a network that is created so that large storage devices can be accessible from servers in a convenient and easy way. There can be various servers connected to a network such as a company's LAN. For example, in Figure 3.8 a LAN is depicted with four clients (two of them wirelessly connected) and three servers all of which are connected with a Hub/Switch. There are three servers because they provide three distinct services to the clients. One server is a

Example 3.5: Compare and contrast the similarities and differences between LAN and WAN.

Answer:

Similarities	Differences
Both allow communication.	A LAN is usually faster.
Both used to connect devices.	A WAN is more expensive.
Both allow sharing of resources.	LAN is easier to maintain than WAN.
	LAN serves local areas while WAN serves large geographic areas.

[9] Wide area network. (2015, May 20). In *Wikipedia, The Free Encyclopedia*. Retrieved 16:47, June 15, 2015, from https://en.wikipedia.org/w/index.php?title=Wide_area_network&oldid=663323837

[10] Storage area network. (2015, May 20). In *Wikipedia, The Free Encyclopedia*. Retrieved 16:51, June 15, 2015, from https://en.wikipedia.org/w/index.php?title=Storage_area_network&oldid=663172345

mail server, responsible for managing emails. The other server is an application server, responsible for managing centralized applications that can be used by clients. Lastly, the third server is a database server that is responsible for managing company data stored in a database (ex. client list with details).

These servers require storage space in order to store their data and create backups to prevent data loss, if any storage space fails. This is where the storage area network is required. The SAN is a network that connects the servers to the storage devices so that they have enough storage space to complete their tasks. In Figure 3.8 the SAN is comprised of three storage devices connected with the three servers described before using a switch and Ethernet cabling. Examples of storage devices are disk arrays and tape libraries.

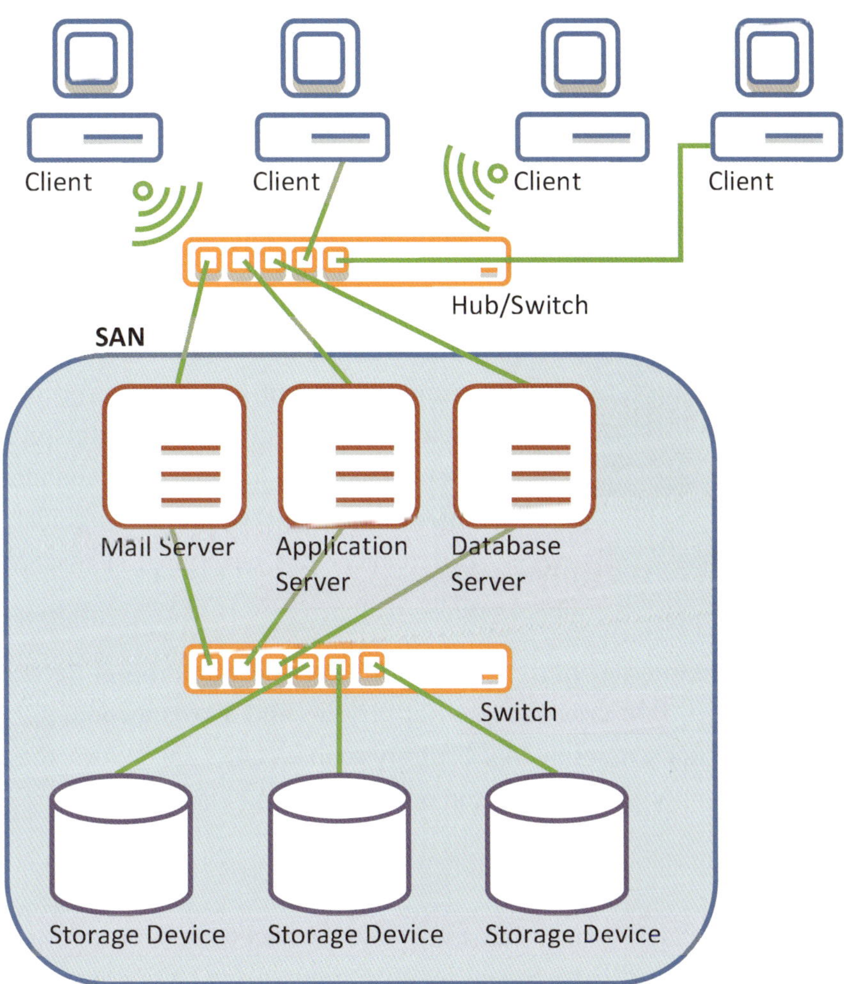

Figure 3.8: A storage area network (SAN) connected to an enterprise LAN

Intranet[11]

An "intranet" is the broad term for a collection of private computer networks within a company, a school or an organization that utilizes standard network protocols like TCP/IP,

[11] Intranet. (2015, June 11). In *Wikipedia, The Free Encyclopedia*. Retrieved 17:16, June 15, 2015, from https://en.wikipedia.org/w/index.php?title=Intranet&oldid=666458905

which will be described in section 3.1.3. It could be considered as a private analogy of the Internet. Its main purpose is to facilitate communication between individuals or work groups and to improve data sharing. Intranet resources and services are not available to the world outside the company. In all cases where an intranet is connected to the internet, a firewall is used for protection.

Internet

The Internet is a global WAN connecting millions of computer systems. Since it is a WAN, the Internet connects a large number of smaller networks together, thereby creating the largest WAN network used by billions of users worldwide.

Image 3.4: Internet of things

The Internet provides an extensive number of services to users such as the *World Wide Web (WWW)*, which consists of websites and webpages, as well as support for email, file transfer and other services. As such, the Internet is not the same as the WWW but rather the WWW is a service of the Internet.

Unlike other networks, the Internet is decentralized by design. That means that its resources are not centrally stored or controlled by a single server. Each computer system that is connected to the Internet is independent and can share services with the global Internet community, thus becoming, in essence, a server of its own.

For most, access to the Internet must go through a commercial Internet Service Provider (ISP), which is a company that provides Internet services and allows a computer system to connect to the Internet for a monthly fee. Contrary to most LANs and WANs, the Internet is not owned by a single entity, such as a person or organization.

Internet of Things (IoT).

It is the network of individual "things" that are able to connect to the Internet, communicate and exchange data. All “things” carry the necessary hardware and software and are assigned an IP-address. Each “thing” is a physical object such as a patient with an implant, a car with an emergency system, an alarm system with advanced warning, a wild animal with a tracking system, etc. Each physical object has a unique embedded system that uniquely identifies it.

Some ways to access the Internet:

- **Broadband access** via DSL or cable modem, a T1 or T3 line.
- **Wi-Fi access** via Wi-Fi router or Wi-Fi hot spots.
- **Dial-up access** via modem. Used where broadband access is not available or too expensive, or no Wi-Fi available.

- **Mobile networks via 3G, 4G networks, etc.**

Extranet[12]

An extranet is a computer network that utilizes the Internet to allow controlled access by specific users to a specific LAN or WAN.

For example, imagine a business that operates a network of computer systems for its everyday operations. This private network is contained within the business, whether it's a LAN or a WAN, and can only be accessed by the personnel that have the required credentials (ex. username and password). The specific business may wish to securely share part of its network (and information) with suppliers, partners, customers or other businesses without making its whole network available to them or the public. This part of the network that is extended to users outside the company is termed as extranet. Extranets require security and privacy techniques so as the public or outside users are not permitted to access any secure data. Extranets could be considered as intranets that are partially accessible to authorized outsiders. A firewall controls the access rights and allows access to the intranet only to people who are authorized.

Virtual Private Network (VPN)[13]

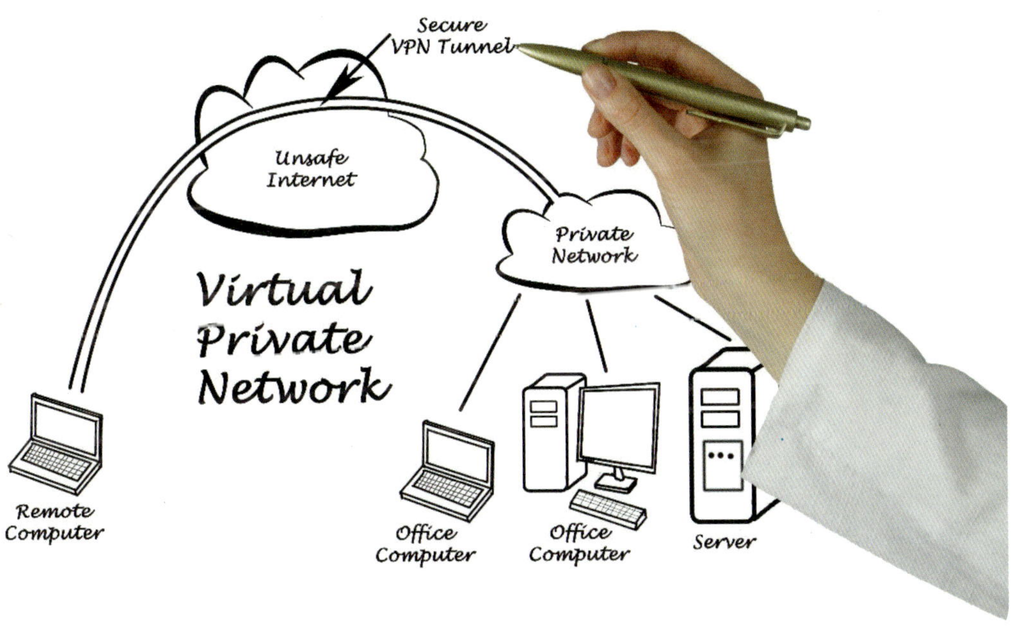

Image 3.5: Virtual Private Network

[12] Mitchell, B. (n.d.). Intranets and Extranets. Retrieved December 23, 2014, from http://compnetworking.about.com/od/filetransferprotocol

[13] Virtual private network. (2015, June 11). In *Wikipedia, The Free Encyclopedia*. Retrieved 16:53, June 15, 2015, from https://en.wikipedia.org/w/index.php?title=Virtual_private_network&oldid=666500623

Example 3.6: Compare and contrast the similarities and differences between VPN and EXTRANET.

Answer:

Similarities	Differences
Both use the internet.	A VPN provides a secure connection to employees of the company, while an extranet limits access to the company network to selected (authenticated) outsiders.
They are both considered inexpensive solutions.	VPN provides more security (data send and received always encrypted).
They both provide some security.	

Imagine that there is a company with a LAN that connects two or more computer systems within a limited geographical area: its office. Imagine that there are some employees that need to travel abroad on work, but still time is needed to access the company's LAN in order to access files and shared resources. That would not be possible with a LAN, or even a WLAN, if the employee is far away and not physically near the LAN or WLAN to connect in a wired or wireless method. VPN solves this problem.

A VPN is a computer network that connects two or more computer systems, similar to a LAN or a WLAN, but also allows clients from remote locations to connect to the network and appear to be inside the LAN as if they were physically present. Thus, a VPN allows the creation of a LAN that is managed through a server software application, to which clients can also connect from a remote location, even through a different network (e.g. the Internet).

A VPN has all the benefits of a LAN, allowing users to share data and resources without compromising security. Furthermore, a VPN can securely and cost-effectively connect geographically disparate offices of a business within a network with all the functionalities of a single LAN.

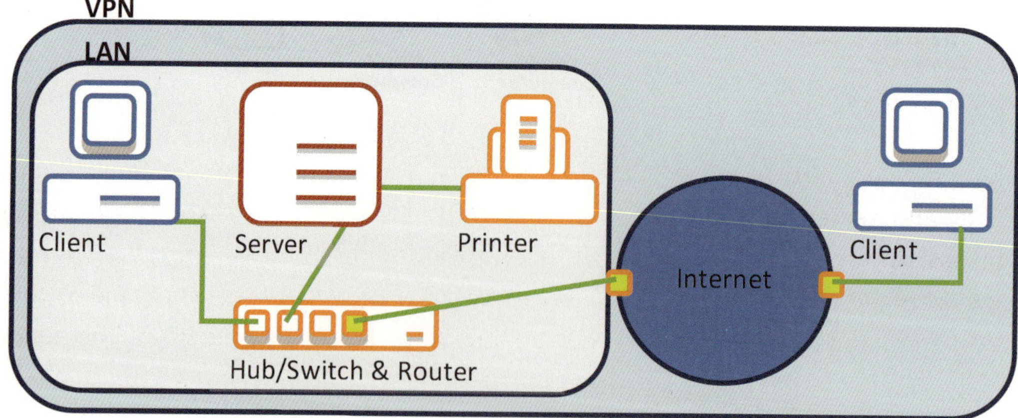

Figure 3.9: A virtual private network (VPN)

Example 3.7: Compare and contrast the similarities and differences between LAN and PAN.

Answer:

Similarities	Differences
Used for data transmission	A LAN connects computers and devices that belong to different people, while a PAN suits the needs of a single person.
	A PAN operates on a smaller area than a LAN
	A PAN does not require a device such as a hub or switch. USB and Bluetooth technologies are used instead.

Figure 3.9 presents a VPN comprised of one server, two clients and a printer connected to the server. One of the clients is connected to the VPN remotely through the Internet using a username and password.

Personal Area Network (PAN)

PAN is a network that interconnects devices that are centered around an individual person's workspace. It can be understood as a LAN that supports only one person, instead of a group of people, and covers a very short range, a maximum of 10 meters. An example of a typical PAN would involve a mobile computer, a smartphone and a tablet all interconnected and sharing data such as emails, calendars, photographs, etc. Devices on PANs can connect both wired (typically through USB) and wirelessly (typically through *Bluetooth*) depending on the technologies used.

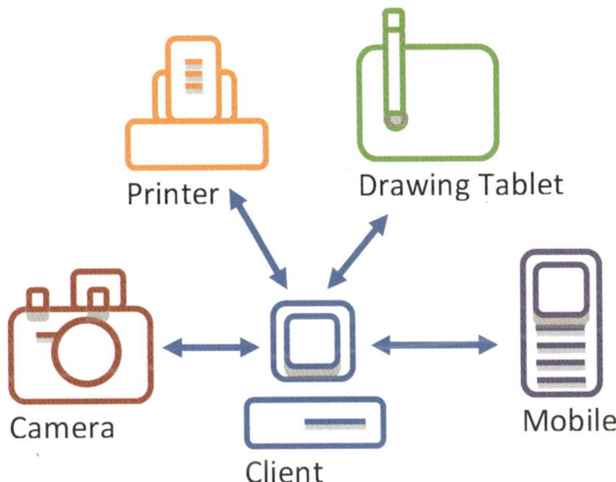

Figure 3.10: A PAN

A PAN using a wireless group of devices using Bluetooth technology in order to interconnect is also known as a *piconet*[14].

Peer-To-Peer (P2P)[15]

P2P is a network that does not utilize the client/server model where clients request resources and servers provide them. Instead, a P2P network uses a distributed network architecture where all the computer systems (called nodes or peers) in the network are decentralized and are both clients and servers at the same time, consuming and supplying resources from and to the other computer systems connected to the network. The need for

---

[14] What is Piconet? - Definition from Techopedia. (n.d.). Retrieved December 23, 2014, from http://www.techopedia.com/definition/5081/piconet

[15] Peer-to-peer. (2015, June 3). In *Wikipedia, The Free Encyclopedia*. Retrieved 16:56, June 15, 2015, from https://en.wikipedia.org/w/index.php?title=Peer-to-peer&oldid=665302579

centralized servers is removed, in order to avoid bottlenecks, while each computer system makes part of its resources available for other network computer systems to use.

Example 3.8: Compare and contrast the similarities and differences between the client-server model and P2P.

Answer:

Similarities	Differences
They both serve a lot of devices and users.	The client-server model offers a centralized control of services. In a P2P model, the control is decentralized
They both can act on different scales (local, wider).	The client-server model is based on a server that provides services and clients that request services, while the P2P model includes computers that act as both servers and clients (suppliers and consumers).
	The client-server model offers better security.

3.1.2 Importance of standards in the construction of networks

Exit skills. Students should be able to[1]:
Define the term standards. Outline the importance of standards. Appreciate the importance of compatibility.

Imagine that a business needs to setup a LAN with a number of clients and servers. If the hardware does not follow some common rules (or specific *standards*), the computer systems may not be able to interconnect together to create the network.

Useful Information: There are two organizations standardize networking protocols: Institute of Electrical and Electronics Engineers (IEEE) and Internet Engineering Task Force (IETF).

If there existed many standards with hardware or software manufacturers following different ones, the result would be incompatible hardware and software. For example, in a hypothetical situation without standards, a computer system might be developed, which only supported USB ports, and a switch might be developed that only supported Ethernet ports. These two hardware elements would be unable to connect to each other, since they would have been using different communication standards.

Standards play an important role in the construction of networks. Standards describe the common ground on which hardware and software manufacturers (Apple, Microsoft, Linux etc.) can depend on in order to build systems that are able to communicate with each other.

As such, *standards* can be thought to provide a common international "language" that enables compatibility for all computer systems throughout the globe.

3.1.3 Networks, communication and layers[16]

Exit skills. Students should be able to[1]:
Explain how communication over networks is analyzed into different layers. List the OSI (reference model) layers. Explain how the OSI model facilitates abstraction. List the TCP/IP (protocol model) layers. Explain the function of TCP/IP.

If only one computer system manufacturer existed, offering one type of computer system to be used everywhere, the communication between computer systems would be easy. There would only be one standard for communication and non other. However, this is not the case in the world today. There are a number of computer system manufacturers and a wide variety of different types of computers. Although hardware in these computer systems differs, we may need these different computer systems to communicate. To achieve this, a specific standard has to be followed.

Software application developers have to abide by some standards in order to develop an application capable of communicating with other software over a WAN (Internet). Imagine a simple program that asks for services from an online database. This process requires the program to:

1. Pass the request through different layers
2. Obtain an answer through different layers

It is clear that different layers serve different functions and use different protocols for information exchange. Organizing a network design in layers makes the process less complex because any problem is broken down into distinct modules. The protocol of a layer carries out a sequence of operations.

Every computer system that is connected to a network uses a specific process to transfer data or receive data from the connection medium (e.g. cable). Imagine that a software application on a computer system creates some data to be sent to another software application on another computer system, both of which are connected to a network. The data to be sent must be placed in a format understandable by both software applications. Once this is done, the data is encoded into a format that is suitable to be placed on the network. Therefore, the data is broken up into small groups that are termed *packets*. Each packet contains a small amount of data, as well as other important information such as the destination of the packet. The packets then travel through the network and reach their final destination. Various procedures handle the routing of packets across a network through

[16] 4 Understanding the Communication Layers. (n.d.). Retrieved December 23, 2014, from https://docs.oracle.com/cd/E18283_01/network.112/e10836/layers.htm

intermediary devices. Only bits, 0s and 1s, travel over media. Finally the receiving application gets the reassembled data in a suitable form.

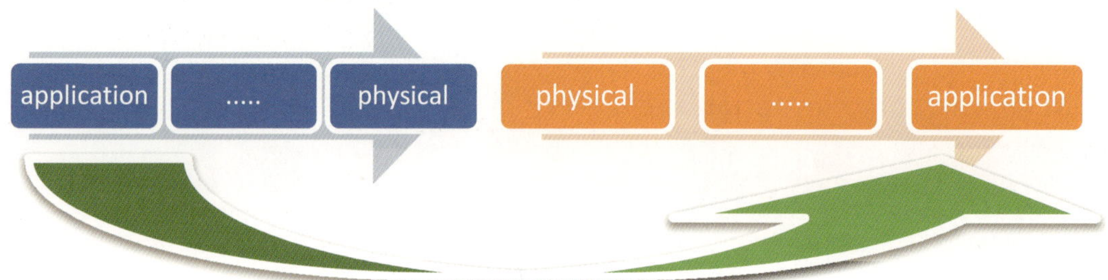

Figure 3.11: Data communication throught different layers

Advantages of Layers

1. Easy to manage.
2. Greater understanding of each layer.
3. Common language for each layer.
4. Makes protocol design easier.
5. A manufacturer can focus on technologies of a particular layer.
6. Products of different manufacturers can work together.
7. Technology advances of a layer are independent of technology advancements of other layers (wireless technology advances are not dependent on advances of media format compression (GIF))

OSI (reference model)[17]

The most-widely used networking standard is the Open Systems Interconnection model (OSI). The OSI Model was established by the International Standards Organization (ISO) and aims to facilitate communication across a variety of systems. It contains seven layers. It should be mentioned that the Open Systems Interconnection model provides an abstract depiction and explanation of the network communication process. It is just a reference model.

---

[17] OSI reference model (Open Systems Interconnection). (n.d.). Retrieved December 23, 2014, from http://searchnetworking.techtarget.com/definition/OSI

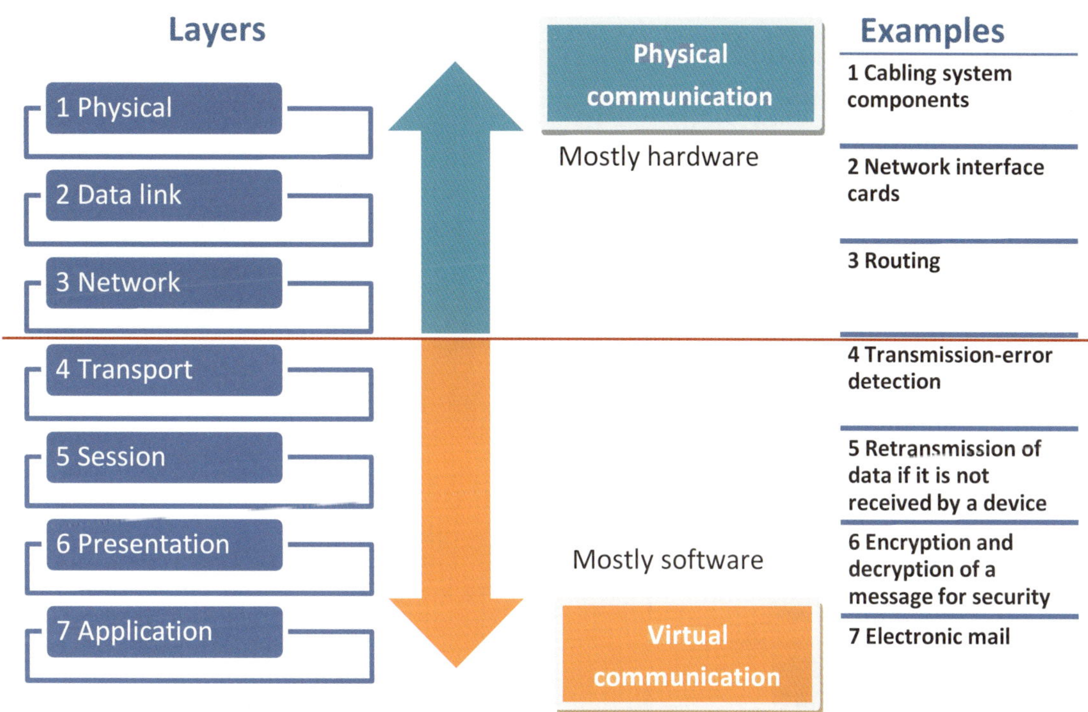

Figure 3.12: OSI MODEL[18]

No	LAYER	Description and protocols used
1	Application	Performs various services for the applications used by the end users. Example protocol: HyperText Transfer Protocol (HTTP)
2	Presentation	Provides data format information, data compression information and data encryption information to the application. Example protocol: Portable Network Graphics (PNG).
3	Session	Manages sessions between two users. Example protocol: UNIX X Window system core protocol.
4	Transport	End to end connections (hosts). Definition of data segments →assignment of numbers→ data transfer→ reassemblage of data at the destination. Example protocol: TCP.
5	Network	Handles routing of packets across a network through intermediary devices. Example protocol: IP.
6	Data Link	Error handling of physical transmission. Builds frames and amends transmission rate according the buffer of the receiver (flow control). Example protocol: Ethernet, HDLC.
7	Physical	Transmits 0s and 1s over media between devices. Definition of media specifications. Voltage levels. Example protocol: RS232-C (serial port).

Table 3.2: OSI Model

[18] The OSI Model: Understanding the Seven Layers of Computer Networks Expert Reference Series of White Papers Introduction. (n.d.). Retrieved December 21, 2014, from http://www.academia.edu/7212126/The_OSI_Model_Understanding_the_Seven_Layers_of_Computer_Networks_Expert_Reference_Series_of_White_Papers_Introduction

TCP/IP (protocol model)[19]

The TCP/IP (Transfer Control Protocol / Internet Protocol) describes all the functions that take place at each layer of protocols within the TCP/IP suite. It is a hierarchical model protocol that models and represents all the functionality required for successful communication between users. Its functionality is structured into four abstraction layers.

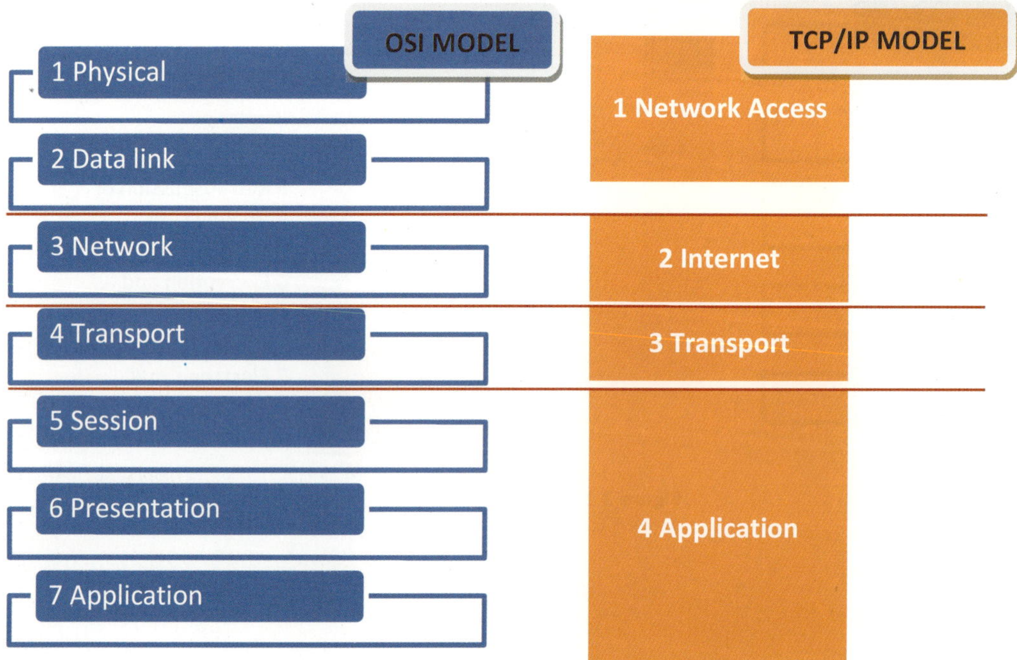

Figure 3.13: Comparison of OSI and TCP/IP models

No	LAYER	Description and protocols used (TCP/IP)
1	Application	Performs various services for the software applications used by the end user. Example protocol: HyperText Transfer Protocol
2	Transport	End to end connections (hosts). Definition of data segments →assignment of numbers→ data transfer→ reassemblage of data at the destination. Example protocol: TCP.
3	Internet	Handles routing of packets across a network through intermediary devices. Example protocol: IP.

[19] OSI reference model (Open Systems Interconnection). (n.d.). Retrieved December 23, 2014, from http://searchnetworking.techtarget.com/definition/OSI

4	Network Access	Media and devices

Table 3.3: TCP/IP Model

3.1.4 Technologies required to provide a VPN

Exit skills. Students should be able to[1]:
Define VPN. **Analyze the technologies needed to set up and provide a VPN.**

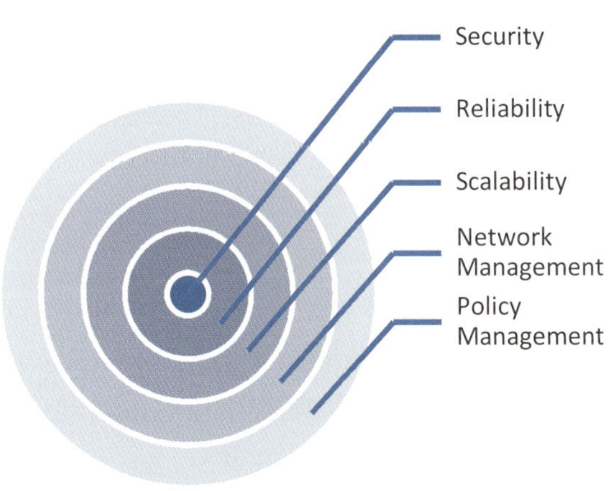

Figure 3.14: Features of a well-designed VPN

A *Virtual Private Network* makes a "tunnelled" network connection through the Internet or any other public network. It is considered ideal for establishing a secure connection between private networks with remote users and remote sites. A VPN enables a device to exchange data across the internet as if it was directly connected to a private network. Users can use a VPN to access data, files, databases and resources that are stored in their computer at work from their computer at home. VPN users can exchange data maintaining privacy through the use of a "tunnelling" protocol and various security procedures.

VPN technologies [20, 21]

A. Hardware and software requirements

1. Internet access
2. VPN software[22] (client software, utilities and server software). VPN software enables private communication over the Internet
3. VPN routers[23]
4. VPN appliances[24]
5. VPN concentrators[25]. A single device to handle a large number of incoming VPN tunnels

---

[20] Cisco. "How Virtual Private Networks Work." Retrieved December 21, 2014, from http://www.cisco.com/application/pdf/paws/14106/how_vpn_works.pdf

[21] What you need to know about VPN technologies. (n.d.). Retrieved December 21, 2014, from http://www.computerworld.com/article/2546283/networking/what-you-need-to-know-about-vpn-technologies.html

[22] Mitchell, B. (n.d.). Free VPN Client and Server Software Downloads. Retrieved December 21, 2014, from http://compnetworking.about.com/od/vpn/tp/vpnsoftwarefree.htm

[23] Cisco RV180 VPN Router. (n.d.). Retrieved December 21, 2014, from http://www.cisco.com/c/en/us/products/routers/rv180-vpn-router/index.html

[24] Barracuda Networks. (n.d.). Retrieved December 21, 2014, from https://www.barracuda.com/products/sslvpn

6. VPN servers[26]

B. Secure VPN

All traffic on the VPN must be encrypted, authenticated and then sent along virtual tunnels.

Secure VPN technologies:

1. Internet protocol security protocol (IPSec) which functions in both transport and tunnel mode:
    - allows the secure transmission of data over public IP-based networks
    - uses standard encryption algorithm to provide confidentiality (AES)
    - provides authentication via digital certificates
2. Secure Sockets Layer (*SSL*) 3.0 or Transport Layer Security (*TLS*) with encryption. SSL/TLS-based VPNs are much simpler than IPSec based VPNs. The use of this technology does not require special client software because all Web servers and Web browsers support this method of providing a VPN.

C. Trusted VPN

All traffic on the VPN relies on the security of a provider's network to protect the network. Modern service providers offer many different solutions of trusted VPNs. These can generally be separated into "layer 2" and "layer 3" VPNs.

Trusted VPN technologies:

1. Technologies for trusted layer 2 VPNs include:
    - Asynchronous Transfer Mode (ATM) circuits
    - Frame relay circuits
    - Transport of layer 2 frames over MultiProtocol Label Switching (*MPLS*)
2. Technologies for trusted layer 3 VPNs include:
    - MultiProtocol Label Switching (*MPLS*) with constrained distribution of routing information through Border Gateway Protocol (BGP)

D. Hybrid VPN

Hybrid VPN technologies: A combination of both secure and trusted technologies or a combination of two VPN technologies.

---

[25] VPN Concentrators: A Must for Small Business -- Redmondmag.com. (n.d.). Retrieved December 21, 2014, from http://redmondmag.com/articles/2008/05/01/vpn-concentrators-a-must-for-small-business.aspx

[26] How to Create a VPN Server on Your Windows Computer Without Installing Any Software. (n.d.). Retrieved December 21, 2014, from http://www.howtogeek.com/135996/how-to-create-a-vpn-server-on-your-windows-computer-without-installing-any-software/

Common VPN types

1. *Site-to-site VPN*[27]

This type of VPN connects entire networks and facilitates secure data interchange between different sites. VPN gateways are used.

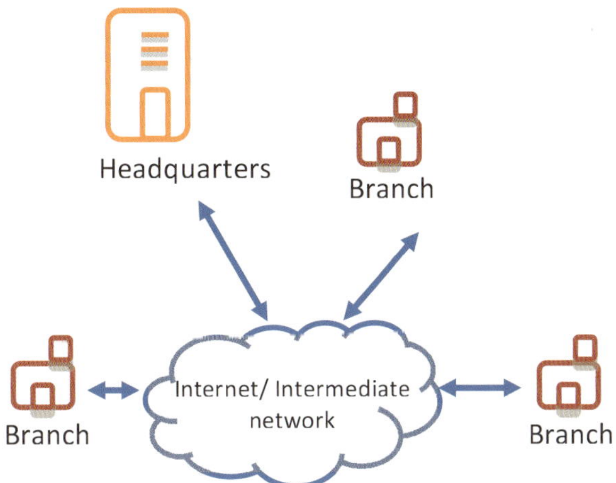

Figure 3.15 Site to site VPN

2. *Remote-access VPN*[26]

This type of VPN connects individual hosts to private networks and facilitates teleworkers who need to access their company's network securely using the Internet. Every host has VPN client software installed.

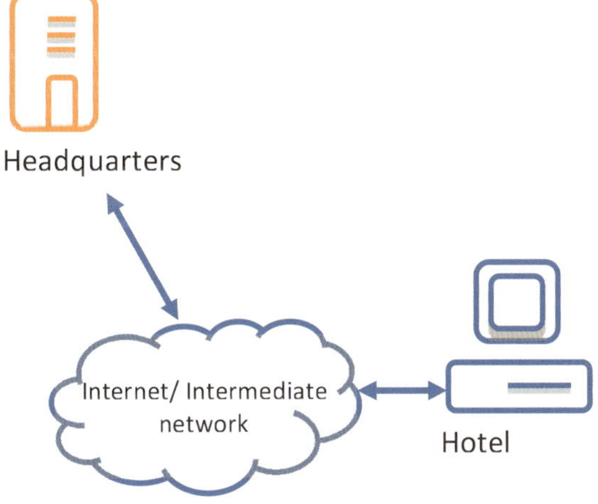

Figure 3.16 Remote access VPN

---

[27] What are the differences between a site-to-site VPN and a VPN client connecting to a VPN server? (n.d.). Retrieved December 21, 2014, from http://searchnetworking.techtarget.com/answer/What-are-the-differences-between-a-site-to-site-VPN-and-a-VPN-client-connecting-to-a-VPN-server-Wh

3.1.5 Use of a VPN

Exit skills. Students should be able to[1]:
List the benefits of VPN. Explain how the use of VPN has changed traditional working patterns.

VPN benefits:

1. Communication is easier
2. Companies take advantage of the Internet to provide secure connections
3. Decreases operational costs versus traditional Wide Area Networks
4. Employees work as if they were directly connected to the company's network
5. Extends connections across numerous geographic sites without the use of a leased line
6. Improves overall productivity
7. Improves productivity of remote employees
8. Improves security
9. Offers the flexibility to employees to take advantage of the company's Intranet over an existing Internet connection
10. Offers flexibility to remote offices
11. Offers global networking opportunities
12. Provides teleworker support
13. Reduces environmental footprint
14. Reduces travel times and traveling costs for remote users
15. Simplifies network topology for administrators and companies
16. Positive changes in working patterns

Example 3.9:

Question: Compare and contrast the similarities and differences between OSI and TCP/IP.

Answer:

Similarities	Differences
Both include a number of different layers.	The OSI has more layers than the TCP/IP.
They are used to describe network functionality.	OSI is a reference model while TCP/IP is a protocol model.

Example 3.10:

Question: What the acronyms OSI and TCP/IP stand for?

Answer:

OSI stands for Open Systems Interconnection and TCP/IP stands for Transfer Control Protocol / Internet Protocol

Example 3.11:

Question: State in which layer does IP belongs.

Answer: Network Layer

Example 3.12:

Question: Which from the layers listed below does not belong to the ISO-OSI model?

1. Security Layer
2. Physical Layer
3. Data Link Layer
4. Network Layer
5. Transport Layer

Answer: Security Layer

Example3.13:

Question: Discuss the differences between VPN and Intranet.

Answer: Although both can be found in modern business environments, they have significant operational and functional differences. VPN utilizes Internet to establish connections between distant offices or between teleworkers and their offices. A VPN connection uses encryption technologies to guarantee security. An Intranet is a network that makes use of Internet technologies to provide various services, access resources and share data. A VPN offers the advantages of a leased line without the extreme cost of a leased line. An Intranet serves a network of computers found in the same area while a VPN serves remote and distant connections. Intranet is a network while VPN is a method of connection that uses a public network.

Example 3.14:

Question: Discuss the main characteristics of cloud storage.

Answer: Cloud storage is provided by cloud storage providers such as Dropbox, Microsoft for OneDrive, Apple for iCloud, and Google for Google Drive. These providers use various servers, infrastructure and software to provide free or paid data storage to individuals and companies. All cloud storage providers have the responsibility for keeping the data available and accessible and maintain in the best possible way their infrastructure.

Data transmission

3.1.6 Protocol and data packet

Exit skills. Students should be able to[1]:
Define the terms protocol and data packet.

Defined in the introduction.

3.1.7 Necessity of protocols

Exit skills. Students should be able to[1]:
Define the terms: data integrity, source integrity, flow control, deadlock, congestion management, error correction and error checking. Explain the importance of network protocols.

Without predefined rules, communication would be impossible. The rules of communication are called *protocols*. Consider them as strict predefined rules.

Some of the protocols required for communication to take place include[28]:

1. The presence of an identified sender
2. The presence of an identified receiver
3. The presence of an agreed-upon method of communicating (email, IM, smartphone, gestures, face-to-face, telephone, fax, letter, photograph, etc.)
4. The presence of a common language
5. The presence of a common grammar
6. The presence of an agreed-upon speed and timing of delivery ("**Slow Down, You're Talking Too Fast!**")
7. The presence of confirmation or acknowledgment requirements (for example, "Does that make sense?" "No, please explain!")

Computer Network Protocols also provide:

1. Rules about the message format
2. Rules about the way intermediary devices should facilitate communication
3. Rules about initiation and termination of a communication session
4. Rules about the type of error checking to be used
5. Rules about the data compression methods and algorithms (if compression takes place)
6. Rules about an error detection and correction mechanism
7. Rules about recovery and resending of data

Computer Network Protocols also guarantee:

Data integrity. This means that the information has not been changed / corrupted deliberately or accidentally during transmission, from source to destination. Checksum mechanisms provide data integrity.

[28] Adapted by: (n.d.). Retrieved December 21, 2014, from http://www.netakademija.rs/pdf/ccna r&s/01.Introduction to Networks/ ITN_instructorPPT_Chapter3_final.pdf

Source integrity. It means that the identity of the sender has been validated. Digital signatures prove source integrity.

Flow Control. Network infrastructures have limited memory and bandwidth. The transport layer is responsible for taking advantage of its protocols and facing situations where an overload of resources occurs. These protocols can request from a sending application to slow down data flow rate. The transport layer controls the reliability of a given link through flow control.

Congestion management. Congestion happens when the request on the network resources exceeds the offered capacity.

Deadlock[29] prevention. Deadlock is a situation in which two or more network competing actions are each waiting for the other to finish, and thus neither ever does. The *persistence timer* is used to resolve the situation.

Error checking. A process to determine the error.

Error correction. The ability to repair the error.

3.1.8 Speed of data transmission across a network.

Exit skills. Students should be able to[1]:
Define the terms: bandwidth, throughput, goodput and bottleneck. **Describe why the speed of data transmission across a computer network is not stable.** **List the factors that affect speed of data transmission.**

It is important to mention that different media support different transfer speeds. The main unit that we use to measure data transfer is bps (bits per second). Nowadays improvements in network technologies have increased transfer speed and so it is more convenient to use kilobits (kbps) or megabits (millions of bits per second (Mbps)).

The theoretical speed of data in a medium is called *bandwidth* and it depends on the signalling technique used and the physical properties of the medium. The actual transfer rate is called *throughput* and it is affected by various factors such as interference, traffic, the number of connected devices and errors (throughput < bandwidth). In a network with many segments the slowest segment creates a *bottleneck* that affects the throughput of the network. In this case throughput is only as fast as the slowest link of the path from source to endpoint. *Goodput* measures the transfer rate of usable data (goodput < throughput).

Factors that affect speed of data transmission[30]

1. Bandwidth of the network
2. Data transfer rate of storage devices
3. Interferences

---

[29] (n.d.). Retrieved December 21, 2014, from http://medusa.sdsu.edu/network/CS576/Lectures/ch12_TCP.pdf

[30] Digital Imaging Tutorial - Delivery. (n.d.). Retrieved December 21, 2014, from https://www.library.cornell.edu/preservation/tutorial/technical/technicalD-04.html

4. Malicious software
5. Number of connected devices
6. Number of users' and users demand at any particular time (traffic)
7. Packet loss and retransmission
8. Read speed of storage devices
9. Slowest segment
10. Speed, technology and capacity of the network server
11. Time required for user authentication and various security checks that take place
12. Type of files send
13. Type of transmission medium
14. User's PC CPU speed
15. User's PC RAM/disk caching
16. User's PC various subsystem performance

3.1.9 Compression of data

Exit skills. Students should be able to[1]:
Define the terms: data compression, lossy data compression and lossless data compression. **Explain the importance of data compression during transmission over a network.** **List some file formats that use data compression.**

All networks have a limited bandwidth. Data compression reduces the size of files to be transmitted over a network. A compressed file takes up less bandwidth. When we reduce the size of a file, the time required to send this file over a network is also reduced. Data *compression* (a.k.a. bit-rate reduction) is the reduction of bits by encoding data using fewer bits than the original representation. File compression is commonly used when sending a file from one computer to another. It makes the file smaller and the transfer faster with no data loss. The receiver must have a program that will decompress the file.

There are two types of data compression:

- *Lossy data compression*: With this compression method, some loss of information is acceptable and there is no way to get the original file back. Examples: JPEG, MPEG2.
- *Lossless data compression*: this compression method reduces the number of bits by first identifying and then eliminating any statistical redundancy. There is no loss of information during lossless compression. Examples: compression- decompression software.

Graphics, sound, music and video formats that use compression algorithms to decrease the size of the original file have become ubiquitous on the Internet. The following are examples of such formats:

- The Graphics Interchange Format (GIF) is a graphic file format that is used extensively on the Web and uses a form of lossless compression algorithm (if we are dealing with a graphic file that has fewer than 256 colours).

- Mp3 is an audio coding format that uses a form of lossy data compression. Almost all music now comes in mp3 format and this format dominates the Internet.
- MPEG-2 combines lossy audio data compression and lossy video data compression methods and is used in the transmission of video over the Internet (e.g. movies).

3.1.10 Characteristics of different transmission media[31]

Exit skills. Students should be able to[1]:
Describe the characteristics and use of metal conductors, fiber optic cables and wireless transmission. Discuss the speed, reliability, cost and security of metal conductors, fiber optic cables and wireless transmission.

Image 3.6: Wired media

1. **Wired communication**

- *Copper Cable* (metal conductors): Copper cable is the most common kind of cabling in computer networks.
- *Coaxial Cable*: It consists of two copper conductors. It was used in computer networks, as well as to carry TV signals. Low cost of installation.
- *Unshielded Twisted Pair Cable (UTP)*: Very popular in LANs. Easy to install. Prone to electrical interference. Low cost of installation. Good for short distances between repeaters. Used in telephone networks. Very secure.
- *Shielded Twisted Pair Cable*: More difficult to install than UTP.

Reduced interference.

- *Fiber Optic Cable*: Optical fiber carries a beam of light. Very expensive. Offers higher speeds. Needs fewer repeaters. Extremely secure. It is used for data transmission and telephone lines.

Image 3.7: RFID

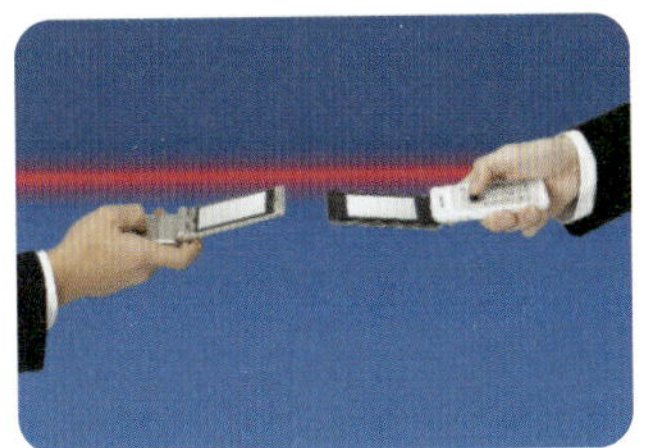

Image 3.8: Infrared connection

2. **Wireless communication**

- *Microwave Radio*: Used extensively for mobile telephone networks and LANs. Information is carried through air. Microwave signals offer high bandwidth (but lower than cables). For optimum results no buildings and other structures should be between the transmitter and the receiver. Weather conditions affect the performance. Difficult to guarantee reliability. Less secure than wired communication.
- *Satellites*: Use microwave signals.

[31] Traditional Transmission Media for Networking and Telecommunications. (n.d.). Retrieved December 21, 2014, from http://www.informit.com/articles/article.aspx?p=683070

- Infrared: Used only for very short distances. Infrared transmission cannot pass through objects and it is directional. A line of sight is required. Advanced security.
- *RFID*: Uses various radio technologies. Active RFID needs internal power. Passive RFID needs no internal power source.
- *Bluetooth*: Bluetooth devices use microwave radio to exchange data. They transmit at very low power levels. Their frequencies change regularly.
- *Free Space Optics*: Use of lasers for wireless computer communication.

Transmission media	Characteristics (scale worst:1- best:3)			
	speed	reliability	cost	security
metal conductor	2	2	2	2
fiber optic	3	3	3	3
wireless	1	1	1	1

Table 3.4: Transmission media characteristics

3.1.11 Packet switching

Exit skills. Students should be able to[1]:

Define the term data packet
Describe the packet switching communication method.

Useful Information: It is important to mention that there are three kinds of switching: circuit switching, packet switching and message switching.

Data packet is a unit of information in a form suitable to travel between computers.

In a packet switching network the *datagram* is the basic transfer unit and sometimes is used instead of the term data packet. The analysis of differences between data packets and datagrams is beyond the scope of this book.

Packet switching refers to a communication method used in computer networks (digital) in which data are grouped into packets. The original file is divided into packets before transmission and each packet may follow a different path to the destination. Each packet is sent individually, possibly reaching the destination via different routes. With packet switching the communication channel can be used more efficiently and delays are minimized. Packet switching can be distinguished in:

1. **Datagram Packet Switching:** with this method, each packet contains the receiver address. The path that datagrams take between the same source and destination can be different.
2. **Virtual Circuit Packet Switching:** with this method, a route from source to destination is set up before any transmission takes place.

3.1 (Additional Section) Network topologies

Exit skills. Students should be able to[1]:

Describe the characteristics and use of metal conductors, fiber optic cables and wireless transmission.
Discuss the speed, reliability, cost and security of metal conductors, fiber optic cables and wireless transmission.

There are eight basic topologies: point-to-point, bus, star, ring, mesh, tree, fully connected and hybrid.

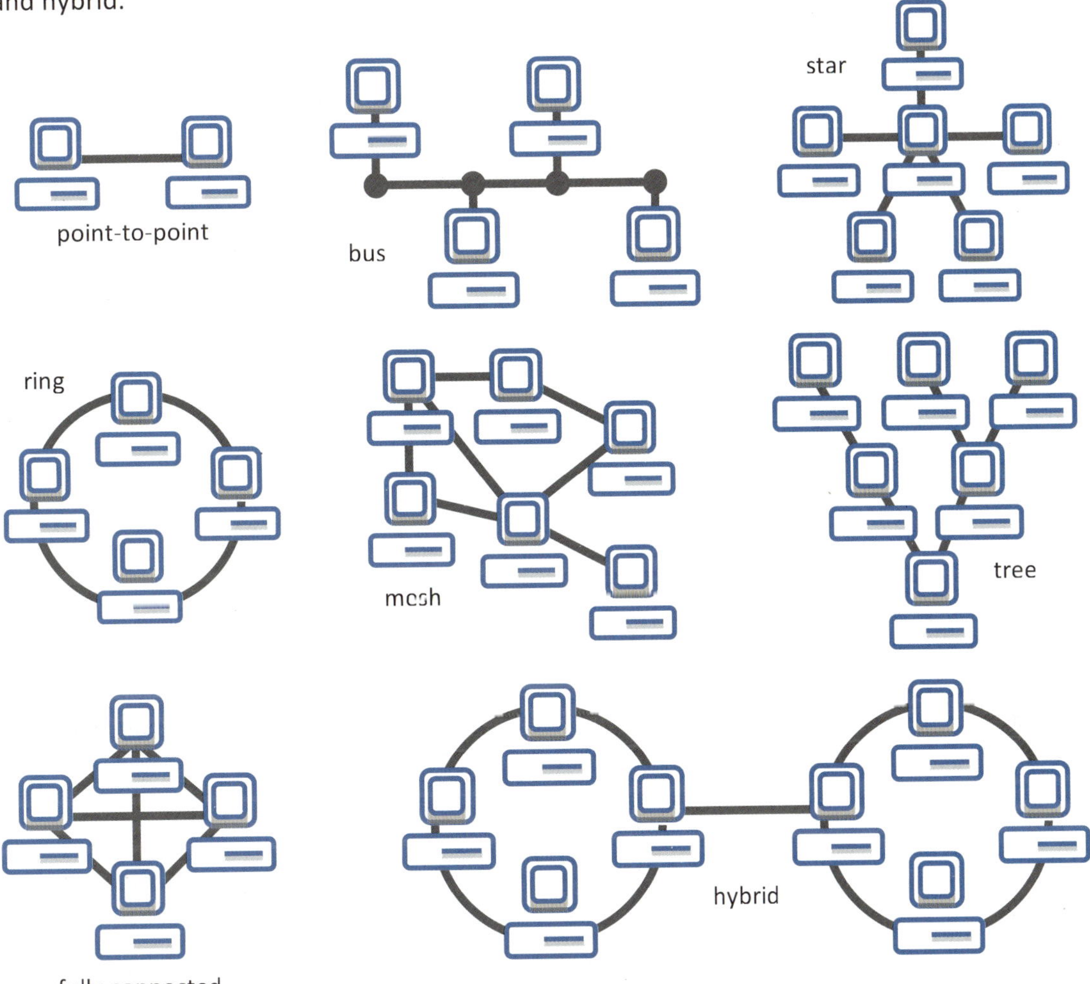

Figure 3.17: Network topologies

Example 3.15:

Question: what is star network topology?

Answer: A star network consists of one central node (computer or hub), to which all other nodes (computers) are connected.

Wireless networking

All wireless devices communicate and exchange data through radio transmissions, without any physical connection or cabling. Wireless systems and devices include cell phones, cordless computer keyboards, local area networks, mouse devices, personal networks, remote controls, wireless headphones, wireless hi-fi stereo headsets, wireless microphones, etc.

Useful Information: Nowadays laptops, smartphones and tablets are equipped with various network adapters and cards that facilitate the integration between Wi-Fi and Mobile Phone Networks.

3.1.12 Advantages and disadvantages of wireless networks

Exit skills. Students should be able to[1]:
Describe advantages and disadvantages of wireless networks and communication. Describe how wireless networks have led to significant changes in working and studying patterns. Describe health concerns that relate to the extensive use of wireless networks. Describe how wireless networks affect social activities.

The extensive use of wireless and mobile devices and networks has raised various concerns:

- **What are the long term health effects of extensive use of mobile phones and Wi-Fi networks? This is a health issue.**

According to World Health Organization (2014)[32]:

Short-term effects:

"To date, research does not suggest any consistent evidence of adverse health effects from exposure to radiofrequency fields at levels below those that cause tissue heating. Further, research has not been able to provide support for a causal relationship between exposure to electromagnetic fields and self-reported symptoms, or "electromagnetic hypersensitivity"."

Long-term effects:

"While an increased risk of brain tumors is not established, the increasing use of mobile

Useful Information: In a recent interview Dr Olle Johansson at the Department of Neuroscience, Karolinska Institute, spoke about exposure to electromagnetic waves from mobile phones causing learning cognitive difficulties in children: https://www.youtube.com/watch?v=bXCCvoiWt0g.

[32] Copied by: WHO, 2014, Electromagnetic fields and public health: Mobile phones. (n.d.). Retrieved December 21, 2014, from http://www.who.int/mediacentre/factsheets/fs193/en/

phones and the *lack of data for mobile phone use over time periods longer than 15 years warrant further research of mobile phone use and brain cancer risk.* In particular, with the recent popularity of mobile phone use among younger people, and therefore a potentially longer lifetime of exposure, World Health Organization (WHO) has promoted further research on this group. Several studies investigating potential health effects in children and adolescents are underway."

- **How many car accidents happen every day due to misuse of mobile phones? This is a social issue.**

According to National Safety Council (2014)[33] report (NSC releases latest injury and fatality statistics and trends) "the use of cellphones causes 26% of all motor vehicle crashes" and "only 5% of cellphone-related crashes involve texting while the majority of the accidents involve drivers talking on handheld or hands-free cell phones."

Image 3.9: Misuse of mobile phones

- **What happens with all these devices when improperly disposed? This is an environmental issue.**

A study reported that the number of active mobile phones will reach 7.3 billion by 2014.[34] Cell phones, tablets, laptops and Wi-Fi devices contain hazardous materials including, mercury and lead. The improper disposal of these materials harms the environment, humans and wildlife. All electronic devices should be recycled and never buried in landfills or burned.[35]

- **Is there a change in working patterns due to wireless technology? This is a social issue.**

A study conducted at MIT (2005)[36] ten years ago indicated that the use of MIT WLANs changed the way students worked and studied. This study indicated that "factors like comfort, convenience, spatial qualities, presence of other people, presence of food etc.

---

[33] Copied by: NSC (2014, March 25). News release. Retrieved December 21, 2014, http://www.nsc.org/NewsDocuments/2014-Press-Release-Archive/3-25-2014-Injury-Facts-release.pdf

[34] Number of mobile phones to exceed world population by 2014. (2013, February 28). Retrieved December 21, 2014, from http://www.digitaltrends.com/mobile/mobile-phone-world-population-2014/

[35] Disclaimer. (n.d.). Retrieved December 21, 2014, from http://www.dec.ny.gov/chemical/8818.html

[36] Copied by: Sevtsuk, A and C. Ratti, 2005, iSPOTS. How Wireless Technology is Changing Life on the MIT Campus. Retrieved December 21, 2014, from http://senseable.mit.edu/papers/pdf/SevtsukRatti2005CUPUM.pdf

Example 3.16: State the advantages and disadvantages of wireless networks.

Advantages	Disadvantages
Installing a cable can often be difficult.	Wireless communication gives relatively low speed.
Installing a cable can often be expensive.	Wireless communication gives high error rates.
Easy to set up a temporary link.	Wireless communication is affected by weather.
Wireless communication is truly wireless. No cables are needed.	Wireless communication offers weakest protection, security, privacy.
It costs less to set up a wireless network.	Wireless networks are less reliable.
Easier to plan a wireless network.	Health concerns.
A lot of public access points exist.	Some old devices don't have wireless connection capability.
It is the only way to connect some devices (tablets, smartphones).	
Flexibility/convenience.	

affected the way laptops were used." The following paragraph copied from this study gives a clear picture of the current trends: "According to graduate resident tutors at the new Simmons Hall dormitory, designed by Steven Hall, most undergraduates spend long evening hours in comfortable lounge spaces, where they can socialize with other students, while working on their laptop computers. Simultaneous physical communication and Internet communication through e-mails, instant messengers, chat forums and videoconferences have become commonplace for most students. The notorious amount of problem sets and homework demanded from MIT students is often facilitated by consulting and checking answers with fellow students through Instant Messengers over the Internet and many homework assignments can be turned in on-line." Similar trends take place in modern software companies like Google, Microsoft etc.

3.1.13 Hardware and software components of a wireless network

Exit skills. Students should be able to[1]:
Describe and explain the hardware and software components needed to set up and run a wireless network.

Hardware devices needed:

- A ***modem*** allows you to connect to the Internet.
- **A wireless router serves a similar function to traditional routers in wired networks.** In most cases it also provides the functions of a Wireless Access Point (used to connect to an existing wired network). A *Wireless Access Point (WAP)* allows

Useful Information: In most cases we buy a single device that integrates a modem, a switch and a router into a single box. This allows the creation of both a wired and a wireless network, as well as a connection of that network to other networks, such as the Internet (a firewall is provided as software or as an integrated hardware component).

wireless data transfer between a device and a network. A router normally has some LAN jacks for other wired devices.

- A ***wireless network adapter*** also known as wireless *NIC (Wireless Network Interface Controller or Wireless Network Interface Card)* is required for each device on a wireless network.
- A **device that has the ability to connect to the wireless network** such as a PC, laptop, sensor, smart phone, printer, game console, tablet, etc.
- ***Wireless antennas.*** Access points and routers frequently utilize Wi-Fi antennas that significantly increase the effective communication area of the wireless network. These antennas are fixed, optional or removable.
- ***A wireless repeater*** (signal boosters or range expanders) connects to a router or access point. Their purpose is to receive an existing signal from a wireless router or access point and to rebroadcast it.
- **Ethernet to Wireless Access Point or Ethernet to wireless repeater**. It uses Ethernet cables to carry the signal to the wireless repeater or WAP.
- **Ethernet over power line to wireless repeater or WAP**. It uses power lines to carry the signal to the wireless repeater or WAP.

Figure 3.18: A WLAN

Software needed:

- ***DHCP***[37]: Dynamic Host Configuration Protocol (DHCP) is a network protocol that allows a server to automatically assign an IP address to a client device. It is very efficient and convenient to let the router automatically assign IP addresses to devices. This client operates in the client-server model, which is widely used in many networks, including local ones. It is important to mention that when a wireless device enters the wireless network it may be able to acquire an IP address from the router. The alternative would be to disable the DHCP functionality and configure each one of the wireless network devices with a static IP address.

- ***Software Firewall***: A network security system that determines what data comes in and goes out of a network or a PC.

- ***Name/SSID***: A service set identification (SSID) is a set of 32 alphanumeric characters. It is used to differentiate one WLAN from another and is case sensitive.

- ***NIC drivers***: A Network Interface Card driver is a device driver for the NIC card. A Network Interface Card driver operates or controls the hardware of the card. It acts like a translator between the wireless card and the applications or operating system of the device.

- **OS:** The Operating System handles system resources and is responsible for managing all the protocols, hardware, and applications that have to cooperate in order that a network can exist and function correctly.

- ***Security Software***[38]: Security software includes all software that prevents unauthorized access, use, disclosure, disruption, modification, perusal, inspection, recording or destruction. It includes access control, firewall, anti-spyware, anti-subversion software, anti-tamper software, antivirus software, cryptographic software, anti-key loggers, intrusion detection system (IDS), intrusion prevention system (IPS) and sandbox.

- ***WAP***[39, 40]: Wireless Application Protocol specifies a set of protocols for accessing information over a mobile wireless network. It allows users to access the Internet, exchange e-mails, surf the web etc. It is used in radio transceivers and cellular phones. The WAP protocol supports most wireless networks and is supported by most operating systems. Most devices in Europe and the USA no longer need WAP

---

[37] Bradley, C. (n.d.). Don't Invite Strange Devices to Play on Your Network. Retrieved December 21, 2014, from http://netsecurity.about.com/od/quicktip1/qt/qtwifistaticip.htm

[38] Security software. (2015, March 24). In *Wikipedia, The Free Encyclopedia*. Retrieved 17:01, June 15, 2015, from https://en.wikipedia.org/w/index.php?title=Security_software&oldid=653304393

[39] Wireless Application Protocol. (2015, June 10). In *Wikipedia, The Free Encyclopedia*. Retrieved 17:04, June 15, 2015, from https://en.wikipedia.org/w/index.php?title=Wireless_Application_Protocol&oldid=666351127

[40] WAP - Wireless Application Protocol. (n.d.). Retrieved December 21, 2014, from http://www.webopedia.com/TERM/W/WAP.html

and its use has almost disappeared. Modern browser approaches for mobile devices support HTML and don't need to use WAP to achieve webpage compatibility.

- ***WEB-BROWSER*:** A Web browser is an application software that is used to find, retrieve and display content on the WWW, including web pages, text, images, audio, videos and other content. Most browsers have functions like "favorites", "history", "search a web page" etc.

Example 3.17: Compare and contrast the similarities and differences between OS and Network OS (NOS).

Answer:

Similarities	Differences
They both manage a system's resources.	A network operating system is more expensive to obtain, install and maintain.
They both manage access and permissions on a system.	A NOS is installed on network servers.
They are both system software.	A NOS can also be found in a router or a hardware firewall.
	A NOS has the ability to manage multiple users, security policies and other functions of a network.

Example 3.18: Compare and contrast the similarities and differences between software and hardware firewall.

Answer:

Similarities	Differences
They both control the data flow.	A hardware firewall is used to protect many devices.
They serve the same purpose.	A hardware firewall is more expensive.

3.1.14 Characteristics of wireless networks.

Exit skills. Students should be able to[1]:
Describe and explain the characteristics of WiFi networks. Describe and explain the characteristics of WiMax networks. Describe and explain the characteristics of 3G, 4G and 5G mobile networks. Describe and explain the characteristics of LTE.

Bit rates		
kilobit per second	kbit/s	10^3
megabit per second	Mbit/s	10^6
gigabit per second	Gbit/s	10^9
terabit per second	Tbit/s	10^{12}

Table 3.5: Bit rates

- ***1G, 2G*:** The first generation of mobile technology (1G/year 1981) used analog transmission, and in 1992 2G appeared and used digital exchange.

- ***3G*[41,42]:** 3G is the third generation of mobile networking and telecommunications technology. 3G is widely used in wireless telephony, GPS and location based services, mobile internet access, video calls and mobile TV. It is based on standards used for mobile devices and mobile telecommunications. It can provide a data transfer rate of 200 kbit/s. 3G networks are more secure than 2G networks. There is a significant difference between Wi-Fi (IEEE 802.11 technology) and 3G. The first one is a short range wireless network that offers high-bandwidth designed for data transfer while the second focuses on cellular telephones and Internet access.

Example 3.19: Compare and contrast the similarities and differences between 1G and 4G.

Answer:

Similarities	Differences
Both are mobile wireless networks	4G is a lot faster than 1G
	1G is an analog telecommunication standard while 4G is a digital telecommunication standard
	4G offers greater telecommunication capabilities and the ability to exchange multimedia

- ***4G*[43]:** 4G mobile is the fourth generation of mobile telecommunications technology that was released after 3G. It is used for mobile Internet access to laptops, smartphones and other devices. The speed requirement for 4G services is at 100 Mbit/s for various forms of high mobility communication such as use from trains, buses and cars, and 1 Gbit/s for low mobility communication that serves walking and static persons. It doesn't support traditional circuit-switched telephony service (2G and 3G did) but only IP-based communication like IP telephony.

- ***LTE*[44, 45]:** LTE (*Long Term Evolution*) is a 4G network, as well as a standard for wireless communication of high-speed data for

[41] 3G. (2015, May 19). In *Wikipedia, The Free Encyclopedia*. Retrieved 17:06, June 15, 2015, from https://en.wikipedia.org/w/index.php?title=3G&oldid=663146953

[42] What is a 3G Network? (n.d.). Retrieved December 21, 2014, from http://www.wisegeek.org/what-is-a-3g-network.htm

[43] 4G. (2015, June 1). In *Wikipedia, The Free Encyclopedia*. Retrieved 17:09, June 15, 2015, from https://en.wikipedia.org/w/index.php?title=4G&oldid=665002346

[44] LTE (telecommunication). (2015, June 12). In *Wikipedia, The Free Encyclopedia*. Retrieved 17:08, June 15, 2015, from https://en.wikipedia.org/w/index.php?title=LTE_(telecommunication)&oldid=666645572

smartphones and mobile data terminals. Its goal is to be fast and to have a large capacity. Its highest download rates are as high as 300 Mbit/s and upload rates 75 Mbit/s. 4G LTE has evolved to LTE Advanced that provides even more data capacity.

- ***WiMAX***[44, 46, 47, 48]: WiMAX (*Worldwide Interoperability for Microwave Access*), is a 4G network originally designed as an alternative to DSL Cable and T1 lines. It is a wireless communications standard intended to provide 30 to 40 mbps data rates for a great number of users. Recently WiMAX 2.0 was released, promising data transfer rates of 1 Gbit/s for fixed devices, and 100 Mbit/s for various mobile devices. WiMax is intended to serve long-range networking (spanning kilometers) as opposed to WLANs. WiMAX is used to provide portable mobile broadband connectivity across cities or even countries through many devices. Its setup has a low cost in comparison with 3G, because the provider does not need to run cables. It provides a line-of-sight connection service which offers more stable connection than the non-line of sight WiFi service which service most users. The most important application of WiMax is that it allows connectivity even in remote and isolated areas where there is no WiFi, dial-up or broadband access. WiMAX poses a great threat to providers of DSL and cable-modem services.

Image 3.10: WiMAX

- ***5G***[49]: 5G is the fifth generation of technology for mobile telecommunication. It is also known as *Tactile Internet*. It has not been made publically available. Samsung has announced that its goal for 2020 is to deliver 5G at 1Gbps. Various analysts estimate that by 2020, 50 billion to 100 billion devices will be connected to the internet, many of which will be every day-devices that now are not network-enabled.

---

[45] WiMAX vs LTE – What is a better 4G technology. (2014, March 4). Retrieved December 21, 2014, from http://thebestwirelessinternet.com/wimax-vs-lte.html

[46] WiMAX. (2015, June 12). In *Wikipedia, The Free Encyclopedia*. Retrieved 17:11, June 15, 2015, from https://en.wikipedia.org/w/index.php?title=WiMAX&oldid=666576611

[47] Mitchell, B. (n.d.). What Is WiMAX Broadband Wireless Networking? Retrieved December 21, 2014, from http://compnetworking.about.com/od/wirelessinternet/g/bldef_wimax.htm

[48] WiMAX Wireless Network - HowStuffWorks. (n.d.). Retrieved December 21, 2014, from http://computer.howstuffworks.com/wimax1.htm

[49] 5G. (2015, June 3). In *Wikipedia, The Free Encyclopedia*. Retrieved 17:12, June 15, 2015, from https://en.wikipedia.org/w/index.php?title=5G&oldid=665329464

- ***Sensor networks***[50], can be used to measure data and parameters, such as temperature, sound, pressure etc. for physical or environmental reasons such as environmental sampling, security and surveillance, health-care monitoring of critical patients, underwater measurements etc. Sensors are placed at fixed locations and are linked by a wireless network to perform distributed sensing tasks. Most modern networks also enable control of the activity of the sensors. Wireless communication enables processing of events at the node, local neighbourhood, and global levels. A wireless sensor network requires multiple nodes to communicate and ensure appropriate coordination and cooperation.

- **WiMAX versus LTE**
    1. WiMAX and LTE are both considered 4G technologies and are both all IP technologies.
    2. They use different channels.
    3. It is important to mention that LTE is compatible with 2G and 3G systems while WiMAX network doesn't support these "legacy" systems.
    4. Building a LTE network is more expensive than the cost of building a WiMAX network.
    5. LTE allows much greater speed for mobile users. LTE-A is the only true 4G technology (according to the 4G specifications).
    6. The WiMAX isn't as popular and LTE is much more widespread.
    7. WiMAX is considered a better choice for low-cost network installation in developing countries.

Image 3.11: various 4G services

[50] Wireless sensor network. (n.d.). Retrieved December 21, 2014, from http://en.wikipedia.org/wiki/Wireless_sensor_network

3.1.15 Different methods of network security[51]

Exit skills. Students should be able to[1]:
Define the terms symmetric key encryption, public key encryption and trusted media access control (MAC) addresses. Explain the use of symmetric key encryption, public key encryption and trusted media access control (MAC) addresses. Describe the different methods that can be used to increase security of the user's data.

As wireless technology improves, innovative devices are being developed to provide advanced functionality, portability, ease of use, smarter features and complex functions. Wireless networks, tablets, laptops, smart-phones and PDAs provide services such as web access, voice, email, text messaging (SMS), multimedia messaging (MMS), paging, GPS, navigation, and voice recognition services. Wireless networks, devices and services are more vulnerable than conventional wired networks. Intruders, hackers and unauthorized users can:

- disable operations
- disturb the privacy of legitimate users
- gain unauthorized access
- insert viruses or malicious code
- launch denial of service attacks
- steal identities
- steal devices and
- steal sensitive information that is stored or transmitted

Encryption[52, 53]

Encryption is absolutely necessary to protect data from unauthorized access during Internet use or any other untrusted network. The process of encryption uses complex mathematical algorithms and encryption keys to alter a message into a form that is not understandable to an unauthorized person. Only the person with the correct key can decode the message and read it. There are two computer encryption categories:

- ***Symmetric-key encryption****, single key encryption or secret key encryption*. The same key is used for encryption and decryption. In this encryption method each device has a secret code that is used to encrypt a packet before it is sent over an untrusted network. The receiving device should know and use the same key to decode the packet received. A well-known symmetric algorithm developed for computers was

---

[51] NETGEAR Support | Answer | Introduction to Wireless Security. (n.d.). Retrieved December 21, 2014, from http://kb.netgear.fr/app/answers/detail/a_id/20049/~/introduction-to-wireless-security
[52] (n.d.). Retrieved December 27, 2014, from https://www.cs.utexas.edu/~byoung/cs361/lecture44.pdf
[53] An Overview of Cryptography. (n.d.). Retrieved December 27, 2014, from http://www.garykessler.net/library/crypto.html

the Data Encryption Standard (DES), which uses a 56-bit key. Although 72,057,594,037,927,936 possible combinations might seem enough, a *brute force* attack of from modern computer can crack the code and reveal the original message. Advanced Encryption Standard (AES), which uses 128 to 256-bit keys offers:

3.4028236692093846346337460743177e+38 to
1.1579208923731619542357098500869e+77 key combinations.

- ***Public-key encryption*** *or asymmetric key encryption*. This uses a public key for encryption and a private key for decryption. These two keys are mathematically linked. This type of encryption is used on the Internet. Transport Layer Security (TLS) and Secure Socket Layer (SSL) encryption protocols, used for secure web communication, are based on public key encryption.

Method	Advantages of method	Disadvantages of method
Public-key encryption	The two sides don't need to have already shared their secret key in order to communicate using encryption.	Messages take more time to encrypt and decrypt. The authenticity of the public key needs to be verified.
Symmetric-Key encryption	Encryption speed is faster than with public-key encryption. Uses less computer resources.	Keys must be shared before they can be used. If the key becomes known by unauthorized individuals then another key must be used.

Table 3.6: Methods of network security

Free access

- **No security:** Wireless data transmission extends beyond walls and window screens. In many cases when you buy a wireless router or an access point, its security features are not enabled. Some public authorities provide free access to their Wi-Fi but this is not normally the case for the average user. When you set up a wireless network you may not want to provide open and free Internet access to your neighbours. So you have to enable some security features.

Methods of network security

- **Use a password to access your device.** Remember, weak passwords are easy to crack. Choose a password with at least eight characters, a combination of numbers, upper and lower case letters, and other keyboard symbols.
- **Install an antivirus program on your device** to prevent, detect and remove malicious software.
- **Use a software firewall installed on each device** that will help keep intruders, hackers and malicious software from getting into your devices.

- **Use a password to access the web interface that is used to setup your wireless routers or access points.**
- **Turn On/ Off Wireless Connectivity.** It is very important to mention that many commercial models of router have a button that enables or disables the wireless connection. This is a very good option if you don't need wireless access.
- **Enable/Disable SSID Broadcast.** A wireless router or an access point broadcasts its wireless network name (SSID). All wireless devices in range can identify it. By disabling this broadcast, devices in range will not be able to find the wireless network unless a user enters the correct SSID manually. Some users think that this provides a security measure against unauthorized access. This is a common mistake, because an intruder can easily detect hidden wireless networks and "sniffer" tools can even discover the SSID.
- **Block access to wireless devices by *MAC address***: Mac stands for *Medium Access Control*, follows MAC protocol and is a sub-layer of the data link layer. Every Network Interface Card (NIC) has a unique MAC address given when it is manufactured. A MAC address is a string of 12 digits/characters, with a size of 48-bit (e.g. in the hex format: *00:40:96:9d:68:16*). Network security can be enhanced by permitting access to only specific trusted wireless devices, based on their MAC addresses. An untrusted device would not be able to connect to the wireless network. MAC address limitation increases the wireless network protection but, it can be very difficult to maintain an up-to-date list of allowed MAC addresses.

Useful Information: All security protocols require a password (key) and the use of encryption algorithms. Any wireless network is vulnerable without the use of an encryption method. All encryption methods and techniques follow certain security protocols.

- ***WEP Wireless Security***: The most common data encryption techniques that have been designed for the 802.11 is the WEP. WEP is a Wireless Encryption Protocol. WEP stands for *Wired Equivalent Privacy*. It was introduced in 1999 to provide data confidentiality and usually provides 40/64bit and 128bit encryption key lengths. WEP adds processing overheads that slow down the wireless connection. WEP *cracking* is possible but novice users are not able to hack it. A key advantage is that it offers interoperability with older devices (access to a legacy wireless device).
- ***WPA, WPA2 Wireless Security***: WEP was superseded by *Wi-Fi Protected Access* (WPA) which was adopted in 2003 by the Wi-Fi Alliance as an interim security measure while the WPA2 wireless security standard was developed. WPA2 was finally approved in June 2004. It uses an Advanced Encryption Standard (AES) block cipher and is now available in a broad range of wireless devices. It is considered the best protection but, the administrator should still use a strong password.
- ***Wireless Protected Setup (WPS)*** sometimes referred as *Quick Security Setup (QSS)*: This protocol is specially designed to allow novice and residential users to securely operate their wireless network. Wireless Protected Setup requires a WPS router and

WPS compatible devices. WPS has known security weaknesses and it is strongly recommended to disable WPS if you are not using it.

WPS methods

a. PIN. A personal identification number (PIN) should be entered in the device that we wish to connect in the network. This must be read from:
    i. a sticker attached on the wireless router or access point or
    ii. a GUI application that helps the setup process.
b. Push button. The user pushes a WPS button on both devices (wireless router or access point and the client device).
c. *Near field communication (NFC)* method. The new device should be close to the access point/router.
d. USB transfer method to transfer data between wireless router or access point and the client device.

- **Prevent physical access:** It is possible for a building to be shielded from electromagnetic interference. Directional antennas can be used to restrict the spread of the signal. Both methods offer great protection but the cost is extreme. In wired networks this process is extremely simple.
- **Use router hardware firewall:** It is very important to mention that the built-in router firewall is the first line of defence that prevents hackers on the Internet from getting access to your device. It protects your connection and is able to block incoming traffic. It can also be used to control or limit the user's own access to the Internet. Most firewall systems can't stop people in range of your Wi-Fi from getting onto your Wi-Fi network.
- **Use encryption software for sensitive information sent over the Internet e.g. attached files sent with email.**

3.1.16 Advantages and disadvantages of each method of network security[54]

Exit skills. Students should be able to[1]:
Evaluate different methods of network security Describe the pros and cons of each method of network security

Each method has advantages and disadvantages. The perfect security method simply does not exist.

	Advantages	Disadvantages
No security	High speeds.	Anyone can access the network.
Use a password to access your device.	Easy to use. It will prevent unauthorized access.	Takes some time to enter the user name and password. If it is weak then it is easy to crack.

[54] Wireless Networking Security. (n.d.). Retrieved December 21, 2014, from http://technet.microsoft.com/en-us/library/bb457019.aspx

Install an antivirus program on your device	Very good protection from malicious software.	May slow down your device.
Use a software firewall installed on each device	It will monitor and control the traffic flow between your computer and the network and prevent unauthorized access to your device.	May slow down your device.
Use a password to access the web interface that is used to setup your wireless routers or access point	If a person has access to the LAN, uses a web browser and enters the IP address of the router, he/she will need a password to log into the web-based Utility page of the modem / router / access point.	Takes some time to enter the user name and password. If it is weak then it is easy to crack.
Turn On/ Off Wireless Connectivity	Complete security.	If the wireless is disabled then there is no wireless network.
Enable/Disable SSID Broadcast	Invisible to novice users.	Experienced attackers can easily find your SSID.
Limit access to wireless devices by MAC address	Extra security.	By sniffing the wireless transmissions, the allowed list of MAC addresses can be easily discovered. Difficult to manage the list.
WEP Wireless Security	Works with legacy systems.	Outdated.
WPA, WPA2 Wireless Security	The best option. Strong encryption.	
Wireless Protected Setup (WPS)	Ease of use. No need to know the SSID and security keys or passphrases.	New technology. Works only with WPS certified devices. Some known security issues.
Prevent physical access (wireless networks)	Limited to the interior of the user's premises.	Very expensive.
Use routers' hardware firewall	Prevents hackers and unauthorized persons on the Internet from getting access to your network.	Can't stop persons in range of your Wi-Fi from getting onto your Wi-Fi network.
Use encryption software for sensitive information sent over the internet	Extremely difficult for an unauthorized person to read your sensitive files.	This process takes some time.

Table 3.7: Advantages and disadvantages of network security methods

Example 3.20:

Example 3.20.a:

Laptops and computers are able to connect to wireless network. State five other devices that are able to connect to a wireless network.

Answer:

Game consoles, smartphones, TVs, printers, PDAs.

Example 3.20.b:

All these devices need a hardware component to connect to the wireless network. State the name of this component.

Answer:

Wireless network interface card.

Example 3.20.c:

State the name of the hardware component that is essential to set up a wireless network.

Answer:

Wireless router

Example 3.20.d:

State one reason to use WEP instead of WPA2.

Answer:

It offers interoperability with older devices (access to a legacy wireless device).

Example 3.20.e:

State why WPA2 is better than WEP.

Answer:

Because it uses an Advanced Encryption Standard (AES) block cipher that allows stronger encryption than WEP. So, it offers greater security.

Chapter References

1. International Baccalaureate Organization. (2012). IBDP Computer Science Guide.
2. Copied by: A quote by Aristotle. (n.d.). Retrieved December 21, 2014, from http://www.goodreads.com/quotes/183896-man-is-by-nature-a-social-animal-an-individual-who
3. International Baccalaureate Organization. (2004). IBDP Computer Science Guide.
4. Client/server (client/server model, client/server architecture). (n.d.). Retrieved December 23, 2014, from http://searchnetworking.techtarget.com/definition/client-server
5. How do hubs, switches, routers, and access points differ? - Windows Help. (n.d.). Retrieved December 23, 2014, from http://windows.microsoft.com/en-us/windows/hubs-switches-routers-access-points-differ#1TC=windows-7
6. Local area network. (2015, May 16). In *Wikipedia, The Free Encyclopedia*. Retrieved 16:43, June 15, 2015, from https://en.wikipedia.org/w/index.php?title=Local_area_network&oldid=662633873
7. Wireless LAN. (2015, June 14). In *Wikipedia, The Free Encyclopedia*. Retrieved 16:46, June 15, 2015, from https://en.wikipedia.org/w/index.php?title=Wireless_LAN&oldid=666879923
8. VLAN (Virtual Local Area Network). (n.d.). Retrieved December 23, 2014, from http://orbit-computer-solutions.com/VLAN-and-Trunking.php
9. Wide area network. (2015, May 20). In *Wikipedia, The Free Encyclopedia*. Retrieved 16:47, June 15, 2015, from https://en.wikipedia.org/w/index.php?title=Wide_area_network&oldid=663323837
10. Storage area network. (2015, May 20). In *Wikipedia, The Free Encyclopedia*. Retrieved 16:51, June 15, 2015, from https://en.wikipedia.org/w/index.php?title=Storage_area_network&oldid=663172345
11. Intranet. (2015, June 11). In *Wikipedia, The Free Encyclopedia*. Retrieved 16:52, June 15, 2015, from https://en.wikipedia.org/w/index.php?title=Intranet&oldid=666458905
12. Mitchell, B. (n.d.). Intranets and Extranets. Retrieved December 23, 2014, from http://compnetworking.about.com/od/filetransferprotocol
13. Virtual private network. (2015, June 11). In *Wikipedia, The Free Encyclopedia*. Retrieved 16:53, June 15, 2015, from https://en.wikipedia.org/w/index.php?title=Virtual_private_network&oldid=666500623
14. What is Piconet? - Definition from Techopedia. (n.d.). Retrieved December 23, 2014, from http://www.techopedia.com/definition/5081/piconet
15. Peer-to-peer. (2015, June 3). In *Wikipedia, The Free Encyclopedia*. Retrieved 16:56, June 15, 2015, from https://en.wikipedia.org/w/index.php?title=Peer-to-peer&oldid=665302579
16. 4 Understanding the Communication Layers. (n.d.). Retrieved December 23, 2014, from https://docs.oracle.com/cd/E18283_01/network.112/e10836/layers.htm
17. OSI reference model (Open Systems Interconnection). (n.d.). Retrieved December 23, 2014, from http://searchnetworking.techtarget.com/definition/OSI
18. The OSI Model: Understanding the Seven Layers of Computer Networks Expert Reference Series of White Papers Introduction. (n.d.). Retrieved December 21, 2014, from http://www.academia.edu/7212126/The_OSI_Model_Understanding_the_Seven_Layers_of_Computer_Networks_Expert_Reference_Series_of_White_Papers_Introduction
19. OSI reference model (Open Systems Interconnection). (n.d.). Retrieved December 23, 2014, from http://searchnetworking.techtarget.com/definition/OSI

20. Cisco. "How Virtual Private Networks Work." Retrieved December 21, 2014, from http://www.cisco.com/application/pdf/paws/14106/how_vpn_works.pdf
21. What you need to know about VPN technologies. (n.d.). Retrieved December 21, 2014, from http://www.computerworld.com/article/2546283/networking/what-you-need-to-know-about-vpn-technologies.html
22. Mitchell, B. (n.d.). Free VPN Client and Server Software Downloads. Retrieved December 21, 2014, from http://compnetworking.about.com/od/vpn/tp/vpnsoftwarefree.htm
23. Cisco RV180 VPN Router. (n.d.). Retrieved December 21, 2014, from http://www.cisco.com/c/en/us/products/routers/rv180-vpn-router/index.html
24. Barracuda Networks. (n.d.). Retrieved December 21, 2014, from https://www.barracuda.com/products/sslvpn
25. VPN Concentrators: A Must for Small Business -- Redmondmag.com. (n.d.). Retrieved December 21, 2014, from http://redmondmag.com/articles/2008/05/01/vpn-concentrators-a-must-for-small-business.aspx
26. How to Create a VPN Server on Your Windows Computer Without Installing Any Software. (n.d.). Retrieved December 21, 2014, from http://www.howtogeek.com/135996/how-to-create-a-vpn-server-on-your-windows-computer-without-installing-any-software/
27. What are the differences between a site-to-site VPN and a VPN client connecting to a VPN server? (n.d.). Retrieved December 21, 2014, from http://searchnetworking.techtarget.com/answer/What-are-the-differences-between-a-site-to-site-VPN-and-a-VPN-client-connecting-to-a-VPN-server-Wh
28. Adapted by: (n.d.). Retrieved December 21, 2014, from http://www.netakademija.rs/pdf/ccna r&s/01.Introduction to Networks/ ITN_instructorPPT_Chapter3_final.pdf
29. (n.d.). Retrieved December 21, 2014, from http://medusa.sdsu.edu/network/CS576/Lectures/ch12_TCP.pdf
30. Digital Imaging Tutorial - Delivery. (n.d.). Retrieved December 21, 2014, from https://www.library.cornell.edu/preservation/tutorial/technical/technicalD-04.html
31. Traditional Transmission Media for Networking and Telecommunications. (n.d.). Retrieved December 21, 2014, from http://www.informit.com/articles/article.aspx?p=683070
32. Copied by: WHO, 2014, Electromagnetic fields and public health: Mobile phones. (n.d.). Retrieved December 21, 2014, from http://www.who.int/mediacentre/factsheets/fs193/en/
33. Copied by: Kratsas, U. (2014, March 28). Cellphone use causes over 1 in 4 car accidents. Retrieved December 21, 2014, from http://www.usatoday.com/story/money/cars/2014/03/28/cellphone-use-1-in-4-car-crashes/7018505/
34. Number of mobile phones to exceed world population by 2014. (2013, February 28). Retrieved December 21, 2014, from http://www.digitaltrends.com/mobile/mobile-phone-world-population-2014/
35. Disclaimer. (n.d.). Retrieved December 21, 2014, from http://www.dec.ny.gov/chemical/8818.html
36. Copied by: Sevtsuk, A and C. Ratti, 2005, iSPOTS. How Wireless Technology is Changing Life on the MIT Campus. Retrieved December 21, 2014, from http://senseable.mit.edu/papers/pdf/SevtsukRatti2005CUPUM.pdf
37. Bradley, C. (n.d.). Don't Invite Strange Devices to Play on Your Network. Retrieved December 21, 2014, from http://netsecurity.about.com/od/quicktip1/qt/qtwifistaticip.htm

38. Security software. (2015, March 24). In *Wikipedia, The Free Encyclopedia*. Retrieved 17:01, June 15, 2015, from https://en.wikipedia.org/w/index.php?title=Security_software&oldid=653304393

39. Wireless Application Protocol. (2015, June 10). In *Wikipedia, The Free Encyclopedia*. Retrieved 17:04, June 15, 2015, from https://en.wikipedia.org/w/index.php?title=Wireless_Application_Protocol&oldid=666351127

40. WAP - Wireless Application Protocol. (n.d.). Retrieved December 21, 2014, from http://www.webopedia.com/TERM/W/WAP.htm l

41. 3G. (2015, May 19). In *Wikipedia, The Free Encyclopedia*. Retrieved 17:06, June 15, 2015, from https://en.wikipedia.org/w/index.php?title=3G&oldid=663146953

42. What is a 3G Network? (n.d.). Retrieved December 21, 2014, from http://www.wisegeek.org/what-is-a-3g-network.htm

43. 4G. (2015, June 1). In *Wikipedia, The Free Encyclopedia*. Retrieved 17:09, June 15, 2015, from https://en.wikipedia.org/w/index.php?title=4G&oldid=665002346

44. LTE (telecommunication). (2015, June 12). In *Wikipedia, The Free Encyclopedia*. Retrieved 17:08, June 15, 2015, from https://en.wikipedia.org/w/index.php?title=LTE_(telecommunication)&oldid=666645572

45. WiMAX vs LTE – What is a better 4G technology. (2014, March 4). Retrieved December 21, 2014, from http://thebestwirelessinternet.com/wimax-vs-lte.html

46. WiMAX. (2015, June 12). In *Wikipedia, The Free Encyclopedia*. Retrieved 17:11, June 15, 2015, from https://en.wikipedia.org/w/index.php?title=WiMAX&oldid=666576611

47. Mitchell, B. (n.d.). What Is WiMAX Broadband Wireless Networking? Retrieved December 21, 2014, from http://compnetworking.about.com/od/wirelessinternet/g/bldef_wimax.htm

48. WiMAX Wireless Network - HowStuffWorks. (n.d.). Retrieved December 21, 2014, from http://computer.howstuffworks.com/wimax1.htm

49. 5G. (2015, June 3). In *Wikipedia, The Free Encyclopedia*. Retrieved 17:12, June 15, 2015, from https://en.wikipedia.org/w/index.php?title=5G&oldid=665329464 Wireless sensor network. (n.d.). Retrieved December 21, 2014, from http://en.wikipedia.org/wiki/Wireless_sensor_network

50. NETGEAR Support | Answer | Introduction to Wireless Security. (n.d.). Retrieved December 21, 2014, from http://kb.netgear.fr/app/answers/detail/a_id/20049/~/introduction-to-wireless-security

51. (n.d.). Retrieved December 27, 2014, from https://www.cs.utexas.edu/~byoung/cs361/lecture44.pdf

52. An Overview of Cryptography. (n.d.). Retrieved December 27, 2014, from http://www.garykessler.net/library/crypto.html

53. Wireless Networking Security. (n.d.). Retrieved December 21, 2014, from http://technet.microsoft.com/en-us/library/bb457019.aspx

54. Wireless Networking Security. (n.d.). Retrieved December 21, 2014, from http://technet.microsoft.com/en-us/library/bb457019.aspx

Chapter 4

TOPIC 4 – COMPUTATIONAL THINKING

© IBO 2012

Topic 4. Computational thinking[1]

Tools used

1. Most IB compatible pseudocode examples of this book have been tested using the EZ Pcode practice tool found at:

   http://ibcomp.fis.edu/pseudocode/pcode.html

   This excellent tool was developed by Mr. Dave Mulkey. The Authors wish to express their gratitude to the developer of this valuable educational resource.

2. Most flowcharts were developed using the Flowgorithm software. It can be downloaded using the following link.

   http://www.flowgorithm.org/

   This software was developed by Mr. Devin Cook and is highly recommended.

3. All Java programs were tested in BlueJ. It can be downloaded using the following link.

   http://www.bluej.org/

   The BlueJ development environment was created by the University of Kent and is ideally suited for students.

The concept of a problem

Exit skills. Students should be able to:
Explain the concept of the problem.

According to the Cambridge dictionary: "A problem is a situation that needs attention and needs to be dealt with or solved."[2] Whenever we have to deal with a problem, we have to take one or more decisions. Herbert A. Simon[3] (Nobel prize in Economic sciences, 1978)[4] was

[1] International Baccalaureate Organization. (2012). IBDP Computer Science Guide.

[2] Problem definition, meaning - what is problem in the British English Dictionary & Thesaurus - Cambridge Dictionaries Online. (n.d.). Retrieved May 30, 2015, from http://dictionary.cambridge.org/dictionary/british/problem

[3] Herbert A. Simon. (2015, June 9). In Wikipedia, The Free Encyclopedia. Retrieved 17:07, June 19, 2015, from https://en.wikipedia.org/w/index.php?title=Herbert_A._Simon&oldid=666130799

[4] Herbert A. Simon - Biographical. (n.d.). Retrieved May 31, 2015, from http://www.nobelprize.org/nobel_prizes/economic-sciences/laureates/1978/simon-bio.html

a pioneer in many fields including decision-making. He originally defined three steps in Decision Making: *Intelligence gathering*, *Design* and *Choice* (Simon 1960[5]). Other researchers (Mintzberg et al, 1976)[6] redefined these three stages as a sequence of *Identification*, *Development* and *Selection*. In both cases an implementation phase follows (Figure 4.1). Every time you need to solve a problem, you have to make a decision according to these steps. Sometimes a person finding a solution to a problem must return to a previous phase and improve the outcome, before proceeding to the next phase. Imagine a situation where during the selection phase the chosen alternative does not return the desired results in an efficient way. It is then necessary to return to the development phase and explore again various alternatives (Figure 4.2).

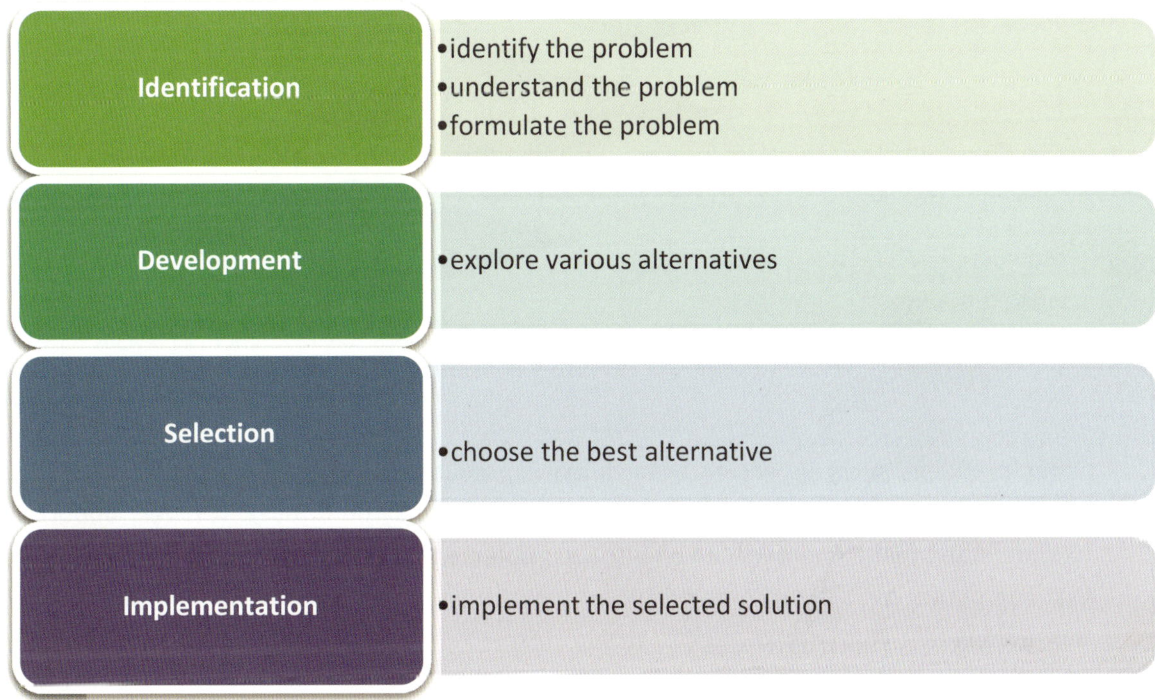

Figure 4.1: Decision making process

Following the above process will solve most problems, but it does not guarantee the solution of all problems.

There are many mathematical problems that remain unsolved. Some mathematical unsolved problems include[7]:

- The Goldbach conjecture
- The Riemann hypothesis
- The conjecture that there exists a Hadamard matrix for every positive multiple of 4
- The twin prime conjecture

---

[5] Simon, H.A. (1960). THE NEW SCIENCE OF MANAGEMENT DECISION. New York, NY: Harper and Row.
[6] Mintzberg, H., D. Raisinghani and A. Téorèt. (1976). The structure of unstructured decision processes. Administrative Science Quartely, 21, pp. 246-275.
[7] (n.d.). Retrieved May 30, 2015, from http://mathworld.wolfram.com/UnsolvedProblems.html

- Determination of whether NP-problems are actually P-problems
- The Collatz problem

However, we can posit that all these will, one day, be solved, and almost certainly by using the decision-making process below.

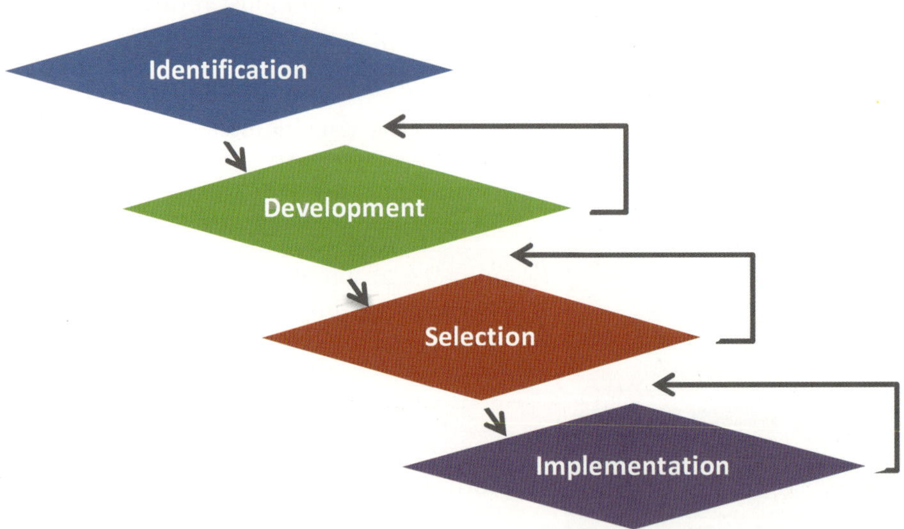

Figure 4.2: Decision making process is not linear. Sometimes it is necessary to return to a previous stage

Other problems such, as accurate earthquake prediction, how the Universe began, and question of "Free Will" are still under examination and may be forever! It is very important to understand that computers can only solve problems that are solvable by humans, but also that computers can't solve some problems that are solvable by humans. Take, for example the *Completely Automated Public Turing test to tell Computers and Humans Apart (CAPTSHA)*. This is a program used to prevent *bots* or automated software from distorting online polls, registering email accounts etc. Some problems need human intelligence, human perception, human intuition and human logic, and only advanced Artificial Intelligence programs can come close to imitating human performance in these areas.

Programming involves the creation of a series of steps that will solve a problem. It is a process of solving a problem in phases. It is very important to understand that a computer program is a sequence of instructions that explains to the computer how to solve a specific problem. Some problems are very complicated, while other problems are easy to solve. Compare the following problems:

1. Write a program that will calculate the probability of an earthquake in USA the following 34 minutes.
2. Write a program that will output "Hello world".

A Google search of the first problem returns 72,200,000 results. It will take you something like 4178 days reading for 10 seconds, half of the results. And the funny thing is that it is practically impossible to write a decent program to address the particular problem.

On the contrary Google will return 1,280,000 results for the second problem, and you will find a perfect answer by clicking the first link[8].

Luckily, all problems that you are going to face during CS IB exams are easily solvable by experienced students and it is easy to write an algorithmic solution!

Algorithm

Exit skills. Students should be able to:
Explain the concept of the algorithm. **Explain the key properties of an algorithm.** **Describe the ways used to express an algorithm.**

An *algorithm* is a series of unambiguous instructions designed in order to solve a problem and achieve a certain goal in a finite number of steps[9]. According to Knuth (1968) an algorithm must possess the following properties[10, 11]:

- ***Finiteness***: "An algorithm must always terminate after a finite number of steps ... a *very* finite number, a reasonable number"
- ***Definiteness***: "Each step of an algorithm must be precisely defined; the actions to be carried out must be rigorously and unambiguously specified for each case"
- ***Input***: "...quantities which are given to it initially before the algorithm begins. These inputs are taken from specified sets of objects"
- ***Output***. "...quantities which have a specified relation to the inputs"
- ***Effectiveness***: "... all of the operations to be performed in the algorithm must be sufficiently basic that they can in principle be done exactly and in a finite length of time by a man using paper and pencil"

Think of an algorithm as a recipe. It's easy to write a recipe for a boiled egg.

1. Start with an egg at room temperature.
2. Bring a small pan of water to the boil.
3. Put the egg in the pan.
4. Boil for 4 minutes.

Now consider a recipe for making an omelette.

1. Whisk two eggs with some milk and some salt and pepper.

---

[8] List of Hello world program examples. (2015, June 14). In Wikipedia, The Free Encyclopedia. Retrieved 17:11, June 19, 2015, from https://en.wikipedia.org/w/index.php?title=List_of_Hello_world_program_examples&oldid=666880519

[9] International Baccalaureate Organization. (2004). IBDP Computer Science Guide.

[10] Knuth, Donald E. (1968). The Art of Computer Programming Second Edition, Volume 1, Fundamental Algorithms (First ed.). Addison-Wesley Publishing Company.

[11] (n.d.). Retrieved May 30, 2015, from http://www.statemaster.com/encyclopedia/Algorithm-characterizations

2. Heat some oil in a frying pan and add the mixture.
3. After one minute, stir and reduce heat.
4. Add ham, mushrooms and cheese onto the surface.
5. Wait for the omelette to set underneath.
6. Fold in half and serve.

Boiling an egg isn't as simple as boiling water. The simpler the problem, the simpler the algorithm will be. The harder the problem, the bigger and more complicated the algorithm will be. It is very important to understand that writing an algorithm is in essence, just problem-solving.

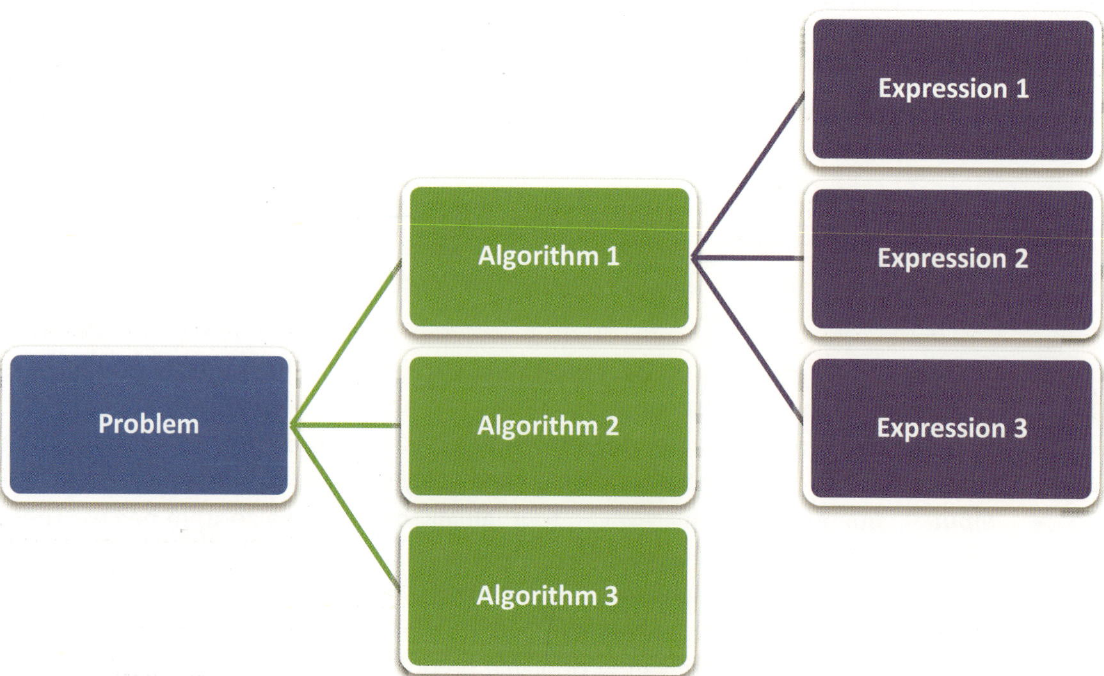

Figure 4.3: Many expressions can solve the same problem

For each problem, there may be many different algorithms and for each algorithm, there may be many different expressions (implementations). An algorithm may be expressed in a number of ways, including:

1. ***Simple English (natural language)****:* Not very common because it is usually verbose and ambiguous.
2. A ***flow chart:*** A formalized graphic representation method which avoids most issues of ambiguity.
3. ***Pseudocode***: is a generic artificial language that describes computer algorithms but does not use the syntax of any particular programming language. Pseudocode may often contain natural language to describe various parts of an algorithm. These parts, written in natural language, are later replaced. [9]
4. ***Programming language***: is an artificial language designed in such a way so that it may be used by humans in order to communicate with a computer system. Various programming languages exist that may be used for different purposes or problems.

One thing that all programming languages have in common is that they may be used to describe algorithms, create programs and control machinery.[12]

Flowcharts

Exit skills. Students should be able to:
Explain the various symbols used in flowcharts.

A flowchart is used to diagrammatically describe an algorithm. The following symbols are widely accepted:

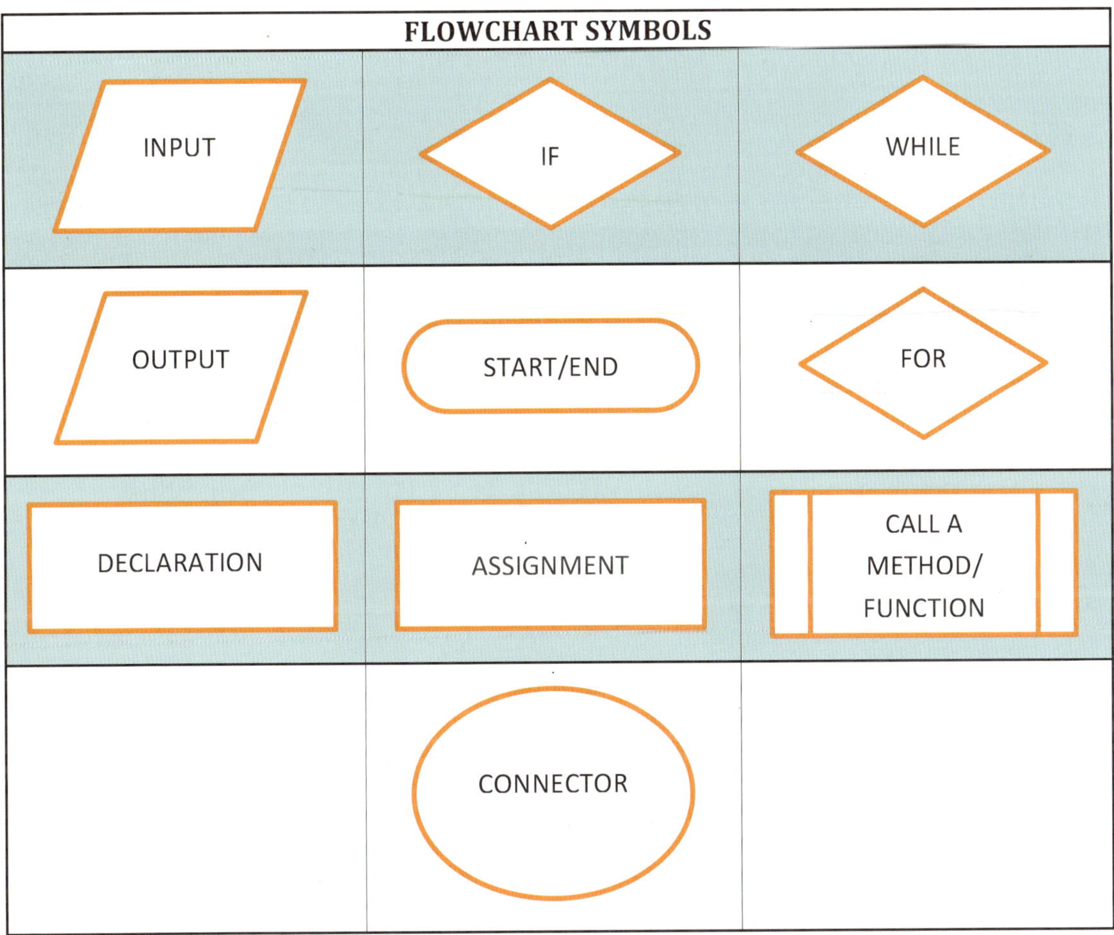

Table 4.1: Flowchart symbols

[12] Programming language. (2015, June 10). In *Wikipedia, The Free Encyclopedia. Retrieved 17:20, June 19, 2015, from https://en.wikipedia.org/w/index.php?title=Programming_language&oldid=666292926*

Pseudocode[13]

Exit skills. Students should be able to:
Explain the concept of the pseudocode.

The main purpose of pseudocode is to help programmers develop computer programs. Because pseudocode is written for humans the syntax used is not as strict as the one used in computer languages. Pseudocode normally omits details that are not important for human understanding of the algorithm. Computers can't interpret a solution in pseudocode form thus it should be converted to a computer language. When a programmer develops pseudocode he/she does not necessarily think of a particular computer language. Normally a pseudocode could be converted to any computer language with relative ease. It is important to understand that writing pseudocode involves paper and pencil.

An algorithm and its expressions

Exit skills. Students should be able to:
Express an algorithm to flowchart, pseudocode and natural language.

An algorithm

```
Begin
    Display the message "THIS WILL BE PRINTED TWICE" two times
…….
    Display the message "THIS MESSAGE WILL BE PRINTED FOUR TIMES"
four times
End
```

The same algorithm expressed in the pseudocode form used in IB syllabus.

```
loop A from 1 to 2
   output "THIS WILL BE PRINTED TWICE"
end loop
C = 1
loop while C < 5
   output "THIS MESSAGE WILL BE PRINTED FOUR TIMES"
   C = C +1
end loop
```

The same algorithm expressed as a Delphi/Pascal program

```
program MyProgram;
uses Math, SysUtils;
{ Headers }
{ Main }
var
    A : integer;
    C : integer;
begin
```

[13] (n.d.). Retrieved May 30, 2015, from https://cs.brown.edu/courses/cs015/labs/Lab6Pseudocode.pdf

```
    for A := 1 to 2 do
    begin
        WriteLn('THIS WILL BE PRINTED TWICE');
    end;
    C := 1;
    while C < 5 do
    begin
        WriteLn('THIS MESSAGE WILL BE PRINTED FOUR TIMES');
        C := C + 1;
    end;
end.
```

The same algorithm expressed as a flowchart is presented:[14]

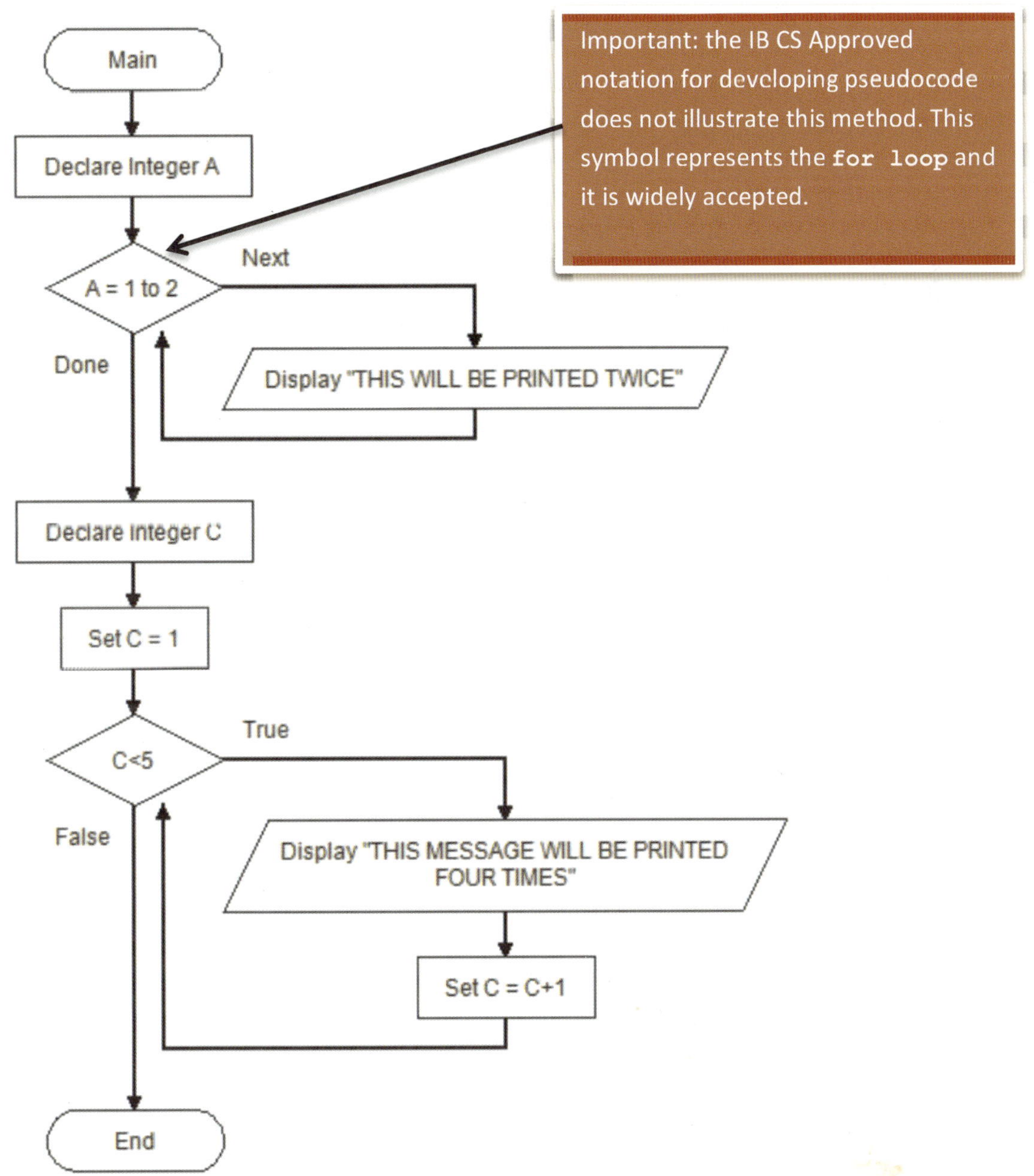

[14] International Baccalaureate Organization. (2012). IBDP Approved notations for developing pseudocode.

The same algorithm expressed as a Java program

```
class MyProgram {
    public static void main(String[] args) {
        int A;
        for (A = 1 ; A <= 2 ; A += 1) {
            System.out.println("THIS WILL BE PRINTED TWICE");
        }
        int C;
        C = 1;
        while (C < 5) {
            System.out.println("THIS MESSAGE WILL BE PRINTED FOUR TIMES");
            C = C + 1;
        }
    }
}
```

The output of the algorithm
THIS WILL BE PRINTED TWICE
THIS WILL BE PRINTED TWICE
THIS MESSAGE WILL BE PRINTED FOUR TIMES
THIS MESSAGE WILL BE PRINTED FOUR TIMES
THIS MESSAGE WILL BE PRINTED FOUR TIMES
THIS MESSAGE WILL BE PRINTED FOUR TIMES

The programming concept

Exit skills. Students should be able to:
Explain the programming concept.

It is very useful to understand the concept of programming. According to etymonline[15]:

- "**program (n.)**

  1630s, "public notice," from Late Latin *programma* "proclamation, edict," from Greek *programma* "a written public notice," from stem of *prographein* "to write publicly," from *pro-* "forth" (see *pro-*) + *graphein* "to write" (see *-graphy*). General sense of "a definite plan or scheme" is recorded from 1837. Meaning "list of pieces at a concert, playbill" first recorded 1805 and retains the original sense. That of "objects or events suggested by music" is from 1854. Sense of "broadcasting presentation" is from 1923. Computer sense (noun and verb) is from 1945. Spelling *programme*, established in Britain, is from French in modern use and began to be used early 19c., originally especially in the "playbill" sense. *Program music* attested from 1877."

[15] Online Etymology Dictionary. (n.d.). Retrieved May 30, 2015, from http://www.etymonline.com/index.php?term=program

- "**program (v.)**

  1889, "write program notes;" 1896, "arrange according to program," from *program* (n.). Of computers from 1945. From 1963 in the figurative sense of "to train to behave in a predetermined way." Related: *Programmed; programming*."

- "**programmer (n.)**

  1890, "event planner," agent noun from *program* (v.). Meaning "person who programs computers" is attested from 1948."

When referring to computer programs it is not acceptable to use the word "programme". A programme or program is a plan of action to accomplish a task. A programme or program includes various activities to be followed. A *computer program* is a sequence of instructions, written to instruct a computer to perform a specified task.

4.1 General principles

Thinking procedurally

4.1.1 Procedure appropriate to solving a problem

Exit skills. Students should be able to[1]:
Explain the importance of various steps to solving a problem. Identify the correct order of steps. Identify the overall procedure for problem solving.

When a particular problem has to be solved, an effective method or procedure should be identified. This procedure reduces the solution to a series of simple steps. These steps have to be followed in the correct order to obtain the desired output. It is impossible to ride a motorcycle if you don't know how to ride a bicycle. So first you have to learn to ride the bicycle and then you will be able to ride the motorcycle.

4.1.2 Order of activities and required outcome

Exit skills. Students should be able to[1]:
Explain the importance of order in which activities are performed.

A company wishes to develop a new information system. The analysis phase will be the one that the company should complete before proceeding to the next stages of the project. If the company tries to implement the new system without first analyzing the problem domain, then a total waste of money, effort and resources will almost certainly occur.

4.1.3 The role of sub-procedures in solving a problem

Exit skills. Students should be able to[1]:
Define the term sub-procedures. Define the term identifier. Explain the importance of sub-procedures.

A good approach for confronting a complex problem is to develop a method of breaking up the problem into smaller sub-problems. This method is very effective and efficient because it is much easier to attack a number of sub-problems instead of a big complex problem. The resulting sub-problems can be further divided to smaller and smaller sub-problems until finally they can be dealt individually. This strategy is often called *top-down design* or *stepwise refinement*.

The very same approach could be used when developing complex computer programs. Using top-down program design, the complex problem is *decomposed* and for each sub-problem, an appropriate sub-procedure is developed. A *sub-procedure* contains a series of commands that perform a task. When a sub-procedure is called all statements included in the particular sub-procedure are executed. All the sub-procedures that represent different parts of the problem solution can be used at the right time using their identifiers. So the procedure is divided into a series of sub-procedures; this process is referred as a *modular programming* approach. An *identifier* is the name that is used by the programmer to uniquely identify a variable, an object a sub-procedure etc.

Programming Example 1: Sub procedure

For example: Let's imagine a program that calculates the solutions of a quadratic equation. A sub procedure called `discriminant` could be used to calculate the discriminant "D". So the algorithmic solution could look like:

```
Input a, b, c
D=Call Sub procedure Discriminant that returns the value D
If D>0 then
    Calculate x1 = (-b+√D)/(2a)
    Calculate x2 = (-b-√D)/(2a)
Else if D=0 then
    Calculate x1 = -b/(2a), x2 = -b/(2a)
Else
    Output no solutions
End if
Output x1, x2
```

```
Sub procedure Discriminant
Calculate D=b^2-4*a*c
Return D
```

4.1.4 Decision-making in a specified situation

Exit skills. Students should be able to[1]:
Identify the importance of alternative decisions. Identify the importance of alternative procedures.

The addition process does not require any decision to be taken. The following algorithm is straight forward:

```
Input A
Input B
C=A+B
Output C
```

Some problems require the use of decisions. Suppose there is a pedestrian crossing that is equipped with a light signal. If the signal is green, then crossing the road is safe and the pedestrian can cross. If the signal is red, then the pedestrian should stop and wait. The following figure illustrates the flowchart and the algorithm that corresponds to this scenario. Two different alternative procedures (WAIT, PASS) could be followed.

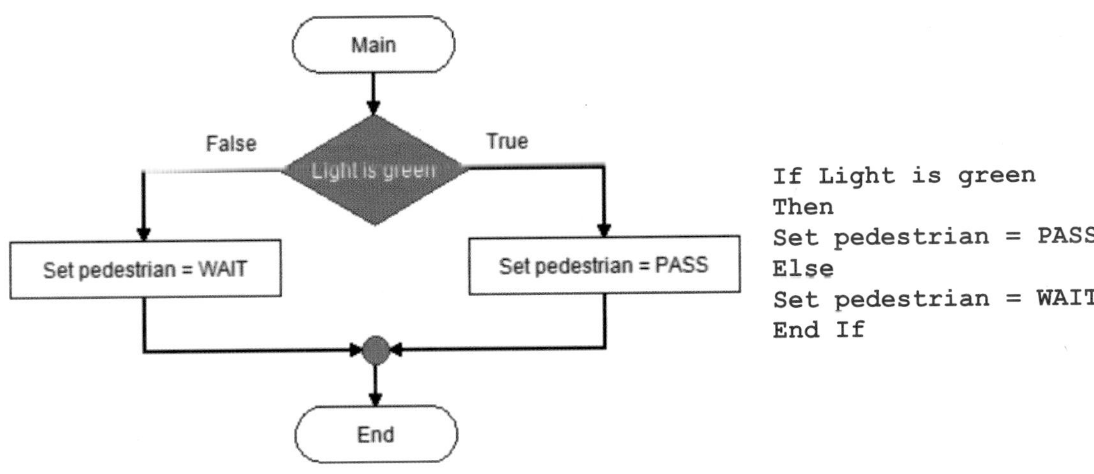

Figure 4.4: Conditional operations

4.1.5 Decisions required for the solution to a specified problem

Exit skills. Students should be able to[1]:
Identify the various decisions and procedures to solve a problem. Identify the cause (conditions) and effect (actions) in a given situation.

In everyday life people are constantly identifying the necessary decisions and the different actions that are relevant to a problem or a situation. It is clear that we take different actions according, to the prevailing conditions.

Programming Example 2: Logic and algorithm

A student is allowed to go to a football game if the following conditions are fulfilled: homework done AND Weather is good. The following truth table illustrates this scenario.

Homework done	Weather is good	Allowed
TRUE	TRUE	TRUE
TRUE	FALSE	FALSE
FALSE	TRUE	FALSE
FALSE	FALSE	FALSE

The logic expression is Allowed = Weather is good AND Homework done

The equivalent algorithm is (this not IB compatible pseudocode):

```
Boolean Homework done
Boolean Weather is good
Boolean Allowed
Input Homework done
Input Weather is good
If Homework done AND Weather is good Then
    Allowed = True
Else
    Allowed = False
End If
```

4.1.6 Iteration associated with a given decision in a specified problem

Exit skills. Students should be able to[1]:

Define iteration.
Identify the importance of iteration in a given situation.
Identify the importance of Boolean tests.

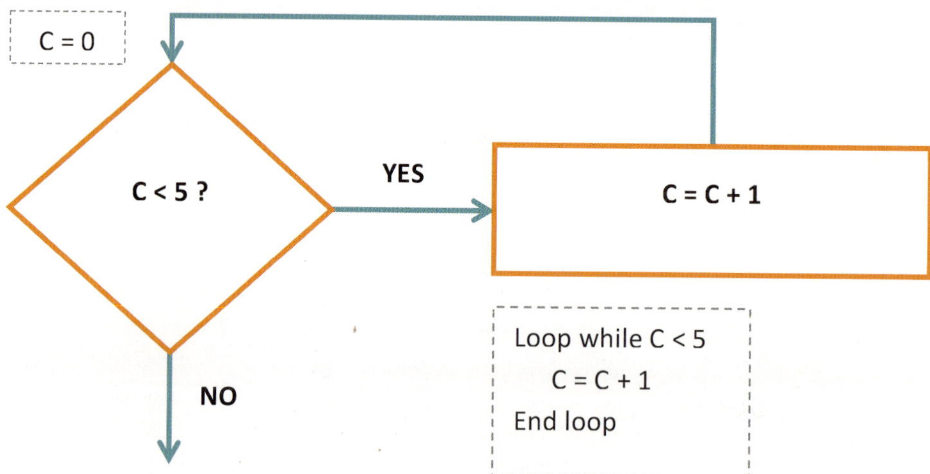

Figure 4.5: The loop while (as illustrated in the approved notation)

Tip: An important difference between the **`while loop`** and the **`from/to loop`** is that the first performs some tasks when the condition is evaluated as true while the second does something when the condition is evaluated as false.

Iteration is the process of repeating a series of instructions. It is extremely useful in programming and is used to repeat a statement or a block of statements within an algorithm. Iteration is expressed using the "**`from to loop`**" and the "**`while loop`**" statements. The IBO approved notation for developing pseudocode[14] includes the following flowcharts and pseudocode to represent these statements. The diamond shape performs a Boolean test, evaluates an expression and returns a Boolean value (true or false).

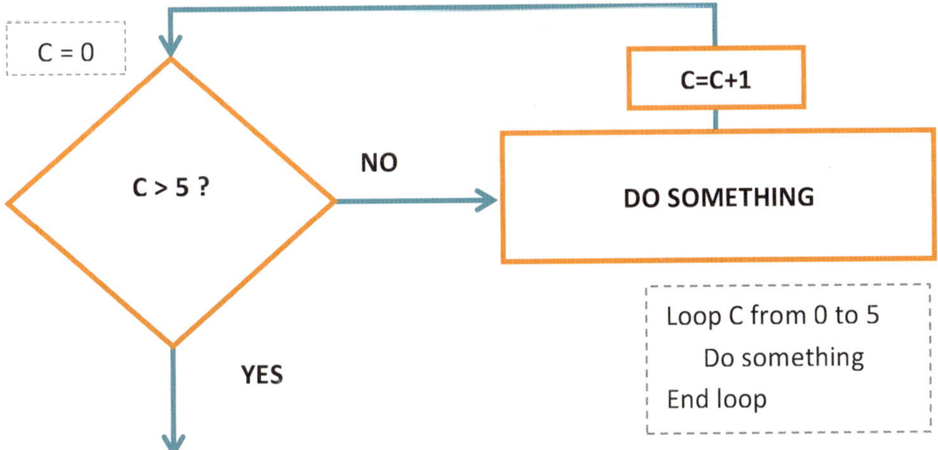

Figure 4.6: The from to loop (as illustrated in the approved notation)

The IB approved notation for developing pseudocode[14] does not include the following flowchart symbol although it is widely accepted.

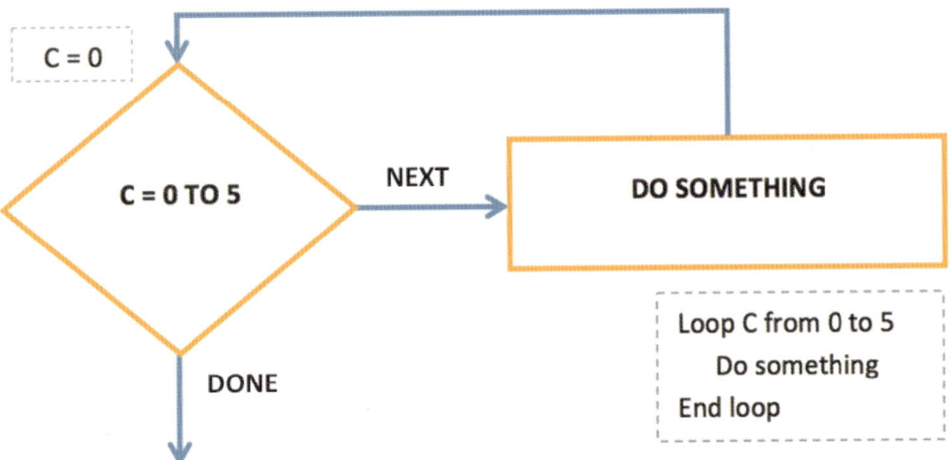

Figure 4.7: The from to loop (the C=C+1 statement is accommodated in the Decision shape)

Programming Example 3: LOOP WHILE

```
//use of while loop
//to print a message
//user selects the number of times
I = 0
X = input("How many times do you want to see the message")
loop while I < X
  I=I+1
output ("it will be printed (number entered) times")
end while
```

Programming Example 4: LOOP FROM TO

```
//use of from to loop
//to print a message
//user selects the number of times
I = 0
X = input("How many times do you want to see the message")
loop I from 1 to X
   output ("it will be printed (number entered) times")
end loop
```

4.1.7 Decisions and conditional statements

Exit skills. Students should be able to[1]:

Define the term conditional statement.
Identify the importance of iteration in a given situation.
Identify the importance of Boolean tests.

A *conditional statement* performs different instructions depending on a *Boolean test*. The `if-then-else` conditional statement is common across many programming languages and human logic. Although some variations are common, the structure in pseudocode form is:

```
IF (Boolean condition) THEN
    (Consequent)
ELSE
    (Alternative)
END IF
```

When an `If` is used in an algorithm a *Boolean condition* is evaluated (`X>0, X=Y` etc.). If the condition is `true`, the (Consequent) statement or statements will be executed. Otherwise, the execution continues to the (Alternative) statement or statements. If there is no `else` branch, the algorithm continues after the `end if`.

Programming Example 5: Convert the following algorithm to an equivalent algorithm that will use only simple conditionals statements.

Initial algorithm	Solution

`A = input("Type a number")`
`if A = 0 then`
`   output "1"`
`else if A+2 > 6 then`
`   output "2"`
	`A = input("Type a number")`
	`if A = 0 then`
	`   output "1"`
	`end if`
	`if A+2 > 6 then`

`else`
`   output "3"`
`end if`
	`   output "2"`
	`end if`
	`if NOT (A+2>6) AND NOT (A=0)`
	`then`
	`   output "3"`
	`end if`

Programming Example 6: Convert the following algorithm to an alternative algorithm that will use multiple conditionals statements.

Initial algorithm	Solution

`A = input("Type a number")`
`if NOT (A = 0) AND NOT (A = 3)`
`then`
`   output "not 0 or 3"`
`end if`
`if A = 0 then`
`   output "0"`
`end if`
`if A = 3  then`
`   output "3"`
`end if`
	`A = input("Type a number")`
	`if A = 0 then`
	`   output "0"`
	`else if A = 3 then`
	`   output "3"`
	`else`
	`   output "not 0 or 3"`
	`end if`

Programming Example 7: IF THEN ELSE (1)

```
//A way to use if-end if
//It finds if a numbered entered is positive, negative or 0
X = input ("Please enter a number")
if X > 0 then
        output "Positive"
end if
if X = 0 then
        output "0"
end if
if X < 0 then
        output "Negative"
end if
```

Programming Example 8: IF THEN ELSE (2)

```
//A way to use if-then-else-end if
//It finds if a numbered entered is positive, negative or 0
X = input ("Please enter a number")
if X > 0 then
       output "Positive"
else if X = 0 then
       output "0"
else
       output "Negative"
end if
```

4.1.8 Logical rules for real-world

Exit skills. Students should be able to[1]:
Derive rules of inference from a real life situation.

Logical rules or *rules of inference* are obvious rules to most humans. Programming and algorithmic thinking involves the translation of these rules into algorithms. The following everyday examples involve the use of common sense: If it rains I will wear a raincoat. I will study all my lessons. I have to pay my bills. Sometimes logic leads to brilliant discoveries, like Einstein's equation $E=m*c^2$, which is a mathematical way to express logic. Einstein was able to successfully combine his logic with scientific knowledge and we really hope all IB students will follow his example!

Thinking ahead

4.1.9 Inputs and outputs required in a solution

Exit skills. Students should be able to[1]:
Define the terms input and output. Identify inputs and outputs in a situation.

Input is something that put into a program while *output* is something that is produced by the program after a *process*.

It is known that Velocity (**V**) is defined as the speed of an object in a given direction. We use the equation **V = s/t** to calculate an objects average velocity **V**.

So **V** equals velocity and is the output of our solution.

s equals the total displacement from the object's starting position, and it is one of the inputs required in the solution.

t equals the time elapsed, and it is one of the inputs required in the solution.

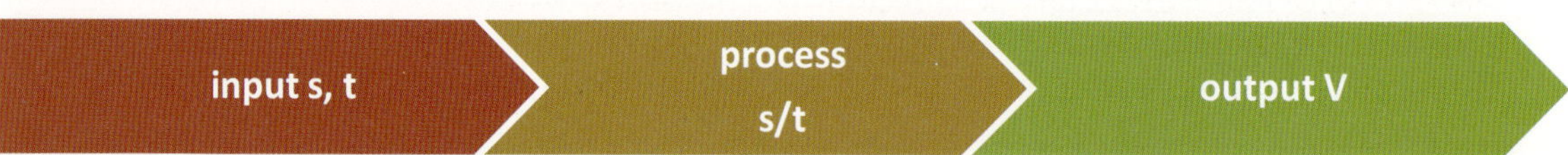

Figure 4.8: Calculation of V

4.1.10 Pre-planning in a suggested problem and solution

Exit skills. Students should be able to[1]:
Define the term pre-planning. Define the term Gantt chart. Define the term pre-fetching. Define the term software libraries. Identify the importance of pre-planning in problem solution.

Pre-planning is the process of planning something in advance.

Suppose a customer desperately wants to buy a gadget as soon as possible. He/she can place an order for this gadget before it is available for purchase. When the gadget comes onto the market he/she will be one of the first to obtain the gadget. This is a typical example of pre-ordering.

A lot of cooking recipes instruct us to put the food in a preheated oven. That means that the cook needs to pre-plan such an action.

Suppose a student wants to find his/her textbook; he/she knows that he/she stores it inside his/her locker in school. So first he/she has to go to school then he/she has to open his/her locker where he/she will eventually find his/her textbook. This is a typical example of procedural thinking and preplanning.

Prefetching in broad terms means getting data or instructions from memory into the cache before they are actually needed. When a program requests data that was previously pre-fetched, it can use the pre-fetched data and continue with execution, instead of waiting for the data from RAM. This is a typical example of preplanning an action so as to save time and improve efficiency.

Another example of effective preplanning is the use of *software libraries*. These consist of pre-formed elements and are ready for future use. A software library consists of pre-written code, classes, procedures, methods etc. that a programmer can use to add more functionality to his/her programs, without having to rewrite the equivalent code.

A *Gantt chart* is a type of bar chart, named after Henry Gantt. It is widely used for project schedule and project management, as a way of showing activities, tasks and events against time. On the left of the chart is a list of the tasks, activities and events. Along the top is an appropriate time scale. All tasks, activities and events are represented by bars. Each bar represents the duration, start day and end day of the task, activity or event. A Gantt chart allows easy inspection of the project's activities, overlapping activities, the total duration of the project etc.

The following Gantt chart represents a construction project. This chart provides details such as: the project includes 8 activities. Site work should take place before plumbing and electrical tasks. Plumbing and electrical are carried out concurrently (that means to do both tasks at the same time). Site work and plumbing are carried out sequentially.

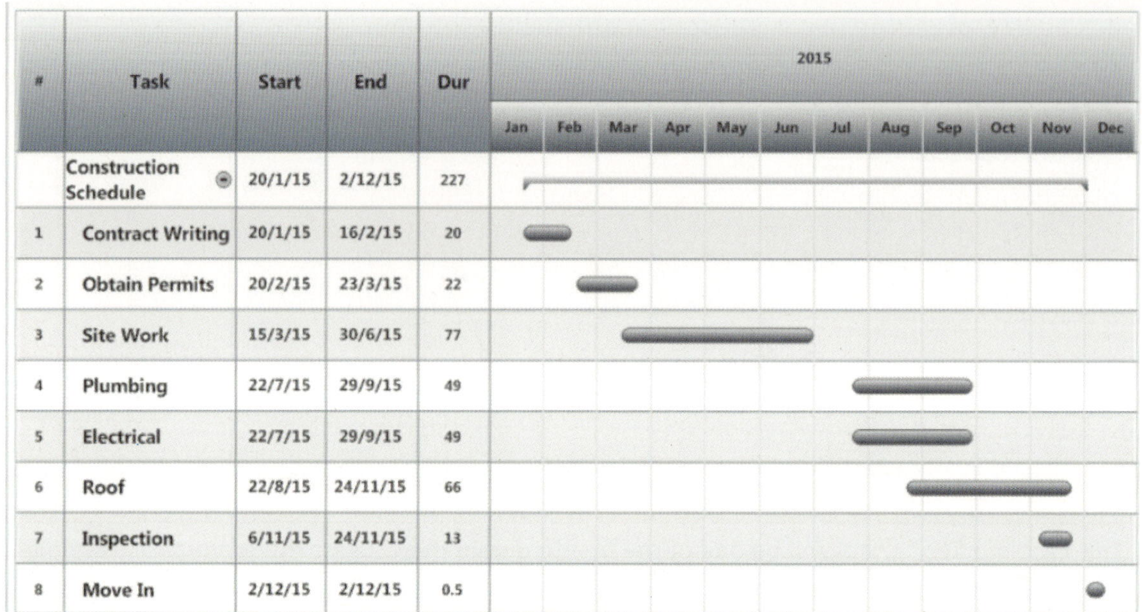

#	Task	Start	End	Dur
	Construction Schedule	20/1/15	2/12/15	227
1	Contract Writing	20/1/15	16/2/15	20
2	Obtain Permits	20/2/15	23/3/15	22
3	Site Work	15/3/15	30/6/15	77
4	Plumbing	22/7/15	29/9/15	49
5	Electrical	22/7/15	29/9/15	49
6	Roof	22/8/15	24/11/15	66
7	Inspection	6/11/15	24/11/15	13
8	Move In	2/12/15	2/12/15	0.5

Figure 4.9: A Gantt chart of a construction project

The following Gantt chart represents a general project. This chart provides details such as: the project consists of four activities. Task 1 and Task 2 are carried out sequentially (the second task cannot begin before the other is completed). The total duration of the project is 21 days. Task 2 is the longest task.

	Task	Start	End	Dur
	PROJECT	1/1/15	29/1/15	21
1	Task 1	1/1/15	7/1/15	5
2	Task 2	8/1/15	16/1/15	7
3	Task 3	14/1/15	20/1/15	5
4	Task 4	22/1/15	29/1/15	6

Figure 4.10: A Gantt chart of a general project

4.1.11 Need for pre-conditions

Exit skills. Students should be able to[1]:

Define the terms pre and post conditions.
Explain the need for pre-conditions in programming.

In most cases, when a programming team deals with a large problem, the large problem is broken down into more easily solvable and controllable sub-problems. Each member of the team will solve one or more of these "easy" sub-problems. Each solution will be a sub-procedure, and it will be expressed as an algorithm. Each sub-procedure will be called using its identifier and will have a certain task to accomplish. The *pre-condition* indicates what must be true before the sub-procedure is called. The post-condition indicates what will be true when the sub-procedure completes its task. *Pre-condition* describes the starting state before the execution of an algorithm; *post-condition* describes the final state after the execution of an algorithm.

4.1.12 Pre- and post-conditions

Exit skills. Students should be able to[1]:
Describe pre- and post-conditions for a specified situation.

When cooking a meal for dinner all the necessary ingredients should be available before cooking. This is the pre-condition of the algorithm cooking. After cooking a table is needed to facilitate eating. This is the post-condition for a proper dinner.

The following algorithm fragment has as pre-condition **A=2** and as post-condition **B=30**

```
//pre-condition A=2
X=3
B= X+A
if A>0 then
  B = B*6
else
  B=0
end if
//post-condition B=30
```

The following algorithm calculates and prints the square root of an integer x. It has as pre-condition **X** accepted >= 0 and as post-condition the calculation of $\sqrt{x}$

```
//Pre-condition: x >= 0
//Post-condition: calculates the square root of x

Sub-procedure square root(accepts x as a parameter)
x=√x
output x
End of Sub-procedure
```

The algorithm fragment `Sub-procedure(9)` will output 3. The output algorithm fragment `Sub-procedure(0)` will output 0. The output algorithm fragment `Sub-procedure(-1)` will violate the preconditions because the square of a number is always positive.

4.1.13 Exceptions that need to be considered

Exit skills. Students should be able to[1]:
Define the term exception. Explain the importance of exceptions in programming.

Exception is an act or event that disrupts the anticipated flow of the program's execution. The exceptions take place during the execution of the program and can be effectively handled by specific mechanisms that most modern programming languages provide. The term exception at this point of the syllabus refers to an occasion or case that is not compatible with the general rule.

The next example clarifies the importance of identifying various exceptions in a specified problem solution.

Programming Example 9: Alternatives and pre-conditions

A company has the following policy to calculate the end-of-year bonus for its employees:
If the employee has worked for the company for 9 months or more then the bonus equals to 30% of his/her monthly salary. If the employee has worked for the company for less than 9 months and his/her salary is less than €2000 then the bonus equals to 20% of his/her monthly salary. If the employee has worked for the company for less than 9 months and his/her salary is equal or more than €2000 then the bonus equals 10% of his/her monthly salary.

A programmer didn't understand the problem and wrote the following pseudocode which apparently violates both pre-conditions and post-condition:

```
//Pre-condition violated: Months = the correct number of months the
employee worked for the company
//Post-conditions violated: the program calculates and outputs the
correct bonus for each employee according to the company's policy.

//Wrong Bonus program
BONUS = 0
TOTAL = 0
SALARY = 1200
   BONUS = (30/100)*(SALARY)
   TOTAL = BONUS+(SALARY * 12)
output "TOTAL IS:" , TOTAL ,"Euros"
output "BONUS IS:" , BONUS ,"Euros"
```

The following pseudocode satisfies the pre- and post-conditions to the specified problem.

```
//Correct Bonus program
MONTHS = 0
SALARY = 0
BONUS = 0
TOTAL = 0
SALARY = input("what is the salary of the employee?")
MONTHS = input("How many months did he/she work?")

if  MONTHS >= 9  then
   BONUS = (30/100)*(SALARY)
   TOTAL = BONUS +(SALARY * MONTHS)
 else if  MONTHS < 9  AND  SALARY < 2000 then
   BONUS = (20/100)*(SALARY)
   TOTAL = BONUS+(SALARY * MONTHS)
 else if  MONTHS < 9  AND  SALARY >= 2000 then
    BONUS = (10/100)*(SALARY)
```

```
    TOTAL = BONUS+(SALARY * MONTHS)

  end if

output "TOTAL IS:" , TOTAL ,"Euros"
output "BONUS IS:" , BONUS ,"Euros"
```

Thinking concurrently

4.1.14 Parts of a solution that could be implemented concurrently

Exit skills. Students should be able to[1]:
Define the term concurrent. Describe tasks that can be performed concurrently.

Concurrent means something that happens at the same time as something else. Imagine a situation where a user replies to his/her e-mails while listening to his/her favorite song. Or imagine another situation where a person is searching for information on the WWW, is printing an essay and is downloading some drivers for his/her PC. In both scenarios, the tasks are implemented concurrently.

In computer science, *concurrent processing* means the execution of different instructions simultaneously by multiple processors so as to achieve the best performance. A *simplified explanation* of this process is that programs are broken down into procedures and procedures are broken down to sub-procedures. These are then assigned to separate processing units to perform simultaneously. Sequential processing is the execution of all sub-procedures one after the other by a single processor.

4.1.15 Concurrent processing and problem solution

Exit skills. Students should be able to[1]:
Describe the importance of concurrent processing in real life.

Imagine a world where there is no concurrent processing; House building would last much longer, people would have to finish their breakfasts before they listen to the morning news, a person would have to either hear or see, to understand or write, and to feel or think.
The famous "pasta with sauce" preparation example can further clarify the situation. There is no need to cook the pasta before the sauce, because most people can use two burners to prepare both pasta and the sauce. The average person saves valuable time and enjoys hot pasta accompanied by warm sauce.

4.1.16 Decision to use concurrent processing in solving a problem

Exit skills. Students should be able to[1]:
Describe the pros and cons of concurrent processing in real life.

Concurrent processing requires better planning and coordination of resources. Without this, concurrent processing may cause serious problems and the decision to use *serial* or concurrent processing in solving a problem should be carefully examined.

For example, an accountant is making changes to an electronic financial database. As he is doing so, a second accountant opens the same database which includes all the modifications made so far by the first accountant, and uses it to retrieve information. The first accountant then decides the changes made so far are invalid and brings the database records to the previous condition. The first accountant saves the database. The information retrieved by the second accountant no longer exists, but the second accountant is not aware of this crucial information. This problem could have been avoided if no one could read the altered database until the first accountant decided that the edits and amendments were final.[16]

Thinking abstractly

4.1.17 Examples of abstraction

Exit skills. Students should be able to[1]:
Define abstract thinking. Describe examples of abstract thinking.

Abstract thinking means reflecting on events, ideas, attributes and relationships in a general manner that hides all unnecessary details of specific objects. All information, that is not necessary to accomplish a goal, is removed and ignored and a generalization technique is implemented. A concrete thinker may identify and count two cats and two cars, while an abstract thinker may identify their common relationship which is the number two.

Abstract art as the name implies, is a typical example of abstraction. An abstract painting represents a principle or idea, but doesn't deal with detailed description and representation of reality.

The explanation of the various components of the motherboard requires the use of abstraction. Although the RAM and the CPU are considered as fundamental physical parts, it is known that they are abstractions of gates and integrated circuits which contain millions of transistors.

---

[16] Concurrency Problems. (n.d.). Retrieved May 30, 2015, from https://technet.microsoft.com/en-us/library/aa213029(v=sql.80).aspx

A level of abstraction occurs in most computer programs. Decades ago, a programmer had to work with the low-level circuitry instructions of the CPU and the computer used. Nowadays, high-level programming languages allow the user to use English-like commands and syntax in which one command statement corresponds to many machine instructions. In Java computer language, **`System.out.println`** displays a message on the screen. The user is not required to understand the function of the monitor and the various procedures, interfaces, graphic card drivers and libraries used to create the corresponding pixels on the screen.

4.1.18 Abstraction and computational solutions for a specified situation

Exit skills. Students should be able to[1]:
Define Object Oriented Programming. Define Collections. Explain the concept of objects. Explain the importance of abstraction in computational solution. Explain the importance of abstraction in programming.

Object-oriented programming

Object-oriented programming uses abstraction, and is based on the principle that all everyday tasks can be considered as entities. These entities are either *objects* or events. The table is an object where we have our dinner. The car is an object; it has wheels and the driver can change the gears. Object-oriented programming uses *programming objects* that describe data (properties) and behavior (methods) of real objects, and facilitates code reusability and abstraction. It makes complex software faster and easier to develop, and facilitates maintenance. It is an evolution of *procedural (structural) programming,* which uses *procedures* that are able to interact and exchange data as building blocks of programs.

The following table shows two different car objects. The first one has two properties (speed and gear) and three behaviors (methods) that could be applied to data. The second one has three properties (colour, equipment level, and availability and manufacturer stock) and three behaviors (change colour, change level of equipment and availability) that could be applied to data (properties of the object). The role of abstraction is profound; the first object (car1) could be used in a program that simulates the driving experience of such a car, while the second (car2) could be used in a program suitable for sales purposes. In each case, the programmer hides the unnecessary details and concentrates only on properties and behaviors that are important to the particular implementation.

Object car1	Object car2

Data:
integer speed = 0;
integer gear = 1;
	Data:
	String Colour = Black
	String Equipment = Silver
	String Availability = True
	Integer ManufacturerStock = 0

Methods: changeGear Accelerate Brake	Methods: changeColour changeEquipment Availability

Suppose a salesman uses a program that facilitates his/her job. When a customer chooses a car and finalizes the deal, a new object is created. Each deal has some unique attributes. The salesman deals with a collection of items (cars). This collection is organized in a particular way to represent the sale of cars. Some common operators could be applied to all items in the collection (add a car, read details of a car etc.). So a collection is a data structure that consists of the data and the predefined methods which operate on the data. A collection as used in the computer science guide[1] is an abstract data type like queues and stacks. An Abstract Data Type, or ADT, is a group of operations and data. In object oriented languages, a collection is an object that assemblies and contains a lot of elements in a single structure. A collection is used to add, store, manage, retrieve, manipulate and communicate the data using predefined methods.

Object manipulation

Suppose a programmer wants to create one object named **Vehicle1** of type **vehicle** with the following data fields: [Colour: "red"-Type: "car"-Engine:2000]. All vehicle objects have the same data fields: Colour, Type and Engine.

The programmer will use the **set** method to define the properties of the particular object:

```
Vehicle1 = new vehicle (setColour = "red", setType = "car", setEngine = 2000)
```

Suppose the programmer wants to retrieve information from this object. The programmer will use the **get** method to retrieve a particular data field of this particular object:

Vehicle1.getColour will return "red"

Vehicle1.getEngine will return 2000

Vehicle1.getType will return "car"

Modelling and simulation

Mathematical modelling refers to a process where a system is understood well enough and scientists describe it using mathematical language. A set of mathematical rules is used to describe the function of the particular system. It is clear that the mathematical model is an abstraction of the real system. A mathematical model contains only the necessary details, rules and objects for studying the real system or an aspect of it. A mathematical model could be transformed into an algorithm and then to a program that replicates the behavior of a real system. A computer simulation runs on a computer and reproduces the behavior of a real system. The simulation uses an abstract mathematical model that is expressed as a computer model (computer program) to simulate the system. A computer simulation is always based on a computer model.

4.1.19 Abstraction from a specified situation

Exit skills. Students should be able to[1]:
Analyze various situations and develop abstraction from real life situations.

A modular program is easier to understand and facilitate the use of abstraction. The programmer is able to focus on the important things and ignore all unnecessary details. Life and programming would be very boring without the use of abstraction. For example, a person can create a list of tasks to finish today:

```
Go to school
Buy a CS book
Visit my uncle
```

Without abstraction, the list would go something like:

```
Wake up
Eat breakfast
Brush my teeth
Put my jacket on
........
........
........
.........
.........
Return to home
```

And so on and so forth.

The "go to school" task could be split to hundreds and even thousands of steps. It is impossible to consider every tiny detail before moving to the next step. So life is easier when tiny insignificant tasks are considered as part of a wider task.

Procedures and sub-procedures facilitate abstraction. For example, the following program can call a sub-procedure named **computeSomething()**. When this sub-procedure is called from the main program, it executes a sequence of instructions and returns a value. If the programmer trusts the performance of **computeSomething()**, then he/she does not have to worry about the details that are contained in this sub-procedure. **So: modularization facilitates abstraction.**

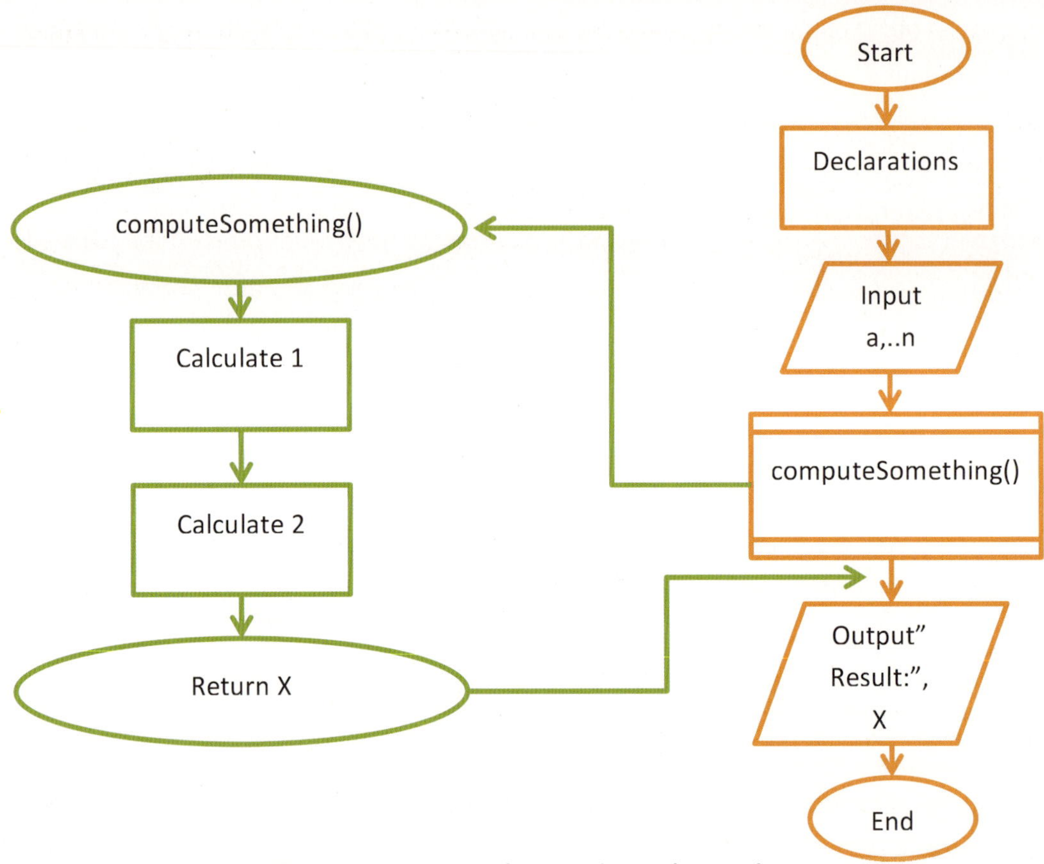

Figure 4.11: A program that contains a sub-procedure

4.1.20 Real-world and abstraction

Exit skills. Students should be able to[1]:
Compare and contrast real-world entities and their abstractions.

A *thematic map* is an abstraction of reality that shows the spatial distribution and emphasizes a particular theme, such as the average distribution of income in a specific geographic area.

Topographic maps show abstractions of selected physical features of the three-dimensional real world at a reduced scale in two-dimensions, paper or a screen.

Political maps are designed to show on data such as the boundaries of countries and states and the location of major cities. These maps are an abstraction of political territory.

In these cases, various levels of abstraction occur. The earth is unique but the point of interest guides the way scientists represent its surface on a piece of paper. This "selective ignorance" approach facilitates the study and understanding of specific components and interactions.

4.2 Connecting computational thinking and program design

4.2.1 Searching, sorting and other algorithms on arrays

Exit skills. Students should be able to[1, 17]:
Define the term variable. Define the term array. Explain the characteristics of sequential search and binary search. Explain the characteristics of bubble sort and selection sort. Develop various algorithms on arrays.

Variables

In computer science, a variable acts as a storage location that can be used to store a value. Each variable has a name (the term *identifier* is also used) that is used to refer to the stored value. The value of the variable can be changed during program execution. Each variable can store a particular type of data like *strings, reals, boolean* and *integers*.

One dimensional arrays or linear arrays

One variable can only store a data element of a program. If a second data element is needed then another variable should be created. The more data elements needed, the more distinct variables should be created by the programmer. An array can hold multiple data elements of the same type (*integers, strings, boolean* etc.). An array has a name, a size that cannot be changed during program execution (in most cases is a static data structure) and a data type that describes the type of data that it can store. A one-dimensional array is a type of linear array. Many programming languages, including Java, always define the lower bound of an array starting with the number 0. The pseudocode described in the IBO Computer Science Guide[1], uses zero-based arrays by default (unless otherwise specified). Consider the following array of integers: The size of the array is 10, the type is integer and the name is A.

Array index 0. A[0]	Array index 1. A[1]...........	Array index 9. A[9]
The first storage area of the array A	The second storage area of the array A	The tenth storage area of the array A

Table 4.2: Array

Programming Example 10: Use of array (array of numbers)

The following program will fill the array A with values from 1 to 10 and then print the values of the array.

```
// ==== Arrays ====

A = new Array()
N = 0
```

[17] Cormen, Thomas H.; Leiserson, Charles E., Rivest, Ronald L. (1990). Introduction to Algorithms (1st ed.). MIT Press and McGraw-Hill. ISBN 0-262-03141-8.

```
loop N from 0 to 9
   A[N] = N+1
end loop

loop N from 0 to 9
   output " Array position " , N , " contains the value", A[N]
end loop
```

Output:

Array position 0 contains the value 1

Array position 1 contains the value 2

Array position 2 contains the value 3

Array position 3 contains the value 4

Array position 4 contains the value 5

Array position 5 contains the value 6

Array position 6 contains the value 7

Array position 7 contains the value 8

Array position 8 contains the value 9

Array position 9 contains the value 10

Programming Example 11: Symmetric 1D array

The following program evaluates if an array is symmetric with respect to its middle element. If the array size is even, then the program stops.

```
ARRAY = new Array()
I = 0
J = 0
X = 0
N = input("Enter the size of array")

if (N mod 2 = 0) then
  output "Works only with odd numbers (eg 3 5 7.....)"
else
  loop I from 0 to N-1
    ARRAY[I] = input("Enter the next element")
  end loop
  I = (N div 2) - 1 // for pseudocode tool div(N,2)-1
  J = (N div 2) + 1 // for pseudocode tool div(N,2)+1
  loop while (I>=0) AND (J<N)
    if ARRAY[I] = ARRAY[J] then
      X = X+1
    end if
    I = I-1
    J = J+1
  end loop
  if X = (N-1)/2 then
    output "Array is symmetric"
  else
    output "Array is not symmetric"
  end if
end if
```

Programming Example 12: Smallest distance between two neighboring numbers of an array

Write an algorithm that finds the two neighboring numbers in an array with the smallest distance to each other. The program should output the distance, index of the first number and the index of the second number. For example, in the array **A = [5,1,4,7,9,-12]** the minimum distance is 2 (between array element 3 and 4). This algorithm should return: distance 2 between element 3 and element 4.

Useful Information: In this problem the use of a function that returns the absolute value of a number is essential. According to the IBO document Pseudocode in Examinations, Standard Data Structures and Examples of Pseudocode[21]: "If such a specialized method is to be used in an examination, it will be fully specified as part of the question in which it is needed."

```
//Use of Math.abs() function that returns the absolute value of a
//number. It is not included in the approved notation.
A = [5,1,4,7,9,-12]

SIZE = 6
MINIMUM  = Math.abs(A[0]-A[1])
MININDEX = 0
loop I from 1 to SIZE-2
         if Math.abs(A[I]-A[I+1])<MINIMUM then
            MINIMUM = Math.abs(A[I]-A[I+1])
            MININDEX = I
         end if
end loop
output "DISTANCE" , MINIMUM, "BETWEEN ELEMENT" , MININDEX, "AND
ELEMENT", MININDEX+1
```

Parallel arrays

Parallel arrays are extremely useful when a programmer wants to store different properties of an entity (fields of a record). All elements of an array should be of the same data type. So, if a programmer wants to store different data types of an entity (e.g. student) parallel arrays offer a convenient solution. The data are organized as a table. Each row represents a particular student and all columns are of the same data type.

Programming Example 13: Parallel arrays (names and grades)

In the following example 10 students' names and their equivalent grades will be used. The array NAMES of type `String` will be used to hold the names of the students, while the array GRADES of type `Integer` will hold the equivalent grades. The index of each array is the same for the same student. It is very important when using parallel arrays to always access each array at the same index when storing or retrieving values. This process guarantees the reference of corresponding data elements.

```
// ==== Arrays ====
NAMES =["May","Eri","Elen","Rit","Rato","More","Epi","Ent","Ronal","Bib"]
GRADES = [99,55,77,45,89,98,76,45,33,75]
MIN =  GRADES[0]
MAX =  GRADES[0]
AV = 0
AVERAGE = 0
M = 0
BEST = "0"
WORST = "0"

output "-----------------------"
output "STUDENTS LIST"
output "-----------------------"
loop M from 0 to 9
   output "No", M+1, "--Student    ", NAMES[M] , "      --Mark ",
GRADES[M]
end loop
loop M from 0 to 9
   if MIN >= GRADES[M] then
     MIN = GRADES[M]
     WORST = NAMES[M]
   end if
end loop
loop M from 0 to 9
   AV = AV + GRADES[M]
   if MAX <= GRADES[M] then
    MAX = GRADES[M]
    BEST = NAMES[M]
   end if
end loop
AVERAGE = AV/10
output "-------------"
output "Statistics"
output "-------------"
output "Minimum mark ", MIN , "Student ", WORST
output "Maximum mark ", MAX , "Student ", BEST
output "Class average ", AVERAGE
```

Output:

STUDENTS LIST

No 1 --Student May --Mark 99

No 2 --Student Eri --Mark 55

No 3 --Student Elen --Mark 77

No 4 --Student Rit --Mark 45

No 5 --Student Rato --Mark 89

No 6 --Student More --Mark 98

No 7 --Student Epi --Mark 76

No 8 --Student Ent --Mark 45

No 9 --Student Ronal --Mark 33

No 10 --Student Bib --Mark 75

Statistics

Minimum mark 33 Student Ronal
Maximum mark 99 Student May
Class average 69.2

Arrays of objects

An array of objects is an array of reference variables. Each reference variable is an element of the array and it's a reference to an object.

Programming Example 14: Use of array of objects

Suppose a programmer wants to create an array of vehicle objects named A. Each vehicle object has the following data fields: Colour, Type and Engine. The programmer wants to construct an array of vehicle objects with the following objects:

Vehicle1 [Colour: "red"-Type: "car"-Engine:2000]

Vehicle2 [Colour: "green"-Type: "bus"-Engine:4000]

Vehicle3 [Colour: "blue"-Type: "motorcycle"-Engine:800]

Elements of array A	OBJECT DATA FIELDS
`A[0] IS A REFERENCE TO Vehicle1` `A[0]= Vehicle1`	[Colour: "red"-Type: "car"-Engine:2000]
`A[1] IS A REFERENCE TO Vehicle2` `A[1]= Vehicle2`	[Colour: "green"-Type: "bus"-Engine:4000]
`A[2] IS A REFERENCE TO Vehicle3` `A[2]= Vehicle3`	[Colour:"blue"-Type:"motorcycle"-Engine:800]

```
//Use of an array of objects vehicle to find the location of
//an object that has data field type = "bus"

Vehicle1= new vehicle (setColour ="red", setType="car, setEngine
=2000)
Vehicle2= new vehicle (setColour ="green", setType="bus, setEngine
=4000)
Vehicle3= new vehicle (setColour ="blue", setType="motorcycle,
setEngine =800)

A = [Vehicle1, Vehicle2, Vehicle3]
loop I from 0 to 2
   if A[I].getType = "bus" then
      output "bus found at array position" , I
   end if
end loop
```

Two dimensional arrays

Although two dimensional arrays do not appear in the SL syllabus it is strongly recommended to study them. The understanding of the structure and function of 2D arrays enhances various algorithmic skills.

A one dimensional array should be considered as a single line of elements. However, in many cases, data come in the form of a data table. A typical example is a table that depicts the average monthly temperature for 10 cities.

		City 1	City 2	City 3	...	City 10
		Index 0	*Index 1*	*Index 2*		*Index 9*
January temperature	*Index 0*	15	28	20		20
February temperature	*Index 1*	14	27	20		19
...	...	...	...	...		...
December temperature	*Index 11*	15	26	21		20

Table 4.3: Two dimensional arrays

2D arrays are indexed by two subscripts. The indices must be integers. The first one refers to the row and the second to the column. **TEMP[1][1]** refers to February temperature of City 2. The value is 27. Each element in a two dimensional array must be of the same data type.

Programming Example 15: Two dimensional array (temperatures)

```
//This program will use the array TEMP which is a 2D ARRAY
//It will print the contents of the array
//12 months 5 cities
TEMP =
[[10,11,12,13,10],
[10,13,14,12,12],
[13,13,14,15,12],
[16,17,17,17,16],
[22,23,24,24,24],
[26,25,24,25,26],
[29,28,26,27,26],
[29,28,27,28,28],
[24,23,24,25,25],
[20,21,22,23,24],
[15,16,17,18,18],
[12,11,13,11,11]]
MONTH = 0
CITY = 0
loop MONTH from 0 to 11
    output MONTH +1, "Month"

    loop CITY from 0 to 4
      output "City", CITY+1, TEMP[MONTH][CITY]
    end loop
end loop
```

Programming Example 16: Extracting information from a 2D array to various one dimensional arrays.

```
//
A = [[0,1,2],
     [2,3,4],
     [5,6,7]]

LINE1 = new Array()
LINE2 = new Array()
```

```
LINE3 = new Array()
COLUMN1 = new Array()
COLUMN2 = new Array()
COLUMN3 = new Array()
DIAGONAL = new Array()

I=0
COUNT1 = 0
COUNT2 = 0
COUNT3 = 0
COUNT4 = 0
COUNT5 = 0
COUNT6 = 0
COUNT7 = 0

loop I from 0 to 2
  loop J from 0 to 2
       if J == 0 then
         COLUMN1[COUNT1] = A[I][J]
         COUNT1 = COUNT1+1
       else if J == 1 then
         COLUMN2[COUNT2] = A[I][J]
         COUNT2 = COUNT2+1
       else
          COLUMN3[COUNT3] = A[I][J]
          COUNT3 = COUNT3+1
       end if
       if I==J then
          DIAGONAL[COUNT4] = A[I][J]
          COUNT4 = COUNT4+1
       end if
       if I == 0 then
          LINE1[COUNT5] = A[I][J]
          COUNT5 = COUNT5+1
       else if I==1 then
          LINE2[COUNT6] = A[I][J]
          COUNT6 = COUNT6+1
       else
         LINE3[COUNT7] = A[I][J]
         COUNT7 = COUNT7+1
       end if
   end loop
end loop

output "LINE1:"
loop I from 0 to 2
   output LINE1[I]
end loop

output "LINE2:"
loop I from 0 to 2
   output LINE2[I]
end loop

output "LINE3:"
loop I from 0 to 2
   output LINE3[I]
end loop

output "COLUMN1:"
loop I from 0 to 2
```

```
   output COLUMN1[I]
end loop

output "COLUMN2:"
loop I from 0 to 2
   output COLUMN2[I]
end loop

output "COLUMN3:"
loop I from 0 to 2
   output COLUMN3[I]
end loop

output "DIAGONAL:"
loop I from 0 to 2
   output DIAGONAL[I]
end loop
```

Programming Example 17: Two dimensional array (lesson grades)

```
//The following table contains the grades of
//three students (x, y, z) for two lessons.
A =  [[85 , 72],
      [82 , 93],
      [75 , 56]]
output
loop J from 0 to 1
 output "next lesson"
  loop I from 0 to 2
    output "lesson", J, "student ", I,  A[I][J]
  end loop
end loop
output "____"
loop J from 0 to 2
 output "next student"
  loop I from 0 to 1
 output "student", J, "lesson ", I,  A[J][I]
  end loop
end loop
```

Programming Example 18: Smallest difference between two neighboring numbers of a 2D array

Write an algorithm that finds the two neighboring numbers in a two dimensional array with the smallest difference to each other. The program should output the difference, index of the first number and the index of the second number. For example in the array

-22, 12,-33
33, 62, 21
54, 22, 42

the smallest difference is 20 = abs(22-42). Between array element [2,1] and [2,2].

```
//Math.abs will be given as a part of the examination question
A = new Array()
A = [[-22,12,-33],
     [33,62,21],
```

```
    [54,22,42]]
N = 3
INDEXROW = 0
INDEXCOLUMN = 0
DIRECTION = ""
MINIMUM = Math.abs(A[0][0]-A[0][1])
loop I from 0 to N-1
  loop J from 0 to N-2
    if Math.abs(A[I][J]-A[I][J+1])<MINIMUM then
      MINIMUM=Math.abs(A[I][J]-A[I][J+1])
      INDEXROW=I
      INDEXCOLUMN=J
      DIRECTION = "ROWS"
    end if
  end loop
end loop
loop J from 0 to N-1
  loop I from 0 to N-2
    if Math.abs(A[I][J]-A[I+1][J])<MINIMUM then
      MINIMUM=Math.abs(A[I][J]-A[I+1][J])
      INDEXROW=I
      INDEXCOLUMN=J
      DIRECTION = "COLUMNS"
    end if
  end loop
end loop

output "DISTANCE" , MINIMUM
if DIRECTION  == "ROWS" then
  output "BETWEEN ELEMENT" , INDEXROW, INDEXCOLUMN, "AND ELEMENT",
INDEXROW, INDEXCOLUMN+1
else
  output "BETWEEN ELEMENT" , INDEXROW, INDEXCOLUMN, "AND ELEMENT",
INDEXROW+1, INDEXCOLUMN
end if
```

Output:
DISTANCE 20
BETWEEN ELEMENT 21 AND ELEMENT 22

Comparison of one-dimensional arrays, two dimensional arrays, parallel arrays and arrays of objects.

Suppose a programmer wants to develop a program that will use a data structure to store lesson grades information for five students. Each student is represented by a record. Four different data fields are used for each student. Two data fields of type string will be used to store Name and Surname while two integer data fields will be used to store the grades for Math and Chemistry respectively. The following table illustrates the scenario described:

	Field 1	Field 2	Field 3	Field 4
	Name	Surname	Math grade	Chemistry grade
Record 1	James	Smith	89	78
Record 2	Mary	Johnson	89	80
Record 3	John	Williams	78	78
Record 4	Patricia	Jones	89	67
Record 5	Linda	Brown	88	70

A one dimensional array is not able to store all the necessary information because it can only store one data type and apparently it can only store one field. So, the programmer should use five different one dimensional arrays, which shall be used as parallel arrays.

A two dimensional array cannot solve the problem because it can only store one data type. So, the programmer will need one two dimensional array to store data for Name and Surname fields and one two dimensional array to store data for Math grade field and Chemistry grade field. The programmer will use these two arrays as parallel arrays.

The creation of an array of Student objects named A can facilitate the situation. Each Student object will have the following data fields: Name, Surname, Math_grade and Chemistry_grade. The programmer will construct an array of student objects with the following objects:

Student1 [Name: "James"-Surname:"Smith"-Math_grade:89-Chemistry_grade:78]

....

Student5 [Name: "Linda"-Surname:"Brown"-Math_grade:88-Chemistry_grade:70]

Sequential search

A sequential or linear search algorithm is a very simple method to find a particular element in an array. It is considered to be the simplest search algorithm. The implementation of this algorithm does not require the use of ordered elements (sorted arrays). It relies on *brute force strategy* to accomplish its purpose.

Programming Example 19: Sequential search

```
//==== Sequential Search ==========
N = [2, 9, 5, 6, 7, 8]//Array elements
X =  7 //Search value
Found= false //Boolean value
Counter = 0 //It will be used for the loop

loop Counter from 0 to 5 //Number of array elements - 1
   if N[Counter] = X then
      Found = true
      output N[Counter],"found at position" , Counter
   end if
end loop

if Found = false then
   output X,"not found"
end if
```

Output:

7 found at position 4

Binary search[18]

Binary search (*or half interval search*) algorithm is a searching method used only in sorted arrays. It relies *on divide and conquer strategy* to accomplish its purpose. In every search iteration, half of the elements of the array are eliminated as possible solutions. Binary search is very efficient for large arrays. Its performance makes it ideal when resorting is not required.

In each iteration, the algorithm

1. Compares the search value with the value of the middle element of the array.
   a. If the values match, then the value was found .
   b. If the search value is less than the middle element of the array,
      - then the algorithm repeats its action on the sub-array to the left of the middle element.
   c. if the search value is greater than the middle element of the array,
      - then the algorithm repeats its action on the sub-array to the right of the middle element.
2. If the remaining array to be searched is empty, then the value was not found.

Programming Example 20: Binary search

```
//==== Binary Search =====
VALUES = [11,12,15,16,112,118,123,145] //sorted array elements
TARGET = 15 //search value
MIN = 0
HIGH = 7 // Number of array elements - 1
FOUND = false
ANSWER = 0
MID =0

loop while FOUND != true AND MIN <= HIGH
  MID = ((MIN + HIGH) div 2)
  if VALUES[MID] = TARGET then
      FOUND = true
      ANSWER = MID
  else if TARGET > VALUES[MID] then
     MIN = MID + 1
  else
     HIGH = MID - 1
  end if
end while
if FOUND = true then
   output TARGET , "FOUND AT ARRAY INDEX" , ANSWER
else
   output TARGET , " was not found"
end if
```

Output: 15 FOUND AT ARRAY INDEX 2

---

[18] Binary search algorithm. (2015, June 11). In Wikipedia, The Free Encyclopedia. Retrieved 06:33, July 1, 2015, from https://en.wikipedia.org/w/index.php?title=Binary_search_algorithm&oldid=666547193

Construct a trace table for the previous algorithm showing what happens after the finish of each loop pass.

	TARGET	MIN	HIGH	FOUND	ANSWER	MID	output
Before the first loop	15	0	7	false	0	0	-
After first loop pass	15	0	2	false	0	3	-
After second loop pas	15	2	2	false	0	1	-
After third loop pass	15	2	2	true	2	2	15 FOUND AT ARRAY INDEX 2

```
START
Declare Array Values and Fill with values
[11,12,15,16,,112,118,123,145]
Declare and Set Integer TARGET =15
Declare and Set Integer MIN = 0
Declare and Set Integer HIGH = 7
Declare and Set Integer ANSWER = 0
Declare and Set Boolean FOUND = true
Declare Integer MID
```

......

......

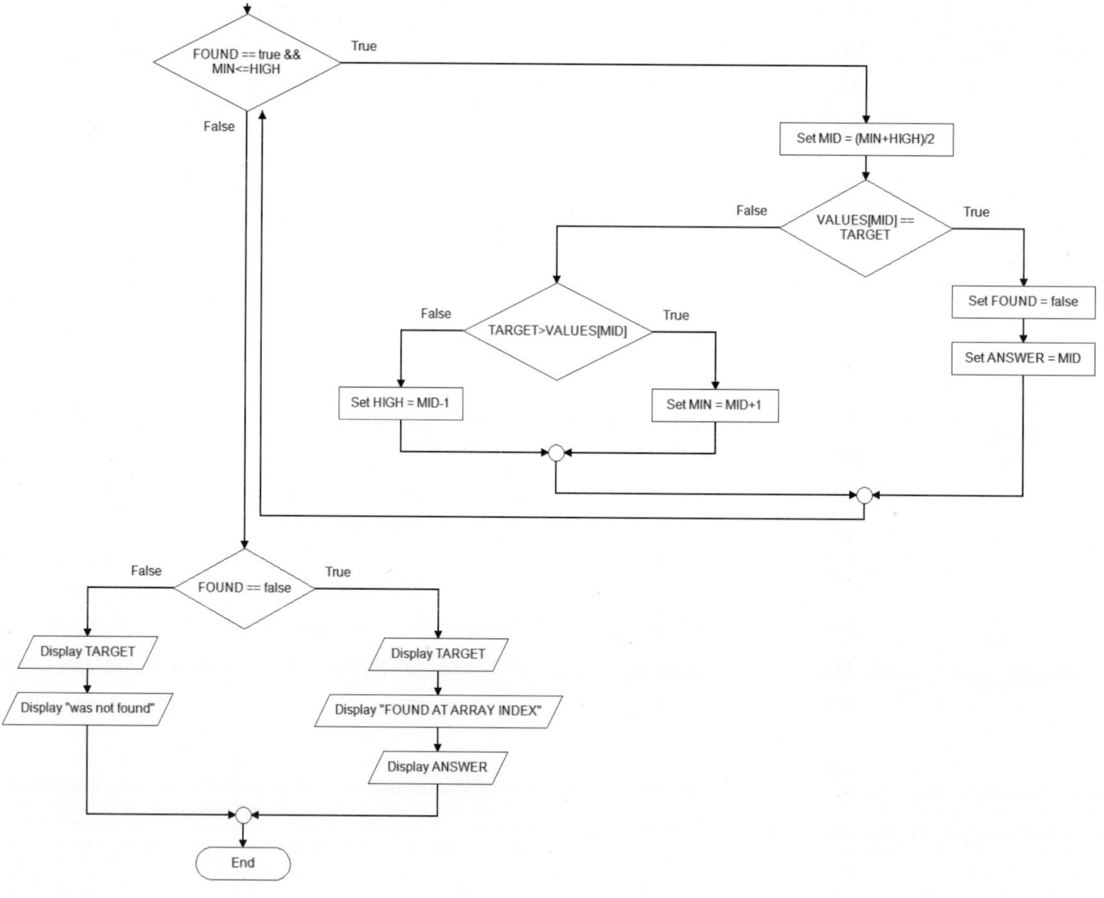

Figure 4.12 Binary search flowchart

Comparison table of linear search and binary search

Binary search	Linear search
Works only on sorted elements	Works on sorted as well as unsorted items.
Generally number of comparisons are less	Efficient for few elements Efficient if the element to be found is located in the beginning of the array or list Generally more number of comparisons are required if the element to be found is not present in the beginning of the array or list
Time complexity: O(log n)	**Time complexity: O(n)**

Bubble sort[19]

Bubble sort is a simple sorting algorithm that repeatedly steps through the array to be sorted. It compares adjacent items (pairs of adjacent array elements) and exchanges them if they are not in the correct order (ascending or descending). The algorithm makes multiple passes until no swaps are necessary and the elements of the array are sorted. The algorithm is named for the way elements "bubble" to the top of the array. After each loop, one less element (the leftmost) needs to be compared. The algorithm is very slow and impractical for most cases.

Programming Example 21: Bubble sort

```
//==== Bubble Sort ====
ELEMENTS = [1,663,8,2,4,1,22,66,20,122]
loop I from 0 to 8// Number of elements - 2
    loop J from 0 to (8-I)
        if ELEMENTS[J] < ELEMENTS[J + 1] then //for descending order
OR
        if ELEMENTS[J] > ELEMENTS[J + 1] then //for ascending order
            TEMP = ELEMENTS[J]
            ELEMENTS[J] = ELEMENTS[J+1]
            ELEMENTS[J+1] = TEMP
        end if
    end loop
end loop

output "Sorted elements"

loop E from 0 to 9
   output ELEMENTS[E]
end loop
```

[19] Bubble sort. (2015, June 15). In *Wikipedia, The Free Encyclopedia*. Retrieved 17:26, June 19, 2015, from https://en.wikipedia.org/w/index.php?title=Bubble_sort&oldid=667050446

if ELEMENTS[J] < ELEMENTS[J + 1] then //for descending order	if ELEMENTS[J] > ELEMENTS[J + 1] then //for ascending order
output: Sorted elements 663 122 66 22 20 8 4 2 1 1	output: Sorted elements 1 1 2 4 8 20 22 66 122 663

Construct a trace table for the previous algorithm showing what happens after the finish of each inner loop pass (descending order).

Loop pass 1	I= 0	J= 0	TEMP= 1	ELEMENTS[J]= 663	ELEMENTS[J+1]= 1
Loop pass 2	I= 0	J= 1	TEMP= 1	ELEMENTS[J]= 8	ELEMENTS[J+1]= 1
Loop pass 3	I= 0	J= 2	TEMP= 1	ELEMENTS[J]= 2	ELEMENTS[J+1]= 1
Loop pass 4	I= 0	J= 3	TEMP= 1	ELEMENTS[J]= 4	ELEMENTS[J+1]= 1
Loop pass 5	I= 0	J= 4	TEMP= 1	ELEMENTS[J]= 1	ELEMENTS[J+1]= 1
Loop pass 6	I= 0	J= 5	TEMP= 1	ELEMENTS[J]= 22	ELEMENTS[J+1]= 1
Loop pass 7	I= 0	J= 6	TEMP= 1	ELEMENTS[J]= 66	ELEMENTS[J+1]= 1
Loop pass 8	I= 0	J= 7	TEMP= 1	ELEMENTS[J]= 20	ELEMENTS[J+1]= 1
Loop pass 9	I= 0	J= 8	TEMP= 1	ELEMENTS[J]= 122	ELEMENTS[J+1]= 1
Loop pass 10	I= 1	J= 0	TEMP= 1	ELEMENTS[J]= 663	ELEMENTS[J+1]= 8
Loop pass 11	I= 1	J= 1	TEMP= 1	ELEMENTS[J]= 8	ELEMENTS[J+1]= 2
Loop pass 12	I= 1	J= 2	TEMP= 2	ELEMENTS[J]= 4	ELEMENTS[J+1]= 2
Loop pass 13	I= 1	J= 3	TEMP= 2	ELEMENTS[J]= 2	ELEMENTS[J+1]= 1
Loop pass 14	I= 1	J= 4	TEMP= 1	ELEMENTS[J]= 22	ELEMENTS[J+1]= 1
Loop pass 15	I= 1	J= 5	TEMP= 1	ELEMENTS[J]= 66	ELEMENTS[J+1]= 1
Loop pass 16	I= 1	J= 6	TEMP= 1	ELEMENTS[J]= 20	ELEMENTS[J+1]= 1
Loop pass 17	I= 1	J= 7	TEMP= 1	ELEMENTS[J]= 122	ELEMENTS[J+1]= 1
Loop pass 18	I= 2	J= 0	TEMP= 1	ELEMENTS[J]= 663	ELEMENTS[J+1]= 8
Loop pass 19	I= 2	J= 1	TEMP= 1	ELEMENTS[J]= 8	ELEMENTS[J+1]= 4
Loop pass 20	I= 2	J= 2	TEMP= 1	ELEMENTS[J]= 4	ELEMENTS[J+1]= 2
Loop pass 21	I= 2	J= 3	TEMP= 2	ELEMENTS[J]= 22	ELEMENTS[J+1]= 2
Loop pass 22	I= 2	J= 4	TEMP= 2	ELEMENTS[J]= 66	ELEMENTS[J+1]= 2
Loop pass 23	I= 2	J= 5	TEMP= 2	ELEMENTS[J]= 20	ELEMENTS[J+1]= 2
Loop pass 24	I= 2	J= 6	TEMP= 2	ELEMENTS[J]= 122	ELEMENTS[J+1]= 2
Loop pass 25	I= 3	J= 0	TEMP= 2	ELEMENTS[J]= 663	ELEMENTS[J+1]= 8
Loop pass 26	I= 3	J= 1	TEMP= 2	ELEMENTS[J]= 8	ELEMENTS[J+1]= 4
Loop pass 27	I= 3	J= 2	TEMP= 4	ELEMENTS[J]= 22	ELEMENTS[J+1]= 4

Loop pass 28	I= 3	J= 3	TEMP= 4	ELEMENTS[J]= 66	ELEMENTS[J+1]= 4
Loop pass 29	I= 3	J= 4	TEMP= 4	ELEMENTS[J]= 20	ELEMENTS[J+1]= 4
Loop pass 30	I= 3	J= 5	TEMP= 4	ELEMENTS[J]= 122	ELEMENTS[J+1]= 4
Loop pass 31	I= 4	J= 0	TEMP= 4	ELEMENTS[J]= 663	ELEMENTS[J+1]= 8
Loop pass 32	I= 4	J= 1	TEMP= 8	ELEMENTS[J]= 22	ELEMENTS[J+1]= 8
Loop pass 33	I= 4	J= 2	TEMP= 8	ELEMENTS[J]= 66	ELEMENTS[J+1]= 8
Loop pass 34	I= 4	J= 3	TEMP= 8	ELEMENTS[J]= 20	ELEMENTS[J+1]= 8
Loop pass 35	I= 4	J= 4	TEMP= 8	ELEMENTS[J]= 122	ELEMENTS[J+1]= 8
Loop pass 36	I= 5	J= 0	TEMP= 8	ELEMENTS[J]= 663	ELEMENTS[J+1]= 22
Loop pass 37	I= 5	J= 1	TEMP= 22	ELEMENTS[J]= 66	ELEMENTS[J+1]= 22
Loop pass 38	I= 5	J= 2	TEMP= 22	ELEMENTS[J]= 22	ELEMENTS[J+1]= 20
Loop pass 39	I= 5	J= 3	TEMP= 20	ELEMENTS[J]= 122	ELEMENTS[J+1]= 20
Loop pass 40	I= 6	J= 0	TEMP= 20	ELEMENTS[J]= 663	ELEMENTS[J+1]= 66
Loop pass 41	I= 6	J= 1	TEMP= 20	ELEMENTS[J]= 66	ELEMENTS[J+1]= 22
Loop pass 42	I= 6	J= 2	TEMP= 22	ELEMENTS[J]= 122	ELEMENTS[J+1]= 22
Loop pass 43	I= 7	J= 0	TEMP= 22	ELEMENTS[J]= 663	ELEMENTS[J+1]= 66
Loop pass 44	I= 7	J= 1	TEMP= 66	ELEMENTS[J]= 122	ELEMENTS[J+1]= 66
Loop pass 45	I= 8	J= 0	TEMP= 66	ELEMENTS[J]= 663	ELEMENTS[J+1]= 122

Programming Example 22: Bubble sort (2)

```
//==== Bubble Sort ====
//version with while loops
//sorts in descending order
ELEMENTS = [1,663,8,2,4,1,22,66,20,122]
N = 10
I = 0
loop while I <= N-1
J = 0
    loop while J <= N-I-2
        if ELEMENTS[J] < ELEMENTS[J + 1] then
          TEMP = ELEMENTS[J]
          ELEMENTS[J] = ELEMENTS[J+1]
          ELEMENTS[J+1] = TEMP
        end if
    J = J+1
    end loop
I = I+1
end loop

output "Sorted elements"

loop E from 0 to 9
   output ELEMENTS[E]
end loop
```

Selection sort[20]

Selection sort is a very simple and inefficient sorting algorithm that divides the input array into two sub-arrays: the first sub-array contains the already sorted elements, and the second

[20] Selection sort. (2015, June 11). In *Wikipedia, The Free Encyclopedia. Retrieved 17:28, June 19, 2015, from https://en.wikipedia.org/w/index.php?title=Selection_sort&oldid=666542512*

sub-array contains the unsorted elements and occupies the rest of the array. The first sub-array is built up from left to right at the lowest index position [I=0]. At the beginning, the sub-array that contains the sorted elements is empty and the sub-array that contains the unsorted element is the entire array. The algorithm continues by finding the smallest (or largest, depending on the sorting order) element in the sub-array that contains the unsorted elements, exchanging it with the leftmost unsorted element (the element located in the lowest index position) and putting it in sorted order. The algorithm then moves the first sub-array borders one element to the right.

Programming Example 23: Selection sort

```
//==== Selection Sort ====

ELEMENTS = [1,5,3,86,256,420,9,510,51,24,60]
MIN = 0
I = 0
TEMP = 0

loop MIN from 0 to 9
    I = MIN
    loop CURRENT from MIN+1 to 10
        if ELEMENTS[CURRENT] > ELEMENTS[I] then//for descending order
OR
        if ELEMENTS[CURRENT] < ELEMENTS[I] then//for ascending order
            I = CURRENT
        end if
    end loop
    TEMP = ELEMENTS[I]
    ELEMENTS[I] = ELEMENTS[MIN]
    ELEMENTS[MIN] = TEMP
end loop

output "SORTED ARRAY"
loop C from 0 to 10
   output ELEMENTS[C]
end loop
```

`if ELEMENTS[CURRENT] > ELEMENTS[I] then`	`if ELEMENTS[CURRENT] < ELEMENTS[I] then`
OUTPUT: SORTED ARRAY	OUTPUT: SORTED ARRAY
510	1
420	3
256	5
86	9
60	24
51	51
24	60
9	86
5	256
3	420
1	510

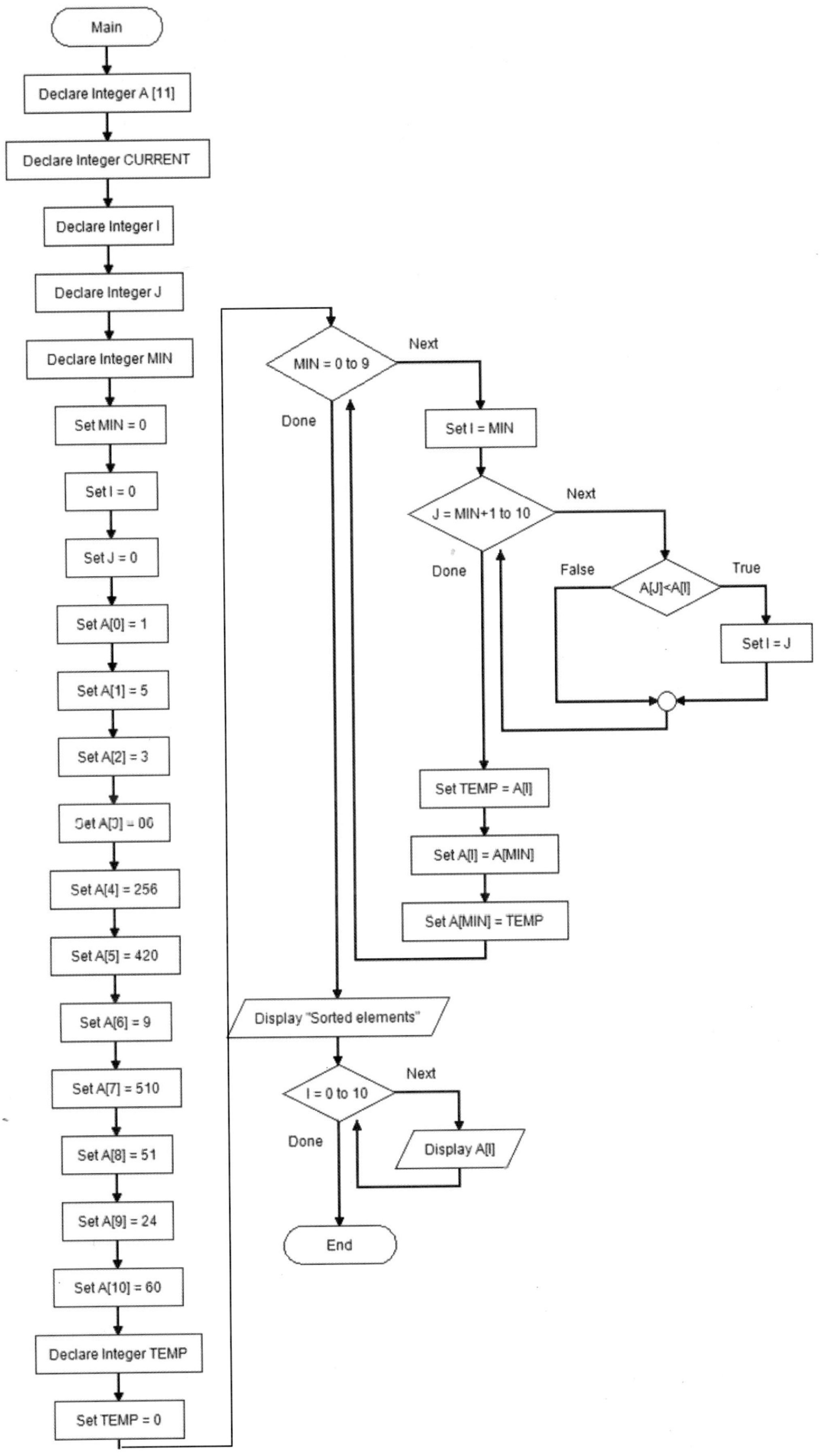

Figure 4.13 selection sort flowchart

4.2.2 Standard operations of collections

Exit skills. Students should be able to[1]:
Explain the standard operations of collections. Explain additional operations of collections.

An array is a perfect choice when a programmer wishes to store the same type of information; a group of strings for example and he/she knows in advance the number of items that he/she wishes to store. But what happens when the programmer wishes to store integers, arrays, objects, booleans and strings in one data structure? The answer is to use *collections* because some collections allow custom specification of the collection item elements. In C# and Visual Basic for example, *generic* collections can only hold data of the same type while *non generic* collections can hold elements of different data types. The most significant advantage of collections is that they act like a resizable array. The programmer does not need to know in advance the number of items that will be placed in the data structure.

The following operations appear in the IBO CS Approved notations for developing pseudocode[14] and IBO CS Pseudocode in examinations[21].

Standard operations

- **`addItem()`**. It is used to add an item in the collection (addition). TEMPERATURES is a collection of temperatures. **`TEMPERATURES.addItem(32)`** will add 32 to the collection TEMPRATURES.
- **`getNext()`**. It is used to return the first item in the collection when it is first called (retrieval). TEMPERATURES is a collection of temperature measurements. **`A=TEMPERATURES.getNext()`** will assign the value of the first item in the collection to the variable A. However, **`getNext()`** will not remove the item from the collection.

Additional operations

- **`resetNext()`**. It is used to restart the iteration through the collection. TEMPERATURES is a collection of temperatures. **`TEMPERATURES.resetNext()`** will restart the iteration through the collection TEMPRATURES.
- **`hasNext()`**. It is used to identify if there are remaining elements in the collection that have not been accessed by the present iteration. TEMPERATURES is a collection of temperatures. **`If TEMPERATURES.hasNext()`** will return **`TRUE`** if there are one or more elements in the collection TEMPRATURES that have not been accessed by the present iteration.

---

[21] International Baccalaureate Organization. (2012). IBDP Pseudocode in examinations.

- **isEmpty()**. It is used to test if the collection is empty. TEMPERATURES is a collection of temperatures. **If TEMPERATURES.isEmpty()** will return **TRUE** if the collection is empty.

4.2.3 Algorithm to solve a specific problem

Exit skills. Students should be able to[1]:

Explain the differences between two or more algorithms.
Explain advantages and disadvantages of algorithms.
Develop and explain an algorithm to address a specific problem.

Programming Example 24: Algorithm to address a specific problem

Suppose a programmer wants to develop a program that records temperatures for four cities. The program should ask for each city name, and highest and lowest temperature for a particular year. Three arrays will be used to store the city names, the low temperatures, and the high temperatures. After storing all the data, the program should display a list of cities with high temperatures above the average high, and a list of cities with low temperatures below the average low. The solution to this problem follows.

```
//A program that outputs the cities with temperatures
//above the average of high temperatures and cities
//below the average of low temperatures
TOTALH = 0 //Variable declaration and initialization (total high)
TOTALL = 0 //Variable declaration and initialization (total low)
AVGH = 0 //Variable declaration and initialization (average of high)
AVGL = 0 //Variable declaration and initialization (average of low)
CITYNAMES = new Array()//Declaration of array that will hold the
names
HIGHTEMP = new Array() //Declaration of array for high temperatures
LOWTEMP = new Array() //Declaration of array for low temperatures

loop I from 0 to 3 //Iteration to serve the data input process

    input CITYNAMES[I] //THIS BLOCK IS EQUIVALENT TO THE NEXT BLOCK
    input HIGHTEMP[I]  //DONT USE BOTH BLOCKS
    input LOWTEMP[I]

    CITYNAMES[I] = input("Type the name of the city")
    HIGHTEMP[I] = input("Type the Maximum temperature of the city")
    LOWTEMP[I] = input("Type the Minimum temperature of the city")

    TOTALH = TOTALH + HIGHTEMP[I];//Calculation of sum of all high
//temperatures
    TOTALL  = TOTALL + LOWTEMP[I]; //Calculation of sum of all low
//temperatures
end loop // end of loop

AVGH = TOTALH/4 //Calculation of average for high temperatures
AVGL = TOTALL/4 //Calculation of average for low temperatures

output "Cities Above Avg. High:" //It will print the message
loop I from 0 to 3 //loop to output the cities Above avg. high
```

```
    if HIGHTEMP[I]>AVGH then //start of if conditional statement. If
true then the following statement will be executed
        output CITYNAMES[I] ,"+" //output of cities that fulfil the
//criteria
    end if //end of if conditional statement
end loop //end of loop


output "Cities Below Avg. Low:" //It will print the message
loop I from 0 to 3 //loop to output the cities below avg. low
    if LOWTEMP[I]<AVGL then //start of if conditional statement. If
true then the following statement will be executed
        output CITYNAMES[I] ,"+"
    end if //end of if conditional statement
end loop //end of loop
```

4.2.4 Analyse an algorithm presented as a flow chart

Exit skills. Students should be able to[1]:
Explain a flowchart. Calculate the output of an algorithm presented as flowchart. Convert a flowchart to pseudocode. Trace a flowchart. Find the output of an algorithm as flowchart.

Programming Example 25 and Example 26: Example of flowchart and explanation

An algorithm that checks if two strings are equal and outputs correct or wrong. (This is an algorithm and not IB pseudocode.)

```
Declare String A
Declare String PASSWORD

Set A = "MORGAN"
Input PASSWORD
If PASSWORD == A Then
    Display "CORRECT"
Else
    Display "WRONG"
End If
```

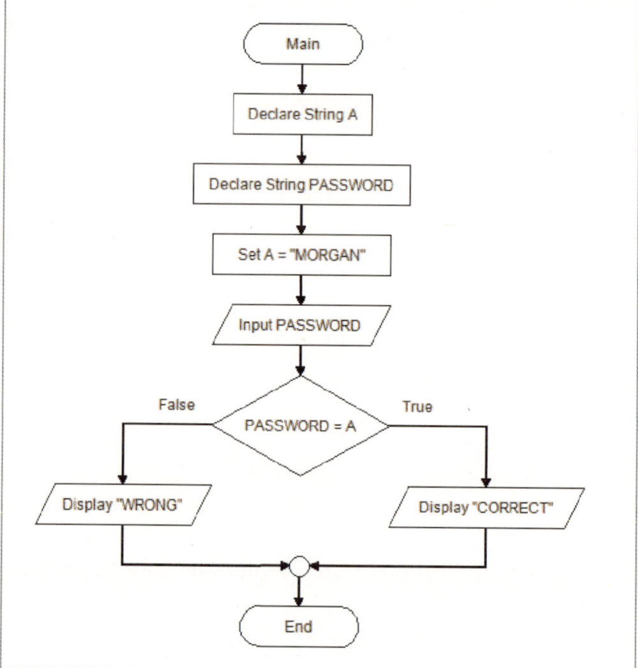

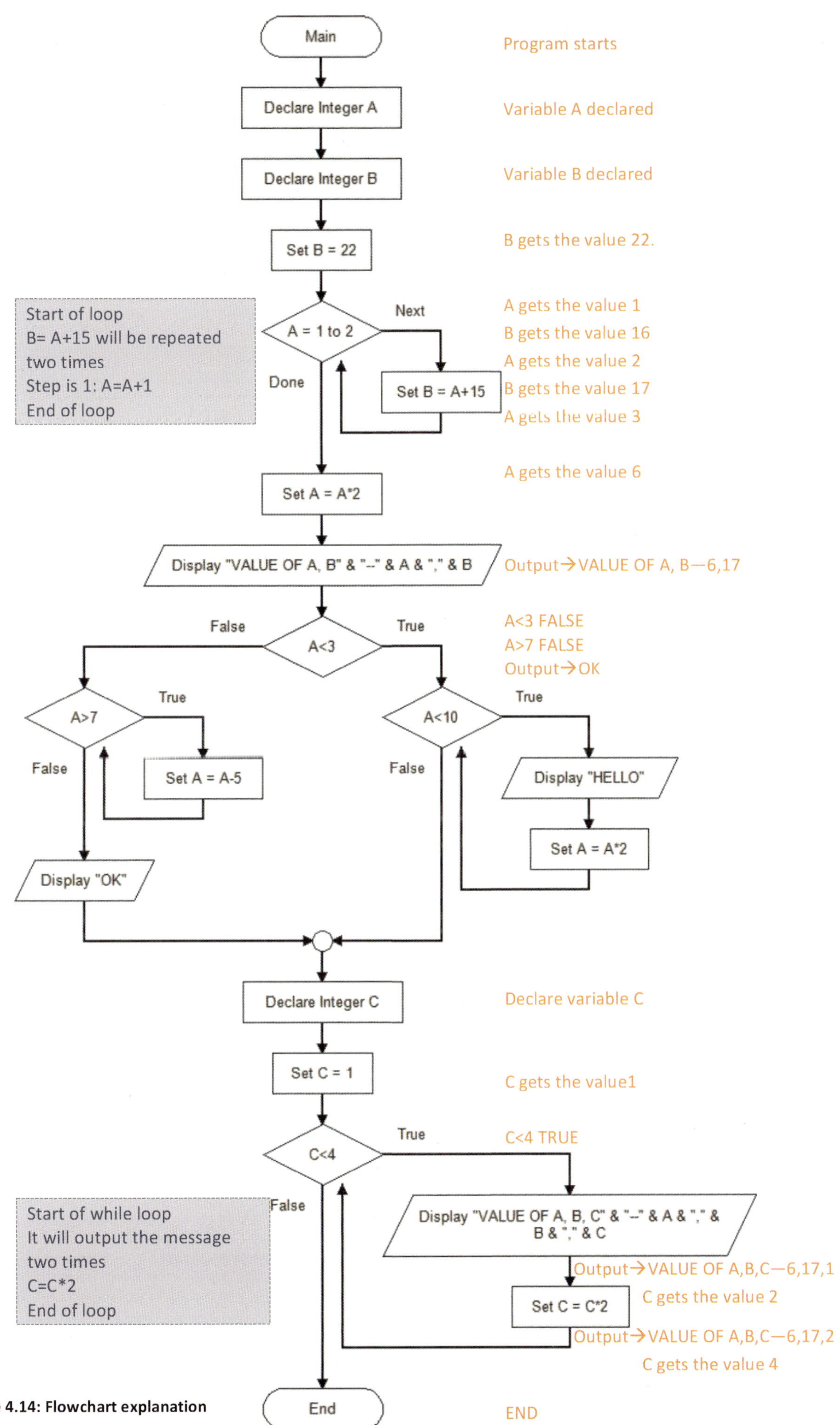

Figure 4.14: Flowchart explanation

Programming Example 27: Example of flowchart

The following algorithms in pseudocode and flowchart form will produce the same output:

```
n = 0
loop while n <= 3
   output "OK"
   n = n +1
end loop
output n
```

```
n = 0
loop n from 0 to 3
   output "OK"
end loop
output n
```

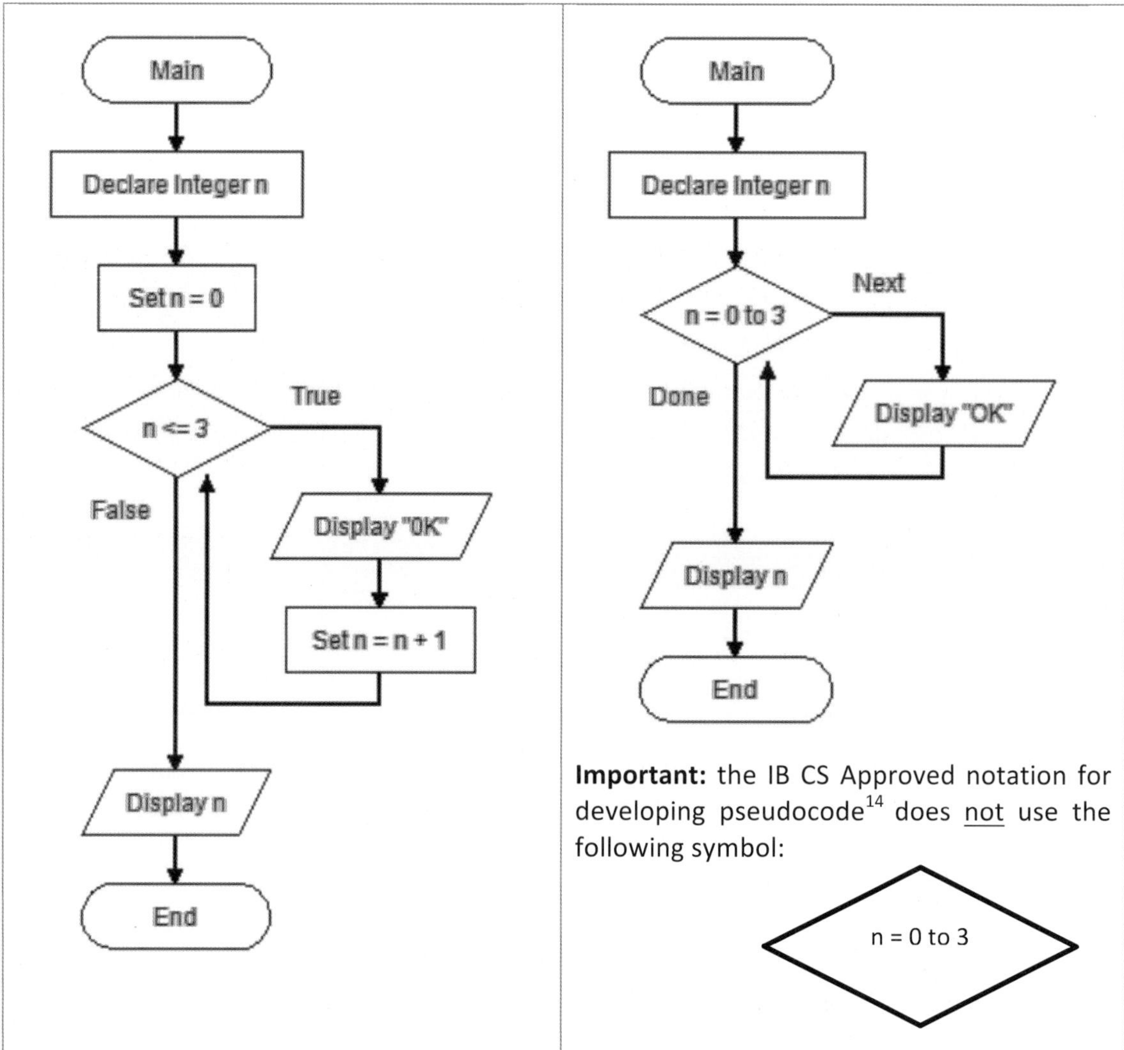

Important: the IB CS Approved notation for developing pseudocode[14] does <u>not</u> use the following symbol:

The following algorithms expressed in Java language will produce the same result:

```
import java.util.Scanner;
import java.util.*;
import java.lang.Math;

class MyProgram {

  public static void
main(String[] args) {

    int n;
    n = 0;
```

```
import java.util.Scanner;
import java.util.*;
import java.lang.Math;

class MyProgram {

  public static void
main(String[] args) {

    int n;

    for (n=0; n<=3; n=n+1) {
```

```
    while (n<=3) {

      System.out.println("OK");
        n=n+1;
      }
    System.out.println(n);
  }
}
```

```
      System.out.println("OK");
    }
    System.out.println(n);
  }
}
```

Output:

OK
OK
OK
OK
4

4.2.5 Analyse an algorithm presented as pseudocode

Exit skills. Students should be able to[1]:
Explain a flowchart Calculate the output of an algorithm presented as pseudocode. Trace an algorithm presented as pseudocode. Find the output of an algorithm presented as pseudocode.

Programming Example 28: Trace an algorithm

Suppose we want to trace the following algorithm

```
//Trace the algorithm

MAX = 10
SUM = 0
COUNT = 0

loop COUNT from 0 to MAX-6
  if COUNT = 0 AND MAX > 0 then
    output "Hello"
  else if COUNT > 2 then
     output "Go for it"
  else
     output "OK"
  end if
end loop
SUM = SUM + COUNT

output "Total = " , SUM
```

The following table is the trace table for the algorithm:

MAX	SUM	COUNT	OUTPUT	COMMENTS
10	0	0	Hello	COUNT = 0 AND MAX > 0 TRUE
10	0	1	OK	COUNT = 0 AND MAX > 0 FALSE

				COUNT > 2 FALSE
10	0	2	OK	COUNT = 0 AND MAX > 0 FALSE COUNT > 2 FALSE
10	0	3	Go for it	COUNT = 0 AND MAX > 0 FALSE COUNT > 2 TRUE
10	0	4	Go for it	COUNT = 0 AND MAX > 0 FALSE COUNT > 2 TRUE
10	0	5		Exit from loop
10	5	5	Total = 5	

Programming Example 29: Calculating the output of an algorithm

What is going to be the output of the following algorithm?

```
//Find the output of the following algorithm
MAX = 10
SUM = 0
COUNT = 0

loop COUNT from 0 to MAX-4
 SUM = MAX - 4
 COUNT = MAX - 3
 loop SUM from 3 to 4
  if COUNT = 0 AND MAX > 0 then
    output "Hello"
  else if COUNT < 4 then
     output "Go for it"
  else
     output "OK"
  end if
 end loop
end loop
SUM = SUM + COUNT

output "Total = " , SUM
output "MAX = " , COUNT
```

Answer:
OK
OK
Total = 13
MAX = 8

Programming Example 30: Identify the error

The following program is supposed to output all the common factors of two numbers. It contains an error. Identify this error.

```
//This program is supposed
//to print the common factors of two numbers
//Find the error!!

FIRST = 14
```

```
SECOND = 12
output "Common factors of numbers" , FIRST , " and " , SECOND
loop COUNT from 1 to SECOND
    if (FIRST mod COUNT = 0) OR (SECOND mod COUNT = 0) then
       output COUNT
    end if
end loop
```

Wrong Output:

Common factors of numbers 14 and 12

1

2

3

4

6

7

12

Answer:

`if (FIRST mod COUNT = 0) OR (SECOND mod COUNT = 0) then` **should be changed to**

`if (FIRST mod COUNT = 0) AND (SECOND mod COUNT = 0) then`

Correct Output:

Common factors of numbers 14 and 12

1

2

Programming Example 31: Identify the error

The following program is supposed to output common elements that appear in two arrays. It contains an error. Identify this error.

```
//This algorithm is supposed to
//compare two arrays and finds
//duplicates that appear in both arrays

ARRAY1 = ["aa","11","34","ff","mm"]
ARRAY2 = ["ff","hh","mn","33","34"]

output "The following items appear in both arrays"

loop A1 from 0 to 4
    loop A2 from 0 to 4
        if ARRAY1[A1] = ARRAY2[A2] then
            output ARRAY2[A1]
        end if
    end loop
end loop
```

Wrong Output:

The following appear in both lists

mn

33

Answer:
`output ARRAY2[A1]` **should be changed to** `output ARRAY2[A2]`

Correct Output:
The following items appear in both arrays
34
ff

4.2.6 Construct pseudocode to represent an algorithm

Exit skills. Students should be able to[1]:
Develop an algorithm in the form of pseudocode to address a specific problem.

Programming Example 32: Pseudocode to represent an algorithm

The following algorithm asks the user to enter five integer values. Then, the values are stored in an array and it is determined if the values entered are in ascending or descending order. The program displays a message indicating whether and how the elements are ordered.

```
//An algorithm that identifies
//if an array is sorted in
//ascending or descending order.

I = 0
SORTEDA = 1
SORTEDD = 1
SAMPLE = new Array()

loop I from 0 to 4
    SAMPLE[I] = input("Enter the measurement")
end loop

loop I from 0 to 3
   if SAMPLE[I] > SAMPLE[I+1] then
     SORTEDA = 0
   end if
   if SAMPLE[I] < SAMPLE[I+1] then
     SORTEDD = 0
   end if
end loop

output "The array is:"

loop I from 0 to 4
  output SAMPLE[I]
end loop

if SORTEDA = 1  then
  output "The array is sorted in ASCENDING order"
else
  output "The array is not sorted in ASCENDING order"
end if
```

```
if SORTEDD = 1  then
  output "The array is sorted in DESCENDING order"
else
  output "The array is not sorted in DESCENDING order"
end if
```

User enters: 3, 5, 6, 4, 4.

Output 1:

The array is:
3
5
6
4
4
The array is not sorted in ASCENDING order
The array is not sorted in DESCENDING order

User enters: 6, 5, 3, 2, 1.

Output 2:

The array is:
6
5
3
2
1
The array is not sorted in ASCENDING order
The array is sorted in DESCENDING order

User enters: 2, 4, 78, 89, 99.

Output 3:

The array is:
2
4
78
89
99
The array is sorted in ASCENDING order
The array is not sorted in DESCENDING order

Programming Example 33: Algorithm and flowchart (array of ten integers)

The following algorithm builds an array of ten integers. The algorithm uses the **Random** function to input random numbers between 0 and 9 to the array. Finally, it outputs the elements of the array. This algorithm is not expressed in IB pseudocode. The equivalent flowchart is illustrated in Figure 4.15.

```
//Declaration of an Integer variable n.
Declare Integer n
//Declaration of an array of integers. Length = 10, Name=RandomM
Declare Integer RandomN[10]

//This loop fills the array with random numbers from 0 to 9.  The
//first index of the array is 0. So, loop from 0 to 9.
For n = 0 To 9
    // It will be repeated 10 times.
    Set RandomN[n] = random(10)
End For

// This loop will print all the array elements.
For n = 0 To 9
    // The message will be repeated 10 times. Each time n changes.
    Display RandomN[n]
End For
Declare Integer n
```

Programming Example 34: Algorithm and flowchart (messages)

The following algorithm uses two **while loops** and an **if** conditional clause. This algorithm is not expressed in IB pseudocode.

The equivalent flowchart is illustrated in Figure 4.16.

```
Set n = 0
Declare Integer m

Set m = n + 3
While n <= 2
    While m < 10
        Set m = 13 - 3
        Display n + 2
        Display "m=", m
    End While
    Display "OK"
    Set n = n + 1
End While
Display "m=", m, " n=", n
If m > n Then
    Display "n=", n
Else
    Display m < n
End If
Display n
```

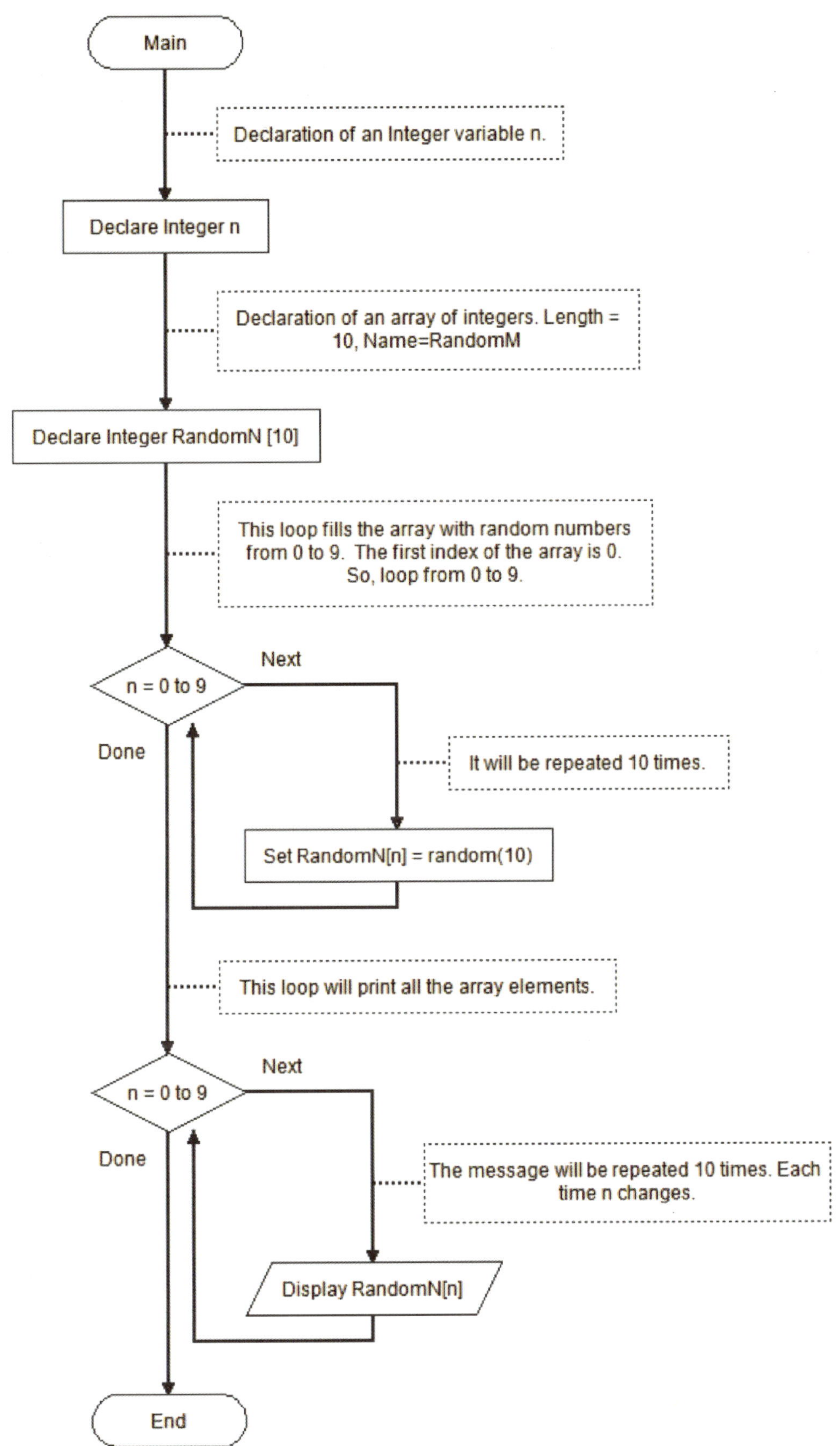

Figure 4.15: Flowchart for the programming example

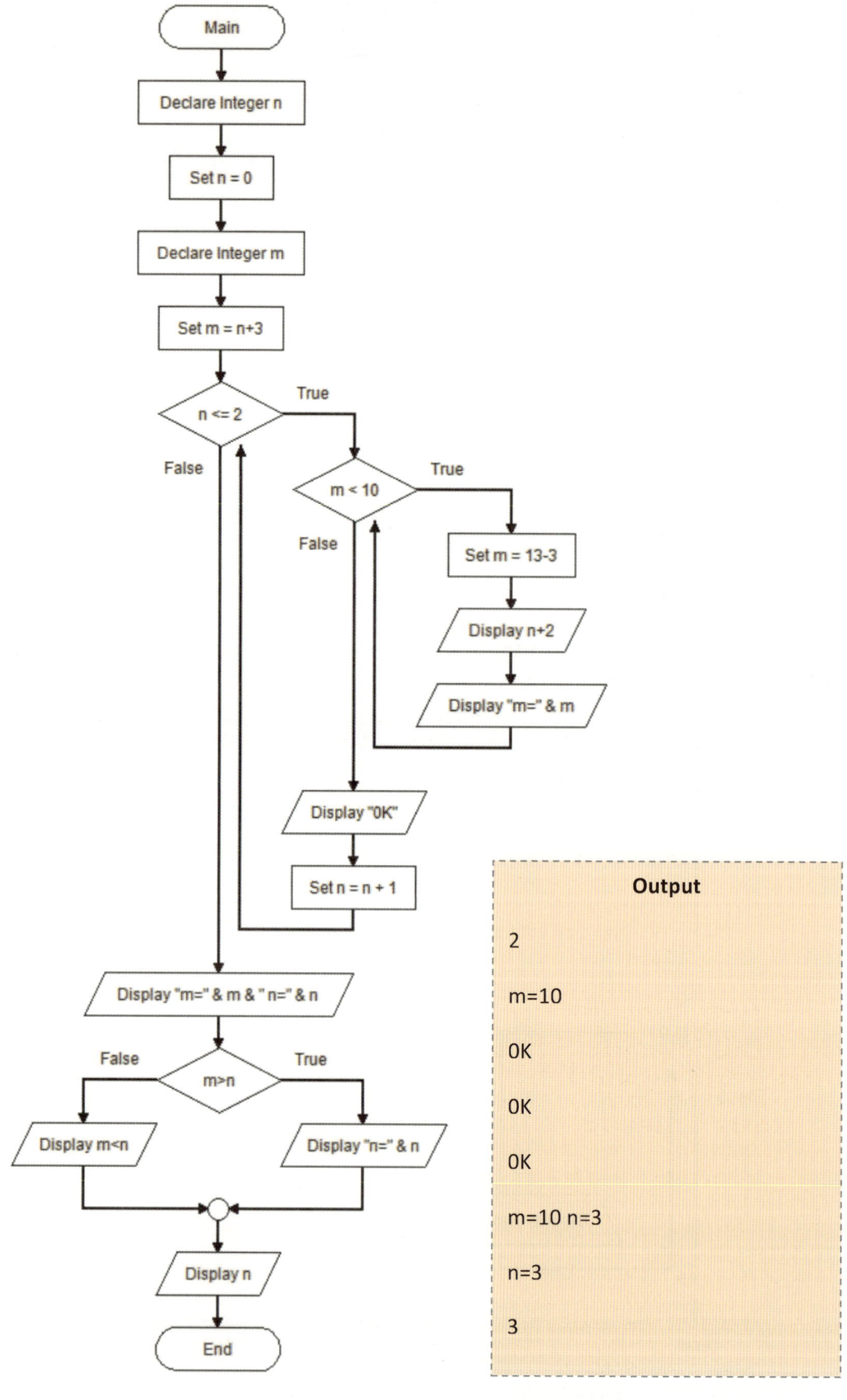

Figure 4.16: Flowchart for the programming example

4.2.7 Suggest suitable algorithms to solve a specific problem

Exit skills. Students should be able to[1]:

Define the terms efficiency, correctness, reliability and flexibility.
Explain the suitability of an algorithm in terms of efficiency, correctness, reliability and flexibility.
Propose suitable algorithms to attack a specific problem

Efficiency of an algorithm refers to the amount of the computer resources required to perform its functions. Minimizing the use of various resources such as the CPU and computer's memory is very important.

Correctness of an algorithm refers to the extent to which the algorithm satisfies its specification, is free from faults, and fulfils all objectives set during the design and implementation phase.

Reliability refers to the capability of the algorithm to maintain a predefined level of performance and perform all required functions under stated conditions, having a long mean time between failures.

Flexibility of an algorithm refers to the effort required to modify the algorithm for other purposes than those for which it was initially developed.

Programming Example 35: Algorithm for a specific problem

Given an array of *n* Integer elements, develop an algorithm that will output the numbers of the array and the frequency of their appearance.

```
//PROGRAM TO CALCULATE THE
//FREQUENCY OF NUMBERS
//IN AN ARRAY
ARRAY = [-30,-13,4,-3,-30,-3,-3,-3,-15]
SIZE = 9
COUNTS = new Array()

loop I from 0 to SIZE-2 //start of bubble sort
  loop J from 0 to SIZE-2
    if ARRAY[J]>ARRAY[J+1] then
       TEMP = ARRAY[J]
       ARRAY[J] = ARRAY[J+1]
       ARRAY[J+1] = TEMP
     end if
  end loop
end loop
//the array is now sorted
PREVIOUS = ARRAY[0]
X = 1 //it will be used to store frequency of appearance

loop I from 1 to SIZE-1
    if ARRAY[I] = PREVIOUS then //condition to check if two or more
                                //subsequent numbers are the same
       X = X+1
       if I == 8 then
```

```
            output "Number:",ARRAY[I],"frequency:",X
         end if
      else
         output "Number:",ARRAY[I-1],"frequency:",X
         PREVIOUS = ARRAY[I]
         X = 1
         if I == 8 then
            output "Number:",ARRAY[I],"frequency:",X
         end if
      end if
   end loop
```

Output:

Number: -30 frequency: 2

Number: -15 frequency: 1

Number: -13 frequency: 1

Number: -3 frequency: 4

Number: 4 frequency: 1

4.2.8 Deduce the efficiency of an algorithm in the context of its use

Exit skills. Students should be able to[1]:
Define and explain the use of Big O notation. Analyze the efficiency of an algorithm Define the term flag. Define the term list. Propose modifications to an algorithm to improve its efficiency.

Big O notation is extremely useful when analyzing algorithms as it is a measure of the *efficiency* of an algorithm. We use to say that an algorithm is *O(n)* what is meant is that the growth rate of the instructions in this particular algorithm shall be executed *n* times.

Programming Example 36: Improving efficiency

The following algorithms finds the sum of numbers 1+2+3+4+5=15 when n=5. If n=7 the algorithms will calculate 1+2+3+4+5+6+7 and the output will be 28. Which algorithm is more efficient?

Algorithm A

```
//An algorithm that outputs the SUM 1+2+3+..+n
//n>0

SUM = 0
n = 5 //n = 5 as input
SUM = n*(n+1)/2
output "The SUM is:" + SUM
```

Algorithm B

```
//An algorithm that outputs the SUM 1+2+3+..+n
//n>0

I = 0
SUM = 0
```

```
n = 5 //n = 5 as input

loop I from 1 to n
    SUM = SUM + I
end loop
output "The SUM is:" + SUM
```

Algorithm C

```
//An algorithm that outputs the SUM 1+2+3+..+n
//n>0

I = 0
SUM = 0
n = 5 //n = 5 as input
m = 0

loop I from 1 to n
    loop m from 1 to I
        SUM = SUM + 1
    end loop
end loop
output "The SUM is:" + SUM
```

The first algorithm does not use a loop (constant time requirement). This algorithm requires time proportional to 1, and its Big O notation is O(1). The time requirement is constant, and is independent of the problem's size. For this particular algorithm, it is independent of the size of n.

The second algorithm uses one loop (linear algorithm-linear time required). This algorithm requires time proportional to *n* and its Big O notation is O(*n*). The time requirement for this algorithm increases directly with the size of the problem. For this particular algorithm, it is dependent on the size of *n*.

The third algorithm use two loops the second inside the first (nested loops (quadratic algorithm-quadratic time required)). This algorithm requires time proportional to n^2 and its Big O notation is $O(n^2)$. The time requirement for this algorithm increases rapidly depending on the size of the problem. For this particular algorithm it is dependent of the size of *n*.
Suppose the first algorithm takes 1 time unit to output the result for *n*=10. The second algorithm will take 10 time units and the third 10^2 time units. For *n*=100 the first algorithm takes 1 time units to output the result, the second algorithm will take 100 time units and the third 100^2 time units.
The following table presents some algorithms and their equivalent Big O notation.

Number of loops (Flowchart)	Big O notation (approx.) *n* = number of iterations	Number of loops (Algorithm)
Main False / If / True End	**O(1)**	// If "expression" Then // End If
Main For / Next Done End	**O(*n*)**	// For "variable" = start To end // End For

Main
For / Next
Done
For / Next
Done
End
	2*O(*n*) ≈ O(*n*)	// For "variable" = start To end
		// End For
		// For "variable" = start To end
		// End For

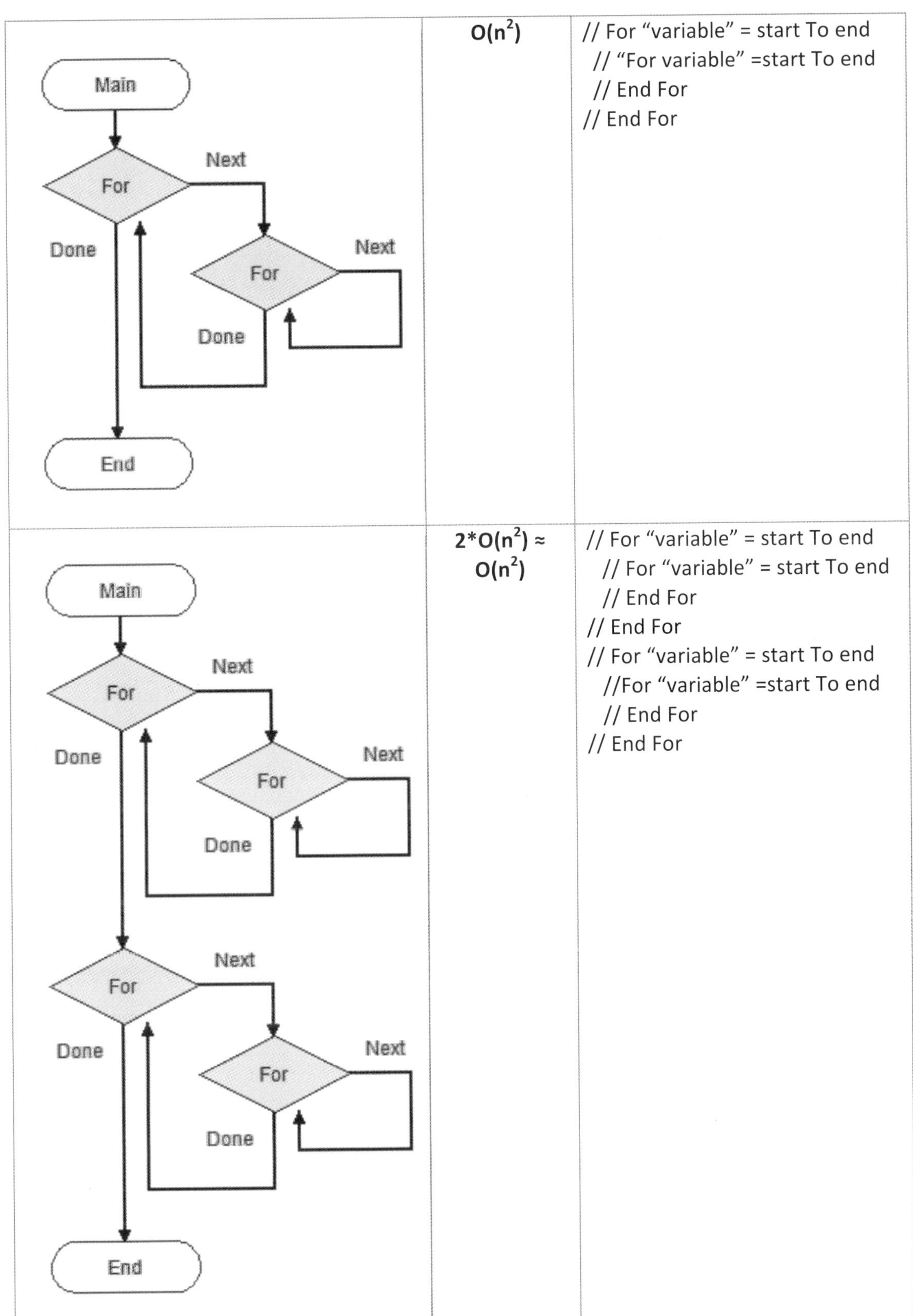

	$O(n^2)$	// For "variable" = start To end
		// "For variable" =start To end
		// End For
		// End For

	$2*O(n^2) \approx O(n^2)$	// For "variable" = start To end
		// For "variable" = start To end
		// End For
		// End For
		// For "variable" = start To end
		//For "variable" =start To end
		// End For
		// End For

Assumption for time estimation based on complexity class

Example 4.1: Suppose a n^2 sorting algorithm needs 4 seconds to run in a particular computer system when n = 1000. For how many elements the same algorithm will need 6 seconds to run?

Answer:

Time1=Constant*Big O notation ⇔ 4=Constant*1000^2 ⇔ Constant=4/1000000

Time2=Constant*n^2 ⇔ 6=Constant*n^2 ⇔ n=sqrt(6/Constant) ⇔ n=1225.

Example 4.2: Assume that a **Bubble Sort** algorithm requires 10 seconds to sort an array containing 1 million numbers. State approximately how long the same algorithm would require to sort 8 million numbers on the same computer system.

Answer:

Time1=Constant*Big O notation ⇔ 10=Constant*1000000^2 ⇔

Constant=10/1000000^2

Time2=Constant*n^2 ⇔ Time2=Constant*8000000^2 ⇔ Time2=640

Example 4.3: Assume that a **Selection sort** algorithm requires 10 seconds to sort an array containing 1 million numbers. State approximately how long an O(*n*) sorting algorithm would require to sort 16 million numbers on the same computer system.

Answer:

Time1=Constant* Big O notation ⇔ 10 =Constant*1000000^2 ⇔

Constant=10/1000000^2

Time2=Constant*n ⇔ Time2=Constant*16000000 ⇔ Time2=0.00016 seconds

Look what a difference a different type of algorithm can make!

Time = Constant * Big O notation, where *Constant* depends on the computer system that runs the program. For the same computer system *Constant* should always be considered to be the same.

The following table shows some useful common complexities.

Common complexities	
Binary search	O(log*n*)
Linear search	O(*n*)
Bubble Sort	O(n^2)
Select Sort	O(n^2)

Table 4.4: Complexities

Programming Example 37: More efficient sequential search

A *flag* in programming is a variable used to indicate a condition. When the condition is changed the value of the flag is changed. The *flag* is usually a *boolean variable* and is used to terminate a *loop*.

Lists in computer science are used to store a sequence of values under a single name. *Lists* allow duplicates to act as containers and to be typically implemented either as linked lists or as arrays. Although the term list appears at this point of the syllabus, it is assumed by the authors that it should be treated as a synonym to the term *array*.

The following algorithm corresponds to an inefficient sequential search. Suppose we run this algorithm searching for 2. This is the first element of the array.

```
//==== Sequential Search ====
N = [2, 9, 5, 6, 7, 8, 19, 3, 4, 17 ,18, 29, 11]//Array elements
X =  2
Found= false
Counter = 0
loop Counter from 0 to 12
   if N[Counter] = X then
      Found = true
      output N[Counter],"found at position" , Counter
   end if
   output Counter, "what a waste!!!!!"
end loop
if Found = false then
   output X,"not found"
end if
```

Output:
2 found at position 0
0 what a waste!!!!!
1 what a waste!!!!!
2 what a waste!!!!!
3 what a waste!!!!!
4 what a waste!!!!!
5 what a waste!!!!!
6 what a waste!!!!!
7 what a waste!!!!!
8 what a waste!!!!!
9 what a waste!!!!!
10 what a waste!!!!!
11 what a waste!!!!!
12 what a waste!!!!!

It is easy to understand that the algorithm found the element and then continued to iterate through all the element of the array. This is a waste of processing recourses. A better solution involves the use of **Found as a flag** that will be used to stop the search immediately when the element is found.

```
//==== Clever Sequential Search ====
N = [2, 9, 5, 6, 7, 8, 19, 3 ,4 ,17 ,18, 29, 11]//Array elements
X =  2
Found= 0
Counter = 0
loop while Counter < 12 AND Found = 0// Use of flag
   if N[Counter] = X then
      Found = 1
      output N[Counter],"found at position" , Counter
```

```
      end if
      Counter = Counter +1
   output Counter, "what a waste!!!!!"
   end loop
   if Found = false then
      output X,"not found"
   end if
```

Output:

2 found at position 0

1 what a waste!!!!!

4.2.9 Determine number of iterations for given input data

Exit skills. Students should be able to[1]:
Calculate the number of iterations that will be performed for given input data Analyze the loops presented in an algorithm (pseudocode, flowchart).

Programming Example 38: Calculation of number of iterations

The following algorithm corresponds to the flowchart illustrated in Figure 4.17:

```
Declare Integer a
Declare Integer b

Input a
Input b
If a > b Then
    Set a = b - 3
    While a < b
        Display "loop 1"
        Set b = a * 2
        While b > 7
            Set b = a - 2
            Display "loop 3"
        End While
        Display "loop 2"
    End While
End If
```

Q1. What is going to be the output when a=10 and b=4?

A1. The program will never end. It will be an infinite loop.

Q2. What is going to be the output when a=4 and b=10?

A2. No output

Q3. What is going to be the output when a=10 and b=9?

A3. Output: loop1 loop2 loop3

Q4. What is going to be the output when a=10 and b=0?

A4. Output: loop1 loop2

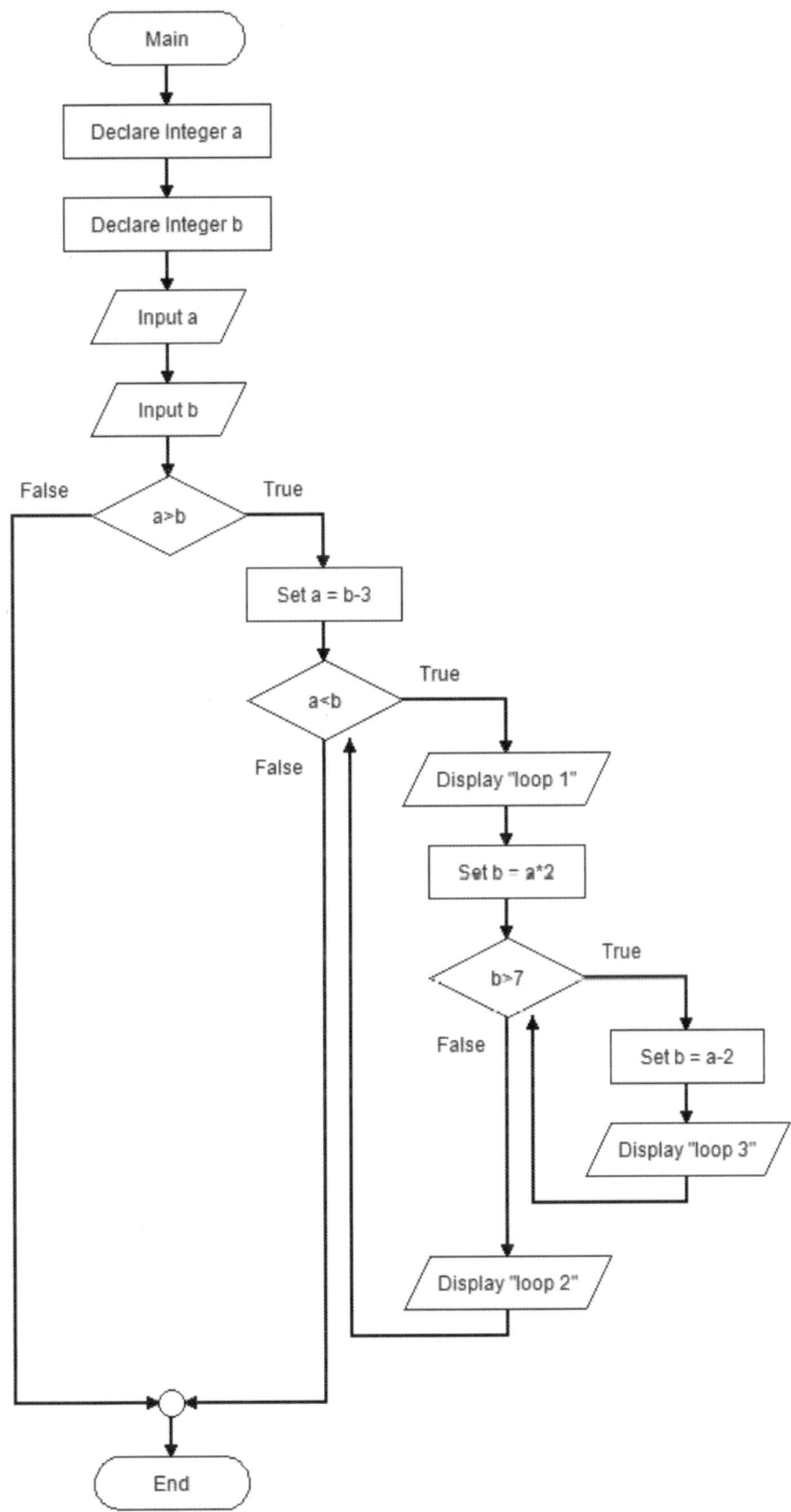

Figure 4.17: Flowchart for the programming example

Programming Example 39: Calculation of number of iterations

Figure 4.18 shows a flowchart. Answer the following questions:

Q1. How many times will the "well done" message appear if the user enters a=20 and b=2?
A1. Two times.

Q2. What is going to be the output of the program if the user enters a=20 and b=2?
A2.

well done

well done

welcome

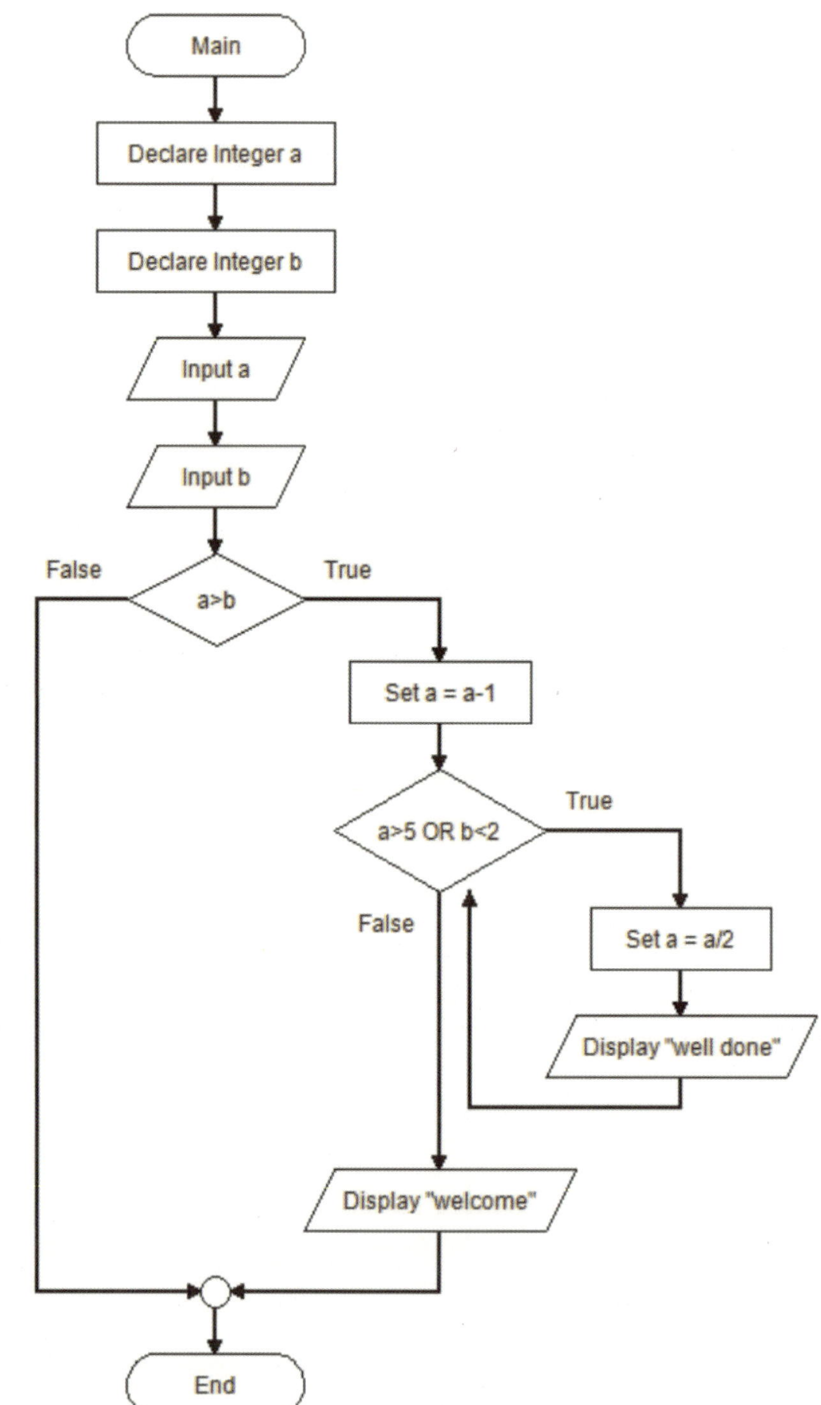

Figure 4.18: Flowchart for the programming example

4.3 Introduction to programming

We can use Java programming language in order to face various problems. Therefore, students can be given the chance to convert algorithms into code what can be executed and tested.

Nature of programming languages

4.3.1 State the fundamental operations of a computer

Exit skills. Students should be able to[1]:
List the fundamental operations (add, compare, retrieve and store) of a computer.

A computer can perform some *fundamental operations*. The following simplified example is used to illustrate some basic computer operations. Suppose that a number is stored as a string of bits in memory location 20 and another number is stored as a string of bits in memory location 30. A LOAD 20 instruction is transferred from RAM into the Control Unit (CU). The contents of the memory location 20 are loaded (retrieved from memory) into the Arithmetic and Logic Unit (ALU). A second instruction is fetched. The CU takes the instruction ADD 30, loads the contents of memory location 30 into the ALU and adds it to the number already there (the number from memory location 20). A final instruction STORE 50 is used to store the output to memory location 50. A variation of this simple code fragment would be to use a statement that would COMPARE (<, >, =) the contents of the memory location 20 to the contents of the memory location 40 and change the course of the program according the result of the comparison. The conditional instructions and basic operations of Boolean algebra (AND, OR, XOR, NOT) are critical for the development of useful programs.

4.3.2 Distinguish between fundamental and compound operations of a computer

Exit skills. Students should be able to[1]:
Outline the differences between fundamental and compound operations of a computer. Suggest an algorithm that acts as a compound operation (e.g. find max).

By combining fundamental computer operations, computers can perform *compound* operations. For example, finding the maximum value of four numbers is a compound operation.

Objective: Find the Maximum value of four numbers

Our goal is to write an algorithm in pseudocode form that will find the maximum of four numbers.
Four numbers as input: a, b, c, d.

It should give the maximum value of these four as output (MAX).
It should always give the Max (actual numbers or order of numbers should not influence our algorithm).

```
Begin by setting MAX = a
Compare MAX and b.
If b > MAX, set b = MAX
Compare MAX and c.
If c > MAX, set c = MAX
Compare MAX and d.
If d > MAX, set d = MAX
Output MAX
```

This algorithm returns correct maximum. Below is JAVA implementation of this algorithm.

Programming Example 40: Compound operations

```
// import of a class that handles input from user (Scanner)
import java.util.Scanner;
//definition of the name of the class (program name)
class LargestOfFourNumbers{
//main method heading
   public static void main(String args[])
   {
//initialization of variables
//all variables are of type integer (int)
      int a, b, c, d, Max;
//System.out.println is equivalent to output
      System.out.println("Enter four integers ");
//use of scanner
      Scanner in = new Scanner(System.in);
      a = in.nextInt();
      b = in.nextInt();
      c = in.nextInt();
      d = in.nextInt();
      Max=a;
      if (b>Max)
         Max = b;
      if (c > Max)
        Max=c;
      if ( d > Max )
        Max = d;
      System.out.println ("Maximum number is "+ Max);
   }
}
```

4.3.3 Explain the essential features of a computer language

Exit skills. Students should be able to[1]:

Define the terms syntax and semantics.

Explain the importance of fixed vocabulary, unambiguous meaning, consistent grammar and syntax for a computer language.

A programming language is described as the combination of its *semantics,* which refers to the meaning of every construction that is possible in the language and its *syntax*, which relates to its structure. A *grammar* is a meta-language that is used to define the syntax of a language, while the rules of statement construction are called syntax. Each high level language has a unique syntax and a specific limited vocabulary. The words `import`, `class`, `int` etc. in Java are *reserved keywords* with special meanings in the Java language. A command written in a computer language always means the same and there is no ambiguity of meaning.

4.3.4 Explain the need for higher level languages

Exit skills. Students should be able to[1]:

Outline the differences and similarities between machine language, assembly language and high-level languages.
Explain the importance of higher level programming languages.
Explain how the use of high level programming languages facilitates abstraction.

Computers can only process 0s and 1s. Each computer has its own *machine language*, which is made up of 0s and 1s. Machine language is a low-level language and is the only language that can be understood directly by a computer. Machine language programs are hard to write, difficult to debug and to maintain. A machine language programmer has to keep track of memory locations and write from the very beginning all the mathematical functions required by a program. Machine language programs written for a computer of one kind are not suitable for a computer of another kind.

The next evolutionary step in programming came with the replacement of binary code for development of instructions and reference to address locations with symbols called mnemonics. These low-level computer languages were referred as *mnemonic* and later as *assembly languages*. An *assembler* was used to convert the assembly language mnemonics to machine code. The development of computer programs was now much easier, but each assembly language was still specific to a specific computer system. The lack of abstraction, the need to focus on problem-solving and to improve efficiency led to the development of high-level languages.

A *high-level programming language* is a programming language that uses elements of natural language, is easy to use, facilitates abstraction by hiding significant areas of computing systems, and makes the program development simpler, faster and more understandable.

4.3.5 Outline the need for a translation process from a higher-level language to machine-executable code

Exit skills. Students should be able to[1]:

Outline the function of compilers, interpreters and combinations of both.
Outline the importance of virtual machine.
Explain the importance of a translation process from a higher level language to machine executable code.

Most applications today are written in one of the *high-level languages*. To execute (RUN) the program on a computer system and get the required job done, a translation method is required. This *translation process* will convert the program into the *machine language* of the computer on which it will run. The original program developed in a selected high-level language is called the *source program* or *source code*. The translated program in *machine language* is called the *object program* or *target program*. Two methods are used for *translation*: *compilation* and *interpretation*.

- A *compiler* is a translator that executes the translation process only once. It normally translates the whole source program into the object program. The object program is saved and next time a programmer wants to use the object program no recompilation is necessary. Compilers issue error messages for all syntax error found and all errors are communicated to the programmer after the entire program is checked. The compilation ends only when all syntax errors have been corrected. Compilers are much faster than interpreters. Examples: C, C++.
- An *interpreter* is a translator that goes through the process of translation every time the program is run. Interpretation refers to the process of reading each line (instruction) of the source program, analyzing it, translating it into the corresponding line of the object program and executing the line. Syntax errors are communicated to the programmer for every instruction that is interpreted. Example: BASIC.
- Java combines compilation and interpretation. Source code is compiled to Java *Virtual Machine bytecode*. When a Java program is compiled from .java file to a .class file, the class file is Java Virtual Machine bytecode. This Java Virtual Machine bytecode can be interpreted by the *Java Virtual Machine interpreter*. The Java architecture allows code to run on any machine to which the Java Virtual Machine interpreter has been installed. In Java architecture, all details of making the code function on a specific hardware platform are handled by the Java Virtual Machine (JVM).

Use of programming languages

The Java programming language is used in many examples of this section.

4.3.6 Variable, constant, operator, object

Exit skills. Students should be able to[1]:
Define the terms: variable, constant, operator and object.

Variable: A variable is used to store a data element of a program. The stored value can be changed during the program execution. A variable has a name (or identifier) and a type. The name of the variable should not clash with reserved keywords and literals of the language. It is highly recommended to use meaningful variable names (e.g. `roomSize`).The type of the variable could be an integer, double, string etc. A variable in most programming languages can only store a data element of the particular type.

Constant: Constants represent things and quantities that don't change. They can be seen as non-modifiable variables. The data element stored in a constant cannot be modified during the execution of the program (e.g. in Java: `final double PI = 3.14159`).

Operator: Operators are used to manipulate operands. The expression 2+3 has as an operator the "+" (sign of addition) and two operands "2", "3". Operands can be variables, literals, boolean values, numerical values, text etc. Operators can be arithmetic, relational, logical etc.

Object: An object is a comprised of *data* and *actions*. Actions refer to the operations that can be performed by the object. Object data may include a number of data members, while actions may also be referred to as *methods*. Data members are used to store the current state of an object and methods are used to change or access those data members.[9]

4.3.7 Define various operators

Exit skills. Students should be able to[1]:
Give the precise meaning of the operators =, ≠, <, <=, >, >=, mod, div.

The following operators appear in the IBO approved notation for developing pseudocode[14].

= Defined as "is equals to". It is also used to assign a value to a variable. `Min = 6` means that the value of 6 is assigned to variable Min

≠ Defined as "not equal to". Min ≠ Max means that Min is not equal to Max

> Defined as "is greater than"

>= Defined as "is greater than or equal to"

< Defined as "is less than"

<= Defined as "is less than or equal to"

div Defined as "integer part of quotient". For example: 22 div 3 = 7.

mod Defined as "modulo operation". It calculates the remainder of division of one number by another. The following table illustrates some examples of mod and div usage.

Operand1	Operator	Operand2	Result
9	mod	3	0
11	mod	3	2
0	mod	3	0
2	mod	44	2

Programming Example 41: Java quotient and remainder program

The following two programs written in Java ask the user to enter two positive integers and then they calculate the quotient and the remainder. The first program does not use "/" or "% (mod)".

```
import java.util.Scanner;
class QuotientRemainderV1
{
   public static void main(String args[])
   {
      int a, b, q=0;
      System.out.println("Enter two positive integers ");
      Scanner in = new Scanner(System.in);
      a = in.nextInt();
      b = in.nextInt();
      int r = a;
      while (!(r<b)){
        r= r-b;
        q=q+1;
      }
     System.out.println ("Quotient: "+ q + " Remainder: " +r);
   }
}
```

```
import java.util.Scanner;
class QuotientRemainderV2
{
   public static void main(String args[])
   {
      int a, b, q=0, r=0;
      System.out.println("Enter two positive integers ");
      Scanner in = new Scanner(System.in);
      a = in.nextInt();
      b = in.nextInt();
      q= a / b;
      r= a % b;
      System.out.println ("Quotient: "+ q + " Remainder: " +r);
   }
}
```

Programming Example 42: Java encryption-decryption example

The following Java program is an encryption algorithm.

```
import java.util.Scanner;
public class Encryption
{
      //Encryption algorithm
      public static void main(String args[])
      {
      int dig_1;
      int dig_2;
      int dig_3;
      int dig_4;
      int a;
      int temp;
      int encrypted;
      System.out.print("Enter a four digit number to be encrypted: ");
      Scanner in = new Scanner(System.in);
      a = in.nextInt();
      //Extract digits using %
      dig_1 = a % 10000 / 1000;
      dig_2 = a % 1000 / 100;
      dig_3 = a % 100 / 10;
      dig_4 = a % 10 / 1;
      //Change digits
      dig_1 = (dig_1 + 5) % 10;
      dig_2 = (dig_2 + 5) % 10;
      dig_3 = (dig_3 + 5) % 10;
      dig_4 = (dig_4 + 5) % 10;
      //Swap digits
      temp = dig_1;
      dig_1 = dig_4;
      dig_4 = temp;
      temp = dig_2;
      dig_2 = dig_3;
      dig_3 = temp;
      //Construct Encrypted Number
      encrypted = dig_1 * 1000 + dig_2 * 100 + dig_3 * 10 + dig_4;
      System.out.print("Encrypted number is: ");
      System.out.print(encrypted);
      }
}
```

Suppose the user enters: 3678.

```
//Extract digits using %
      dig_1 = a % 10000 / 1000 gets the value 3
      dig_2 = a % 1000 / 100 gets the value 6
      dig_3 = a % 100 / 10 gets the value 7
      dig_4 = a % 10 / 1 gets the value 8
//Change digits
      dig_1 = (dig_1 + 5) % 10 gets the value 8
      dig_2 = (dig_2 + 5) % 10 gets the value 1
      dig_3 = (dig_3 + 5) % 10 gets the value 2
      dig_4 = (dig_4 + 5) % 10 gets the value 3
//Swap digits
      temp = dig_1;
      dig_1 = dig_4;
      dig_4 = temp;
      temp = dig_2;
```

```
        dig_2 = dig_3;
        dig_3 = temp;
```

After this digit 1=3, digit2=2, digit 3=1 and digit 4=8.

So the encrypted integer is: 3218.

The following Java program is the decryption algorithm for the previous algorithm.

```
import java.util.Scanner;
public class Decryption

{
        // Decryption algorithm
        public static void main(String args[])
        {
        int dig_1;
        int dig_2;
        int dig_3;
        int dig_4;
        int a;
        int temp;
        int decrypted;
        System.out.print("Enter a four digit number to be decrypted: ");
        Scanner in = new Scanner(System.in);
        a = in.nextInt();
        //Extract digits using %
        dig_1 = a % 10000 / 1000;
        dig_2 = a % 1000 / 100;
        dig_3 = a % 100 / 10;
        dig_4 = a % 10 / 1;
        //Change dig_s
        dig_1 = (dig_1 + 5) % 10;
        dig_2 = (dig_2 + 5) % 10;
        dig_3 = (dig_3 + 5) % 10;
        dig_4 = (dig_4 + 5) % 10;
        //Swap digits
        temp = dig_1;
        dig_1 = dig_4;
        dig_4 = temp;
        temp = dig_2;
        dig_2 = dig_3;
        dig_3 = temp;
        //Construct Decrypted Number
        decrypted = dig_1 * 1000 + dig_2 * 100 + dig_3 * 10 + dig_4;
        System.out.print("Decrypted number is: ");
        System.out.print (decrypted);
        }
}
```

If the user inputs "3218" the program will return the original integer "3678".

4.3.8 Analyse the use of variables, constants and operators in algorithms

Exit skills. Students should be able to[1]:
Explain the use of variables in various algorithms. Explain the use of constants in various algorithms. Explain the use of operators in various algorithms.

It is clear that a constant is a variable whose value does not change during the execution of the program.

Constant name	Value of the constant
Pi (π)	3.141592653
e (Natural log)	2.718281828
c (speed of light)	299,792,458 (m/sec)

Table 4.5: Examples of constants and their values

In some cases when developing a computer program, it is more convenient and more secure to use constants instead of variables. When you use the keyword **`final`**, Java is instructed that the data element cannot be changed. If you try to change a constant "Pi" a message "cannot assign a value to final variable Pi" will appear.

Programming Example 43: Java use of constants

The following inefficient program written in Java clarifies the use of constants. The contents of the variables ratio and area change many times, but there is no reason for the content of the constant Pi to be changed during the execution of the program.

```
import java.util.Scanner;
class AreaOfCircle
{
   public static void main(String args[])
   {
      final double Pi= 3.1415926535;
      double ratio = 0, area;
      while (ratio!=999){
      System.out.println("Enter the ratio of the circle. Enter 999
to exit ");
      Scanner in = new Scanner(System.in);
      ratio = in.nextDouble();
      if (ratio == 999){
      System.out.println ("See you ");
    }
      else{
      area = Pi * ratio * ratio;
      System.out.println ("Area: "+ area);
    }

   }
  }
}
```

Local and global value

The *scope* of a variable defines the visibility of that variable. It defines which parts of the algorithm can store, access and retrieve the data of the variable. Sometimes it is very useful to limit the scope of a variable. A *global* variable is visible to all parts of your program while a *local* variable has a limited scope.

Programming Example 44: Java scope of variables

Now consider the following program in JAVA. If this program is executed, the following will happen.

```
import java.util.Scanner;
import java.util.*;
import java.lang.Math;
class MyProgramwhile {
   public static void main(String[] args) {
      int n;
      n = 0;
      while (n < 2) {
         System.out.println("OK");
         n = n + 1;
         int m = n+1;
         System.out.println("INSIDE
LOOP");
         System.out.println(n);
         System.out.println(m);
      }
      System.out.println("OUTSIDE
LOOP");
      System.out.println(n);
      //System.out.println(m);
   }
}
```

First loop pass

n variable is initialized (global)
n gets the value 0
loop starts (0<2)=TRUE
output→OK
n gets the value 1
m variable is initialized (local), m gets the value 1
output→INSIDE LOOP
output→1
output→2

```
import java.util.Scanner;
import java.util.*;
import java.lang.Math;
class MyProgramwhile {
   public static void main(String[] args) {
      int n;
      n = 0;
      while (n < 2) {
         System.out.println("OK");
         n = n + 1;
         int m = n+1;
         System.out.println("INSIDE
LOOP");
         System.out.println(n);
         System.out.println(m);
      }
      System.out.println("OUTSIDE
LOOP");
      System.out.println(n);
      //System.out.println(m);
   }
}
```

Second loop pass

loop continues (1<2)=TRUE
output→OK
n gets the values 2
m variable is initialized (local), m gets the value 2
output→INSIDE LOOP
output→2
output→3

```
import java.util.Scanner;
import java.util.*;
import java.lang.Math;
class MyProgramwhile {
   public static void main(String[] args) {
      int n;
      n = 0;
      while (n < 2) {
         System.out.println("OK");
         n = n + 1;
         int m = n+1;
         System.out.println("INSIDE
LOOP");
         System.out.println(n);
         System.out.println(m);
      }
      System.out.println("OUTSIDE
LOOP");
      System.out.println(n);
```

Exit from the loop

loop ends (2<2)=false

m variable is destroyed (local). n variable exists (global)
output→OUTSIDE LOOP
output→2
Important: if we remove the comments symbol (//) a message “cannot find symbol variable m” will

//System.out.println(m);
    }
}
	appear. Variable m is not available here.

4.3.9 Develop algorithms using loops, branching

Exit skills. Students should be able to[1]:

Develop various algorithms, explain their use and justify their purpose.
Develop algorithms that include loops and branching to address a problem.

Programming Example 45: Java leap year program analysed

A leap year is a year containing one additional day (an extra day for February).

The algorithm that calculates if a year is a leap year is the following:

```
if (year is divisible by 400, year % 400 = 0)then it is a leap year
else if (year is divisible by 100, year % 100 = 0)then it is not a
leap year
else if (year is divisible by 4, year % 4 = 0)then it is a leap year
else, not a leap year
```

By analyzing the same problem using boolean algebra the following boolean variables as inputs can be set:

A= year is divisible by 400

B= year is divisible by 100

C= year is divisible by 4

The following truth table shows if a year is a leap year or not

A	B	C	Leap year
0	0	0	0
0	0	1	1
0	1	0	0
0	1	1	0
1	0	0	1
1	0	1	1
1	1	0	1
1	1	1	1

The boolean expression is: Leap year=CA'B'+A=A+CB'=

=year is divisible by 400 **OR** $\overline{\text{year is divisible by 100}}$ **AND** year is divisible by 4

The modulo operator (%) calculates the remainder after division of one number by another.

So the Leap year=CA'B'+A=A+CB' can be written as:

Leap year =Year % 400 = 0 OR Year % 100 != 0 AND Year % 4 = 0

Notice: **!=** *in Java means not equal*

A Java version of the algorithm follows:

```
import java.util.Scanner;
public class LeapYearCalc
{
    public static void main(String args[])
    {
      int year = 0;
      while (year!=-999){
        System.out.println("Enter the year. Enter -999 to exit ");
        Scanner in = new Scanner(System.in);
        year = in.nextInt();
        if (year == -999){
          System.out.println ("See you ");
        } else {
          boolean isLeap = false;
          if((year % 400 == 0)||(year % 100 != 0)&& (year % 4 == 0)){
            isLeap = true;
          }

          if(isLeap){
            System.out.println("Year "+year+" is a leap year");
          } else {
            System.out.println("Year "+year+" is not a leap year");
          }
        }
      }
    }
}
```

A simplified flowchart is the following (Figure 4.19):

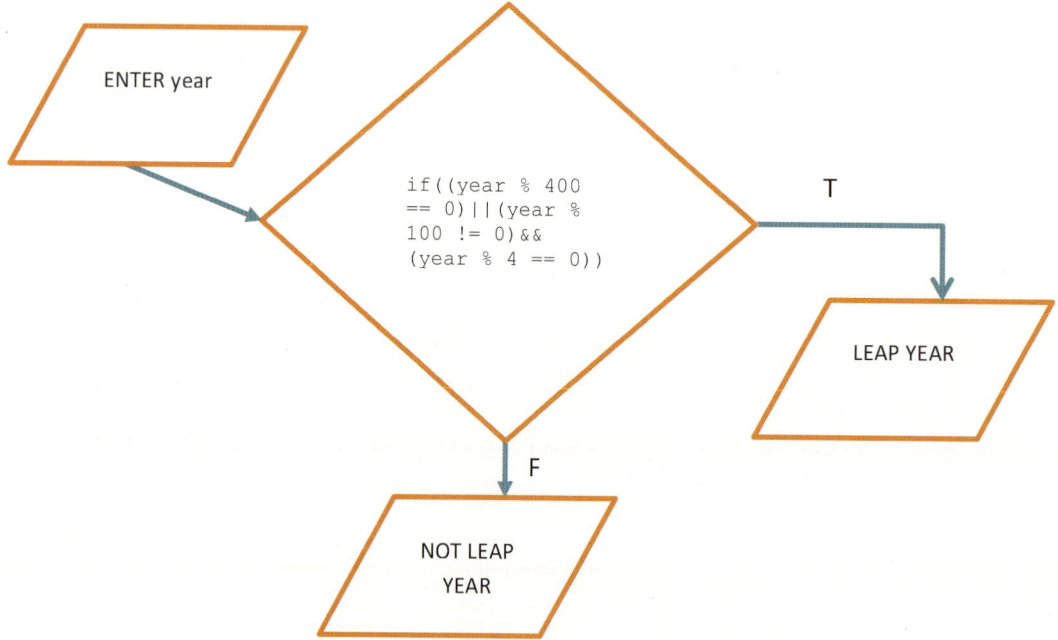

Figure 4.19: Flowchart of the LeapYear program

The following test cases are examined:

Suppose the user enters 2006. The variable **Year** gets the value 2006. So,

```
Leap year =2006 % 400 = 0 OR 2006 % 100 != 0 AND 2006 % 4 = 0.
Leap year =FALSE OR TRUE AND FALSE=FALSE
```

Suppose the user enters 2000. The variable **Year** gets the value 2000. So,

```
Leap year =2000% 400 = 0 OR 2000 % 100 != 0 AND 2000 % 4 = 0.
Leap year =TRUE OR FALSE AND TRUE=TRUE
```

Suppose the user enters 2008. The variable **Year** gets the value 2008. So,

```
Leap year =2008% 400 = 0 OR 2008 % 100 != 0 AND 2008 % 4 = 0.
Leap year =FALSE OR TRUE AND TRUE=TRUE
```

Another Java implementation is the following:

```
import java.util.Scanner;
public class LeapYearCalc
{
    public static void main(String args[])
    {
      int year = 0;
      while (year!=-999){
        System.out.println("Enter the year. Enter -999 to exit ");
        Scanner in = new Scanner(System.in);
        year = in.nextInt();
        if (year == -999){
          System.out.println ("See you ");
        } else {
         boolean isLeap = false;
         if(year % 400 == 0){
           isLeap = true;
         } else if (year % 100 == 0){
            isLeap = false;
          } else if(year % 4 == 0){
            isLeap = true;
          } else{
            isLeap = false;
          }
          if(isLeap){
            System.out.println("Year "+year+" is a leap year");
          } else {
            System.out.println("Year "+year+" is not a leap year");
         }
        }
      }
    }
  }
```

A simplified flowchart is the following.

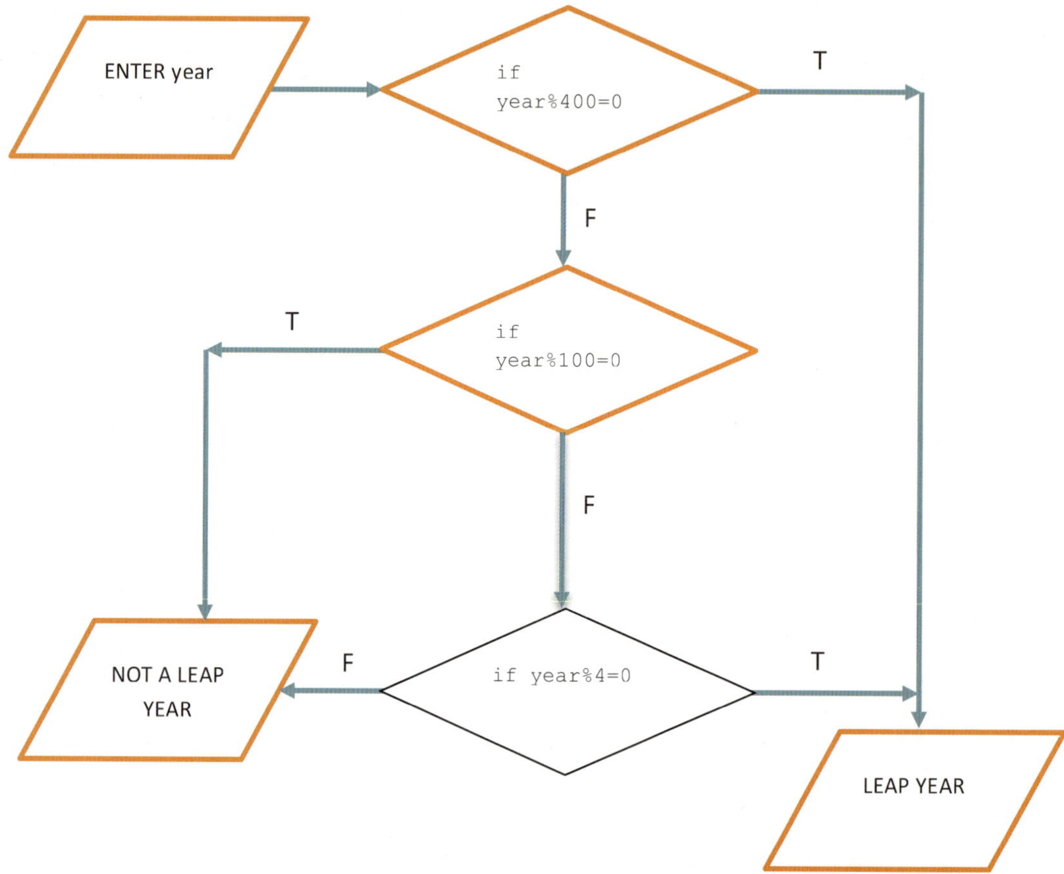

Figure 4.20: The equivalent flowchart

Dry run of the LeapYearCalc Java program:

`import java.util.Scanner;`				
`public class LeapYearCalc`				
`{`				
`public static void main(String args[])`				
`{`				
`int year = 0;`				
`while (year!=-999){`				
`System.out.println("Enter the year. Enter -999 to exit ");`	**User enters 1989**	**User enters 2004**	**User enters 1500**	**User enters -999**
`Scanner in = new Scanner(System.in);`				
`year = in.nextInt();`				
`if (year == -999){`	1989# -999,false	false	false	true
`System.out.println ("See you ");`				OUTPUT
`}`				
`else {`				
`boolean isLeap = false;`	isLeap set to false	isLeap set to false	isLeap set to false	
`if(year % 400 == 0){`	false	false	false	

isLeap = true;				
}				
else if (year % 100 == 0){	false	false	true	
isLeap = false;			isLeap set to false	
}				
else if(year % 4 == 0){	false	true		
isLeap = true;		isLeap=true		
}				
else{				
isLeap = false;	false			
}				
if(isLeap){	false	true	false	
System.out.println("Year "+year+" is a leap year");		OUTPUT		
}				
else {				
System.out.println("Year "+year+" is not a leap year");	OUTPUT		OUTPUT	
}				
}				
}				
}				
}				

Programming Example 46: Java print a diamond

The following Java program prints the following diamond shape with efficient use of loops:

```
    #
   ###
  #####
 #######
#########
 #######
  #####
   ###
    #
```

```
public class Symbol_1
{
   //Shape creation

   public static void main(String args[])
   {
      int row;
      //top part
      for (row = 1; row <= 5; row=row+1)
      {
         for (int space = 1; space <= 5 - row; ++space)
         {
            System.out.print(' ');
         }
```

```
            for (int symbol = 1; symbol <= 2 * row - 1; ++symbol)
            {
                System.out.print('#');
            }
            System.out.print('\n');
        }
        //bottom part
        for (row = 4; row >= 1; row=row-1)
        {
            for (int space = 1; space <= 5 - row; space=space+1)
            {
                System.out.print(' ');
            }
            for (int symbol = 1; symbol <= 2 * row - 1; symbol=symbol+1)
            {
                System.out.print('#');
            }
            System.out.print('\n');
        }
        System.out.print("\n");
    }
}
```

4.3.10 Describe the characteristics and applications of a collection

Exit skills. Students should be able to[1]:
Outline the characteristics of collections. Explain the importance of collections in programming.

Frequently in computer programming there is a need to group and store data that will be used for the problem solution. A *collection* or *container* is consisted of zero or more elements such as objects and values and it is equipped with the necessary operations to handle data. Collections allow duplicate elements and may contain ordered and unordered data elements. Important operations of a collection are **`add`**, **`remove`** etc. Each type of collection is equipped with its own specific operations. The elements of a particular collection are typically all of the same type and represent an entity. A fixed-size array is usually not considered a collection because it holds a fixed number of items.

4.3.11 Develop algorithms using the access methods of a collection

Exit skills. Students should be able to[1]:
Develop various algorithms, explain their use and justify their purpose. Develop algorithms that include the access methods of collections to address a problem.

Programming Example 47: Use of collections (surname collection)

Note: The use of Surname.substring(0,1) will be given as an explanation during examination

SURNAMES = new Collection()
SURNAMES.addItem("Pappas")
SURNAMES.addItem("Percy")
SURNAMES.addItem("Brox")
SURNAMES.resetNext()
output "These names start with P"
loop while SURNAMES.hasNext()
    Surname = SURNAMES.getNext()
    if Surname.substring(0,1) = "P" then
      output Surname
    end if
end loop
	It will return:
	These names start with P
	Pappas
	Percy

Programming Example 48: Use of collection of objects

Suppose a programmer wants to create a collection of vehicle objects. Each vehicle object has the following data fields: Colour, Type and Engine. The programmer wants to manipulate the following objects:

Vehicle1 [Colour: ”red”-Type: ”car”-Engine:2000]

Vehicle2 [Colour: ”green”-Type: ”bus”-Engine:4000]

Vehicle3 [Colour: ”blue”-Type: ”motorcycle”-Engine:800]

The following program adds the objects in the collection and outputs the one that is of type “bus”.

```
Vehicle1= new vehicle (setColour =”red”, setType=”car, setEngine
=2000)
Vehicle2= new vehicle (setColour =”green”, setType=”bus, setEngine
=4000)
Vehicle3= new vehicle (setColour =”blue”, setType=”motorcycle,
setEngine =800)

VEHICLES = new Collection()
VEHICLES.addItem(Vehicle1)
VEHICLES.addItem(Vehicle2)
VEHICLES.addItem(Vehicle3)
VEHICLES.resetNext()
output "This Vehicle is a bus"
loop while VEHICLES.hasNext()
    VehicleV = VEHICLES.getNext()
    if VehicleV.getType =”bus” then
      output VehicleV
    end if
end loop
```

Programming Example 49: Use of collection of arrays

The following program uses a collection of arrays. Each array contains student names. The following program finds the number of times “Bob” is found in the collection of arrays.

```
//Array1.length returns the length of the Array used
Monday = ["Tom", "John", "Mary", "Bob"]
Tuesday = ["Bob", "Tom", "Eri"]
X=0
Array1 = new Array()
ABSENCES = new Collection()
ABSENCES.addItem(Monday)
ABSENCES.addItem(Tuesday)
ABSENCES.resetNext()
loop while ABSENCES.hasNext()
    Array1 = ABSENCES.getNext()
        loop N from 0 to Array1.length - 1
          if Array1[N]="Bob" then
            X=X+1
          end if
        end loop
end loop
output " Bob found " , X , " times"
```

4.3.12 Discuss the importance of sub-programmes and collections within programmed solutions.

Exit skills. Students should be able to[1]:

Define the term sub-program.
Discuss the importance and advantages of sub-programs.
Discuss the importance and advantages of collections.
Discuss the importance of the use of reusable code and program organization for the individual programmer, team members and future maintenance.

A *sub-program* is a unit that contains a sequence of computer instructions that perform a specific and predefined task. *Code reuse* is very useful because it allows programmers to take advantage of existing code and solutions developed by other programmers (or by themselves) to speed up their tasks. Code reuse saves time and resources and allows the completion of demanding projects in the shortest period of time. Authors of new programs can take advantage of *software libraries,* which contain subprograms that can be used by different types of programs[22].

Advantages of breaking a program into sub-programs:

- Breaking down a complex programming job into simpler jobs
- Distributing a very large programming problem among various programmers all over the world
- Enabling code reuse across multiple programs
- Facilitation of abstraction by hiding implementation details from users of the subprogram
- Improving maintainability and traceability
- Reducing programming code duplication within the same program

[22] Ambler, Scott (1 January 1998). "A Realistic Look at Object-Oriented Reuse". Retrieved 2 July 2014, www.drdobbs.com.

Advantages of using collections:

- The methods of collections are predefined algorithms that the programmer can immediately use
- Performance is increased by the data management capabilities provided by the collection
- Software reuse is facilitated because the use of methods is based on a common language and a standard interface

Programming Example 50: Java and main method (palindrome)

The following program in Java checks if a string entered by the user is a palindrome or not. This program has only one method: the main method.

```
import java.util.*;
/**
 * This is a program that checks if a string is a palindrome or
not.
 */
class Palindrome_String
{
   public static void main(String args[])
   {
      String original_string, reverse_string = "";
      Scanner in = new Scanner(System.in);

      System.out.println("Type a string to check if it is a
palindrome or not");
      original_string = in.nextLine();
      int string_length = original_string.length();
      for ( int i = string_length - 1; i >= 0; i=i-1 )
         reverse_string = reverse_string +
original_string.charAt(i);

      if (original_string.equals(reverse_string))
         System.out.println("String entered is a palindrome.");
      else
         System.out.println("String entered is not a palindrome.");

   }
}
```

Programming Example 51: Java and methods (reverse of an integer)

The following program finds the reverse of an integer. It uses the main method to enter the integer, calls the method that returns the reverse of a number, and outputs the reversed number. It also uses a method that actually finds and returns the reversed number. This method could be reused in many other problems that require the calculation of the reverse of an integer.

```
import java.util.Scanner;
/**
```

```
 * This a program that finds the reverse of a number
 */
public class Invert_Integer_A
{

    public static void main(String args[])
    {
        System.out.println("Please Enter an integer : ");
        int number = new Scanner(System.in).nextInt();
        System.out.println( "The reserve of the integer :" + number
+ " entered, is "+ (Find_Reverse(number)));

    }

    //Java method to return the reverse of a number
    public static int Find_Reverse(int number)
    {
        int reverse = 0;
        int palindrome = number;
        while (palindrome != 0)
        {
            int remainder = palindrome % 10;
            reverse = reverse * 10 + remainder;
            palindrome = palindrome / 10;
        }
    return reverse;
    }

}
```

Programming Example 52: Java and methods (palindrome and reverse)

The following program checks if an integer is a palindrome or not. The method that was developed in the previous example, which returns the reverse of an integer, is now reused. Therefore, the programmer does not need to rewrite this method. This is a typical example of reusable code.

```
import java.util.Scanner;
/**
 * This a program that checks if an integer is palindrome or not.
 */
public class Palindrome_Integer_A
{

    public static void main(String args[])
    {
        System.out.println("Please enter the number to check : ");
        int palindrome = new Scanner(System.in).nextInt();

        if(Find_Reverse(palindrome)==(palindrome)){
            System.out.println("So, number : " + palindrome + " is
a palindrome");
        }else{
            System.out.println("So, number : " + palindrome + " is
not a palindrome");
        }

    }
```

```
    //Java method to return the reverse of a number
    public static int Find_Reverse(int number)
    {
        int reverse = 0;
        int palindrome = number;


        while (palindrome != 0)
        {
            int remainder = palindrome % 10;
            reverse = reverse * 10 + remainder;
            palindrome = palindrome / 10;
        }
        System.out.println( "The reserve of Number :" + number + "
entered, is " + reverse  );
        return reverse;
    }

}
```

Programming Example 53: Use of methods

The following trivial algorithm developed in IB compatible pseudocode uses four methods. The objective of the algorithm is to perform basic arithmetic calculations and outputs the result. The user enters two numbers (operands) and then selects the desired operation (operator). The main part of the program utilizes four different methods to perform the equivalent operations. Each method accepts the two numbers, performs the equivalent operation and returns the result to the main part. All methods could be reused in many problems that require basic arithmetic calculations

```
output "Enter first number"
input NUMA
output "Enter second number"
input NUMB
output "Enter operation symbol"
input OPERATION
if OPERATION == "+" then
            output ADD(NUMA,NUMB)
end if
if OPERATION == "-" then
            output SUBTRACT(NUMA,NUMB)
end if
if OPERATION == "*" then
            output MULTIPLY(NUMA,NUMB)
end if
if OPERATION == "/" then
            output DIVIDE(NUMA,NUMB)
end if

method ADD(A,B)
            return A+B
end method
method SUBTRACT(A,B)
            return A-B
end method
```

```
method MULTIPLY(A,B)
            return A*B
end method

method DIVIDE(A,B)
            return A/B
end method
```

Programming Example 54: Use of collections (fire stations 1)

Two parallel arrays named FIRE_STATIONS and PERSONNEL hold the names of the fire stations in a city and the number of their personnel. The arrays are as shown:

Array: FIRE_STATIONS	Array: PERSONNEL
Alpha	12
Beta	13
Theta	23
Center	44
Railway	23
Harbor	11
Suburbs	43

Each week one fire station is on night duty. A collection named FIRE_DUTY retrieves the names from the array FIRE_STATIONS and uses an automatic procedure to keep track of the fire station on night duty. The mayor of the city activates this automatic procedure every Monday morning by writing "true" in an input device located in his/her office. The procedure iterates through the collection FIRE_DUTY and changes the name of the fire station on night duty. When the procedure reaches the end of the collection, it returns to the first fire station and the procedure starts from the beginning. This process is repeated for one year (52 weeks). The Mayor has also asked for an alarm message when the selected on duty station is understaffed which means that it has the minimum personnel if compared to all stations. He has also asked for an emergency procedure that will stop the entire process immediately by writing "false" in the input device.

```
FIRE_STATIONS = ["ALPHA", "BETA", "THETA", "CENTER", "RAILWAY",
"HARBOR", "SUBURB"]
PERSONNEL = [2, 13, 23, 44, 23, 11, 43]
FIRE_DUTY = new Collection()
STATION_ON_DUTY = ""
M = 0
MIN = PERSONNEL[0]
UNDERSTAFFED = ""
INPUT_DEVICE = ""

FIRE_DUTY.resetNext()
loop I from 0 to 6
   FIRE_DUTY.addItem(FIRE_STATIONS[I])
end loop

loop M from 0 to 6
   if MIN >= PERSONNEL[M] then
```

```
      MIN = PERSONNEL[M]
      UNDERSTAFFED = FIRE_STATIONS[M]
    end if
end loop

I = 0
loop while I < 52
  input INPUT_DEVICE
  if INPUT_DEVICE == "true" then
   if FIRE_DUTY.hasNext() then
    STATION_ON_DUTY = FIRE_DUTY.getNext()
     if STATION_ON_DUTY = UNDERSTAFFED then
        output "This station is understaffed"
     end if
    output STATION_ON_DUTY
   else
    FIRE_DUTY.resetNext()
    STATION_ON_DUTY = FIRE_DUTY.getNext()
     if STATION_ON_DUTY = UNDERSTAFFED then
       output "This station is understaffed"
     end if
    output STATION_ON_DUTY
   end if
  else if INPUT_DEVICE == "false" then
   I=53
   output "Emergency stop of procedure"
  end if
   I = I+1
end loop
```

4.3.13 Construct algorithms using pre-defined sub-programmes, one-dimensional arrays and/or collections

Exit skills. Students should be able to[1]:
Present synonyms of the term sub-program used in programming Develop various algorithms that include pre- defined sub-programmes, one-dimensional arrays and/or collections, explain their use and justify their purpose.

Different computer programming languages use the terms *procedure, sub-procedures, function, routine, method, subroutines, modules* etc. to refer to *subprograms*. A *sub-program* is a unit that contains a sequence of computer instructions that perform a specific and predefined task. This unit can then be used in various computer programs wherever that specific and predefined task should be implemented. Subprograms may be defined within programs, or separately in libraries that can be used by multiple programs. In C++ programming language, for example, a *procedure* performs a task whereas a *function* produces information and returns a value. It is important to mention that in most cases a function returns a value and a procedure just executes commands. Java uses *methods* to represent subprograms. A Java method may return a value and the main program may pass one or more variables to a method. A *parameter* is the name of the information that is used in a method, function or procedure while an *argument* is the value that is passed into a method, function or procedure. Usually, a *module* refers to a small section of a program that is customized to perform a particular task. Modules can be customised by a programmer to do a particular task.

Programming Example 55: Pre-defined sub-programs, one-dimensional arrays and collections (fire stations 2)

The mayor of the previous example asked for an extra functionality. He believes that a fire station should have at least 25 firefighters. The program should calculate the fire stations that have less than 25 firefighters and displays a message. This message should include the number of personnel that the particular station lacks.

```
//A method named calculate is used for this additional
//functionality.
FIRE_STATIONS = ["ALPHA", "BETA", "THETA", "CENTER", "RAILWAY",
"HARBOR", "SUBURB"]
PERSONNEL = [12, 13, 23, 44, 23, 11, 43]
FIRE_DUTY = new Collection()
STATION_ON_DUTY = ""
M = 0
MIN = PERSONNEL[0]
UNDERSTAFFED = ""
INPUT_DEVICE = ""
INFO = new Array()

calculate() //call method calculate

FIRE_DUTY.resetNext()
loop I from 0 to 6
   FIRE_DUTY.addItem(FIRE_STATIONS[I])
end loop

loop M from 0 to 6
   if MIN >= PERSONNEL[M] then
     MIN = PERSONNEL[M]
     UNDERSTAFFED = FIRE_STATIONS[M]
   end if
end loop

I = 0
loop while I <= 52 //weeks of a year
  input INPUT_DEVICE
  if INPUT_DEVICE == "true" then
   if FIRE_DUTY.hasNext() then
    STATION_ON_DUTY = FIRE_DUTY.getNext()
     if STATION_ON_DUTY = UNDERSTAFFED then
        output "This station has to few personnel!!!"
     end if
    output STATION_ON_DUTY
   else
    FIRE_DUTY.resetNext()
    STATION_ON_DUTY = FIRE_DUTY.getNext()
     if STATION_ON_DUTY = UNDERSTAFFED then
        output "This station has to few personnel!!!"
     end if
    output STATION_ON_DUTY
   end if
  else if INPUT_DEVICE == "false" then
   I=53
```

```
    output "Emergency stop of procedure"
  end if
   I = I+1
end loop
```

```
method calculate()
 loop M from 0 to 6
   if PERSONNEL[M]<25 then
     INFO[M] = 25-PERSONNEL[M]
   else
     INFO[M] = 0
   end if
   if INFO[M]>0 then
     output "________________________________"
     output FIRE_STATIONS[M],"lacks", INFO[M], "firefighters"
   end if
 end loop
end method
```

Programming Example 56: Pre-defined sub-programs, one-dimensional arrays and collections (players ranking)

The following algorithm uses three parallel arrays to store players' names, ages and rankings. The algorithm adds the names of players that are over or equal to 15 and at the same time belong to category rank A to a collection named "PASS". If a player is less than 15 and at the same time belongs to category rank C then he/she is added to a collection named "FAIL". All other players are not classified and the judgment upon them is pending. The algorithm also outputs the total number of players added to collection PASS. Three methods are used: the first and the second take as a parameter the name of the player, and the third returns the number of items stored in the collection PASS.

```
NAMES = ["AL", "BETY", "THALIA", "CERNER", "RAY", "HARI", "SOFI"]
AGES = [18, 13, 18, 15, 16, 18, 11]
CATEGORY= ["A", "B", "C", "C", "B", "A", "C"]
PASS = new Collection()
FAIL = new Collection()
X = 0

loop M from 0 to 6
   if (AGES[M] >= 15 AND CATEGORY[M] = "A") then
     CALC1(NAMES[M])
   else if  (AGES[M] < 15 AND CATEGORY[M] = "C") then
     CALC2(NAMES[M])
   else
     output "Decision for", NAMES[M],"pending"
   end if
end loop
output CALC3(), "persons pass this stage"
```

```
method CALC1(a)
     PASS.addItem(a)
     output "Person ",a, "added to collection PASS"
end method
```

```
method CALC2(b)
     FAIL.addItem(b)
     output "Person ",b, "added to collection FAIL"
```

```
end method
```

```
method CALC3()
  PASS.resetNext()
   loop while PASS.hasNext()
      PASS.getNext()
      X=X+1
   end loop
return X
end method
```

Output

Person AL added to collection PASS
Decision for BETY pending
Decision for THALIA pending
Decision for CERNER pending
Decision for RAY pending
Person HARI added to collection PASS
Person SOFI added to collection FAIL
2 persons pass this stage

Programming Example 57: Body Mass Index algorithm and Java program explained

The following algorithm is used to calculate the *Body Mass Index*, which is an indicator of body fatness[23]. The formula used for adults is Formula: weight (kg) / [height (m)]^2. It is very difficult to use the same formula for kids and teenagers so the program uses a different approach for them. The main program uses two sub-programs (modules). The algorithm (not IB pseudocode) used is the following:

```
Module main()
    Declare Integer A
    Display "Enter your age"
    Input A
    If A > 18 Then
        Call OVER18()
    Else
        Call CHILD()
    End If
End Module

Module CHILD()
    Display "It is difficult to compute BMI for kids and teens"
    Declare Boolean Diet

    Display "Do you have a healthy diet (TRUE or FALSE)?"
    Input Diet
    If Diet == true Then
        Display "Continue...congratulations!!!!"
```

[23] About BMI for Adults. (2015, April 17). Retrieved May 30, 2015, from http://www.cdc.gov/healthyweight/assessing/bmi/adult_bmi/index.html

```
    Else
        Display "Eat more vegetables!!!"
    End If
End Module

Module OVER18()
    Declare Integer mass
    Declare Integer height
    Declare Real BMI

    Display "Enter your weight in kg"
    Input mass
    Display "Enter your height in cm"
    Input height
    Set BMI = height / (mass / 100 * (mass / 100))
    If BMI > 25 Then
        Display "Change your diet!!"
    Else
        Display "Very good!!"
    End If
End Module
```

If the program is written in Java, the Main method will call two methods to achieve the desired result. The algorithm expressed in the Java language is the following. The two methods are of type **void** meaning that they do not return any result (value) to the main program. Both methods have no parameters in the method signature, which means no values are passed to these methods.

```
import java.util.Scanner;
import java.util.*;
import java.lang.Math;

public class BMI {

    public static Scanner input = new Scanner(System.in);

    public  static void main(String[] args) { //MAIN METHOD
        int A;
        System.out.println("Enter your age");
        A = input.nextInt();
        if (A > 18) {
            OVER18(); //Call of method OVER18
        } else {
            CHILD(); //Call of method CHILD
        }
    }

    public static void CHILD() { //Method CHILD
        System.out.println("It is difficult to compute BMI for kids
and teens");
        boolean Diet;

        System.out.println("Do you have a healthy diet (TRUE or
FALSE)?");
        Diet = input.nextBoolean();
        if (Diet == true) {
            System.out.println("Continue...congratulations!!!!");
        } else {
```

```
            System.out.println("Eat more vegetables!!!");
        }
    }
```

```
    public static void OVER18() { //Method OVER18
        int mass;
        int height;
        double BMI;

        System.out.println("Enter your weight in kg");
        mass = input.nextInt();
        System.out.println("Enter your height in cm");
        height = input.nextInt();
        BMI = (double) height / ((mass/100)*(mass/100));
        if (BMI > 25) {
            System.out.println("Change your diet!!");
        } else {
            System.out.println("Very good!!");
        }
    }
}
```

The same algorithm expressed as three flowcharts is illustrated in Figures 4.21, 4.22 and 4.23.

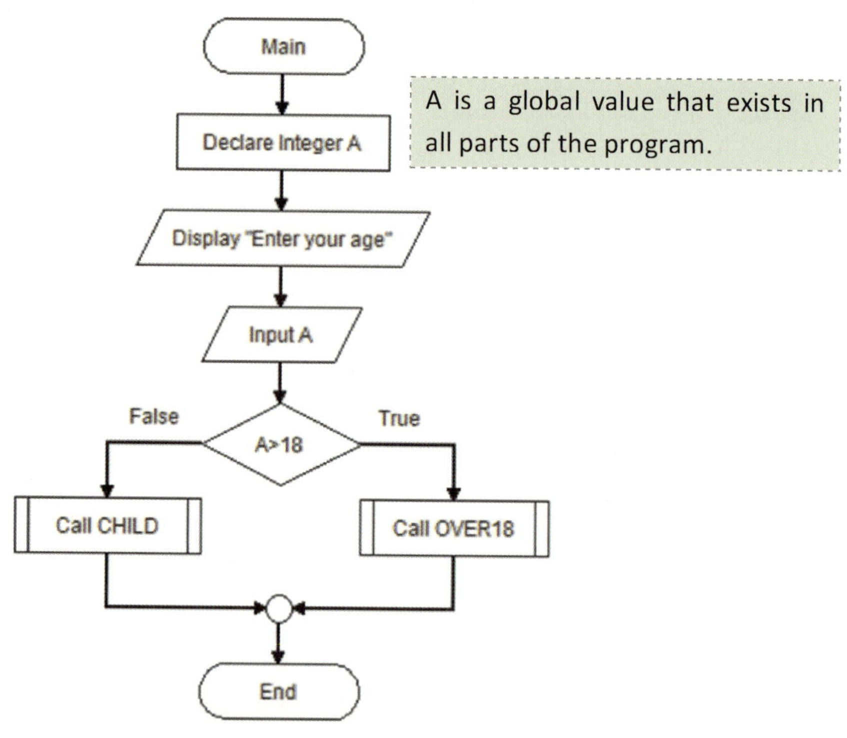

Figure 4.21: Flowchat for the programming example

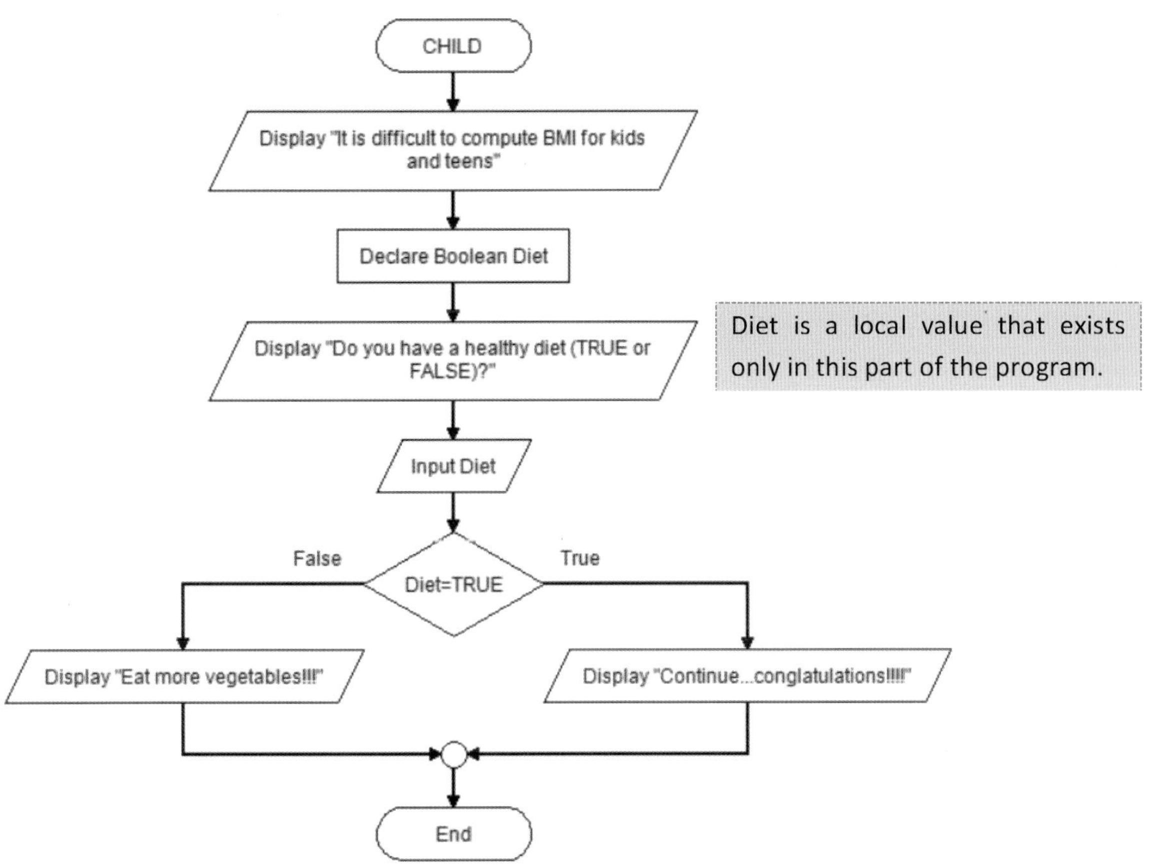

Figure 4.22: Flowchat for the programming example

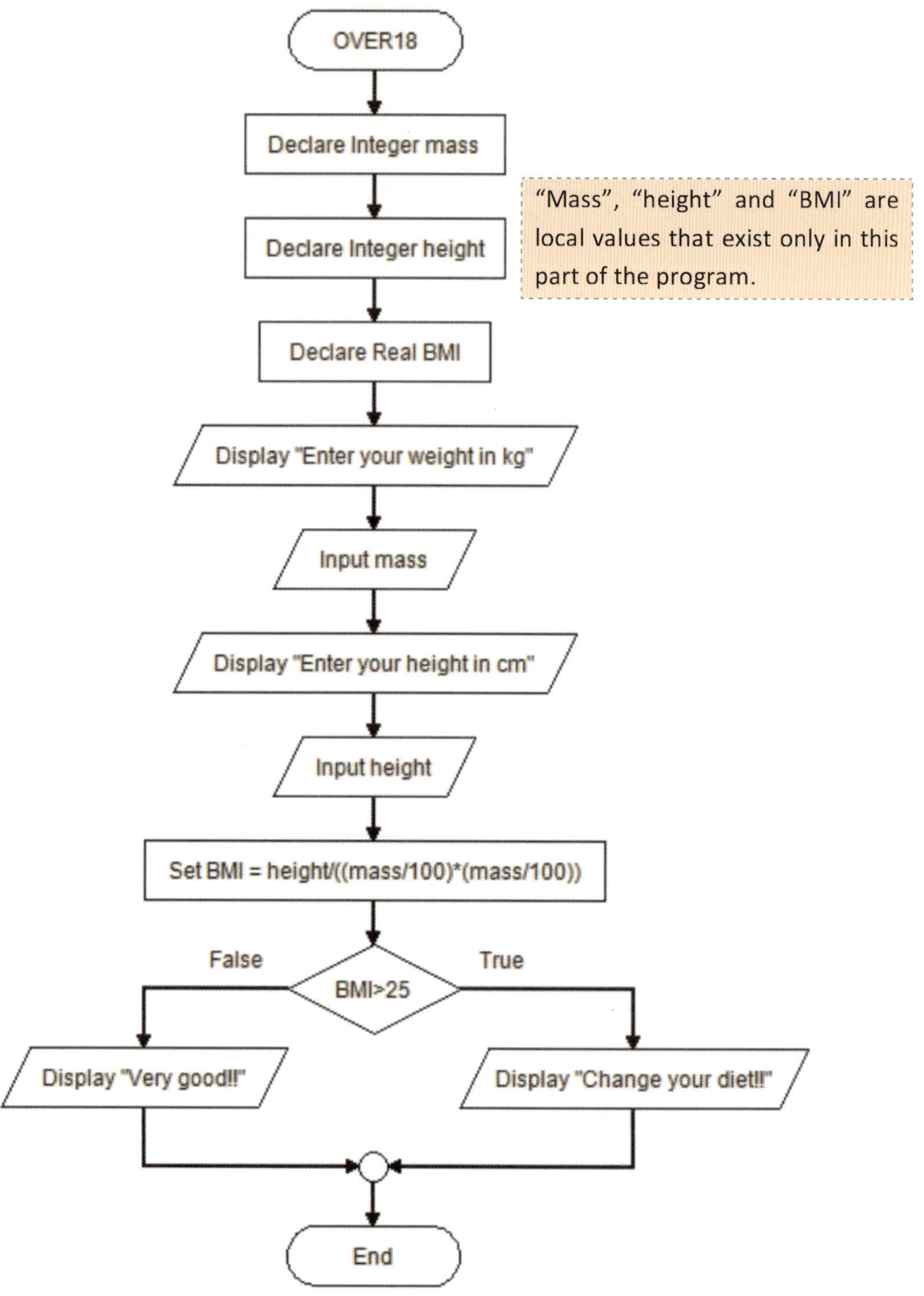

Figure 4.23: Flowchat for the programming example

The following algorithm (not IB pseudocode) is another version that produces the same result as the previous algorithm. The main program (Module main) uses two sub-programs. The Function Boolean CHILD() returns a Boolean value while the Module OVER18 (Real BMI) accepts a parameter (BMI). The algorithm used is the following:

```
Module main()
    Declare Integer Age

    Display "Enter your age"
```

```
    Input Age
    Declare Integer mass
    Declare Integer height
    Declare Real BMI

    Display "Enter your weight in kg"
    Input mass
    Display "Enter your height in cm"
    Input height
    Set BMI = height / (mass / 100 * (mass / 100))
    If Age > 18 Then
        Call OVER18(BMI)
    Else
        If CHILD() == true Then
            Display "Continue...congratulations!!!!"
        Else
            Display "Eat more vegetables!!!"
        End If
    End If
End Module

Function Boolean CHILD()
    Display "It is difficult to compute BMI for kids and teens"
    Declare Boolean Diet

    Display "Do you have a healthy diet (TRUE or FALSE)?"
    Input Diet

    Return Diet
End Function

Module OVER18(Real BMI)
    If BMI > 25 Then
        Display "Change your diet!!"
    Else
        Display "Very good!!"
    End If
End Module
```

If the program is written in Java, the Main method will be used to call two methods so as to achieve the desired result. The first method will return a Boolean value (Diet). This method does not receive any parameter from the main method. The second method is of type **void** meaning that it does not return any result (value) to the main method. This method receives a parameter (double BMI) from the main method. The algorithm, expressed in the Java language, is the following.

```
import java.util.Scanner;
import java.util.*;
import java.lang.Math;


class BMI_2 {
    private static Scanner input = new Scanner(System.in);

    public static void main(String[] args) {
        int Age;

        System.out.println("Enter your age");
```

```
        Age = input.nextInt();
        int mass;
        int height;
        double BMI;

        System.out.println("Enter your weight in kg");
        mass = input.nextInt();
        System.out.println("Enter your height in cm");
        height = input.nextInt();
        BMI = height / ((double) mass / 100 * ((double) mass /
100));
        if (Age > 18) {
            OVER18(BMI);
        } else {
            if (CHILD() == true) {
System.out.println("Continue...congratulations!!!!");
            } else {
                System.out.println("Eat more vegetables!!!");
            }
        }
    }

    public static boolean CHILD() {
        System.out.println("It is difficult to compute BMI for kids
and teens");
        boolean Diet;

        System.out.println("Do you have a healthy diet (TRUE or
FALSE)?");
        Diet = input.nextBoolean();

        return Diet;
    }

    public static void OVER18(double BMI) {
        if (BMI > 25) {
            System.out.println("Change your diet!!");
        } else {
            System.out.println("Very good!!");
        }
    }
}
```

The same algorithm expressed as three flowcharts is illustrated in Figure 4.24.

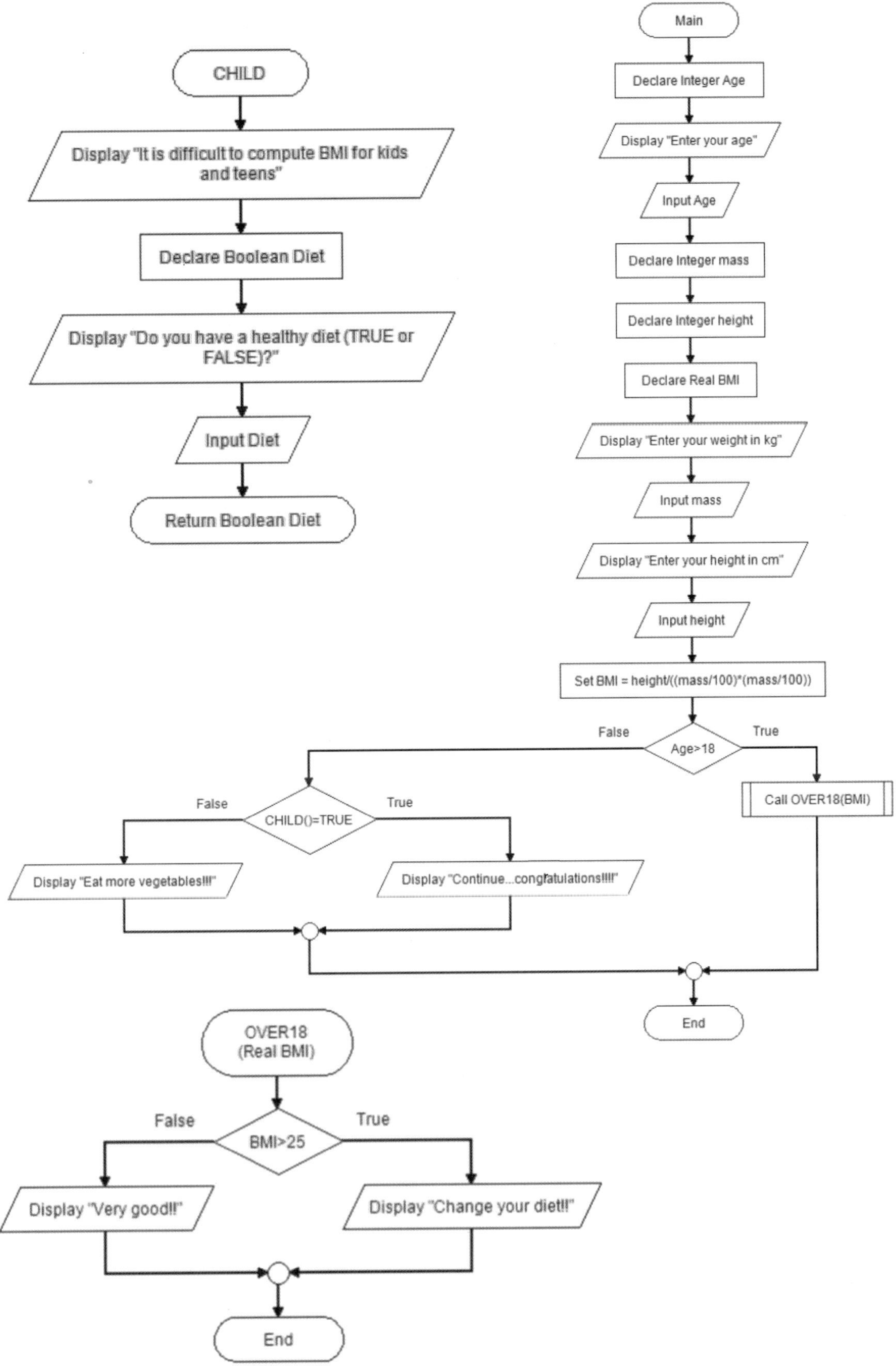

Figure 4.24: Flowchart for the programming example

Programming Example 58: Use of collections and 2D array (weight of children)

The weight (in Kilos) of five children was recorded every year, for 5 years. The following table depicts a two-dimensional array that is used to store the values.

WEIGHTS		Boy 1	Girl 2	Boy 3	Girl 4	Girl 5
		[0]	[1]	[2]	[3]	[4]
Year 2010	[0]	9	8	10	9	8
Year 2011	[1]	13	2	12	13	2
Year 2012	[2]	16	14	14	15	14
Year 2013	[3]	18	16	16	17	16
Year 2014	[4]	19	17	17	18	17

A scientist wants to perform various statistical analyses, to which end, he/she

1. wants to store the information to a collection WEIGHTSEXPERIMENT sequentially
2. takes the items from the collection WEIGHTSEXPERIMENT and gets them to an one dimensional array named FINAL
3. adds WEIGHTS elements to five one dimensional arrays (column by column), one for each child
4. outputs elements of GIRL2 array
5. constructs two different methods that will compare the weight of two children (two arrays comparison)

```
BOY1 = new Array()
GIRL2 = new Array()
BOY3 = new Array()
GIRL4 = new Array()
GIRL5 = new Array()
FINAL = new Array()
WEIGHTSEXPERIMENT = new Collection()
WEIGHTS =                [[9,  8,   10, 9,     8],
                         [13,  2,   12, 13,    2],
                         [16,  14,  14, 15,   14],
                         [18,  16,  16, 17,   16],
                         [19,  17,  17, 18,   17]]

YEAR = 0
CHILD = 0
//Adding WEIGHTS elements to collection WEIGHTSEXPERIMENT(line by
//line)
WEIGHTSEXPERIMENT.resetNext()
loop YEAR from 0 to 4
    loop CHILD from 0 to 4
     WEIGHTSEXPERIMENT.addItem(WEIGHTS[YEAR][CHILD])
    end loop
end loop

//Adding collection elements to array FINAL (line by line)
WEIGHTSEXPERIMENT.resetNext()
I = 0
loop while WEIGHTSEXPERIMENT.hasNext()
FINAL[I] = WEIGHTSEXPERIMENT.getNext()
I = I+1
end loop
```

```
//Adding WEIGHTS elements to 5 arrays (column by column)
loop YEAR from 0 to 4
            BOY1[YEAR] = WEIGHTS[YEAR][0]
                GIRL2[YEAR] = WEIGHTS[YEAR][1]
                BOY3[YEAR] = WEIGHTS[YEAR][2]
                GIRL4[YEAR] = WEIGHTS[YEAR][3]
                GIRL5[YEAR] = WEIGHTS[YEAR][4]
end loop

//Output array GIRL2 elements
output "ARRAY GIRL2 ELEMENTS"
loop YEAR from 0 to 4
             output GIRL2[YEAR]
end loop

//Use of method 1
output "COMPARISON OF TWO ARRAYS FIRST METHOD"
loop YEAR from 0 to 4
  COMPARE_ARRAYS(GIRL2[YEAR],GIRL5[YEAR])
end loop

//Use of method 2
output "COMPARISON OF TWO ARRAYS SECOND METHOD"
Z = 0
loop YEAR from 0 to 4
   Z = Z + COMPARE_ARRAYS_B(GIRL4[YEAR],GIRL5[YEAR])
end loop
if Z = 0 then
  output "All elements are equal"
else
   output "Arrays are not equal"
end if
```

```
//Method 1
method COMPARE_ARRAYS(A,B)
  if A = B then
     output "Year ", YEAR, "elements are equal"
  else
     output "Year ", YEAR, "elements are not equal"
  end if
end method
```

```
//Method 2
method COMPARE_ARRAYS_B(A,B)
X = 0
  if A = B then
     X = 0
  else
     X = 1
  end if
return X
end method
```

Output:

ARRAY GIRL2 ELEMENTS

8

2

14
16
17
COMPARISON OF TWO ARRAYS FIRST METHOD
Year 0 elements are equal
Year 1 elements are equal
Year 2 elements are equal
Year 3 elements are equal
Year 4 elements are equal
COMPARISON OF TWO ARRAYS SECOND METHOD
Arrays are not equal

Programming Example 59: Use of collections of objects

A smart weighing scale has four buttons and can store different weights for four different users. These values are stored within a microprocessor as an array shown in the table below.

Weights

[0]	[1]	[2]	[3]
87.5	62.3	77.2	43.6

A display in the smart scale displays the name and weight of the user when the appropriate button is pressed. The name is manually entered once when the user is initially weighed.

1. Outline how a collection of objects could be used to store the name and weight data in the scale
2. Construct a pseudocode algorithm to access and display the name and weight of a user when a button is pressed

Answer:

1. A new object named SELECTION is created, containing both name and weight. This object is stored in a collection named COLLECTION.
2.

```
BUTTON = input("# button pressed")
COLLECTION.resetNext()
loop while COLLECTION.hasNext()
  SELECTION = COLLECTION.getNext()
  if SELECTION.getWeight() = WEIGHTS[BUTTON] then
    output (SELECTION.getName())
    output(SELECTION.getWeight())
  endif
endloop
```

Various one dimensional array operations (no methods)

Programming Example 60: Java useful 1D array operations

The following program demonstrates various useful array operations. This program in Java does not use methods to accomplish its goals. Data are obtained by an array that contains five elements.

```
import java.util.*;
public class Array_Operations
{
   static Scanner console = new Scanner(System.in);
   public static void main(String[] args)
  {
   int[] elements = new int[5]; //declare an array of five elements
   int sum;
   System.out.println("Enter five integers:");
   sum = 0;
      for (int counter = 0; counter < elements.length; counter++)
     {
      elements[counter] = console.nextInt();

      //used to calculate the sum of the array elements
      sum = sum + elements[counter];
     }
     System.out.println("The sum of the numbers = " + sum);

      //used to print the contents of the array in reverse order
      System.out.print("The numbers in the reverse "+ "order are: ");
      for (int counter = elements.length - 1; counter >= 0;
counter=counter -1)
          System.out.print(elements[counter] + " ");
          System.out.println();

      //used to print the contents of the array
      System.out.println("Contents of the array " );
      for (int i = 0; i< elements.length; i=i+1)
      {
       System.out.println(elements[i] + " ");
      }
      //used to find the largest element
      int max = elements[0];
      for (int i = 0; i< elements.length; i=i+1)
      {
          if (elements[i]>max) max = elements[i];
      }
       System.out.println("Max = " + max);

      //used to find the minimum element
      int min = elements[0];
      for (int i = 0; i< elements.length; i=i+1)
      {
          if (elements[i]<min) min = elements[i];
      }
       System.out.println("Min = " + min);

      //used to find the smallest index of the largest element
      max = elements[0];
      int index_of_max = 0;
      for (int i = 0; i< elements.length; i=i+1)
      {
          if (elements[i]>max)
          {
              max = elements[i];
```

```
                index_of_max = i;
            }
        }
         System.out.println("Max = " + max + "  Smallest Index= " +
index_of_max);

        //used to find the largest index of the largest element
        max = elements[0];
        index_of_max = 0;
        for (int i = 0; i< elements.length; i=i+1)
        {
            if (elements[i]>=max)
            {
                max = elements[i];
                index_of_max = i;
            }
        }
         System.out.println("Max = " + max + "  Largest Index= " +
index_of_max);

        //used to randomly shuffle the elements of the array
        System.out.println("Randomly shuffled elements ");
        for (int i = 0; i< elements.length; i=i+1)
        {
          int random = (int)(Math.random()*elements.length);
          int temp = elements[i];
          elements[i]=elements[random];
          elements[random]=temp;
        }

        //used to print the contents of the array
        System.out.println("Contents of the array " );
        for (int i = 0; i< elements.length; i=i+1)
        {
         System.out.println(elements[i] + " ");
        }

        //used to shift the elements of the array one position left
        //the last element will take the value of the first element
        //the shuffled array is used
        //the original array elements have permanently changed
        System.out.println("Shifted elements left");
        int temp=elements[0];
        for (int i = 1; i< elements.length; i=i+1)
        {
          elements[i-1]=elements[i];
        }
        elements[elements.length-1]=temp;

        //used to print the contents of the array
        System.out.println("Contents of the array " );
        for (int i = 0; i< elements.length; i=i+1)
        {
         System.out.println(elements[i] + " ");
        }
        //used to shift the elements of the array one position right
        //the first element will take the value of the last element
        //the shifted array is used
        //the previous array elements have permanently changed
        System.out.println("Shifted elements right");
        temp=elements[elements.length-1];
```

```
        for (int i = elements.length-1; i>0; i=i-1)
        {
          elements[i]=elements[i-1];
        }
        elements[0]=temp;

        //used to print the contents of the array
        System.out.println("Contents of the array " );
        for (int i = 0; i< elements.length; i=i+1)
        {
         System.out.println(elements[i] + " ");
        }
    }
}
```

Output:

Enter five integers:
23
45
111
1
345
The sum of the numbers = 525
The numbers in the reverse order are: 345 1 111 45 23
Contents of the array
23
45
111
1
345
Max = 345
Min = 1
Max = 345 Smallest Index= 4
Max = 345 Largest Index= 4
Randomly shuffled elements
Contents of the array
45
23
345
111
1
Shifted elements left
Contents of the array
23
345
111
1
45
Shifted elements right
Contents of the array
45
23
345

111
1

Various two-dimensional array operations (use of methods)

Programming Example 61: Various matrix operations (pseudocode)

```
//Declaration of a 2-D array
//Fill the array with zeros
A = [[0,0,0],
     [0,0,0],
     [0,0,0]]
//The size of columns and rows
SIZE = 3
//loop to fill the array with the desired values
loop I from 0 to SIZE-1
 loop J from 0 to SIZE-1
  input A[I][J]
 end loop
end loop
//loop to repeat the menu
//stops if 10 entered
SELECT = 0
loop while SELECT != 10
  output "Options"
  output "Please select 0 to check if the matrix is a (0,1) matrix"
  output "Please select 1 to check if the matrix is an Arrowhead
  matrix"
  output "Please select 2 to check if the matrix is a Binary
  matrix"
  output "Please select 3 to check if the matrix is a Boolean
  matrix"
  output "Please select 4 to check if the matrix is a Diagonal
  matrix"
  output "Please select 5 to check if the matrix is an Identity
  matrix"
  output "Please select 6 to check if the matrix is a Integer
  matrix"
  output "Please select 7 to check if the matrix is a Nonnegative
  matrix"
  output "Please select 8 to check if the matrix is a Permutation
  matrix"
  output "Please select 9 to check if the matrix is a Symmetric
  matrix"
  output "Press 10 to exit"
  CHOICE = input("Please choose an operation")
  //selection of desired operation
  if CHOICE == 0 OR  CHOICE == 2 OR CHOICE == 3 then
     Binary()
  else if CHOICE == 1 then
     Arrowhead()
  else if CHOICE == 4 then
     Diagonal()
  else if CHOICE == 5 then
     Identity()
  else if CHOICE == 6 then
     Integer()
  else if CHOICE == 7 then
     Nonnegative()
  else if CHOICE == 8 then
```

```
    Permutation()
  else if CHOICE == 9 then
    Symmetric()
  else
    SELECT = 10
  end if
end loop

//the following part contains the various methods
//use of from to loop
method Binary()
output
output "Also called logical matrix, binary matrix, relation matrix,
Boolean matrix, or (0,1) matrix."
output "This matrix contains only Boolean values (0,1)."
output "It can be used to symbolize a binary relation between a
pair of finite sets."
output
X = 0
loop I from 0 to SIZE-1
  loop J from 0 to SIZE-1
   if A[I][J] == 1 OR A[I][J] == 0 then
    X = X+1
   end if
  end loop
end loop
if X == (SIZE*SIZE) then
  output "It is such a matrix"
else
  output "It is not such a matrix"
end if
end method

//use of from to loop
method Arrowhead()
output
output "An arrowhead matrix is a square matrix"
output "containing zeros in all entries except for the first row,
first column, and main diagonal."
output "They are considered as an essential tool for the
computation of the eigenvalues."
output
X = 0
loop I from 0 to SIZE-1
 loop J from 0 to SIZE-1
  if (A[0][J] != 0) AND (A[I][0] != 0) AND (A[I][J] != 0) then
   X= X+1
 else
  if (A[I][J] = 0) then
   X= X+1
  end if
 end if
 end loop
end loop
if X == (SIZE * SIZE) then
 output "It is an Arrowhead matrix"
else
 output "It is not an Arrowhead matrix"
end if
end method
```

```
//use of from to loop
method Diagonal()
output
output "In linear algebra, a diagonal matrix is a matrix "
output "in which the entries outside the main diagonal are all
zero."
output "Any square diagonal matrix is also a symmetric matrix."
output
X = 0
loop I from 0 to SIZE-1
 loop J from 0 to SIZE-1
 if (I != J) AND (A[I][J] == 0) then
   X = X+1
 end if
 if (I = J) then
  X = X+1
  output "x", X
 end if
 end loop
end loop
 if X == (SIZE*SIZE) then
  output "It is a Diagonal matrix"
 else
  output "It is not a Diagonal matrix"
 end if
end method

//use of from to loop
method Identity()
output
output "It is a square matrix with"
output "ones on the main diagonal and zeros elsewhere."
output
X = 0
loop I from 0 to SIZE-1
 loop J from 0 to SIZE-1
  if I==J then
   if A[I][J] == 1 then
    X = X+1
   end if
  else
   if A[I][J] == 0 then
    X = X+1
   end if
  end if
 end loop
end loop
if X == (SIZE*SIZE) then
 output "It is an Identity matrix"
else
 output "It is not an Identity matrix"
end if
end method

//use of from to loop
method Integer()
output
output " An integer matrix is a matrix"
output " whose entries are all integers."
output
X = 0
```

```
loop I from 0 to SIZE-1
 loop J from 0 to SIZE-1
   if (div(A[I][J],1) == A[I][J]) then
    X = X+1
   end if
  end loop
end loop
if X == (SIZE*SIZE) then
 output "It is an Integer matrix"
else
 output "It is not an Integer matrix"
end if
end method

//use of while loop
method Nonnegative()
output
output "A nonnegative matrix is a matrix in which "
output "all the elements are equal to or greater than zero"
output
X = 1
I = 0
loop while X = 1 AND I < SIZE
  J = 0
  loop while X = 1 AND J < SIZE
   if A[I][J] < 0 then
    X = 0
   end if
   J = J+1
  end loop
  I = I+1
end loop
if X == 1 then
 output "It is an Nonnegative matrix"
else
 output "It is not an Nonnegative matrix"
end if
end method

//use of while loop
method Permutation()
output
output "A permutation matrix is a square binary matrix that has"
output "exactly one entry 1 in each row and each column and 0s
elsewhere. "
output
X = 1
I = 0
loop while X = 1 AND I < SIZE
  J = 0
  SUMC = 0
  SUMR = 0
   loop while X = 1 AND J < SIZE
    SUMR = SUMR + A[I][J]
    SUMC = SUMC + A[J][I]
    J = J+1
   end loop
  if (SUMR != 1) OR (SUMC != 1) then
    X = 0
    output "x", X
  end if
```

```
  I = I+1
end loop
if X == 1 then
 output "It is a Permutation matrix"
else
 output "It is not a Permutation matrix"
end if
end method

//use of from to loop
method Symmetric()
output
output "In linear algebra, a symmetric matrix is a "
output "square matrix that is equal to its transpose."
output
X = 0
loop I from 0 to SIZE-1
 loop J from 0 to SIZE-1
  if A[I][J] == A[J][I] then
   X = X+1
  end if
 end loop
end loop
if X==(SIZE*SIZE) then
 output "It is a Symmetric matrix"
else
 output "It is not a Symmetric matrix"
end if
end method
```

Programming Example 62: Java useful 2D array operations

The following program in Java uses methods. It performs various calculations on a two dimensional array. The 2D array contains lake measurements.

```
//Solution to Lake Statistics Problem
//Use of a 2D array to store temperatures
//1 sample every 6 hours (00:00, 6:00, 12:00, 18:00)
//4 samples per day
//A total of 28 samples

public class Lake_problem
{

    public static void main(String[] args)
    {
        int[][] Lake_Temp ={{23,22,24,24},
                            {22,23,25,25},
                            {23,22,24,23},
                            {20,23,25,25},
                            {23,22,24,24},
                            {24,23,25,25},
                            {19,21,22,22}};

        printTwo_D_Array(Lake_Temp);
        System.out.println("--------------");
        SumDate(Lake_Temp);
        System.out.println("--------------");
        SumTime(Lake_Temp);
```

```
        System.out.println("--------------");
        MaxDate(Lake_Temp);
        System.out.println("--------------");
        MaxTime(Lake_Temp);
        System.out.println("--------------");
        MinDate(Lake_Temp);
        System.out.println("--------------");
        MinTime(Lake_Temp);
        System.out.println("--------------");
        AvDate(Lake_Temp);
        System.out.println("--------------");
        AvTime(Lake_Temp);
        System.out.println("--------------");
        AvAll(Lake_Temp);
    }

    public static void printTwo_D_Array(int[][] TDarray)
    {
        int date, time;

        for (date = 0; date < TDarray.length; date=date+1)
        {
            for (time = 0; time < TDarray[date].length;
time=time+1)
                System.out.printf("%7d", TDarray[date][time]);

            System.out.println();
        }
    }

    public static void SumDate(int[][] TDarray)
    {
       int date, time;
       int sum;

       //sum of each individual date
       for (date = 0; date < TDarray.length; date=date+1)
       {
           sum = 0;

           for (time = 0; time < TDarray[date].length; time=time+1)
                sum = sum + TDarray[date][time];

           System.out.println("The sum of the temperatures of date
   " + (date + 1) + " = " + sum);
       }
    }

    public static void AvDate(int[][] TDarray)
    {
    int date, time;
    int sum = 0;
    int average = 0;

      //sum of each individual date
      for (date = 0; date < TDarray.length; date=date+1)
      {
         for (time = 0; time < TDarray[date].length; time=time+1)
              sum = sum + TDarray[date][time];
               average = sum/TDarray[time].length;
               sum = 0;
```

```
        System.out.println("The average temperature for date " +
(date + 1) + " = " + average);
      }

    }


    public static void SumTime(int[][] TDarray)
    {
        int date, time;
        int sum;

        //sum of each individual time
        for (time = 0; time < TDarray[0].length; time=time+1)
        {
            sum = 0;
            for (date = 0; date < TDarray.length; date=date+1)
                sum = sum + TDarray[date][time];
            System.out.println("The sum of the temperatures of time
" + (time + 1) + " = " + sum);
        }
    }


    public static void AvTime(int[][] TDarray)
    {
       int date, time;
       int sum = 0;
       int average = 0;

       //sum of each individual date
       for (time = 0; time < TDarray[0].length; time=time+1)
       {
         sum = 0;
         for (date = 0; date < TDarray.length; date=date+1)
              sum = sum + TDarray[date][time];
              average = sum/TDarray.length;
              sum = 0;
         System.out.println("The average temperature for time " +
(time + 1) + " = " + average);
       }
    }

    public static void MaxDate(int[][] TDarray)
    {
    int date, time;
    int maximum;

       //The maximum temperature for each date
       for (date = 0; date < TDarray.length; date=date+1)
       {
           maximum = TDarray[date][0];
           for (time = 1; time < TDarray[date].length; time=time+1)
               if (maximum < TDarray[date][time])
                   maximum = TDarray[date][time];

           System.out.println("The maximum temperature of date " +
   (date + 1) + " = " + maximum);
       }
    }
```

```
    public static void MaxTime(int[][] TDarray)
    {
        int date, time;
        int maximum;

        //The maximum temperature for each time
        for (time = 0; time < TDarray[0].length; time=time+1)
        {
            maximum = TDarray[0][time];
            for (date = 1; date < TDarray.length; date=date+1)
                if (maximum < TDarray[date][time])
                    maximum = TDarray[date][time];
            System.out.println("The maximum temperature of time " +
(time + 1) + " = " + maximum);
        }
    }

    public static void MinDate(int[][] TDarray)
    {
        int date, time;
        int minimum;

        //The minimum temperature for each date
        for (date = 0; date < TDarray.length; date=date+1)
        {
            minimum = TDarray[date][0];
            for (time = 1; time < TDarray[date].length; time=time+1)
                if (minimum > TDarray[date][time])
                    minimum = TDarray[date][time];

            System.out.println("The minimum temperature of date " +
(date + 1) + " = " + minimum);
        }
    }

    public static void MinTime(int[][] TDarray)
    {
        int date, time;
        int minimum;

        //Minimum temperature for each time
        for (time = 0; time < TDarray[0].length; time=time+1)
        {
            minimum = TDarray[0][time];
            for (date = 1; date < TDarray.length; date=date+1)
                if (minimum > TDarray[date][time])
                    minimum = TDarray[date][time];
            System.out.println("The minimum temperature of time " +
(time + 1) + " = " + minimum);
        }
    }

    public static void AvAll(int[][] TDarray)
    {
        int date, time;
        int sum = 0;
        int average = 0;
        int i = 0;

        for (date = 0; date < TDarray.length; date=date+1)
        {
```

```
            for (time = 0; time < TDarray[date].length; time=time+1)
               {
                sum = sum + TDarray[date][time];
                i = i + 1;
               }
        }
          average = sum/i;
          System.out.println("The overall average temperature is " +
" = " + average);
        }
    }
```

Output:

The maximum temperature of date 2 = 25
The maximum temperature of date 3 = 24
The maximum temperature of date 4 = 25
The maximum temperature of date 5 = 24
The maximum temperature of date 6 = 25
The maximum temperature of date 7 = 22

The maximum temperature of time 1 = 24
The maximum temperature of time 2 = 23
The maximum temperature of time 3 = 25
The maximum temperature of time 4 = 25

The minimum temperature of date 1 = 22
The minimum temperature of date 2 = 22
The minimum temperature of date 3 = 22
The minimum temperature of date 4 = 20
The minimum temperature of date 5 = 22
The minimum temperature of date 6 = 23
The minimum temperature of date 7 = 19

The minimum temperature of time 1 = 19
The minimum temperature of time 2 = 21
The minimum temperature of time 3 = 22
The minimum temperature of time 4 = 22

The average temperature for date 1 = 23
The average temperature for date 2 = 23
The average temperature for date 3 = 23
The average temperature for date 4 = 23
The average temperature for date 5 = 23
The average temperature for date 6 = 24
The average temperature for date 7 = 21

The average temperature for time 1 = 22
The average temperature for time 2 = 22
The average temperature for time 3 = 24
The average temperature for time 4 = 24

The overall average temperature is = 23

Programming Example 63: Java use of a method for another problem (average)

Use of **AVall** method for another problem:

```
//Solution to Lake Statistics Problem
//Use of a 2D array to store temperatures

public class Lake_problem2
{

    public static void main(String[] args)
    {
        int[][] Lake_Temp ={{11,12,14,14},
                            {12,13,15,15},
                            {13,12,14,13}};


        System.out.println("--------------");
        AvAll(Lake_Temp);
    }

    public static void AvAll(int[][] TDarray)
    {
      int date, time;
      int sum = 0;
      int average = 0;
      int i = 0;

      for (date = 0; date < TDarray.length; date=date+1)
      {
          for (time = 0; time < TDarray[date].length; time=time+1)
              {
               sum = sum + TDarray[date][time];
               i = i + 1;
              }
      }
        average = sum/i;
        System.out.println("The overall average temperature is " +
" = " + average);
      }
    }
```

Chapter References

1. International Baccalaureate Organization. (2012). IBDP Computer Science Guide.
2. Problem definition, meaning - what is problem in the British English Dictionary & Thesaurus - Cambridge Dictionaries Online. (n.d.). Retrieved May 30, 2015, from http://dictionary.cambridge.org/dictionary/british/problem
3. Herbert A. Simon. (2015, June 9). In Wikipedia, The Free Encyclopedia. Retrieved 17:07, June 19, 2015, from https://en.wikipedia.org/w/index.php?title=Herbert_A._Simon&oldid=666130799
4. Herbert A. Simon - Biographical. (n.d.). Retrieved May 31, 2015, from http://www.nobelprize.org/nobel_prizes/economic-sciences/laureates/1978/simon-bio.html
5. Simon, H.A. (1960). THE NEW SCIENCE OF MANAGEMENT DECISION. New York, NY: Harper and Row.
6. Mintzberg, H., D. Raisinghani and A. Téorèt. (1976). The structure of unstructured decision processes. Administrative Science Quartely, 21, pp. 246-275.
7. (n.d.). Retrieved May 30, 2015, from http://mathworld.wolfram.com/UnsolvedProblems.html
8. List of Hello world program examples. (2015, June 14). In Wikipedia, The Free Encyclopedia. Retrieved 17:11, June 19, 2015, from https://en.wikipedia.org/w/index.php?title=List_of_Hello_world_program_examples&oldid=666880519
9. International Baccalaureate Organization. (2004). IBDP Computer Science Guide.
10. Knuth, Donald E. (1968). The Art of Computer Programming Second Edition, Volume 1, Fundamental Algorithms (First ed.). Addison-Wesley Publishing Company.
11. (n.d.). Retrieved May 30, 2015, from http://www.statemaster.com/encyclopedia/Algorithm-characterizations
12. Programming language. (2015, June 10). In *Wikipedia, The Free Encyclopedia. Retrieved 17:20, June 19, 2015, from https://en.wikipedia.org/w/index.php?title=Programming_language&oldid=666292926*
13. (n.d.). Retrieved May 30, 2015, from https://cs.brown.edu/courses/cs015/labs/Lab6Pseudocode.pdf
14. International Baccalaureate Organization. (2012). IBDP Approved notations for developing pseudocode.
15. Online Etymology Dictionary. (n.d.). Retrieved May 30, 2015, from http://www.etymonline.com/index.php?term=program
16. Concurrency Problems. (n.d.). Retrieved May 30, 2015, from https://technet.microsoft.com/en-us/library/aa213029(v=sql.80).aspx
17. Cormen, Thomas H.; Leiserson, Charles E., Rivest, Ronald L. (1990). Introduction to Algorithms (1st ed.). MIT Press and McGraw-Hill. ISBN 0-262-03141-8.
18. Binary search algorithm. (2015, June 11). In Wikipedia, The Free Encyclopedia. Retrieved 06:33, July 1, 2015, from https://en.wikipedia.org/w/index.php?title=Binary_search_algorithm&oldid=666547193
19. Bubble sort. (2015, June 15). In *Wikipedia, The Free Encyclopedia*. Retrieved 17:26, June 19, 2015, from https://en.wikipedia.org/w/index.php?title=Bubble_sort&oldid=667050446
20. Selection sort. (2015, June 11). In *Wikipedia, The Free Encyclopedia. Retrieved 17:28, June 19, 2015, from https://en.wikipedia.org/w/index.php?title=Selection_sort&oldid=666542512*
21. International Baccalaureate Organization. (2012). IBDP Pseudocode in examinations.
22. Ambler, Scott (1 January 1998). "A Realistic Look at Object-Oriented Reuse". Retrieved July 2, 2014, from www.drdobbs.com.
23. About BMI for Adults. (2015, April 17). Retrieved May 30, 2015, from http://www.cdc.gov/healthyweight/assessing/bmi/adult_bmi/index.html

Chapter 5

OPTION D – OBJECT ORIENTED PROGRAMMING

Topic 5 Object oriented programming[1]

D.1 Objects as a programming concept

The paradigm of object-oriented programming should be introduced through discussion and examples.

D.1.1 The general nature of an object

Exit skills. Students should be able to:[1]
Define the terms: object, objects' data and objects' actions. Describe the conceptual framework of objects in programming. Explain the use of objects as an abstract entity.

Person
DATA
Name Height Weight Gender Age Eye Colour Hair Colour
ACTIONS
Sleep Wake up Walk Run Climb stairs

Figure D.1: Person's Object Data and Actions

We begin this chapter by having a short conceptual discussion of the idea on an "object" before going into *object-oriented programming (OOP)*. To understand objects, we can bring an example from real life to help us along: people. Each person in the world might be different but they also have some traits which define them as humans. For example, a person looks a certain way; he/she has a height, weight, gender, age, eye/hair colour, etc. All these are general properties (data) that a person has. Furthermore, he/she also has the ability to perform certain actions, mainly, do things. For example, a person can sleep, wake up, walk, run, climb stairs, etc. Certainly, there might be some actions that some people can do that others cannot, like playing the piano, but there are some actions which are common for all people. According to these data and actions, we construct Figure D.1 that depicts these components clearly.

An *object* is thus an *abstract entity* that describes the data that this entity has (a.k.a. properties or attributes) and the actions that this entity can perform (a.k.a. methods).

[1] International Baccalaureate Organization. (2012). IBDP Computer Science Guide.

Example D.1: What are the components (data and actions) of an abstract **`Vehicle`** object?

Answer: Think about the abstract concept of a vehicle for a moment. This concept should describe any type of vehicle that is available. An example of such a concept could include the following components:

Vehicle
DATA
Number of wheels
Power source
Brand name
Model name
Model year
ACTIONS
Go forward
Go backward
Stop moving
Turn
Sound horn
Change gear

Objects can correspond to real world entities (e.g. a computer game can have one or more **`Person`** objects as different characters of the game). This notion has helped the evolution of good design practices and are a core aspect of OOP.

D.1.2 Distinguishing between object and instantiation

Exit skills. Students should be able to: [1]
Define the terms: class, template and instantiation. Distinguish between an object and instantiation. Discuss memory use and code definitions that relate to object and instantiation.

In the **`Vehicle`** example of the previous section, we presented an abstract **`Vehicle`** object that described the data (a.k.a. properties or attributes) that this entity has and the actions that this entity can perform. All vehicles have, at the very least, the data and actions presented in the abstract **`Vehicle`** object. However, all the vehicles created in the world are not identical, since they can differ in any of their data or how they perform their actions. For example, a small hybrid city car will have different data from a large truck, as shown in Figure D.2. The actions that these two Vehicle objects can perform may appear the same to the user (ex. the driver presses down the accelerator pedal to go forward) but the mechanics may be different. The large truck, with its eight wheels, will have a different acceleration system from the city car. The inner workings of these systems are "hidden" from the driver, which allows people to drive a vehicle easily even if they do not have any knowledge of how engines work.

Vehicle	City car	Large truck
DATA	**DATA**	**DATA**
Number of wheels	4	8
Power source	Petrol & Electric	Diesel
Brand name	X	A
Model name	Y	B
Model year	2010	2008
ACTIONS	**ACTIONS**	**ACTIONS**
Go forward	Go forward	Go forward
Go backward	Go backward	Go backward
Stop moving	Stop moving	Stop moving
Turn	Turn	Turn
Sound horn	Sound horn	Sound horn
Change gear	Change gear	Change gear

Figure D.2: Two different Vehicle objects

An abstract **`Vehicle`** entity can be considered as a general blueprint. It cannot be driven, as it physically does not exist, but it can be used as a guide to build any type of specific vehicle, such as a city car or a large truck, which can be driven, as they will be physical entities.

In OOP an abstract entity, such as the abstract **`Vehicle`** entity, is called a *class*. Just as we cannot drive a general blueprint, we cannot "drive" a class. As someone has to build a specific vehicle entity from the blueprints in order to be driven, in OOP one has to build a specific object of a class before the object can be used. As such, classes are abstract object entities. Figure D.3 presents the **`Vehicle`** class and two specific objects, **`City Car`** and **`Large Truck`**, which have been created using the class. Specific objects are known as "instantiations" of classes. As such, the **`City Car`** and the **`Large Truck`** objects are instantiations of the **`Vehicle`** class.

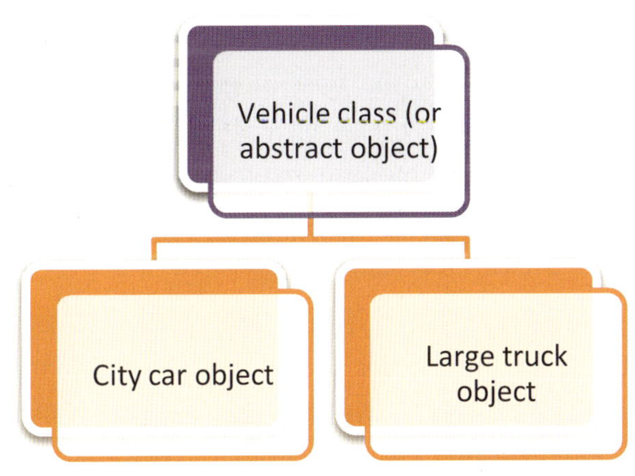

Figure D.3: Two instantiations of the Vehicle class

A class houses data (a.k.a. properties or attributes) as well as actions (a.k.a. methods).

When a driver drives a specific *instantiation* of a **`Vehicle`** blueprint (ex. a **`City Car`**) he/she "sends" messages to the car to perform some actions (ex. pressing the acceleration pedal "sends" the message to go faster). Likewise, in OOP messages are sent to an object in order to perform actions, which are also known as calling methods.

Every specific object cannot only perform actions but also has some specific data (a.k.a. properties or attributes). These data are associated with a specific car and the car maintains its attributes. For example, a car has a petrol indicator and as such can calculate the amount of petrol that it has inside its petrol tank, but it cannot calculate the amount of petrol in other cars. Similarly, every specific object (such as the *city car*) has data that are specific to the object and accompany it throughout the execution of a program.

Up to now, we have used the vehicle analogy to introduce classes (abstract object entities), objects, data and actions. Furthermore, we have shown how multiple objects can be instantiated from a single class (both the **`City Car`** and **`Large Truck`** were instantiated from the **`Vehicle`** class). We now look at the issue of memory use for these elements. Classes, from which specific objects can be instantiated, do not occupy any memory in a program. They are similar to blueprints, which do not occupy any space. When the object in the blueprint gets built however, it occupies space. Similarly, even though classes do not occupy memory space in a program, a specific object that is instantiated from the class (ex. the **`City Car`** that is instantiated from the **`Vehicle`** class) occupies enough memory to accommodate the object's data and actions. As such, classes (abstract object entities) do not occupy any space in memory, whereas specific instantiated objects occupy the necessary memory to store their data and actions.

D.1.3 & D.1.4 UML diagrams

Exit skills. Students should be able to:[1]
Define UML diagrams. Use UML diagrams to facilitate object design. Construct and interpret UML diagrams.

The *unified modeling language (UML[2])* provides a way to visualize the design of any software system and has evolved into the standard for modeling object-oriented programs. UML defines a number of different types of diagrams, but only the class diagram is within the scope of this book. UML diagrams should not be confused with flow charts presented in section 4.2. UML activity diagrams can be considered as a modern extension of flow charts and as such, UML can be thought of as a superset of flowcharts.

UML class diagrams

The goal of the *UML class diagram* is to depict the classes within an object-oriented program, as well as their collaborations. As we presented in the previews sections, a class has data (a.k.a. properties or attributes) and actions (a.k.a. methods). The UML class diagram illustrates classes as three tier compartments, rectangles divided into three compartments, as shown in Figure D.4.

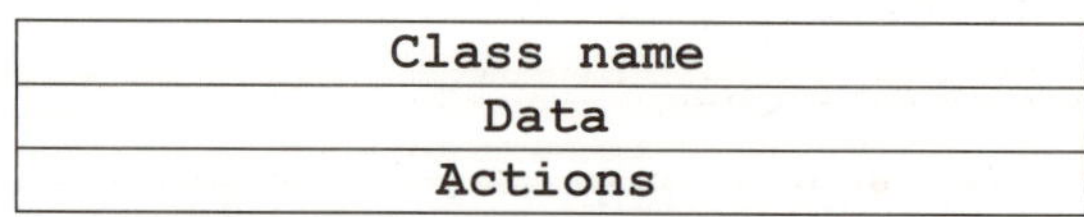

Figure D.4: UML description class template

[2] Unified Modeling Language™ (UML®) Resource Page. Retrieved January 30, 2015, from http:// http://www.uml.org

Vehicle
int: wheels Engine: powerSource String: brand String: model int: year
goForward(int d) goBackward(int d) boolean: stopMoving() turn(int r) boolean: soundHorn() changeGear(int g)

Figure D.5: Vehicle class

The top compartment signifies the name of the class. The middle compartment contains a list of all the data that an object of this class will hold. The last compartment contains a list of all the actions that an object of this class will be able to perform.

Figure D.5 depicts a UML description of the **Vehicle** class presented in the previous sections. The **Vehicle** class has data and actions associated with it. Its data are presented in the **dataType:dataName** form, where **dataName** is the name of the data that belong to the class, and **dataType** is the type of the **dataName** variable. This may be a primitive or non-primitive data type. The data associated with the **Vehicle** class are described below:

- **int: wheels**. The number of wheels a **Vehicle** object will have. Typical values of this variable could be **2**, **3**, **4**, etc.
- **Engine: powerSource**. The type of power source (engine) a **Vehicle** object will use. Typical values of this variable could be **Gas Engine**, **Electric Engine**, etc.
- **String: brand**. The type of brand a **Vehicle** object will be. Typical values of this variable could be "**Ford**", "**Ferrari**", "**BMW**", etc.
- **String: model**. The type of model a **Vehicle** object will be. Typical values of this variable could be "**Fiesta**", "**Spider**", "**316i**", etc.
- **int: year**. The year of make of the **Vehicle** represented as an integer. Typical values of this variable could be **2010**, **1983**, etc.

Apart from the data, the **Vehicle** class also has actions. These actions are presented in the **returnType: actionName(inputType)** form. **inputType** is the type of data that is required by the specific action, whereas **returnType** is the type of data that is returned by the specific action after it has completed its execution. If the **returnType** is missing that depicts an action that does not return any data (a.k.a. it returns **void**). The actions associated with the **Vehicle** class are described below:

- **goForward(int d)**. The action that when called will move the **Vehicle** a number of meters equal to the inputted integer number d. An example of this action being called could be **goForward(50)**, signifying that the **Vehicle** class will move 50 meters forward.
- **goBackward(int d)**. This action is similar to the **goForward(int)** action, but will move the **Vehicle** class backward instead of forward.
- **boolean: stopMoving()**. The action that when called will stop the **Vehicle** from moving. This action has a **boolean** return type that will return a **true** or **false** value depending on whether the **Vehicle** class performed the action **stopMoving()** appropriately and stopped or something went wrong respectively.

- **turn(int r)**. The action that when called will turn the **Vehicle** a number of degrees equal to the inputted integer number **r**. An example of this action being called could be **turn(90)**, signifying that the **Vehicle** class will turn 90 degrees.
- **boolean: soundHorn()**. The action that when called will sound the horn of the **Vehicle**. This action has a **boolean** return type that will return a **true** or **false** value depending on whether the **Vehicle** class performed the action **soundHorn()** appropriately or something went wrong respectively.
- **changeGear(int g)**. The action that when called will change the gear of the **Vehicle** to the inputted integer number **g**. An example of this action being called could be **changeGear(3)**, signifying that the **Vehicle** class will be on gear 3.

UML class diagrams depict classes but also display how those classes collaborate. Classes within an object-oriented program are connected in various ways with each other and UML class diagrams represent those connections. They describe the static structure of the system. Figure D.6 presents a UML diagram that includes the **Vehicle** class described previously, as well as its connection to the **Engine** class.

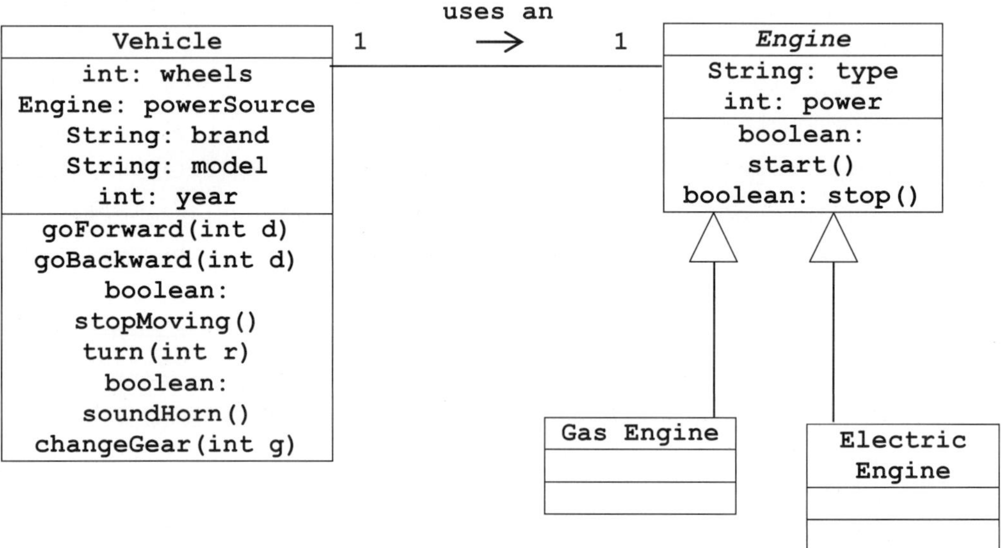

Figure D.6: UML class diagram

The UML class diagram can be read as follows: There exists a **Vehicle** class that uses an **Engine** class. The **Engine** class can be one of two types, either a **Gas Engine** or an **Electric Engine**. Both the **Gas** and the **Electric Engines** are like the **Engine** class (signified by the hollow arrows) and so we say that the **Gas** and **Electric Engines** have an *is a* or *is like* relationship with the **Engine** class. Since both the **Gas** and the **Electric Engines** have an *is a* relationship with the **Engine** class, they also share data and actions with the **Engine** class. We say that the **Gas** and the **Electric Engine** classes **inherit** the data and actions from the **Engine** class. As such, by inheritance, **Gas** and **Electric Engines** have **type** and **power** as data, as well as **start()** and **stop()** actions as actions. These data and actions do not appear in the **Gas** or **Electric Engine** class diagram because they are inherited from the **Engine** class diagram. Any data or actions appearing in the **Gas** or **Electric class** diagram would be specific to that class.

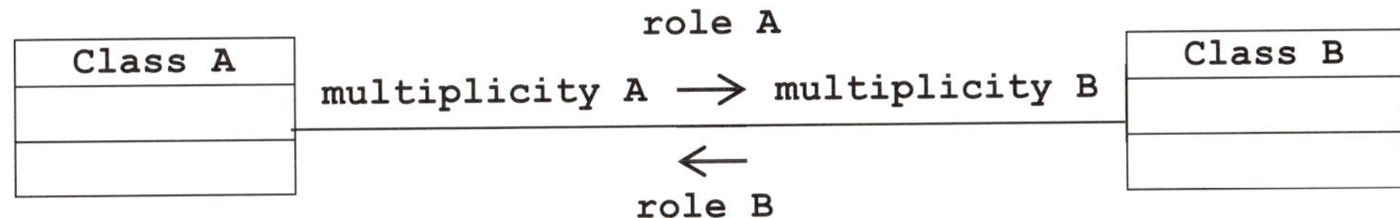

Figure D.7: Generic UML class diagram

Classes, as shown in Figure D.6, may be associated with, or related to, other classes. A **Vehicle** class uses one engine. In the same manner, an **Engine** class is part of only one **Vehicle**. A line connecting the two classes presents this *association*. Since UML class diagrams can become quite complex, as programs increase in size and incorporate more classes, information can be attached to these associations so as to make things easier. This information is displayed in a generic UML class diagram in Figure D.7.

Each association has two roles and each role has a direction. In Figure D.6, the **Vehicle** class has an association with the **Engine** class and the role has a label of *has a* meaning, in that the **Vehicle** class has an **Engine** class associated with it. On the other hand, there is no role label signifying the relationship of the **Engine** class to the **Vehicle** class. Thus, a role does not have to be explicitly named. It is given a name only if that makes things clearer. In this example, one could have added an *is part of* explicit role from the **Engine** class to the **Vehicle** class, signifying that the **Engine** class is part of the **Vehicle** class.

Associations between classes also have multiplicities, as shown in Figure D.7. These are placed at each end of an association line and indicate the number of objects of one class linked to one object of the other class. In our example in Figure D.6, one **Vehicle** class uses only one **Engine** class associated with it. Similarly, one **Engine** class has only one **Vehicle** class associated with it, since an engine can only be part of one vehicle at a time. Another example is displayed in Figure D.8. Here, an association between a **Company** class and a **Person** class is displayed. From the multiplicities we understand that a **Company** may have 1 or more **Person** classes but a **Person** may only have one **Company**. Note that the example is simple enough that no role labels are needed.

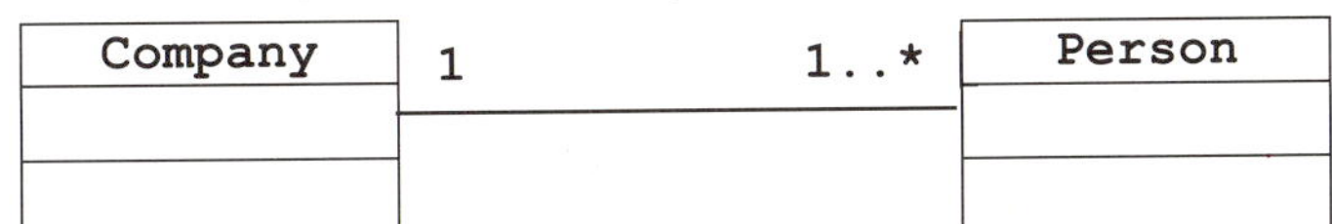

Figure D.8: UML class diagram

In Figure D.9 the most commonly used multiplicities are shown. Note that these are not the only multiplicities that can be used. Single numbers (ex. 11 to denote players in a soccer team) or ranges of any kind (ex. 7..9) can be used.

Common Multiplicities	
1	Exactly one
0..1	Zero or one
*	Many
0..*	Zero or many
1..*	One or many

Figure D.9: Common Multiplicities

Classes may have similarities. In Figure D.6 there are two **`Engine`** classes, the **`Gas Engine`** and the **`Electric Engine`** class. These classes have similar data and actions. In an object-oriented program it would be confusing and difficult to maintain repeated code in various classes and as such, writing similar code for both the **`Gas Engine`** and the **`Electric Engine`** class would resolve in unwanted repetition. The mechanism that takes advantage of these similarities is known as *inheritance* (a.k.a. generalization). **Inheritance can be thought of as an *is a* or *is like* relationship. In UML class diagrams inheritance is displayed with hollow arrows**, as those that appear in Figure D.6, which connect the **`Gas Engine`** and the **`Electric Engine`** class to the **`Engine`** class. Since both the **`Gas Engine`** and the **`Electric Engine`** would have the same data (**`type`** and **`power`**), as well as the same actions (**`start`** and **`stop`**), it makes sense to create a more general class: the **`Engine`** class that would include these data and actions and from which the **`Gas Engine`** and the **`Electric Engine`** class would inherit. The **`Engine`** class is written in italics to denote that it is an abstract class. Objects cannot be instantiated from these classes. There cannot exist a generic **`Engine`**, it has to either be a **`Gas`** or an **`Electric Engine`** in our example.

UML class diagrams can also be created using just the name of the classes that participate in the diagram. For example, the UML diagram depicted in Figure D.6 could also be presented as shown in Figure D.10. UML class diagrams that are created in this manner focus on the associations, roles, multiplicities and inheritances that take part between the classes and not in the actual data or actions that each of these classes may contain.

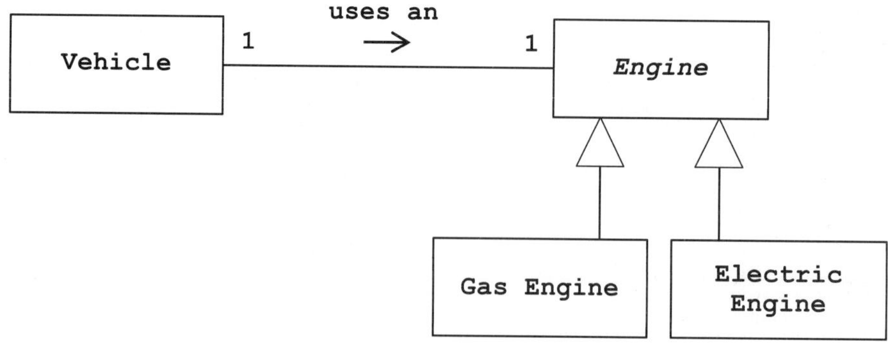

Figure D.10: UML class diagram

Example D.2: Describe the following UML class diagram paying attention to the associations, roles, multiplicities and inheritance.

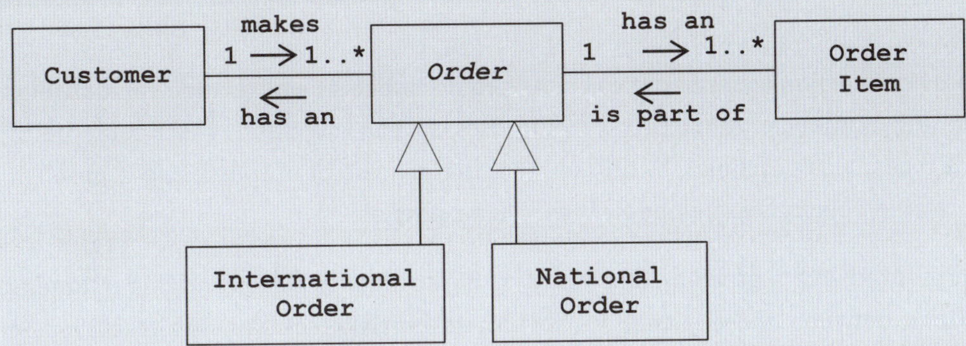

Answer: There are three classes in the UML class diagram, which can be read in one of the two ways:

- There is a **Customer** that makes one or more **Orders**. Each **Order** has one or more **Order Items**.
- There is an **Order Item** that is part of an **Order**. Each **Order** has one **Customer**.

The **Order** class is an abstract class. An order is either an **International** or **National Order**. Thus, **International** and **National Order** classes inherit from the **Order** class.

Example D.3: Construct a UML class diagram from the following scenario (class names begin with a capital letter): A **Person** has one or more home **Addresses**, as well as zero or more **Pets**. A home **Address** has zero or more **Person** owners. A **Pet** can only have at most one owner and can either be a **Cat** or a **Dog**.

Answer: The UML class diagram that derives from the above scenario is the following:

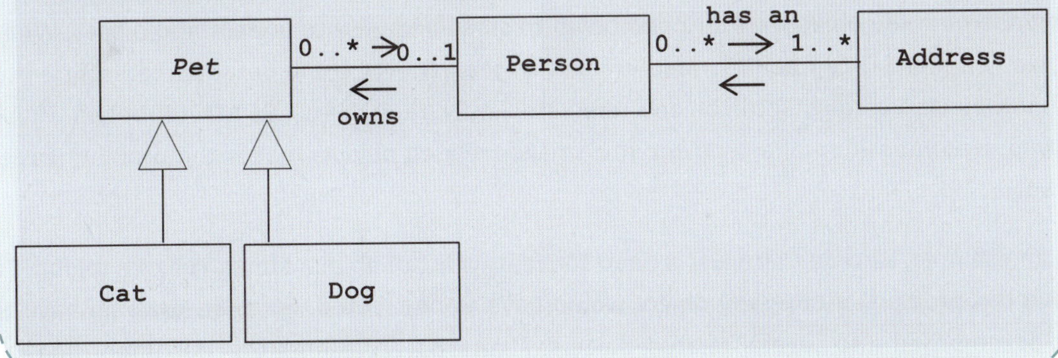

D.1.5 Process of decomposition

Exit skills. Students should be able to: [1]
Describe the decomposition process of an object to several related objects. Explain how the decomposition process facilitates abstraction. Use the objects' decomposition process in real life situations.

In the previous section a number of objects were described as well as their relationships. For example, a hypothetical **`Vehicle`** class that uses an **`Engine`** class, which could be of two different types, was described. In this section, the process of *decomposing a problem* into several related objects is examined further using examples.

When presented with a problem, decomposing it into smaller pieces and understanding the connections between those pieces is vital in its efficient solution. As discussed in the previous sections, objects allow us to describe these smaller pieces, as well as their connections, which we depict as UML diagrams. Decomposing a problem into several related objects and then decomposing those objects again into even simpler related objects allows for the reduction of the complexity of a problem and as such makes it easier to deal with. This can be seen in Figure D.11, where the Main Problem has been decomposed into four objects and the first object has been decomposed into two more. This decomposition can

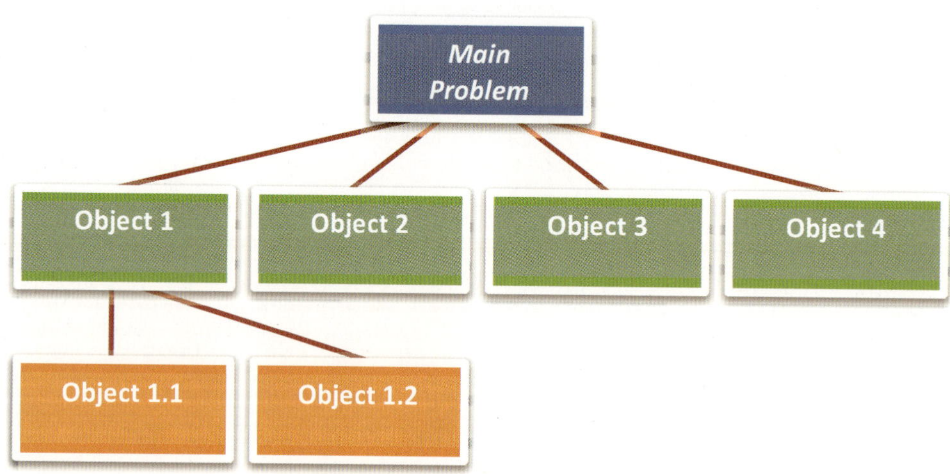

Figure D.11: The decomposition of a problem into related objects

continue until the objects are stripped down to small-and-easy to understand pieces. When Object 1.1 and 1.2 can be described efficiently, then Object 1 will be described efficiently. When Objects 1 through 4 can be described efficiently, then the whole Main Problem will be solved. Decomposition of a problem into smaller related objects makes the problem easier to solve.

As an example, assume there was a need to create a list of all the companies of a region. To solve this problem, a **`Company`** object would have to be created. For that, it would have to be decomposed into several related objects. Figure D.12 presents this decomposition. A **`Company`** object could be decomposed into several smaller objects that, all of them together, describe the company. This, of course, is a simplified example, which nevertheless presents the process of decomposing a problem into several related objects effectively.

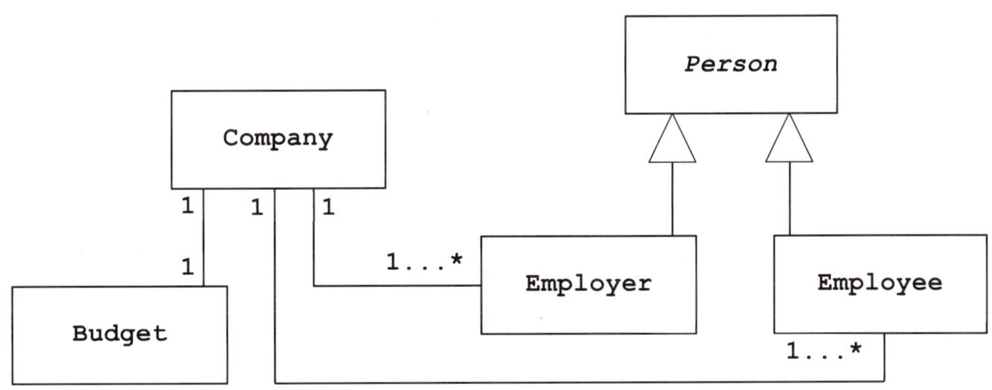

Figure D.12: The decomposition of a problem into related objects

The **Company** object depicted in Figure D.12 has one or more **Employer** objects as well as one or more **Employee** objects connected to it. Both the **Employer** and **Employee** objects inherit their data and actions from the **Person** object, since any **Employer** or **Employee** in our example will be a person. **Employers** and **Employees** will most probably have a number of data in addition to those inherited from the **Person** object, such as job title or salary. The **Company** object also adheres to a **Budget** object that describes the budget of the company. A real life **Company** object would probably have to be decomposed into a large number of related objects in order to be described fully, but even through this short example, the basic principle of thinking abstractly and selecting objects that can be used to describe a larger object can be understood.

Another example that adequately describes the process of decomposition into several related objects could be that of a traffic simulation model. Engineers use traffic simulation models in order to understand how current or future road networks will work. Models such as this become extremely complicated and are sometimes hard to describe. However, we will look into a simplified traffic simulation model to understand how it could be decomposed into several related objects. As shown in Figure D.13, three objects could describe a simplified traffic simulation model: **Vehicle**, **Traffic Light** and **Road**. These objects would have their own data and actions and they could in turn be decomposed into other objects. For example, the **Vehicle** object could be decomposed into **City Car** and **Large Truck** (as well as other vehicle types) and the **Road** could be decomposed into **Highway**, **City Road** and **Country Road** (as well as other road types). Understanding and efficiently modeling these decomposed simpler objects would tackle the problem of creating a traffic simulation model.

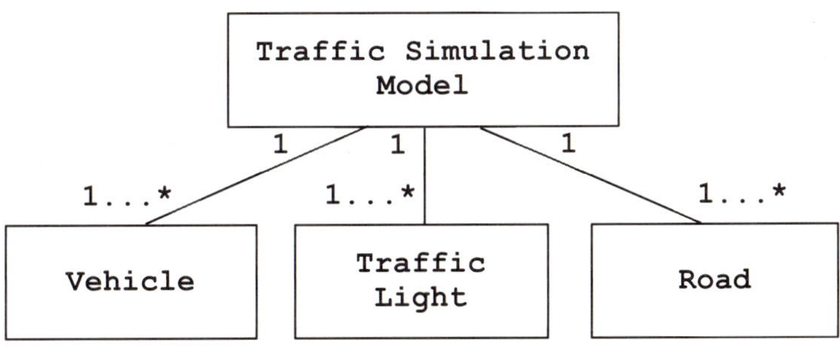

Figure D.13: The decomposition of a problem into related objects

Example D.4: Describe how a **Calendar** object could be decomposed into several related objects.

Answer: The decomposition of a **Calendar** object into several related objects is presented below in a UML diagram. The **Calendar** object is decomposed into a **Year** object, a **Month** object, a **Day** object and an **Hour** object.

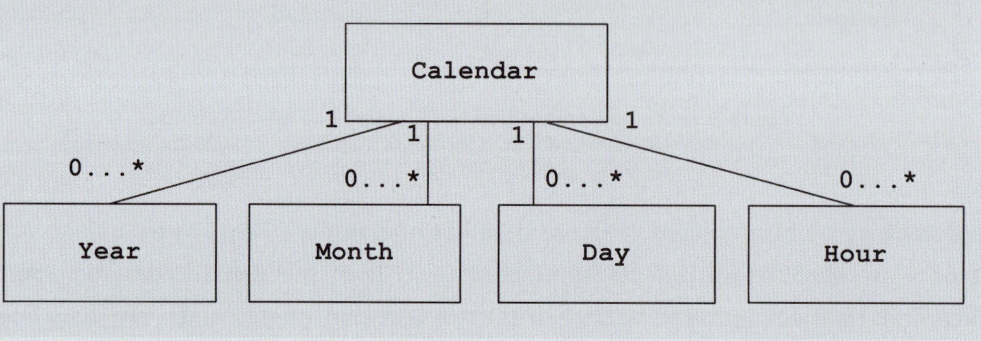

D.1.6 Relationships between objects

Exit skills. Students should be able to:[1]
Explain the dependency ("uses"), aggregation ("has a") and inheritance ("is a") relationship between objects in a given situation. Explain how relationships can facilitate abstraction.

In sections D.1.3 and D.1.4 the UML class diagram was described. It was used to depict how various objects associated with each other, as well as how some classes could inherit data and actions from other classes that were termed generalizations. For example, a **Vehicle** class was presented to have used an **Engine** class. The **Engine** class was an abstract class that could be instantiated as either a **Gas** or **Electric Engine** class. Thus, the **Gas** and **Electric Engine** classes inherited their data and actions from the **Engine** class.

In this section, a closer look into the relationships between objects takes place. These relationships are described as UML class diagram examples and are the following four: association, dependency, aggregation and inheritance.

Association

The association relationship is the simplest relationship that can be present between two or more objects and has been discussed in sections D.1.3 and D.1.4. It is represented with a solid line as can be seen in Figure D.14. One or two role labels may be present to signify the type of association that takes place between the two objects. In Figure D.14, the role label **employs** signifies that a **Company** object employs one or more **Person** objects.

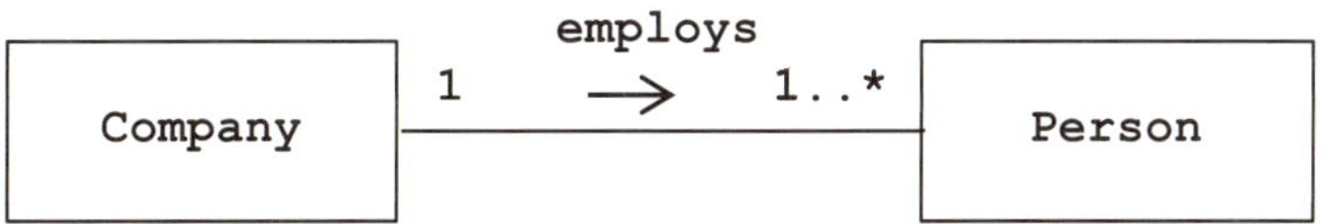

Figure D.14: Association relationship

Dependency – "uses" relationship

The dependency relationship signifies that one object is dependent on one or more objects in order to function. In other words, the implementation of an object depends on one or more other objects. This occurs when one class links to one or more other classes. The dependency relationship is represented with a dashed arrow. The arrow leaves the object that depends on the object that the arrow points to. An example of a dependency relationship can be seen in the UML class diagram in Figure D.15. This dependency can be described as "a client *uses* a supplier" (i.e. a client is dependent on the supplier). A dependency is said to be a *uses* relationship. In this example, if the supplier changes or seizes to exist and as a result is not able to supply what the client needs anymore, the client will not be able to use those products. Thus, the client is dependent on the supplier.

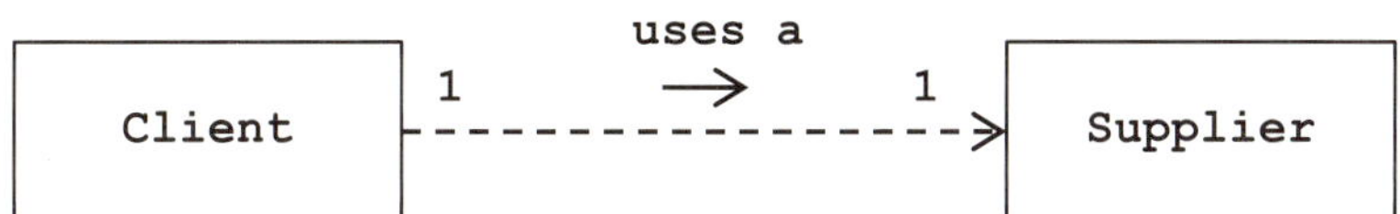

Figure D.15: Dependency relationship

In sections D.1.3 and D.1.4 a *uses* relationship was introduced in the **Vehicle** UML class diagram in Figure D.6. That relationship was depicted as a simple association between the **Vehicle** and the **Engine** classes, but in fact is a dependency. Figure D.16 presents the updated Vehicle UML class diagram that includes that dependency. The **Vehicle** class uses an **Engine** class and as such is dependent on it. If the **Engine** class ceases to exist, the **Vehicle** class will not be able to operate.

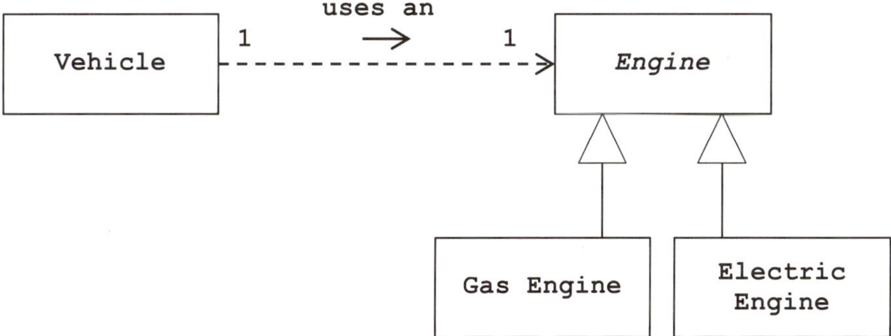

Figure D.16: Updated UML class diagram

Aggregation – "has a" relationship

The aggregation relationship signifies that one object belongs to another object and none other. That is, there exists a special kind of association between two objects, the parent and the child object, and the child object cannot belong to another parent object. The lifecycles of the parent and the child object are independent. An example of an aggregation relationship can be seen in the UML class diagram in Figure D.17. This aggregation can be described as "a department *has a* teacher" (i.e. a department has a teacher and the teacher cannot be part of another department). An aggregation is said to be a *has a* relationship. In this example, the department has a teacher (i.e. the teacher is an employee of the department). The teacher cannot be employed by anyone else, but if the department or the teacher ceases to exist, the other side, the teacher or the department respectively, will not cease to exist as well, since they have their own lifecycles. Their lifecycles do not depend on each other. A hollow diamond followed by a line represents the aggregation relationship.

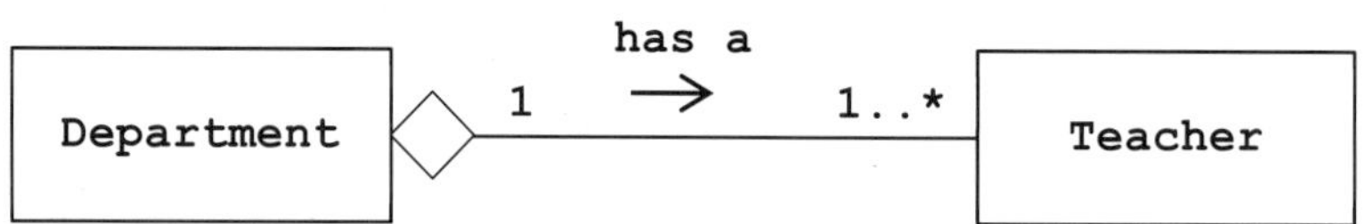

Figure D.17: Aggregation relationship

Inheritance – "is a" relationship

The inheritance relationship (a.k.a. generalization) signifies that one object (a.k.a. child or subclass) is a specialized form of another object (a.k.a. parent or superclass). An example of an inheritance relationship, between a parent class and two child classes can be seen in the UML class diagram in Figure D.18. This inheritance can be described as "a student *is a* person and a professor *is a* person." A hollow triangle followed by a line represents the inheritance

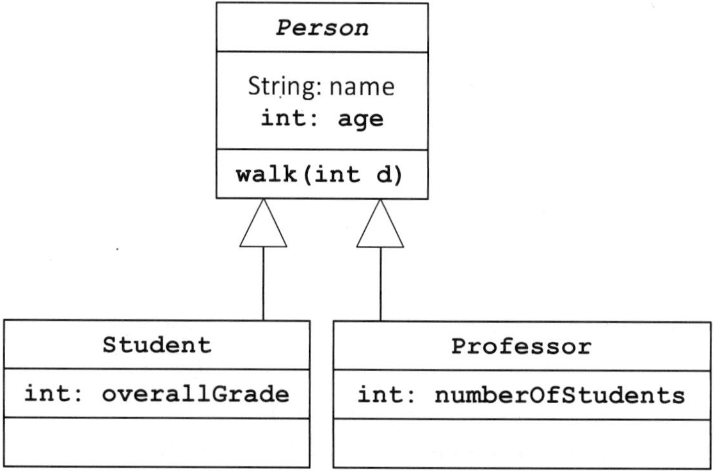

Figure D.18: Inheritance relationship

relationship. Both the **`Student`** and the **`Professor`** class inherit the data and actions of the **`Person`** class. From this, simplified version, of the **`Person`** class, both the student and the professor inherit and can use the data **string: name** and **int: age**, as well as the action **walk(int d)**. Both the **Student** and the **Professor** class can have additional data and actions associated with their classes that are not inherited from the **Person** class. For example, the **Student** class also has an overall grade as data (**int: overallGrade**), whereas the **Professor** class also has a number of students as data (**int: numberOfStudents**).

In sections D.1.3 and D.1.4 two *is a* relationships were introduced in the **Vehicle** UML class diagram in Figure D.6. Those relationships were depicted between the **Engine** and the **Gas Engine** class, as well as the **Engine** and the **Electric Engine** class. Figure D.19 presents the **Engine** UML class diagram that included those relationships. Both the **Gas** and the **Electric Engine** are subclasses, children of the superclass, parent, **Engine**.

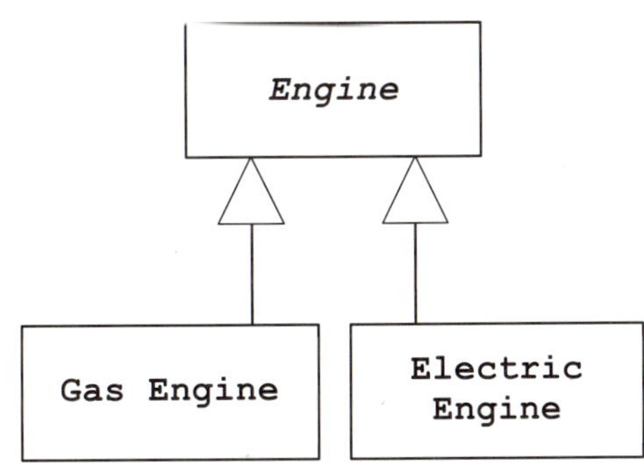

Figure D.19: Inheritance relationship

D.1.7 Need to reduce dependencies between objects

Exit skills. Students should be able to:[1]
Explain the negative effects that unnecessary dependencies between objects cause. Discuss the increase of maintenance overheads because of increased dependencies

Dependencies between objects are what the name suggests: when one object uses another object, the first object depends on the second, since it cannot function without it. Whenever the first object needs to be used, the second object will be used as well. Dependencies are directional, in that an object can depend on another object, but the second object does not necessarily need to depend on the first object as well. For example, if object A depends on object B, it does not necessarily mean that B also depends on A.

As most problems are complex, finding a solution using object-oriented programming involves dealing with a number of interdependent objects. As such, dependencies always appear in such programs. However, dependencies decrease the ability of code reuse, as well as increase maintenance overheads. Code reuse means the use of existing code to build new software. Chunks of code that are regularly used do not need to be rewritten again and again in a project or other new projects. Code reuse takes place so that there is no need to reinvent the wheel in every project. For example, a developer that has created a login screen, with two text fields where the user enters his/her credentials (username and password), will not have to redevelop another login screen from scratch if it appears anywhere else in the same project or another project that needs similar functionality. Code reuse allows the developer to use the same code again if the same functionality is needed.

The following example demonstrates how dependencies between objects in a problem increase the complexity and maintenance overheads, as well as how the reduction of these generate a clearer solution that can be more easily modified, reused and maintained. An address book program is needed that will be able to handle the storage and display of a number of contacts for a user. The program should be able to read a contact card (a list of elements that describe a contact, such as name, date of birth, telephone number and email) from a file stored locally on a computer, a database or from a network connection. The objects that would be responsible for the solution to this problem, as well as their dependencies, are shown in Figure D.20.

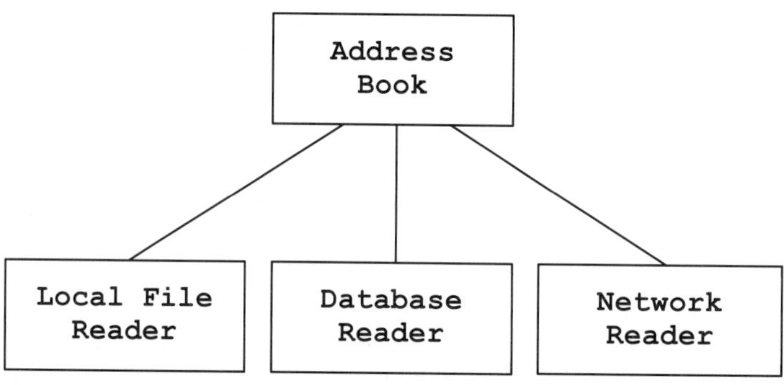

Figure D.20: Dependencies between objects

The **`Address Book`** object would handle the displaying and storage of the data, as well as the interaction with the user. However, in order to receive the data, the **`Address Book`** object would have to read the data from a local file, a database or a network. The **`Address Book`** object thus depends on all three objects (**`Local File Reader`**, **`Database Reader`** and **`Network Reader`**) in order to function properly. If any of these three objects changes how it interacts with other objects then the **`Address Book`** object will need to be updated to account for those changes as well. That would mean extra maintenance work for the developer that will need to make sure that the program works correctly when an update takes place.

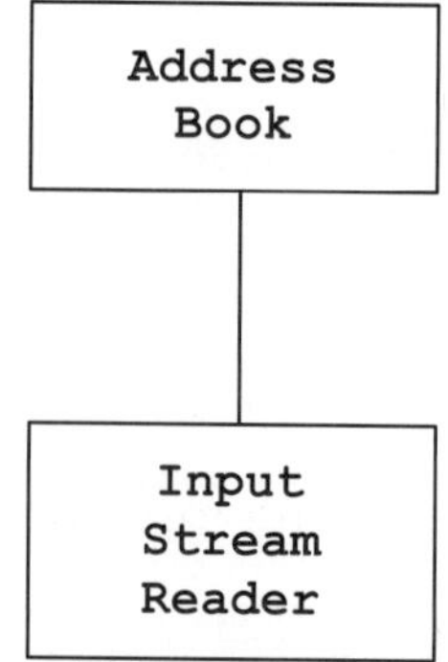

Figure D.21: Dependencies between objects

On the other hand, if the developer could depend on a single object, as shown in Figure D.21, which was responsible and flexible enough to incorporate all three objects (**Local File Reader**, **Database Reader** and **Network Reader**) then the **Address Book** object would only depend on one other object (**Input Stream Reader**) and that would reduce the maintenance overheads for the developer. Incorporating similar objects, with similar functionalities and coding, into a single object, so as to reduce duplication of code as much as possible, creates easy-to-use, easy-to-maintain, and easy-to-update code.

D.1.8 Constructing related objects

Exit skills. Students should be able to: [1]
Develop objects for a given scenario. Develop various object definitions. Explain the relationships of objects to each other and to any additional classes defined by a given scenario.

This section is presented through an example. A large store that sells all kinds of different vehicles needs to develop a computer program to keep track of all its vehicles. Since different types of vehicles have common as well as unique characteristics, it was decided that the computer program would classify the vehicles as a tree structure depicted in Figure D.22. A vehicle could be any one of three different types that share similar characteristics: car, truck or motorcycle. That is, the **VehicleType** object *inherits* from the **Vehicle** class. A separate object, **Automobile**, is used to represent each individual vehicle in the store. The **Automobile** class is *associated* with the **VehicleType** object through a member variable.

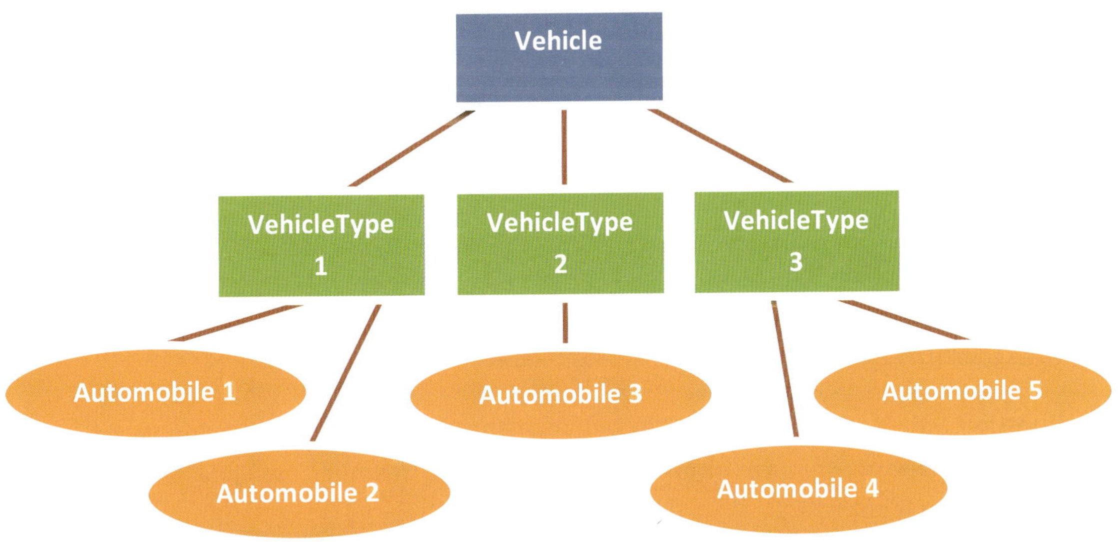

Figure D.22: Dependencies between objects

The example presented could be described in a unified modeling language (UML) diagram as depicted in Figure D.23. The **VehicleType** objects *extend* the **Vehicle** object and the

Automobile objects are *associated* with a **VehicleType** through a variable (**VehicleType: type**). The data and actions provided for these objects in Figure D.23 are, of course, simplified versions of real world examples and are used to describe the relationships between the objects.

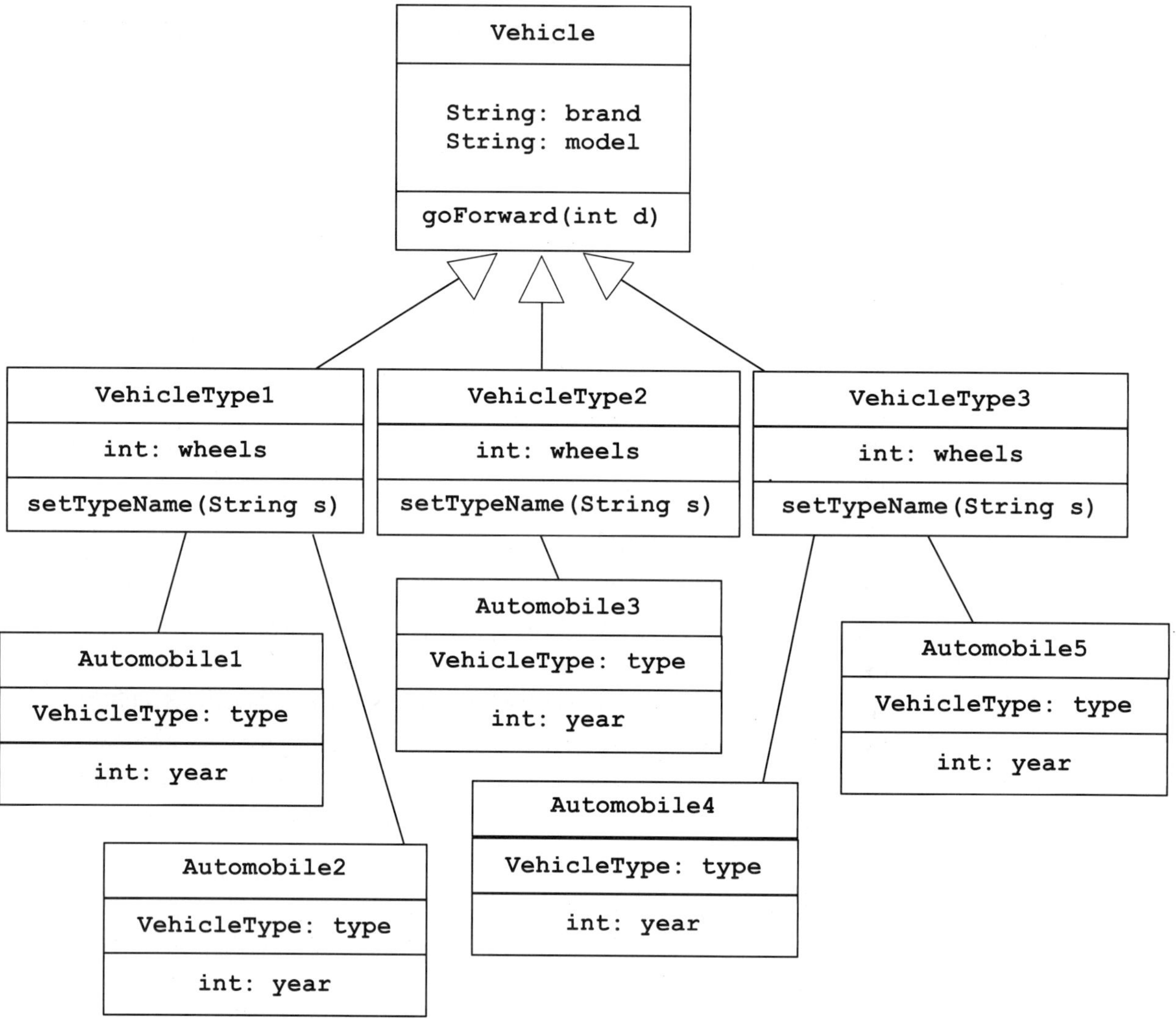

Figure D.23: UML diagram

Example D.5: State the relationship between the **Vehicle** and the **VehicleType** objects. **Answer:** The **VehicleType** object inherits from the **Vehicle** object. The **VehicleType** extends **Vehicle**.

Question 5.6: State the relationship between the **VehicleType** and **Automobile** objects. **Answer:** The **Automobile** object has a member variable that is a **VehicleType** object.

D.1.9 Data types

Exit skills. Students should be able to:[1]
Explain the need of integer, real, string and Boolean data types. **Explain how real world items are represented, store and manipulated by different data types.**

All computer programs store and manipulate data in one way or another. *Data types* allow programs to classify these data into different types, which is crucial as to the meaning of the data, as well as to how they can be stored and manipulated. This section describes some common data types that are available in most programming languages.

The data types presented in this section are the following:

- ***integer numbers***: represent a finite subset of the mathematical integers. They may or may not include negative values. Depending on the hardware and programming language used, every integer is represented by a specific number of bits. For example, in the Java programming language, 32-bits are used to represent integer numbers (`int`) and as such integer values can range from -2,147,483,648 to 2,147,483,647. For larger or smaller values than those provided by `int`, another data type is used, named `long`, that can represent even wider values.
- ***real numbers***: (a.k.a. floating point numbers) represent numbers that contain fractional values. Computers actually represent approximations of real numbers with a trade-off between range and precision. There are mainly two primitive data types that can represent floating point numbers: `float` and `double`. The `double` data type has more precision and can represent larger numbers than the `float`.
- ***booleans***: represent only two possible values, `true`/`false`.
- ***strings***: represent a series of characters and are mainly used to display information. For example, in the Java programming language, the command `String s = "this is a string";` would build a new `String` object that could be used to display the information between the quotes to the user.

The need for different data types to represent various data items is clearly evident from the fact that, as discussed above, different data types can represent different data. For example, in a program that stores student information in a school, an integer number (`int` data type) could be used to hold the age or the telephone number of each student. On the other hand, a floating-point data type (such as `float` or `double`) would be needed to hold the height or weight of each student. The names would be represented using a `String` data type and a simple `boolean` could be used to store gender information. As such, different data types can represent different types of information in a more efficient manner.

D.1.10 Data items passed as parameters

Exit skills. Students should be able to:[1]
Define the term parameter. Explain the use of parameters. Explain the pass-by-value process. Explain how data items are passed to and from actions (methods in Java) as parameters.

As discussed in previous sections, objects have both data and actions. Figure D.24 depicts a UML diagram of a number of objects that are related to each other. The **`Vehicle`** class is dependent on the **`Engine`** class, while the **`Gas`** and **`Electric Engine`** classes are of type **`Engine`**. When a **`Vehicle`** object is instructed to move some distance, its action (method) **`goForward(int d)`** is called. In order that the **`Vehicle`** class will know how much distance it will need to travel an argument of type **`int`** (as such, an integer value) is provided along with the action. The **`Vehicle`** class calls the **`start()`** action from the **`Engine`** so that the **`goForward(int d)`** action will take place. The **`start()`** action does not have any parameters and as such does not need to have any additional information in order to perform its action. When the **`start()`** action completes it returns a value, of Boolean type, back to the **`Vehicle`** class to notify whether the action completed successfully or not.

For example, if the **`Vehicle`** class was instructed to move 5 meters forward, its **`goForward(5)`** action would be called with an argument of 5 representing 5 meters. The **`start()`** action, from the **`Engine`** class, would then be called and return a true value if everything went according to plan. The **`Vehicle`** class would then move 5 meters forward and the **`goForward(5)`** action would complete successfully.

Data items can be passed to and from actions (methods) as parameters. This was previously discussed in Chapter 4. Different computer programming languages use the terms ***procedure, sub-procedure, function, routine, method, subroutine, module, subprogram etc.*** to refer to ***actions.*** An object action, when implemented, is a unit that contains a sequence of computer instructions that perform a specific and predefined task. This unit can then be used in various computer programs wherever that specific and predefined task should be implemented. It is important to mention that in most cases a function returns a value and a procedure just executes commands. Java uses methods to represent subprograms. A Java method may return a value and the main program may pass one or more variables to a method.

A *parameter* is the name of the information that is used in a method, function or procedure while an *argument* is the value that is passed into a method, function or procedure.

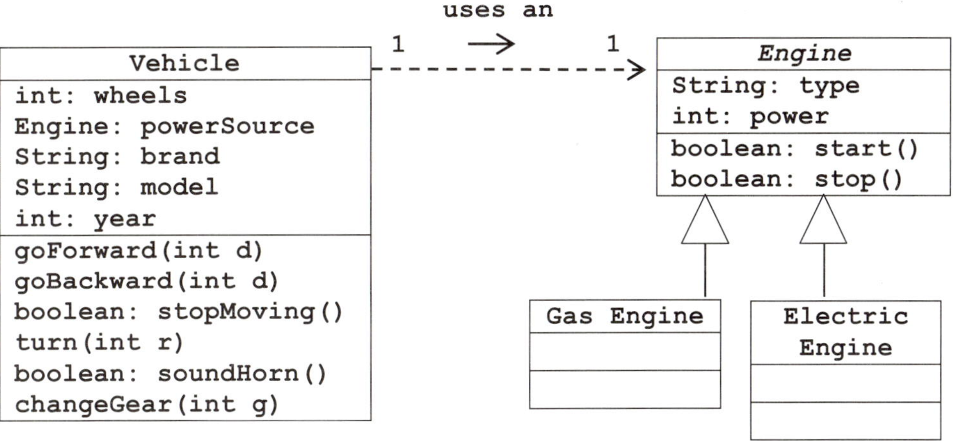

Figure D.24: UML class diagram

Any action may be designed so as to take as many parameters as necessary for it to complete its given task but may return only one value at most. Values passed as arguments to an action may be used as parameters within the action. Any changes performed to those parameters will not affect the arguments that were passed to the action.

Calculator
int: x int: y
int: add(int a, int b) int: increment(int a)

Figure D.25: Calculator object

For example, the **`Calculator`** object presented in Figure D.25 has integers **`x`** and **`y`** as data and actions **`add`** and **`increment`**. The **`add`** action takes two integer parameters (**`a`** and **`b`**), adds them together and returns the result of the addition. The **`increment`** action takes one integer parameter (**`a`**), increases it by one and returns the result.

The **`add`** action illustrates the fact that any number of parameters may be passed to an action, but only one value may be returned.

Take the following pseudocode program into consideration:

```
NUMBER1 = 3
NUMBER2 = 4
CAL = new Calculator()
NUMBER3 = CAL.increment(NUMBER2)
output "NUM1: ", NUMBER1, "NUM2: ", NUMBER2, "NUM3: ", NUMBER3
RESULT1 = CAL.add(NUMBER1, NUMBER2)
RESULT2 = CAL.add(NUMBER1, NUMBER3)
output "RESULT1: ", RESULT1, "RESULT2: ", RESULT2
```

Output:

```
NUM1: 3 NUM2: 4 NUM3: 5
RESULT1: 7 RESULT2: 8
```

Two numbers, **NUMBER1** and **NUMBER2**, are initialized to values **3** and **4** respectively. A new **Calculator** object is instantiated and the action increment is called with an argument of **NUMBER2**. The value of **NUMBER2** is incremented, returned, and stored as **NUMBER3**. Although **NUMBER2** is provided as an argument to the increment action, which increases the value of its parameter by one and returns it, **NUMBER2** is not affected as a variable. When the increment action is called with the **NUMBER2** argument, the **NUMBER2** value is passed to the action and not the actual variable. As such, changing the value passed to the increment action does not affect the value of **NUMBER2**. When variables are used as arguments to actions and only their values are passed, this is known as pass-by-value.

D.2 Features of OOP

Students should be able to explain the major features of Object Oriented Programming that differentiate it from other programming approaches.

D.2.1 Encapsulation

Exit skills. Students should be able to:[1]
Define the term encapsulation. Explain how encapsulation restricts access to some of the object's data and actions.

Encapsulation refers to the inclusion of both data and actions into a single component[3]. Classes contain data and actions that are built-in such a way so that their structure is hidden and can only be accessed outside the class via specific methods.

Employee
double: salary
double: getSalary()

Figure D.26: Employee object

Figure D.26 demonstrates the term encapsulation with a simple example. An employee can access the **Employee** objects within a company and can check the salary through the **getSalary()** action, but he/she should not be able to manipulate the value. As such, by using encapsulation, users only have access to specific data and actions.

D.2.2 Inheritance

Exit skills. Students should be able to:[1]
Define the term inheritance. Explain the parent child relation of data and actions between parent child objects.

[3] Encapsulation (object-oriented programming). (2015, March 26). In *Wikipedia, The Free Encyclopedia*. Retrieved 20:26, March 25, 2015, from http://en.wikipedia.org/wiki/Encapsulation_(object-oriented_programming)

The term *inheritance* was discussed in sections 1.3, 1.4 and 1.6 through UML diagrams. The inheritance relationship (a.k.a. generalization) signifies that one object (a.k.a. child or subclass) is a specialized form of another object (a.k.a. parent or superclass). An example of an inheritance relationship, between a parent class and two children classes can be seen in the UML class diagram in Figure D.27. This inheritance can be described as "a student *is a* person and a professor *is a* person."

Inheritance has been widely used in OOP and allows new classes to be derived from an existing class. The derived classes inherit the data and actions of the existing class. That is, the child or subclass inherits the data and actions of the parent or superclass. In Figure D.27, both the **Student** and **Professor** classes inherit the data **name** and **age**, as well as the action **walk(int d)** from the **Person** class, which is the parent class.

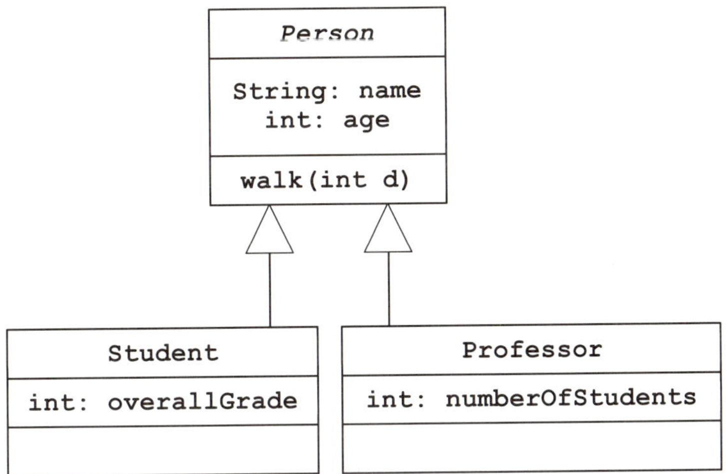

Figure D.27: Inheritance relationship

D.2.3 Polymorphism

Exit skills. Students should be able to:[1]
Define the term polymorphism. Explain how methods have the same name but different signatures.

Calculator
int: x int: y int: z
int: add(int a, int b) int: add(int a, int b, int c) float: add(float a, float b) int: increment(int a)

Figure D.28: Static polymorphism

The term *polymorphism* comes from the Greek word "πολύς", meaning "many", and "μορφή", meaning "form". The word polymorphism thus literally means "the ability to have many forms".

To understand how this applies to OOP, an extended **Calculator** object is presented in Figure D.28. The extended **Calculator** object has integers **x**, **y** and **z** as data and **add** and **increment** as actions. However, there are three **add** actions included, each one having different parameters. These three **add** actions process data in the following manners:

- **int: add(int a, int b)**: Takes in two integer parameters, **a** and **b**, adds them together and returns the result as an integer
- **int: add(int a, int b, int c)**: Takes in three integers, **a**, **b** and **c**, adds them together and returns the result as an integer
- **float: add(float a, float b)**: Takes in two float numbers, **a** and **b**, adds them together and returns the result as a float

The compiler is able to understand the method signatures and decide the method that needs to be invoked for a particular method call depending on the number and types of parameters passed. This kind of polymorphism is known as static polymorphism.

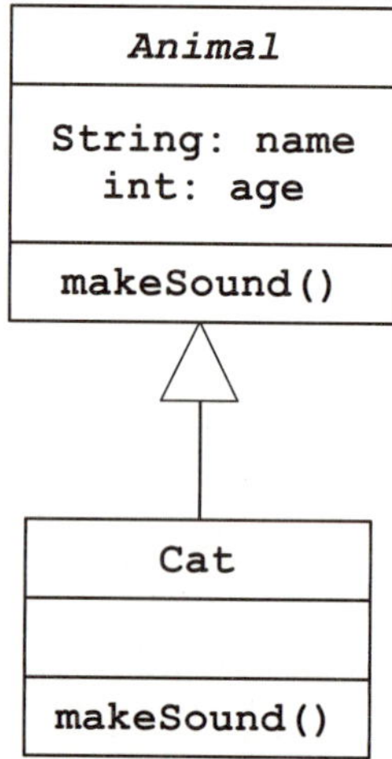

Figure D.29: Dynamic polymorphism

Dynamic polymorphism also exists, where a subclass overrides actions of the superclass. Figure D.29 demonstrates the use of dynamic polymorphism. A **Cat** class extends the **Animal** class. The **Animal** class provides data **name** and **age**, as well as action **makeSound()**, which can be used by the **Cat** class, since the **Cat** class inherits all data and actions from the parent class. The sound each animal creates however is not the same. A cat goes "meow" whereas a dog "woof". As such, each class that inherits the **Animal** class needs to have a specialized **makeSound()** action that will be specific to its needs. Thus, the **Cat** class contains a **makeSound()** action that will be used each time the **makeSound()** action is called for a **Cat** object. Dynamic polymorphism allows for subclasses to alter any parent class actions and make them specific to their needs.

Another example could be derived from Figure D.27. The **Person** class has a **walk(int d)** action that is inherited by both the **Student** and the **Professor** classes. However, since students are generally younger than professors they would tend to walk faster. As such, student's **walk(int d)** action would need to be altered for students and professors in order to account for this difference in pace. These **walk(int d)** actions, which would be specific to the **Student** and the **Professor** classes, would override the **walk(int d)** action of the superclass.

D.2.4 Advantages of encapsulation

Exit skills. Students should be able to: [1]
Explain the use and advantages of encapsulation. Explain how encapsulation could be used to minimize side-effects and dependencies.

Before continuing, read section D.2.1 where the term 'encapsulation' is defined. Encapsulation plays the role of a protective wall that prevents data and actions from being accessed from outside a class, resulting in unwanted behavior. Data and actions are only accessible in specific predefined ways. This fact allows for the following advantages:

- Data in a class can be made read or write only
- A class restricts the ways that its data and actions can be altered or called
- A class can hide the way that data is stored
- Easier to maintain, as changes to data and actions in a class can take place without being apparent on the outside, as long as data and actions can still be accessed through the same way
- Increase in usability

Encapsulation creates a "black box" for an object, separating its behavior and implementation by restricting access to data and actions as necessary. Outside the object, only the behavior of the object is apparent, hiding and protecting its internal workings.

D.2.5 Advantages of inheritance

Exit skills. Students should be able to:[1]
Explain the use and advantages of inheritance. **Explain how inheritance could be used to minimize maintenance overheads and to increase code reuse.**

Before continuing, read section D.2.2 where the term inheritance is defined. Inheritance has a number of benefits associated with it:

- **Extensibility:** as discussed in section D.2.2, all child classes inherit the actions and data of a parent class. Furthermore, child classes may add new functionality, extending the parent's actions and data, or even redefining them.
- **Reusability:** child classes that inherit the actions and data of a parent class will not need to be altered in the event that an inherited action or data needs to be upgraded. When parent class actions are upgraded, all child classes that inherit from the parent class will automatically use the new upgraded version of these actions. This fact reduces maintenance overheads as an action needs only to be changed once and all the dependent child classes will use it.
- **Information hiding:** the parent class determines what actions and data are available to the child classes.
- **Overriding of actions:** child classes may override parent actions in order to implement meaningful actions for their needs. As such, for a child class, inheriting from a parent class means that it can use whichever data and actions needed, as well as implement or improve on any parent actions.

D.2.6 Advantages of polymorphism

Exit skills. Students should be able to: [1]
Explain the use and advantages of polymorphism. Explain how encapsulation could be used to override actions. Explain how encapsulation could be used to hide implementation details.

Before continuing, read section D.2.3 where the term *polymorphism* is defined. Polymorphism has a number of benefits associated with it:

- Object actions can have the same name but different parameter lists and processes
- Subclasses can have their own unique actions, as well as being able to override or improve on parent actions
- Subclasses inherit all parent data and actions, without rewriting code, and can alter the actions that they deem necessary. This allows for *code reusability*
- Polymorphism provides a high degree of decoupling since, to an external program, the implementation behind actions is hidden. That is, a common interface exists for a family of objects that abstracts and hides the details of the implementation. In the examples of section D.2.3 an external program would use the **`makeSound()`** or the **`walk(int d)`** actions without being interested as to which object implements the specific action.

D.2.7 Advantages of libraries

Exit skills. Students should be able to: [1]
Explain how code reusability in the form of libraries of objects facilitate programming.

Libraries of objects are collections of classes that have already been written in code and can be used by a programmer while developing a program. The availability of libraries, as well as their use, simplifies the work that has to be put into a project, since standard, tested, working code is available for various functions. These libraries are used as "**black boxes**".

The usage of libraries of objects allows for the reuse of code. Many different applications have, in part, the same essential functionalities. The way an application may connect to a database or the login functions of a website are examples where a library of objects would be useful. Another example is the need to sort and search various collections of objects. Instead of writing code from scratch, developers may use libraries of objects to perform some standard functionalities and spend more time on the parts of their applications that have to be unique.

D.2.8 Disadvantages of OOP

Exit skills. Students should be able to: [1]
Explain the disadvantages of OPP when addressing small projects.

Object oriented programming (OOP) presents all its advantages when working on large-scale projects that can be broken down into multiple modules and developed by multiple developers at the same time. However, for small projects, with few developers and modules, OOP may increase complexity, development time and maintenance costs. Programming in OOP requires care in order not to make projects too abstract, which would lead to unnecessarily large and complex programs.

D.2.9 Use of programming teams

Exit skills. Students should be able to: [1]
Explain the importance of programming teams. Explain how programming teams speed up the completion of a project. Discuss various issues that relate to cooperative programming work.

Working as a solo developer allows for one person to be in charge of the whole development cycle from design to implementation, testing and maintenance. This approach is reasonable for small-scale projects and in fact does have some advantages, since the developer is aware of every aspect of the project. This allows the developer to have an overall view of the whole project and be able to make changes quickly and without the need to communicate with anyone else. Thus, decisions are generally quicker for a single individual than for a team that has to coordinate. Furthermore, the solo developer does not need to develop a common "language" with his/her peers, since he/she is working alone, and will not face any of the coordination or collaboration problems that may arise in a team. However, groups of developers need to be formed for larger projects, since in many of those projects a single developer would need much more time than he/she would have available in order to finish the project within a deadline.

The use of programming teams provides the following advantages:

- Larger projects can be taken, since more developers can work on them.
- Compared to a solo developer, members of a team may bring various ideas to the table that would not have come about without member collaboration.
- The strengths of some team members may offset the weaknesses of other members.
- Team members do not need to know the workings of the whole project, and can thus concentrate their time and energy in developing part of a project to a higher standard.

The use of programming teams comes with the following disadvantages:

- Since there is more than one developer working on a project, there needs to be honest, well-mannered communication between team members. A common "language" to enable collaboration when resolving problems needs to be established.
- If not managed properly, the weaknesses of some team members may end up undermining the group as a whole.
- Since team members will not be aware of the project as a whole and because members will be working on different aspects, decisions and project planning takes longer compared to a single developer project.

D.2.10 Advantages of modularity in program development

Exit skills. Students should be able to: [1]
Explain the importance of modularity in program design and development. Explain how modularity facilitates debugging, testing and decreases completion time.

Modularity in program development is related to the process of dividing a computer program into separate smaller sub-programs that can be implemented and tested on their own before combining them all together to build the final program. When a program increases in size and complexity, designing, implementing and testing it becomes cumbersome. Modularity in program development is meant to solve this drawback by separating the program into smaller pieces. The division of a program into smaller sub-programs is more effective when there are logic boundaries between the sub-programs and there are very few dependencies with each other.

The use of modularity in program development provides the following advantages:

- A sub-program developed for one application may be reused in other applications that need to have the same functionality. Libraries of objects (see D.2.7) may be created using this approach.
- Less new code needs to be written for a program.
- Team support. By dividing a program into several sub-programs that have few dependencies between them, different teams can work on these sub-programs separately.
- The code of a program is comprised of short, simple and easy to understand smaller sub-programs that are easier to maintain and debug.
- The structure of a program is easier to understand.
- Sub-programs work as "black boxes" that can be changed or updated, without other team members needing to be involved.
- Speedier completion of the sub-programs, and as a result the whole program itself, compared to taking on the program as one large problem.

D.3 Program development

D.3.1 Class, identifier and variables

Exit skills. Students should be able to: [1]
Define the terms class, identifier, primitive, instance variable, parameter variable and local variable.

Person
String:name double:height double:weight String:gender int:age
sleep(int hours) boolean: wakeup() walk(double distance) run(double distance, double speed)

Figure D.30: Person UML class diagram with data and actions

The **Person** UML class diagram, described in Figure D.30, will be used to define the following terms: class, identifier, primitive, instance variable, parameter variable and local variable.

- ***Class***: In OOP a class defines a template through which objects may be created. Classes provide specific data and actions. For example, the **Person** class described in Figure D.30 defines a template through which **Person** objects may be created. When an object is created, it is known as an instance of the class. For example, a **Person** object could be created to represent an imaginary person known as **Mike**. That instance of the **Person** class will have its own name, "**Mike**", with a height of "1.8m", weight of "80kgs", gender "**male**", and age "18". These data are specific to the **Mike** object, which is an instance of the **Person** class, and are thus called instance variables.
- ***Identifier***: In programming an identifier is exactly what the name suggests: a name that identifies an entity. For example, **Person** is the identity of the class presented by the UML class diagram in Figure D.30. Identifiers also denote data and actions (**name**, **height**, **weight**, **sleep**, **wakeUp**, etc are all identifiers). In general, identifiers are generated by alphanumeric sequences, as well as underscore, and should not begin with a digit.
- ***Primitive***: In section D.1.9 various common data types that are available in most programming languages were described, as well as the need for different data types to represent data items. The term *primitive* in programming denotes a predefined identifier (keyword) that is provided by a programming language as a basic building block. Common primitive types include:
  - Characters (**char**): Primitive type that represents a character
  - Integers (**int**, **short**, **long**, **byte**): Four primitive types that identify integers depending on the range of integers that need to be represented
  - Floating-point numbers (**float**, **double**): Two or more primitive types that identify floating-point numbers depending on the range and precision that is required
  - Boolean (**bool**): Primitive type that may take only one of two values, **true** or **false**

- ***Instance variable***: As discussed in the Class definition before, Figure D.30 describes a template through which **Person** objects may be created. Every person in the world is unique and will have his/her own data that describes him/her. Thus, every instance of the **Person** class, every object created from the **Person** class, will have a **name**, **height**, **weight**, **gender** and **age** but their values will be different, specific to each instance. This is shown in Figure D.31. Each instantiated object has separate instance variables that are properties that the object knows about itself. Every instance of an object has its own instance variables, even if the value of some of those variables is identical between some objects. Every instance can alter its own instance variables without affecting other instances. For example, in Figure D.31 two instances of the **Person** class are presented with their instance variables. **Mike** has his own instance variables and **Sara** has her own instance variables. Even though their age is the same, their instance variables can be changed independently. For example, if **Sara** was born earlier in the year than **Mike**, at some point, right after her birthday, her **age** instance variable would be **19**, whereas Mike's would be **18**.

Person	name	height	weight	gender	age
Mike	Mike	1.8m	80kgs	male	18
Sara	Sara	1.65m	52kgs	female	18

Figure D.31: Two object instances from the Person class

- ***Parameter variable***: In section D.1.10 data items and how they can be passed to and from actions as parameters were presented. Data items passed to and from actions are called parameter variables. For example, the **Person** class described in Figure D.30 includes a **sleep(int hours)** action that takes one integer parameter named hours. When the **sleep(int hours)** action is called, a value is passed and assigned to the hours parameter variable. For example, if a **Person** object instance needed to go to sleep for 8 hours the **sleep(8)** action would be called and the **hours** parameter would take the integer value **8**. Parameter variables are only accessible inside the actions (methods) that declare them.
- ***Local variable***: Local variables are variables that are declared inside blocks of code, such as in actions (methods) that are used within the specific blocks of code, and are then destroyed and cease to exist. They are only visible within the declared block of code.

D.3.2 Method, accessor, mutator, constructor, signature and return value

Exit skills. Students should be able to: [1]
Define the terms method, accessor, mutator, constructor, signature and return value.

The Person UML class diagram, described in Figure D.30, will be used to define the following terms: method, accessor, mutator, constructor, signature and return value.

- ***Method***: Objects in OOP have data and actions. Methods are the actions that are associated with an object. They provide the interface an object depicts to the outside world in that through those methods other classes can access and modify its data properties. For example, actions **`sleep`**, **`wakeup`**, **`walk`** and **`run`** of the **`Person`** class are all methods.
- ***Accessor***: A special kind of method that is called in order to read a specific data value of an object. For example, in order to access the age of a **`Person`** object, the accessor method **`getAge()`** may be used to get the value of the **`age`** property.
- ***Mutator***: A special kind of method that is called in order to modify a specific data value of an object. For example, in order to modify the **`age`** of a **`Person`** object the mutator method **`setAge(int age)`** may be used to set the value of the **`age`** property to be equal to the provided **`age`** integer.
- ***Constructor***: A special kind of method that is called when an object is instantiated so that it initializes its data with specific values. Constructors are run only once, when an object is created. They use the name of the class and have no return type. For example, a constructor for the **`Person`** class could have the following signature: **`Person(String name, double height, double weight, String gender, int age)`**
- ***Signature***: Every method in a class has its own unique method signature that identifies the method. A signature includes the name of the method, as well as its parameters, their number and types. Return types are not considered part of the signature. For example, all the actions of Figure D.30, without their return types, describe method signatures.
- ***Return value***: Value that is passed back, returned, to the code that called the specific method which returns the value. This value is returned after the execution of the method has taken place. For example, the **`wakeUp()`** action of Figure D.30 returns a boolean value after it has been executed, signifying whether or not the **`Person`** object woke up or not.

D.3.3 Private, protected, public, extends and static

Exit skills. Students should be able to:[1]
Define the terms private, protected, public, extends and static.

- ***Private, protected, public***: These three terms are strongly related to each other in that they are access modifiers that allow for the implementation of encapsulation. Sections D.2.1 and D.2.4 define encapsulation (a.k.a. information hiding) and explain its benefits. Access modifiers provide the compiler with information as to which other classes can have access to class data (properties) and actions (methods).
    - ***Private***: If some data or action is classified as *private,* then it can be accessed only by the class that defines it.
    - ***Protected***: If some data or action is classified as *protected,* then only the class that defines it and its subclasses can access it.

- **Public:** If some data or action is classified as *public*, then any class can access it.

- ***Extends***: Sections D.1.6, D.1.8, D.2.2 and D.2.3 have looked into the subject of inheritance, as well as how one class can extend from another class. For example, in Figure D.27, the classes `Student` and `Professor` extend from the `Person` class. As such, both the `Student` and the `Professor` classes inherit the data and actions of the `Person` class and can also define their own, unique data and actions.
- ***Static***: Every class has both data and actions. When a class object is instantiated, values are provided for the class data that can change later on without affecting other instances of the class. However, if some data or action is termed static it then belongs to the class instead of a specific instance. This means that all instance objects of the class share the same value and if that value is altered, it is altered for all the instance objects. For example, imagine that car company, "BestCar", creates a computer program to hold all of the information it needs for every new car manufactured. It thus creates a Car class and instantiates a Car class object for every new car. Every instance will have its own unique ID, as well as other instance properties (data), such as colour and mileage. However, the manufacturing company of each of these cars is the same and every instance of the Car class will have the same value. As such, the manufacturer data should be termed static so that each instantiated object has the same value and if that value changes, it will change for all the instances of the Car class.

D.3.4 Uses of the primitive data types and the string class

Exit skills. Students should be able to: [1]
Explain the use of primitive data types (int, long, double, char and Boolean) and class string which is not a primitive data type.

Before reading this section a revision of section D.1.9, where the need for different data types to represent data items was explained, is advised. There are mainly eight primitive data types, which are the following:

- **Byte:**
  - Minimum value: -128
  - Maximum value: 127
  - It occupies 8 bits of memory
  - Typically used for saving memory in large arrays of small numbers
- **Short:**
  - Minimum value: -32,768
  - Maximum value: 32,767
  - It occupies 16 bits of memory
  - Typically used for the same reasons as a byte, but for a wider range of numbers

- **Int**
    - Minimum value: -2^{31}
    - Maximum value: $2^{31}-1$
    - It occupies 32 bits of memory
    - Most commonly used primitive data type to represent integer numbers
- **Long**
    - Minimum value: -2^{63}
    - Maximum value: $2^{63}-1$
    - It occupies 64 bits of memory
    - Primitive data type used to represent integer numbers when the range of the int data type is not sufficient
- **Float**
    - The minimum and maximum values are beyond the scope of this book. However, in the Java programming language the float primitive data type ranges from 1.4^{-45} to 3.4^{38}
    - It occupies 32 bits of memory
    - Typically used for saving memory in large arrays of floating point numbers. Should not be used as a data type for numbers that need precision
- **Double**
    - The minimum and maximum values are beyond the scope of this book. However, in the Java programming language the double primitive data type ranges from 4.9^{-324} to 1.7^{308}
    - It occupies 64 bits of memory
    - Most commonly used data type for the representation of decimal values. Should not be used as a data type for precise values such as currency
- **Char**
    - Minimum value: '\u000' - 0
    - Maximum value: '\uffff' – 65,535
    - It occupies 16 bits of memory
    - Represents a Unicode character
- **Boolean**
    - Can take only one of two values: true or false
    - Typically used for conditions that may have one of two outcomes
- **String**
    - It is not a primitive data type but rather a reference class
    - Typically used to represent series of characters (ex. a word or a sentence)
    - Once it is created its value cannot change and it is thus immutable

Code construction

In sections D.3.5 through D.3.8 the use of working code constructs are presented using the IBO Java Examination Tool Subset (JETS[4]). The JETS[4] platform allows students to learn and develop algorithms using a small controlled subset of the Java programming language.

[4] International Baccalaureate Organization. (2012). IBDP Java Examination Tool Subset

Examination questions will only include the commands, symbols and constructs specified in JETS[4].

For sections D.3.5 through D.3.8 a simple but functional program, written in JETS[4], that simulates a Bookstore library is to be used. The program uses text input and output and allows the user to:

- List all the books in the bookstore
- Add a book to the bookstore
- Sort books by price (either in descending or ascending order)
- Find a book with a specific title
- Exit the program

Because Java does not provide input/output commands as part of its core functionality, while JETS[4] takes as granted that some standard input/output commands are available, a class with simplified input and output methods has been provided by the IBO[5]. The name `InputOutput` is given to this class and can be studied in detail in Appendix A.

Useful Information: The Bookstore library project is presented here in some detail. However, a full working version of the project can be found in Appendix B, as well as on the book website at:

http://www.expresspublishing.co.uk/ibcorecomputerscience.

All readers are advised to download this functional version of the project, try it out and study it thoroughly. In order to compile and run Java code a Java Development Environment (JDE) is necessary. A free JDE designed for beginners is BlueJ, which can be found at: http://www.bluej.org.

A simplified UML diagram describing the Bookstore program is presented in Figure D.32. It consists of eight classes, one of which is the `InputOutput` class from Appendix A that is responsible for the input/output commands necessary to implement the Bookstore program. The simplified UML diagram in Figure D.32 does not include association roles or multiplicities. Data and actions of classes are also hidden and only class names appear. Even though the UML diagram is simplified it still becomes quite complex. Exam programs and UML diagrams will certainly be simpler. However, programs constructed for the program dossier will require this kind of complexity and as such, sections D.3.5 through D.3.8 will use code examples of the Bookstore program.

The functionality of the eight classes used to implement the Bookstore program are described below:

[5] International Baccalaureate Organization. (2004). IBDP Computer Science Guide.

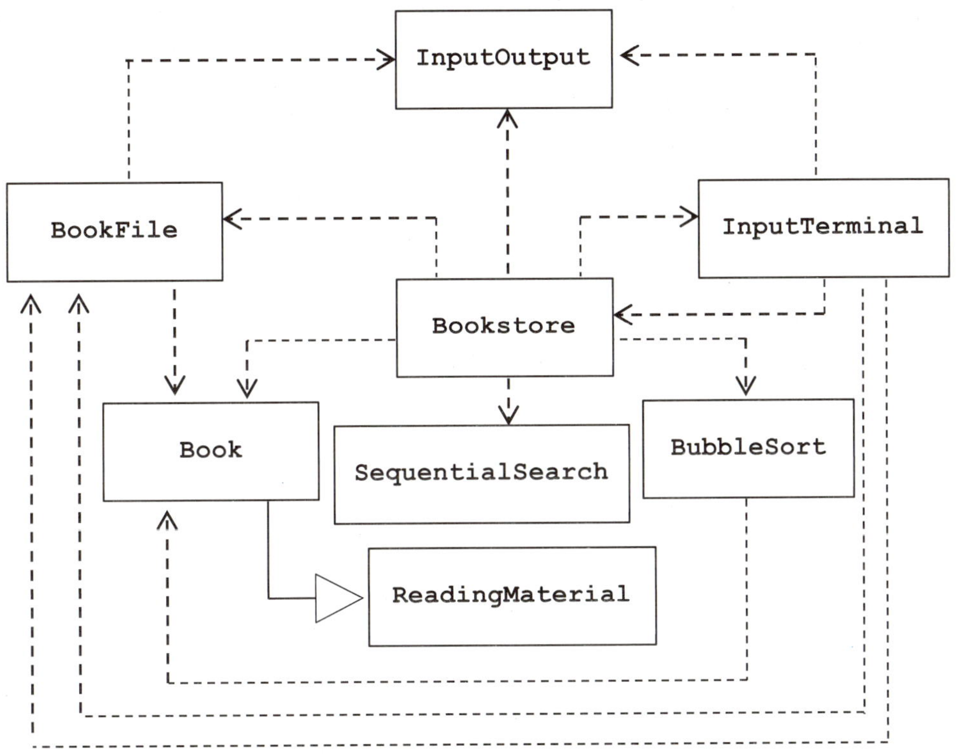

Figure D.32: Bookstore simplified UML diagram

- **InputOutput:** Provides input/output functionality through specific actions (methods). The code provided in this class should be used as a "black box", meaning that understanding is not required regarding the exact implementation.
- **ReadingMaterial:** Every Bookstore has some reading material, such as books and magazines. All reading material will include the following instance variables: **`id`**, **`title`**, **`pages`**, **`price`**. The **`ReadingClass`** includes these instance variables, as well as mutator and accessor methods to allow for their alteration. A constructor is also present and allows for the initialization of a **`ReadingMaterial`** object. The **`ReadingMaterial`** class is an abstract class, in that it should not be instantiated. There cannot be a general **`ReadingMaterial`** object, it has to be a book, a magazine or something else. The **`ReadingMaterial`** class needs to be extended and initialized by another, more specific class. This is done by the **`Book`** class.
- **Book:** Every **`Bookstore`** has books and as such a **`Book`** class is necessary to describe the basic information of a book. It includes instance variables **`chapters`** and **`author`** and inherits variables **`id`**, **`title`**, **`pages`**, and **`price`** from the **`ReadingMaterial`** class, which it extends. Mutator and accessor methods are also available to allow for the alteration of these instance variables. Furthermore, a constructor is called every time a **`Book`** object is instantiated, where all the instance variables are initialized.
- **BubbleSort:** Provides sorting functionality to allow for an array of **`Book`** objects to be sorted in ascending or descending order according to their price.
- **SequentialSearch:** Provides searching functionality to allow for an array of **`Book`** objects to be searched according to a specific **`Book title`**.

- **InputTerminal:** Provides user input functionality to allow for the input of information of a new **Book** and the instantiation of a new **Book** object with the inputted information.
- **BookFile:** Provides reading/writing functionality to and from a file in the file system. In order that a Bookstore will have persistent data, which means that data should not be lost every time the program quits, all the data needs to be stored in an external text file, which is used as a simple database.
- **Bookstore:** This class is the main class in that it is the first class which is run when the Bookstore program is run. It displays the main menu of the application in the terminal and receives user input as to what actions the user wants to perform. It then calls the necessary classes needed to perform the requested actions.

D.3.5 Code examples for D.3.1 - D.3.4

Exit skills. Students should be able to:[1]
Construct code examples, trace code fragments and explain code fragments using class, identifiers, primitives, instance variables, parameter variables, local variables, methods, accessors, mutators, constructors, signatures, return values, private, protected, public, extends, static, int, long, double, char, Boolean and string.

In order to understand how the terms defined in assessment statements D.3.1 through D.3.4 may be implemented in actual working JETS[4] code the **ReadingMaterial** and Book classes are presented. The **ReadingMaterial** class below is initially discussed:

```
public class ReadingMaterial //1
{
    protected static String bookstoreName;
    private int id; //2
    private String title; //2
    private int pages; //2
    private int price; //2

//3
    ReadingMaterial(int id, String title, int pages, int price)
    {
        bookstoreName = "K&M Bookstore";

        this.id = id;
        this.title = title;
        this.pages = pages;
        this.price = price;
    }

    public String getBookstoreName()
    { return bookstoreName; }

    public void setBookstoreName(String bookstoreName)
    { this.bookstoreName = bookstoreName; }

    public int getId()
    { return id; }
```

```
    public void setId(int id)
    { this.id = id; }

    public String getTitle()
    { return title; }

    public void setTitle(String title)
    { this.title = title; }

    public int getPages()
    { return pages; }

    public void setPages(int pages)
    { this.pages = pages; }

    public int getPrice()
    { return price; }

    public void setPrice(int price)
    { this.price = price; }

    public void changePriceBy(int increase)
    {
        int newPrice = price + increase; //4

         if(newPrice >= 0) {
            this.price = newPrice;
         }
    }
}
```

Terms defined in assessment statement D.3.1 and implemented in the `ReadingMaterial` class above:

- **Class:** A class is implemented using the statement in //1.
- **Identifier:** All the names that are included in the class as well as the actual class name are identifiers. For example, identifiers in this class include the following: `ReadingMaterial`, `bookstoreName`, `id`, `title`, `pages`, `price`, as well as all the names of the mutator and accessor methods.
- **Primitive:** Primitive data types are used throughout the class, to define the types of instance variables, parameter variables, as well as return types.
- **Instance variable:** Instance variables are implemented using the statements in //2
- **Parameter variable:** Parameter variables are included in the constructor of the class in //3 as well as all the mutator methods.
- **Local variable:** A local variable of type `int` and identifier `newPrice` is presented in //4. The instance variable `price` is added to the parameter variable `increase` and their result is stored into the local variable `newPrice`. The value of `newPrice`, if greater or equal to zero, is stored in the `price` instance variable and the local variable seizes to exist when the `changePriceBy(int increase)` method finishes.

Terms defined in assessment statement D.3.2 and implemented in the `ReadingMaterial` class above:

- **Method:** The **`ReadingMaterial`** class includes a number of methods, most of which are accessor and mutator methods. Examples of such methods are **`getBookstoreName`**, **`setBookstoreName(String bookstoreName)`**, **`changePriceBy(int increase)`**.
- **Accessor:** Accessor methods can generally be distinguished by the prefix **`get`** in the method name. **`getBookstoreName`**, **`getId`**, **`getTitle`** are all examples of accessor methods
- **Mutator:** Mutator methods can generally be distinguished by the prefix **`set`** in the method name. **`setBookstoreName(String bookstoreName)`**, **`setId(int id)`**, **`setTitle(String title)`** are all examples of mutator methods
- **Constructor:** **`ReadingMaterial(int id, String title, int pages, int price)`** is the signature of the constructor of the **`ReadingMaterial`** class. The constructor is run only once, when a new **`ReadingMaterial`** object is instantiated, and initializes the object's data. For example, a new **`ReadingMaterial`** object could be instantiated as follows:

```
ReadingMaterial(1025, "A Title", 99, 15)
```

The above code would create a **`ReadingMaterial`** object with an id of 1025, title "A Title", 99 pages and a price of 15.

- **Signature:** All methods in a class have their own unique method signature. Return types are not considered part of the signature. As such, a method signature includes the name, as well as the parameters, their number and types. For example, the following are all method signatures from the `ReadingMaterial` class:

```
ReadingMaterial(int id, String title, int pages, int price)
getBookstoreName()
setBookstoreName(String bookstoreName)
changePriceBy(int increase)
```

- **Return value:** The value that is returned after the execution of the method has taken place. For example, the following method returns a `String` that depicts the bookstore name:

```
public String getBookstoreName()
{ return bookstoreName; }
```

Another example is the following method that does not return anything and as such includes the keyword **`void`** as a return type:

```
public void setPrice(int price)
{ this.price = price; }
```

Terms defined in assessment statement D.3.3 and implemented in the **ReadingMaterial** class above:

Private: The object data in //2 **(id, title, pages, price)** are all termed **private**. Accessor and mutator methods are in place in order that other classes will have access.

- **Protected:** The **bookstoreName** object data is termed **protected** so that it can also be accessed and manipulated directly by any subclasses of the ReadingMaterial class. All other classes need to use the accessor and mutator methods that are in place in order to access the bookstoreName object data.
- **Public:** Apart from the constructor, all the other methods are termed **public** so that any class can access them and use their functionalities. These **public** methods constitute the interface of the class to the "outside world", in that these are the only methods that other classes can use in order to interact with the **ReadingMaterial** class.
- **Static:** Apart from **protected** the **bookstoreName** object data is also termed **static**. All instantiations of the class therefore share the same value of the **bookstoreName** and if that value is altered, it is altered for all the instance objects. Since the current example simulates one specific Bookstore library, all **ReadingMaterial** objects will have a single **bookstoreName** that will be identical to all objects.

In order to understand how the term *extends* (defined in assessment statement D.3.3) may be implemented in actual working JETS[4] code the **Book** class is presented below:

```
public class Book extends ReadingMaterial //1
{
    private int chapters;
    private String author;

    public Book(int id, String title, int pages, int price, int
chapters, String author) {
          //Calls the ReadingMaterial constructor.
         super(id, title, pages, price);

         this.chapters = chapters;
         this.author = author;
    }

    public int getChapters()
    { return chapters; }

    public void setChapters(int chapters)
    { this.chapters = chapters; }

    public String getAuthor()
    { return author; }

    public void setAuthor(String author)
    { this.author = author; }
}
```

- **Extends:** A bookstore may contain several types of reading material, such as books and magazines. The **ReadingMaterial** class is used to specify general reading material. However, specific types of reading materials should be defined in order to be stored in a bookstore. As such, the **Book** class exists to describe the basic information about a book. Since the **Book** class is reading material and needs all the data and actions of the **ReadingMaterial** class, it extends the class with the keyword depicted in `//1`. The **Book** class specifies its own data and actions but also inherits all the data and actions of the parent **ReadingMaterial** class.

In assessment statement D.3.4, the uses of the primitive data types and the reference class String were described. In the **ReadingMaterial** class above, primitive types are defined in `//2` and used throughout the class to store data. The use of primitive data types can also be seen in the `Book` class.

D.3.6 Code example for selection statements

Exit skills. Students should be able to:[1]
Construct code examples, trace code fragments and explain code fragments using simple and compound if ... else constructs.

In programming, code is executed sequentially, in that each line of code is executed one after the other. However, sometimes code needs to be executed only if certain conditions are met and omitted otherwise. For example, an ATM (Automated Teller Machine) cash dispenser should only allow access to a bank account if the correct card and PIN number are inserted, otherwise an error message should be displayed. Controlling the flow of a program is possible through the use of conditional logic, such as the `if` statement.

The structure of the if statement is the following:

```
if(logic statement) {
        //do something
}
```

If the logic statement is true then the section of code inside the curly brackets is run. For example:

```
if(cardIsValid == true && pinIsValid == true) {
        //allow access to the account
}
```

The code inside the curly brackets of the `if` statement is run if the card inserted into the ATM is valid and the PIN given is valid for the card. If the card, the PIN or both are invalid then the code between the curly brackets will be skipped.

In a logic statement:

- `&&` symbols signify an AND. For example, `A && B` means that both `A` and `B` need to be true in order that the logic statement can be true
- `||` symbols signify an OR. For example, `A || B` means that if either `A` or `B` is true then the logic statement is true

An **`if`** statement is present in the **`changePriceBy(int increase)`** method of the **`ReadingMaterial`** class. The **`newPrice`** calculated is checked so that, if it is equal to or greater than zero, the price variable is given the value of the **`newPrice`**. The **`newPrice`** would not make any sense if it were less than zero.

The method is presented below:

```
public void changePriceBy(int increase) {

        int newPrice = price + increase; //4

        if(newPrice >= 0) {
                        this.price = newPrice;
        }
}
```

```
public class Example6 {

   public static void main(String[] args) {

        int user = 17;

        if(user <= 18) {

             InputOutput.output("The age of the user is less than
             or equal to 18");

        }

   }

}
```

What happens when the project is run?

Answer: The statement "`The age of the user is less than or equal to 18`" is displayed.

Compound **if...else** statements may also be created. The ATM example described before is used, where an ATM should only allow access to a bank account if the correct card and PIN number are inserted, otherwise an error message should be displayed. The code is improved so that an error message is displayed if the card is not valid, or the PIN is not correct, or something else went wrong.

```
if(cardIsValid == true && pinIsValid == true) {

       //allow access to the account
} else if (cardIsValid == false || pinIsValid == false) {

       //card or PIN is not valid
       System.out.println("Card or PIN is not valid, please try
again.");

} else {

       //Something else went wrong (ex. connection to the bank
       //network is unavailable)
       System.out.println("ATM currently unavailable, please try again
later.");

}
```

The structure of the compound **if...else** statement is the following:

```
if(logic statement 1) {

       //do something 1
} else(logic statement 2) {

       //do something 2
} else {

       //do something 3
}
```

The **if**...**else** compound statement may have as many **else** clauses as necessary. It always begins with an **if** clause and a logic statement. It continues with zero or more **else** statements and logic statements, which may be followed by an **else** clause without a logic statement.

Example D.8: Create a new project in JETS[4] and include the InputOutput class from Appendix A. Create an Example7 class and insert the following code:

```
public class Example7 {

   public static void main(String[] args) {

        int grade = 78;

        if(grade > 80) {

             InputOutput.output("A+");

        } else if(grade > 70) {

             InputOutput.output("A");

        } else if(grade > 60) {

             InputOutput.output("B");

        } else if(grade > 50) {

             InputOutput.output("C");

        } else {

             InputOutput.output("F");

        }

   }

}
```

What happens when the project is run?

Answer: The statement "A" is displayed.

D.3.7 Code examples for repetition statements

Exit skills. Students should be able to:[1]
Construct code examples, trace code fragments and explain code fragments using for, while or do ... while loops.

Three basic looping mechanisms are available in most programming languages. The **for** loop, the **while** loop and the **do**...**while** loop. All three mechanisms are described below:

- **The `for` loop:** The specific number of times the **for** loop is to be run should be known beforehand.

```
for(initialization; boolean expression; update) {
        //do something
}
```

The **for** loop is run by declaring and initializing any loop control variables in the initialization step. The Boolean expression is evaluated in the beginning of every loop. If it is **true**, the **for** loop is executed, otherwise the flow of control jumps to the statement that comes after the **for** loop. If the Boolean expression is **true**, after the loop is run, the control flow returns to the **update** statement. Variables are updated as required and the Boolean expression is re-evaluated. If it is **true** the **for** loop is executed, and so on. At some point the Boolean expression needs to evaluate to **false** so that the **for** loop terminates and the execution of the program continues. Otherwise, if the Boolean expression is always **true**, the **for** loop will result in an infinite loop that will cause the program to crash. This is a common bug that may arise during code development.

An example is displayed below of a working **for** loop that prints numbers from 0 to 10 (exclusive):

```
for(int i = 0; i < 10; i = i+1) {
        System.out.println(i);
}
```

In the initialization phase, the integer variable **i** is initialized to `0`. The Boolean expression to be evaluated in every loop of this **for** loop is **i < 10**, while the update that takes place is **i = i + 1** (which can also be written as **i++**). The trace table for this **for loop** is displayed in Figure D.33.

i	i < 10	i = i + 1	output
0	true	1	0
1	true	2	1
2	true	3	2
3	true	4	3
4	true	5	4
5	true	6	5
6	true	7	6
7	true	8	7
8	true	9	8
9	true	10	9
10	false		

Figure D.33: Trace table for simple for loop

Example D.9: Create a new project in JETS[4] and include the InputOutput class from Appendix A. Create an Example8 class and insert the following code:

```
public class Example8 {

   public static void main(String[] args) {

       for(int i = 10; i > 0; i = i - 1) {

              System.out.print(i + " ");

       }

   }

}
```

What happens when the project is run?
Answer: The following results appear:

10 9 8 7 6 5 4 3 2 1

Example D.10: Create a new project in JETS[4] and include the InputOutput class from Appendix A. Create an Example9 class and insert the following code:

```
public class Example9 {

   public static void main(String[] args) {

       for(int i = 0; i < 20; i = i + 2) {

              System.out.print(i + " ");

       }

   }

}
```

What happens when the project is run?

Answer: The following results appear:

0 2 4 6 8 10 12 14 16 18

- **The `while` loop:**

```
while(Boolean expression) {

   //do something
}
```

The **while** loop is run if the Boolean expression evaluates to **true**. While the Boolean expression evaluates to **true** the **while** statement will continue to loop. The code within the **while loop** should at some point force the Boolean expression to become **false** so that the **while** loop is not stuck in an infinite loop.

An example of a working **while** loop that prints numbers from 0 to 10 (exclusive) is displayed below:

```
int i = 0;

while(i < 10) {
    System.out.println(i);
    i = i + 1;
}
```

There is a number of similarities with a **for** loop. The initialization phase happens before the **while** loop, while the update phase takes place inside the **while** loop. Otherwise, both **for** loop and **while** loop examples that print numbers from 0 to 10 (exclusive) are identical. They both print the same results and their trace table is the same (Figure D.33).

The **InputTerminal** class of the **Bookstore** program, which can be found in Appendix B, uses **while** loops in order to check if the input that is received by the user is logical and within the accepted limits. For example, when entering a new **Book** to the **Bookstore** the user is asked to enter the number of pages the new **Book** has using the following code segment:

```
int pages = InputOutput.inputInt("pages: "); //1

while(pages < 0 || pages == 0) { //2

    InputOutput.output("Error: The number of pages you entered
  was not a positive number"); //3

    pages = InputOutput.inputInt("pages: "); //4

}
```

The pages of the new book are inputted by the user in //1. While the pages entered are either zero or less than zero //2 the program outputs an error //3. The program finally asks the user to try again and input another number for the pages //4. The **while** loop will stop only if the pages entered by the user are greater than zero.

Example D.11: Create a new project in JETS[4] and include the InputOutput class from Appendix A. Create an Example10 class and insert the following code:

```
public class Example10 {

   public static void main(String[] args) {

      int i = 10;

      while(i > 0) {

            System.out.print(i + " ");

            i = i - 1;

      }

   }

}
```

What happens when the project is run?

Answer: The following results appear:
10 9 8 7 6 5 4 3 2 1

Example D.12: Create a new project in JETS[4] and include the InputOutput class from Appendix A. Create an Example11 class and insert the following code:

```
public class Example11 {

   public static void main(String[] args) {

      int i = 0;

      while(i < 20) {

            System.out.print(i + " ");

            i = i + 2;

      }

   }

}
```

What happens when the project is run?

Answer: The following results appear:
0 2 4 6 8 10 12 14 16 18

- **The do while loop:** Similar to the **while** loop, apart from the fact that it will certainly execute at least one time, since the boolean expression is at the end of the loop.

```
do {
   //do something
} while(boolean expression)
```

The **do...while** loop is run once and then the boolean expression is evaluated. If it evaluates to **true** the **do...while** statement will continue to loop. The code within the **do...while** loop should at some point force the boolean expression to become **false** so that the **do...while** loop is not stuck in an infinite loop.

An example of a working **do...while** loop that prints numbers from 0 to 10 (exclusive) is displayed below:

int i = 0;

```
do {
   System.out.println(i);
   i = i + 1;
} while(i < 10)
```

The **do...while** and **while** loops examples that print numbers from 0 to 10 (exclusive) are very similar. They both print the same results and their trace table is the same (Figure D.33).

The **InputTerminal** class of the Bookstore program, which can be found in Appendix B, could have used **do...while** loops, instead of **while** loops, in order to check if the input that is received by the user is logical and within the accepted limits. For example, when entering a new book to the Bookstore the user could have been asked to enter the number of pages the new book has, using the following code segment:

```
do {

  pages = InputOutput.inputInt("pages: "); //1

  if(pages < 0 || pages == 0) { //2

      InputOutput.output("Error: The pages you entered was not a
      positive number"); //3

  }

} while(pages < 0 || pages == 0) //4
```

The pages of the new book are inputted by the user in //1. If the pages entered are either zero or less than zero //2 the program outputs an error //3. While the pages entered are either zero or less than zero the program asks the user to try again and input another number for the pages //4. The **do...while** loop will stop only if the pages entered by the user are greater than zero.

D.3.8 Code examples of arrays

Exit skills. Students should be able to:[1]
Construct code examples, trace code fragments and explain code fragments using static arrays.

Static arrays hold a fixed number of elements of the same type. Since the array has a fixed number of elements, the length of the array is established during the array initialization phase. The array is created with a fixed length. Figure D.34 displays an array of length 10, which contains 10 integer numbers. Note that every cell has an index that can be used to reference it and that the first cell has an index of 0. Thus, an array of length 10 has indexes 0 to 9.

Index	0	1	2	3	4	5	6	7	8	9
Array	15	10	99	125	3	1	322	1024	97	2

Figure D.34: An array with 10 integers

Arrays are very helpful in storing a number of same type variables under one name, instead of declaring many individual variables. For example, ten individual variables (**number0**, **number1** ... **number9**) would be needed to hold the information of the array displayed in Figure D.34.

An array is declared in the following manner:

```
dataType[] arrayName;
```

dataType signifies the type of data that the array will hold, while arrayName is the name that will be used to reference the array. A working example for the array of Figure D.34, could have been the following:

```
int[] numbers;
```

An array of integers called numbers is declared. The size of the array needs to be provided when the array is created, which happens after the declaration of the array in the following way:

```
arrayName = new dataType[arraySize];
```

An array of type dataType with size arraySize is created and assigned to the variable arrayName. A working example for the array of Figure D.34, could have been the following:

```
numbers = new int[10];
```

The declaration and creation of the array, as well as its assignment to a variable name, can be combined in one statement as follows:

```
dataType[] arrayName = new dataType[arraySize];
```

If the values of the array elements are known, as is the case of the example in Figure D.34, the array can be also created in the following way:

```
dataType[] arrayName = {value0, value1, …, valueN};
```

For example, the array of Figure D.34 could be created in the following way:

```
int[] numbers = {15, 10, 99, 125, 3, 1, 322, 1024, 97, 2};
```

Another way of creating the array of Figure D.34 is the following:

```
int[] numbers = new int[10];

numbers[0] = 15;

numbers[1] = 10;

numbers[2] = 99;

numbers[3] = 125;

numbers[4] = 3;

numbers[5] = 1;

numbers[6] = 322;

numbers[7] = 1024;

numbers[8] = 97;

numbers[9] = 2;
```

To initialize, access or mutate elements in arrays, a **for** loop is commonly used since the number of elements in the arrays are known. The following code presents how **for** loops could be used to display the elements of an array, sum all the elements or find the minimum element in an array of numbers. The array of Figure D.34 is used as an example.

```
public class Figure34 {

	public static void main(String[] args) {

		int[] numbers = {15, 10, 99, 125, 3, 1, 322, 1024,
	97, 2};


		//Display array elements

		for(int i = 0; i < 10; i++) {
```

```
            System.out.print(numbers[i] + " ");
        }

        //Sum array elements
        int sum = 0;
        for(int i = 0; i < 10; i++) {
            sum = sum + numbers[i];
        }
        System.out.println("Sum is: " + sum);

        //Minimum
        int minimum = numbers[0];
        for(int i = 1; i < 10; i++) {
            if(numbers[i] < minimum) {
                minimum = numbers[i];
            }
        }
        System.out.println("Min is: " + minimum);
    }
}
```

The output of the program above would be the following:

```
15 10 99 125 3 1 322 1024 97 2
Sum is: 1698
Min is: 1
```

Example D.13: Since arrays hold elements there come times that an array needs to be searched so as to determine whether it holds an element or not. Create a new project in JETS[4] and include the **InputOutput** class from Appendix A. Create an Example13 class and insert the following code:

```
public class Example13 {

   public static void main(String[] args) {

       int[] numbers = {5, 10, 15, 20, 25};

       boolean found = false;

       for(int i = 0; i < numbers.length; i++) {

             if(numbers[i] == 20) {

                    found = true;

             }

       }

       if(found) {

             System.out.println("Number found");

       } else {

             System.out.println("Number not found");

       }

   }

}
```

What happens when the project is run?

Answer: The following results appear:

```
Number found
```

The program looks through all the elements of the **numbers** array and checks whether they are equal to 20. If at least one element is equal to twenty, then when the **for** loop stops, the message "**Number found**" is displayed. Otherwise, the message "Number not found" is displayed.

Question: Construct a program (the Team Builder System) that will allow you to build a list of people, output this list, as well as the oldest and the youngest person in the list. The program will do the following:

1) When the user starts the program by running its main method the system will first output the following welcome message:

```
Welcome to the Team Builder System

==================================
```

2) After the welcome message the user will be asked to input the number of members in the team as follows:

```
How many members are there in the team?
```

For example:

```
How many members are there in the team? 5
```

3) Following the number of team members the program will ask the user to input every team member. Each member will have to be added in the following specific format:

```
Name:Surname:Sex:DD/MM/YYYY
```

So, for example, if I wanted to add George Georgiou born in 18/4/1954 I would input the following:

```
George:Georgiou:m:18/04/1954
```

4) As far as input is concerned, the following is an example run of the program:

```
Welcome to the Team Builder System

==================================

How many members are there in the team? 3

Input the team members (Name:Surname:Sex:DD/MM/YYYY):

George:Georgiou:m:18/04/1954

Alexia:Georgiou:f:19/05/1957

Notis:Katsanis:m:04/01/1982
```

Question cont.:

5) You should include the **InputOutput** class from Appendix A in your project, so as to use the following code for every team member during input:

```
String member = InputOutput.input();
```

The **member** String will hold the team member details, for example:

George:Georgiou:m:18/04/1954

Every element of the team member details is separated by a ':' character. That allows us to search through the **String** using the **.charAt(int index)** method and compare every letter to the ':' character using the **.equals(String s)** method. After we find at which index each ':' exists, we can retrieve each element of the team member using the **.substring(int from, int to)** method. As such, we can separate into different variables the **name**, **surname**, **gender**, **date**, **month** and **year** of birth of each member.

Do not forget that we can find the length of a **String** using the **length()** method.

6) A class named **Member** should be created that will hold the details for each team member, defined by the following UML class diagram:

Member
-name:String -surname:String -sex:char -date:int -month:int -year:int
+Member(String name, String surname, char sex, int date, int month, int year) +getName():String +getSurname():String +getSex():char +getDate():int +getMonth():int +getYear():int

Create a **Member** object for each team member and put every object into an array that will hold all the members. The array initialization will be the following:

```
Member[] teamMembers = new Member[i];
```

Where **i** is the number of members (which the user has input in the beginning).

Question cont.:

7) After you have created the `Member` objects and array you should output the following menu to the user:

```
Team Builder Menu:

==================================

1) List the team members

2) Find the oldest member

3) Find the youngest member
```

- If the user picks 1), the team members will be displayed as output one under the other.
- If the user picks 2), the age of each team member will be calculated and the oldest member will be displayed as output.
- If the user picks 3), the age of each team member will be calculated and the youngest member will be displayed as output.
- If more than one member have the same age and are the oldest (or youngest), only one will be displayed as output.

Trial run example:

```
Welcome to the Team Builder System

==================================

How many members are there in the team? 3

Input the team members (Name:Surname:Sex:DD/MM/YYYY):

George:Georgiou:m:18/04/1954

Alexia:Georgiou:f:19/05/1957

Notis:Katsanis:m:04/01/1982


Team Builder Menu:

==================================

1) List the team members

2) Find the oldest member
```

Question cont.:

```
3) Find the youngest member
```

If the user chooses:

```
1
George Georgiou, male, born 18/04/1954
Alexia Georgiou, female, born 19/05/1957
Notis Katsanis, male, born 04/01/1982
```

If the user chooses:

```
2
Oldest member is: George Georgiou, age 57.
```

If the user chooses:

```
3
Youngest member is: Notis Katsanis, age 29.
```

Finally, after the result has been shown, the program ends.

Answer: The solution to this example is in Appendix C, as well as in http://www.expresspublishing.co.uk/ibcorecomputerscience in digital form.

D.3.9 Features of programming languages that enable internationalization

Exit skills. Students should be able to: [1]
Discuss characteristics of modern high level programming languages as Java that support internationalization

Modern programming languages enable *internationalization* in a variety of ways, which include:

- Support for the display of international fonts and text
- Support for language and local specific needs, such as date and time formatting
- Support for different keyboard layouts, as well as complex characters and symbols
- Support for a variety of written languages with the use of Unicode, allowing the representation and handling of text in most languages
- Support for user language auto detection and tailoring of the user experience according to it
- Support for global deployment of software that includes localized content

D.3.10 Ethical and moral obligations of programmers

Exit skills. Students should be able to: [1]
Discuss the ethical and moral obligations of programmers. **Explain the obligation of every programmer to adequately test the program before its release.** **Discuss the obligation of every programmer to properly cite and acknowledge the work of other programmers.** **Explain the main aims of the Open Source Initiative.**

Alongside the design, implementation and testing of software, programmers have *ethical and moral obligations*. For example, programmers should thoroughly test their products before providing them to the public. This ensure that they are working as expected and that any possibility of commercial or other damage has been minimized. As such, programmers have an obligation to act professionally and perform all the tasks that they have agreed to, without trying to deceive any of the parties involved. Programmers are also obliged to give credit to the intellectual property of others when they include such work in their projects. If they are not authorized to do so, they should not include it at all. Furthermore, programmers have an obligation to honour the principles of confidentiality and security, since data may be personally or commercially sensitive.

A growing number of programmers and other individuals support the Open Source movement. That creates open source software that is available for anyone to use or modify. The source code of these open source projects is free for anyone to use or alter. One of the main goals of the Open Source movement is to promote learning and understanding. Users have rights to both the functionality and methodology of an open source program, in contrast to proprietary software programs where users only have functionality rights. Examples of open source programs include OpenOffice[6] (as an alternative to Microsoft Office[7]) and Mozilla Firefox[8] (as an alternative to Internet Explorer[9]). Programmers involved in the Open Source movement write, exchange and share their programming code openly and voluntarily.

---

[6] Apache OpenOffice. (n.d.). Retrieved June 3, 2015, from https://www.openoffice.org

[7] Welcome to Office. (n.d.). Retrieved June 3, 2015, from https://products.office.com/

[8] We're building a better Internet. (n.d.). Retrieved June 3, 2015, from https://www.mozilla.org/

[9] Touch the web - Internet Explorer. (n.d.). Retrieved June 3, 2015, from http://windows.microsoft.com/en-us/internet-explorer

Chapter references

1. International Baccalaureate Organization. (2012). IBDP Computer Science Guide.
2. Unified Modeling Language™ (UML®) Resource Page. Retrieved January 30, 2015, from http:// http://www.uml.org
3. Encapsulation (object-oriented programming). (2015, March 26). In Wikipedia, The Free Encyclopedia. Retrieved 20:26, March 25, 2015, from http://en.wikipedia.org/wiki/Encapsulation_(object-oriented_programming)
4. International Baccalaureate Organization. (2012). IBDP Java Examination Tool Subset
5. Apache OpenOffice. (n.d.). Retrieved June 3, 2015, from https://www.openoffice.org
6. Welcome to Office. (n.d.). Retrieved June 3, 2015, from https://products.office.com/
7. We're building a better Internet. (n.d.). Retrieved June 3, 2015, from https://www.mozilla.org/
8. Touch the web - Internet Explorer. (n.d.). Retrieved June 3, 2015, from http://windows.microsoft.com/en-us/internet-explorer

APPENDIX A – INPUT/OUTPUT CLASS

Appendix A – Input/Output class

All appendix A was copied from the document: International Baccalaureate Organization. (2004). IBDP Computer Science Guide.[1]

```
/**
 * class InputOutput
 *
 * Input/output methods
 *
 * @author
 * @version
 */
public abstract class InputOutput
{
    //Output methods
    static void output(String info)
    { System.out.println(info); }

    static void output(char info)
    { System.out.println(info); }

    static void output(byte info)
    { System.out.println(info); }

    static void output(int info)
    { System.out.println(info); }

    static void output(long info)
    { System.out.println(info); }

    static void output(double info)
    { System.out.println(info); }
```

[1] International Baccalaureate Organization. (2004). IBDP Java Examination Tool Subset

```
static void output(boolean info)
{ System.out.println(info); }

//Input methods
static String input(String prompt)
{ String inputLine = "";
    System.out.print(prompt);
    try
    {inputLine = (new java.io.BufferedReader(
                new java.io.InputStreamReader(System.in))).readLine();}
    catch (Exception e)
    { String err = e.toString();
        System.out.println(err);
        inputLine = "";
    }
    return inputLine;
}

static String inputString(String prompt)
{ return input(prompt); }

static String input()
{ return input(""); }

static int inputInt()
{ return inputInt(""); }

static double inputDouble()
{ return inputDouble(""); }

static char inputChar(String prompt)
{ char result=(char)0;
    try{result=input(prompt).charAt(0);}
    catch (Exception e){result = (char)0;}
    return result;
}
```

```
static byte inputByte(String prompt)
{ byte result=0;
    try{result=Byte.valueOf(input(prompt).trim()).byteValue();}
    catch (Exception e){result = 0;}
    return result;
}

static int inputInt(String prompt)
{ int result=0;
    try{result=Integer.valueOf(
            input(prompt).trim()).intValue();}
    catch (Exception e){result = 0;}
    return result;
}

static long inputLong(String prompt)
{ long result=0;
    try{result=Long.valueOf(input(prompt).trim()).longValue();}
    catch (Exception e){result = 0;}
    return result;
}

static double inputDouble(String prompt)
{ double result=0;
    try{result=Double.valueOf(
            input(prompt).trim()).doubleValue();}
    catch (Exception e){result = 0;}
    return result;
}

static boolean inputBoolean(String prompt)
{ boolean result=false;
    try{result=Boolean.valueOf(
            input(prompt).trim()).booleanValue();}
    catch (Exception e){result = false;}
```

```
        return result;
    }
}
```

Appendix A references

International Baccalaureate Organization. (2004). IBDP Computer Science Guide..

APPENDIX B - BOOKSTORE PROGRAM

Appendix B – Bookstore Program

ReadingMaterial class

```
/**
 * Abstract class ReadingMaterial
 * This class describes the basic information of a reading material in the
 * bookstore. It is an abstract method that can be extended to describe a
 * more concrete type of reading material such as a book or a magazine.
 * @author
 * @version 1.0
 */
public class ReadingMaterial
{
    protected static String bookstoreName;

    // Instance variables
    private int id;
    private String title;
    private int pages;
    private int price;

    /**
     * Constructor
     *
     * @param  id     the id of the ReadingMaterial
     * @param  title     the title of the ReadingMaterial
     * @param  pages     the number of pages of the ReadingMaterial
     * @param  price     the price of the ReadingMaterial
     */
    ReadingMaterial(int id, String title, int pages, int price)
    {
        bookstoreName = "K&M Bookstore";
```

```
    this.id = id;
    this.title = title;
    this.pages = pages;
    this.price = price;
}

/**
 * Accessor method
 *
 * @return         the name of the Bookstore
 */
public String getBookstoreName()
{ return bookstoreName; }

/**
 * Mutator method
 *
 * @param  name    the name of the Bookstore
 */
public void setBookstoreName(String bookstoreName)
{ this.bookstoreName = bookstoreName; }
/**
 * Accessor method
 *
 * @return         the id of the ReadingMaterial
 */
public int getId()
{ return id; }

/**
 * Mutator method
 *
 * @param  id    the id of the ReadingMaterial
 */
public void setId(int id)
{ this.id = id; }
```

```
/**
 * Accessor method
 *
 * @return        the title of the ReadingMaterial
 */
public String getTitle()
{ return title; }

/**
 * Mutator method
 *
 * @param  title    the title of the ReadingMaterial
 */
public void setTitle(String title)
{ this.title = title; }

/**
 * Accessor method
 *
 * @return        the number of pages of the ReadingMaterial
 */
public int getPages()
{ return pages; }

/**
 * Mutator method
 *
 * @param  pages    the number of pages of the ReadingMaterial
 */
public void setPages(int pages)
{ this.pages = pages; }

/**
 * Accessor method
 *
```

```
     * @return         the price of the Reading material
     */
    public int getPrice()
    { return price; }


    /**
     * Mutator method
     *
     * @param  price     the price of the ReadingMaterial
     */
    public void setPrice(int price)
    { this.price = price; }

    /**
     * Mutator method
     *
     * @param  increase    increase the price of the ReadingMaterial by a number
     */
    public void changePriceBy(int increase)
    {
        int newPrice = price + increase;

        if(newPrice >= 0) {
            this.price = newPrice;
        }
    }
}
```

Book class

```
/**
 * class Book
 * This class describes the basic information of a book in the
 * bookstore. It extends the ReadingMaterial class.
 *
 * @author
 * @version 1.0
 */

public class Book extends ReadingMaterial
{
    // instance variables
    private int chapters;
    private String author;

   /**
     * Constructor
     *
     * @param  id    the id of the book
     * @param  title    the title of the book
     * @param  pages    the number of pages of the book
     * @param  price    the price of the book
     * @param  chapters the number of chapters in the book
     * @param  author  author of the book
     */


    public Book(int id, String title, int pages, int price, int chapters, String author)
    {
        //Calls the ReadingMaterial constructor.
        super(id, title, pages, price);
```

```
        this.chapters = chapters;
        this.author = author;
    }

    /**
     * Accessor method
     *
     * @return         the number of chapters in the Book
     */
    public int getChapters()
    { return chapters; }

    /**
     * Mutator method
     *
     * @param  chapters    the number of chapters in the Book
     */
    public void setChapters(int chapters)
    { this.chapters = chapters; }

    /**
     * Accessor method
     *
     * @return         list of the author of the book
     */
    public String getAuthor()
    { return author; }

    /**
     * Mutator method
     *
     * @param  authors      list of the author of the book
     */
    public void setAuthor(String author)
    { this.author = author; }
}
```

BubbleSort class

```
/**
 * BubbleSort class contains methods to sort various data structures in specific orders using the
 * bubble sort algorithm.
 *
 * @author
 */
public class BubbleSort
{
    /**
     * bubbleSortA - sorts the books in the bookstore by price.
     *
     * @param books   an array containing the books to be sorted
     */
public static Book[] bubbleSortA(Book[] books, boolean ascending)
    {
        int size = books.length;
        int last, current;
        Book temp;
        for(last = size-1; last > 0; last = last - 1)
        { for(current = 0; current < last; current = current + 1)
            {
                if(ascending) {
                    if (books[current].getPrice() > books[current + 1].getPrice())
                    {
                        temp = books[current];
                        books[current] = books[current+1];
                        books[current+1] = temp;
                    }
                } else {
                    if (books[current].getPrice() < books[current + 1].getPrice())
                    {
                        temp = books[current];
                        books[current] = books[current+1];
                        books[current+1] = temp;
```

```
                        }
                    }
                }
            }

            return books;
        }
    }
```

SequentialSearch class

```
/**
 * SequentialSearch holds the methods needed for sequential search for this program.
 *
 * @author
 */
public class SequentialSearch
{
    /**
     * sequentialSearchTitle - searches an array of Book records for a specific title.
     *
     * @param  target   the title to be found
     * @param  nums     the array of Book records to be searched
     * @return     -1 if element not found, else the index where our element resides in the Book[] array.
     */
    public static int sequentialSearchTitle(String target, Book[] nums)
    {
        int size = nums.length;
        boolean found = false;
        int place = 0;
        while (place < size && !found)
        {
            String toFind = nums[place].getTitle();
```

```
        String toFindTrim = toFind.trim();
        if (target.equals(toFindTrim))
        { found = true; }
        else
        { place = place + 1; }
    }
    if (found)
    { return place; }
    else
    { return -1; }
}

/**
 * sequentialSearchAuthor - searches an array of Book records for a specific author.
 *
 * @param  target   the author to be found
 * @param  nums     the array of Book records to be searched
 * @return     -1 if element not found, else the index where our element resides in the Book[] array.
 */
public static int sequentialSearchAuthor(String target, Book[] nums)
{
    int size = nums.length;
    boolean found = false;
    int place = 0;
    while (place < size && !found)
    {
        String toFind = nums[place].getAuthor();

        String toFindTrim = toFind.trim();

        if (target.equals(toFindTrim))
        { found = true; }
        else
        { place = place + 1; }
    }
    if (found)
```

```
        { return place; }
        else
        { return -1; }
    }
}
```

InputTerminal class

```
/**
 * class InputTerminal
 * Allows the user to add a book or a magazine to the Bookstore through the terminal.
 *
 * @author
 * @version 1.0
 */
public class InputTerminal
{
    // instance variables
    private String title, author;
    private int id, pages, price, chapters;
    private String[] authorList;
    /**
     * bookEntry method
     *
     * Responsible for getting user input for a new book entry in the bookstore.
     */
    public Book bookEntry()
    {
        InputOutput.output("");
        InputOutput.output("");
        InputOutput.output("==================");
        InputOutput.output("New bookstore entry");
```

```
InputOutput.output("===================");
InputOutput.output("");
InputOutput.output("");
InputOutput.output("");
InputOutput.output("Book details");
InputOutput.output("------------");
InputOutput.output("");

id = InputOutput.inputInt("id: ");
while(id < 0 || id == 0) {
    InputOutput.output("Error: The id you entered was not a proper id number");
    id = InputOutput.inputInt("id: ");
}

title = InputOutput.inputString("title: ");
while(title.trim().length() == 0 || title.trim().length() > 25) {
    InputOutput.output("Error: The title you entered was empty or has more than 25 characters");
    title = InputOutput.inputString("title: ");
}

pages = InputOutput.inputInt("pages: ");
while(pages < 0 || pages == 0) {
    InputOutput.output("Error: The pages you entered was not a positive number");
    pages = InputOutput.inputInt("pages: ");
}

price = InputOutput.inputInt("price ($): ");
while(price < 0 || price == 0) {
    InputOutput.output("Error: The price you entered was not a positive number");
    price = InputOutput.inputInt("price: ($)");
}

chapters = InputOutput.inputInt("chapters: ");
while(chapters < 0 || chapters == 0) {
    InputOutput.output("Error: The chapters you entered was not a positive number");
    chapters = InputOutput.inputInt("chapters: ");
```

```
        }

        author = InputOutput.inputString("author: ");

        while(author.trim().length() == 0  || title.trim().length() > 25) {
                InputOutput.output("Error: The author name you entered was empty or has more than 25 
characters");
                author = InputOutput.inputString("author: ");
        }


        Book b = new Book(id, title, pages, price, chapters, author);

        return b;
    }
}
```

BookFile class

```
/**
 * class BookFile
 * This class is responsible for reading the file where all the books are stored.
 * Furthermore, this class can also write a book entry to the file.
 *
 * @author
 * @version v1.0
 */


import java.io.PrintWriter;
import java.io.BufferedReader;
import java.io.FileReader;
```

```
public class BookFile
{
    static final String FILENAME = "bookFile";
    /**
     * readBookFile - reads all the book entries from the bookstore
     *
     * @return     DynamicQueue with all the contents of the bookFile (i.e. all the books in our bookstore)
     */
    public Book[] readBookFile()
    {
        Book[] arrayOfBooks = new Book[999];
        int length = 0;

        try {
            FileReader theBookFile = new FileReader(FILENAME);
            BufferedReader input = new BufferedReader(theBookFile);

            String line;

            while((line = input.readLine()) != null) {
                length = length + 1;

                int token = line.indexOf(":");
                int nextToken = line.indexOf(":", token+1);

                int id = Integer.parseInt(line.substring(0, token));
                String title = line.substring(token+1, nextToken);

                token = nextToken;
                nextToken = line.indexOf(":", token+1);

                int pages = Integer.parseInt(line.substring(token+1, nextToken));

                token = nextToken;
```

```
            nextToken = line.indexOf(":", token+1);

            int price = Integer.parseInt(line.substring(token+1, nextToken));

            token = nextToken;
            nextToken = line.indexOf(":", token+1);

            int chapters = Integer.parseInt(line.substring(token+1, nextToken));

            token = nextToken;
            nextToken = line.indexOf(":", token+1);

            String author = line.substring(token+1, nextToken);

            Book entry = new Book(id, title, pages, price, chapters, author);

            arrayOfBooks[length-1] = entry;
        }

    } catch (Exception e) {
        //bookFile does not exist or cannot be created.
        String err = e.toString();
        InputOutput.output("");
        InputOutput.output("The file does not exist or cannot be created.");
        InputOutput.output("");
    }

    Book[] properArrayOfBooks = new Book[length];



    for(int i=0; i<length; i++) {
        properArrayOfBooks[i] = arrayOfBooks[i];
    }

    return properArrayOfBooks;
```

```
}


/**
 * writeToBookFile - writes a new book entry to the book file.
 *
 * @param  b   a new book entry
 */
public void writeToBookFile(Book b)
{
    Book[] books = readBookFile();
    Book[] booksWithAddedBook;

    if(books != null) {

        booksWithAddedBook = new Book[books.length+1];

        for(int i=0; i < books.length; i++) {
            booksWithAddedBook[i] = books[i];
        }

        booksWithAddedBook[booksWithAddedBook.length-1] = b;
    } else {
        booksWithAddedBook = new Book[1];
        booksWithAddedBook[0] = b;
    }

    writeBooksToBookFile(booksWithAddedBook);
}

/**
 * writeBooksToBookFile - writes an array of books to the book file.
 *
 * @param  books   an array of books
 */
public void writeBooksToBookFile(Book[] books)
```

```
{
    PrintWriter output = null;


        try {
            output = new PrintWriter(FILENAME);
        } catch (Exception e) {
            //bookFile does not exist or cannot be created.
            String err = e.toString();
            InputOutput.output("");
            InputOutput.output("The file cannot be created.");
            InputOutput.output("");
        }

    if(books != null && books.length != 0) {
        for(int i=0; i < books.length; i++) {

            Book temp = books[i];

            int id = temp.getId();
            String title = temp.getTitle();
            int pages = temp.getPages();
            int price = temp.getPrice();
            int chapters = temp.getChapters();
            String author = temp.getAuthor();

            //append them to the bookFile file.
            output.print(id + ":");
            output.print(title + ":");
            output.print(pages + ":");
            output.print(price + ":");
            output.print(chapters + ":");
            output.println(author + ":");
        }

    } else {
```

```
            output.print("");
        }

        output.close();
    }

    /**
     * outputAllBooksToTerminal - outputs all the books in the bookstore to the terminal without sorting
     *
     */
    public void outputAllBooksToTerminal()
    {
        Book[] books = null;

        books = readBookFile();

        if(books != null) {

            if(books.length == 0) {
                InputOutput.output("");
                InputOutput.output("The bookstore is empty.");
                InputOutput.output("");
            }

            for(int i=0; i < books.length; i++) {

                Book temp = books[i];

                int id = temp.getId();
                String title = temp.getTitle();
                int pages = temp.getPages();
                int price = temp.getPrice();
                int chapters = temp.getChapters();
                String author = temp.getAuthor();

                InputOutput.output("");
```

```
                InputOutput.output("=================================");
                InputOutput.output("ID:" + id);
                InputOutput.output("TITLE:" + title);
                InputOutput.output("PAGES:" + pages);
                InputOutput.output("PRICE ($):" + price);
                InputOutput.output("CHAPTERS:" + chapters);
                InputOutput.output("AUTHOR(S):" + author);


                InputOutput.output("=================================");
                InputOutput.output("");
            }

        } else {
            InputOutput.output("");
            InputOutput.output("There are no books in the bookstore.");
            InputOutput.output("");
        }
    }
}
```

Bookstore class

```
/**
 * Bookstore class is the main class for the Bookstore example.
 *
 * @author
 * @version 1.0
 */
public class Bookstore
{
    // instance variables
    BookFile bf;
```

```
/**
 * Main method
 */
public static void main(String[] args)
{
    new Bookstore();
}

/**
 * Constructor for objects of class Bookstore
 */
public Bookstore()
{
    //sequentially
    bf = new BookFile();

    showMenu();
}
/**
 * showMenu method - displays the start menu in the Terminal.
 *
 */
public void showMenu()
{
    InputOutput.output("========================");
    InputOutput.output("Welcome to the Bookstore");
    InputOutput.output("========================");
    InputOutput.output("");
    InputOutput.output("Select one of the following actions:");
    InputOutput.output("a) List all the books in the bookstore");
    InputOutput.output("b) Add a book to the boostore");
    InputOutput.output("c) Sort books by price (descending)");
    InputOutput.output("d) Sort books by price (ascending)");
    InputOutput.output("e) Find book with title");
    InputOutput.output("f) Exit");
```

```
        InputOutput.output("");
        InputOutput.output("");

        char selection = InputOutput.inputChar("Which action do you want to perform? ");

        switch (selection) {
            case 'a' : listAllBooks();
            break;
            case 'b' : addBook();
            break;
            case 'c' : sortByPrice(false);
            break;
            case 'd' : sortByPrice(true);
            break;
            case 'e' : findBookTitle();
            break;
            case 'f' : System.exit(0);
            break;
            default :
            break;
        }
    }
    /**
     * listAllBooks method - lists all the books of the bookstore in the terminal.
     */
    public void listAllBooks()
    {
            //sequentially
            bf.outputAllBooksToTerminal();
            InputOutput.output("");
            InputOutput.input("Press ANY BUTTON to continue.");
            InputOutput.output("");
            showMenu();
    }

    /**
```

```
 * addBook method - allows the user to add a book through the terminal
 */
public void addBook()
{
    InputTerminal addBook = new InputTerminal();
    Book b = addBook.bookEntry();

    bf.writeToBookFile(b);

    InputOutput.output("");
    InputOutput.input("Press ANY BUTTON to continue.");
    InputOutput.output("");
    showMenu();
}

/**
 * sortByPrice method
 *
 * @param ascending     whether the Bookstore list is sorted in an ascending or descending way.
 */
public void sortByPrice(boolean ascending)
{

    Book[] books = null;

    //sequentially
    books = bf.readBookFile();

    if(books == null || books.length == 0)
        InputOutput.output("There are no books in the bookstore to sort.");
    else {
        if(ascending) {
            books = BubbleSort.bubbleSortA(books, true);
            InputOutput.output("");
            InputOutput.output("Sorted books by price (ascending):");
            InputOutput.output("");
```

```
        } else {
            books = BubbleSort.bubbleSortA(books, false);
            InputOutput.output("");
            InputOutput.output("Sorted books by price (descending):");
            InputOutput.output("");
        }

        for(int i=books.length-1; i>=0; i--) {
            int id = books[i].getId();
            String title = books[i].getTitle();
            int pages = books[i].getPages();
            int price = books[i].getPrice();
            int chapters = books[i].getChapters();
            String author = books[i].getAuthor();

            InputOutput.output("");
            InputOutput.output("=================================");
            InputOutput.output("ID:" + id);
            InputOutput.output("TITLE:" + title);
            InputOutput.output("PAGES:" + pages);
            InputOutput.output("PRICE ($):" + price);
            InputOutput.output("CHAPTERS:" + chapters);
            InputOutput.output("AUTHOR(S):" + author);

            InputOutput.output("=================================");
            InputOutput.output("");
        }
    }

    InputOutput.output("");
    InputOutput.input("Press ANY BUTTON to continue.");
    InputOutput.output("");
    showMenu();
}

/**
```

```
 * findBookTitle method
 *
 * @return     find a Book with a given book title.
 */
public void findBookTitle()
{
    InputOutput.output("");
    InputOutput.output("Search for a book.");
    String searchParameter = InputOutput.input("Title to search: ");
    InputOutput.output("");

    Book[] books = null;

    //sequentially
    books = bf.readBookFile();

    int toShow = SequentialSearch.sequentialSearchTitle(searchParameter, books);

    do {

        if(toShow == -1)
            InputOutput.output("There is no book in the bookstore with such a title.");
        else {
            int id = books[toShow].getId();
            String title = books[toShow].getTitle();
            int pages = books[toShow].getPages();
            int price = books[toShow].getPrice();
            int chapters = books[toShow].getChapters();
            String author = books[toShow].getAuthor();

            InputOutput.output("");
            InputOutput.output("=================================");
            InputOutput.output("ID:" + id);
            InputOutput.output("TITLE:" + title);
            InputOutput.output("PAGES:" + pages);
            InputOutput.output("PRICE ($):" + price);
```

```
                InputOutput.output("CHAPTERS:" + chapters);
                InputOutput.output("AUTHOR(S):" + author);
                InputOutput.output("==================================");
                InputOutput.output("");

                int ltemp = books.length - toShow - 1;
                Book[] temp = new Book[ltemp];

                for(int i=0; i<temp.length; i++)
                    temp[i] = books[toShow+i+1];

                books = temp;

                toShow = SequentialSearch.sequentialSearchTitle(searchParameter, books);

            }
        } while(toShow != -1);

        InputOutput.output("");
        InputOutput.input("Press ANY BUTTON to continue.");
        InputOutput.output("");
        showMenu();
    }
}
```

Appendix B references

Chua Hock-Chuan. (n.d.). Programming notes. Retrieved June 23, 2015, from http://www.ntu.edu.sg/home/ehchua/programming/index.html

APPENDIX C – TEAM BUILDER SYSTEM

Appendix C – Team Builder System

Team Builder class

```
/**
 * TeamBuilder.java
 *
 */
public class TeamBuilder
{


    public static void main(String[] s){
        InputOutput.output("Welcome to the Team Builder System");
        InputOutput.output("==================================");

        int i = InputOutput.inputInt("How many members are in the team? ");

        Member[] teamMembers = new Member[i];

    InputOutput.output("Input the team members (Name:Surname:Sex:DD/MM/YYYY):");

        for(int j = 0; j < i; j++) {

            String member = InputOutput.input();
            InputOutput.output("");

            int indexSeperator = member.indexOf(":");
            String name = member.substring(0, indexSeperator);
            member = member.substring(indexSeperator+1, member.length());
```

```
    indexSeperator = member.indexOf(":");
    String surname = member.substring(0, indexSeperator);
    member = member.substring(indexSeperator+1, member.length());

    indexSeperator = member.indexOf(":");
    char sex = member.charAt(0);
    member = member.substring(indexSeperator+1, member.length());

    indexSeperator = member.indexOf("/");
    String dateString =  member.substring(0, indexSeperator);
    member = member.substring(indexSeperator+1, member.length());

    indexSeperator = member.indexOf("/");
    String monthString =  member.substring(0, indexSeperator);
    member = member.substring(indexSeperator+1, member.length());

    String yearString =  member.substring(0, member.length());

    Integer dateInteger = new Integer(dateString);
    Integer monthInteger = new Integer(monthString);
    Integer yearInteger = new Integer(yearString);

    int date = dateInteger.intValue();
    int month = monthInteger.intValue();
    int year = yearInteger.intValue();

    teamMembers[j] = new Member(name, surname, sex, date, month, year);
}


int selection = 0;

while (selection != 1 && selection != 2 && selection !=3){
    InputOutput.output("");
    InputOutput.output("Team Builder Menu: ");
    InputOutput.output("");
```

```
            InputOutput.output("=================");
            InputOutput.output("");
            InputOutput.output("1) List the team members");
            InputOutput.output("2) Find the oldest member");
            InputOutput.output("3) Find the youngest member");

            selection = InputOutput.inputInt("");
        }

        switch(selection) {
            case 1: InputOutput.output("");
                    outputTeamMembers(teamMembers);
                    break;
            case 2: InputOutput.output("The oldest member is: " + oldest(teamMembers));
                    break;
            case 3: InputOutput.output("The youngest member is: " + youngest(teamMembers));
            default: break;
        }
    }

    public static void outputTeamMembers (Member[] teamMembers) {

        for(int i = 0; i < teamMembers.length; i++) {
                String name = teamMembers[i].getName();
                String surname = teamMembers[i].getSurname();
                char sex = teamMembers[i].getSex();
                int date = teamMembers[i].getDate();
                int month = teamMembers[i].getMonth();
                int year = teamMembers[i].getYear();

                String sLong;

                if(sex == 'm') {
                    sLong = "male";
                } else {
                    sLong = "female";
```

```
                }

                InputOutput.output(name + " " + surname + ", " + sLong + ", " + "born " + date + "/" + month +
"/" + year);
            }
        }

        public static String oldest (Member[] teamMembers){

            //initialization.
            int max = 0;
            int oldest = 0;

            for(int i = 0; i < teamMembers.length; i++) {

                int age = (2011 - teamMembers[i].getYear());

                if(age > max) {
                        max = age;
                        oldest = i;
                }

            }

            int age = (2011 - teamMembers[oldest].getYear());
            String toReturn = teamMembers[oldest].getName() + " " + teamMembers[oldest].getSurname() + ", age " +
age;

            return toReturn;
        }


        public static String youngest (Member[] teamMembers){

            //initialization.
            int min = 999;
```

```
        int youngest = 0;

        for(int i = 0; i < teamMembers.length; i++) {

            int age = (2011 - teamMembers[i].getYear());

            if(age < min) {
                    min = age;
                    youngest = i;
            }

        }

        int age = (2011 - teamMembers[youngest].getYear());
        String toReturn = teamMembers[youngest].getName() + " " + teamMembers[youngest].getSurname() + ", age
" + age;

        return toReturn;
    }
}
```

Member class

```
/**
 * Member class
 *
 */
public class Member
{
   private String name;
   private String surname;
   private char sex;
   private int date;
   private int month;
   private int year;
```

```
    public Member(String name, String surname, char sex, int date, int month, int year) {
         this.name = name;
         this.surname = surname;
         this.sex = sex;
         this.date = date;
         this.month = month;
         this.year = year;
    }

    public String getName()
    { return name; }

    public String getSurname()
    { return surname; }

    public char getSex()
    { return sex; }

    public int getDate()
    { return date; }

    public int getMonth()
    { return month; }

    public int getYear()
    { return year; }
}
```

Appendix C references

Chua Hock-Chuan. (n.d.). Programming notes. Retrieved June 23, 2015, from http://www.ntu.edu.sg/home/ehchua/programming/index.html

Index of Terms

Q

R

S

T

U

V

W